D1245195

Ideas, Interests, and
American Trade Policy

A volume in the series

Cornell Studies in Political Economy

EDITED BY PETER J. KATZENSTEIN

A full list of titles in the series appears at the end of the book.

Ideas, Interests, and American Trade Policy

JUDITH GOLDSTEIN

CORNELL UNIVERSITY PRESS

Ithaca and London

First published 1993 by Cornell University Press.

International Standard Book Number 0-8014-2695-2 (cloth)
International Standard Book Number 0-8014-9988-7 (paper)
Library of Congress Catalog Card Number 93-29481
Printed in the United States of America
*Librarians: Library of Congress cataloging information appears
on the last page of the book.*

⊗ The paper in this book meets the minimum requirements of the
American National Standard for Information Sciences—Permanence
of Paper for Printed Library Materials, ANSI Z39.48-1984.

Contents

Tables and Figures   ix
Preface   xi

1. Ideas, Institutions, and the Politics of Protectionism   1
2. Generation and Selection: Antebellum Ideas, Politics, and
   the Tariff   23
3. Institutionalization: Putting Protectionism in Place,
   1870–1930   81
4. Reforming Institutions: The Liberalization of Trade Policy   137
5. The Pattern of Protectionism: Conflicting Rules,
   Conflicting Incentives   183
6. Ideas and American Foreign Policy   237

   Index   261

204

26 IDEAS
42 Congress
73 Republic

Tables and Figures

TABLES

2.1.	Price changes, 1800–1820	46
2.2.	Growth of the federal budget, 1810–1820	48
2.3.	Average tariff rates, 1821–1857	48
2.4.	House votes on major tariff legislation, 1816–1842	50
2.5.	Partisan control of the House, Senate, and presidency, 1815–1860	51
3.1.	Growth in GNP, imports, and exports, 1810–1930	94
3.2.	European tariff rates, 1875 and 1913	95
3.3.	Average tariff rates, 1870–1929	95
3.4.	Partisan control of the House, Senate, and presidency in years of major trade legislation, 1870–1929	96
3.5.	Budget surplus/deficit, 1870–1930	99
3.6.	Growth of U.S. productivity, 1870–1930	105
3.7.	Price changes, 1870–1930	109
3.8.	Growth in GNP, agriculture, and industry, 1869–1929	115
4.1.	Average tariff rates compared with changes in GNP and imports, 1934–1991	163
4.2.	Partisan control of the House, Senate, and presidency, and House votes on liberal trade legislation, 1934–1988	165
4.3.	U.S. share of Organization of Economic Cooperation and Development trade, 1950–1990	168
4.4.	Percent change in import penetration, 1955–1990	168
5.1.	Escape-clause cases (in effect 1958–1991)	209
5.2.	Trade adjustment under the 1962 and 1974 trade adjustment assistance statutes, 1963–1989	211
5.3.	Predicting escape-clause aid, 1958–1978	212
5.4.	Adjustment assistance model, 1963–1978	213

5.5.   Section 301 petitions, 1975–1991   217
5.6.   Antidumping (AD), countervailing duty (CD), and
        Section 337 cases, 1958–1991   217
5.7.   Final outcomes of EC, AA, and U.S. unfair trade cases
        by legislation period, 1963–1991   219
5.8.   Unfair trade aid model, 1958–1978   220
5.9.   Change in U.S. real GNP, imports, and tariffs,
        1948–1991   234
5.10.   Rates of change in U.S. trade by sector, 1958–1988   235

FIGURE

1.   The determinants of American trade policy   242

Preface

This book was motivated by an empirical anomaly. As early as the mid-1970s, analysts both in and outside academia began to predict the imminent end of the international trade regime. Its demise, always just around the corner, would reflect America's relative decline in power and the inability of U.S. decision makers to fend off private interests hurt by import competition. Yet, while academics were writing about the end of liberalism, policy makers were signing accords that *increased* foreign access to the American market. Not only did Congress accept the Tokyo Round agreements, but as imports reached unprecedented levels, elected officials instigated the Uruguay Round, the most far-reaching trade talks to date. My research began as an attempt to explain America's continued commitment to free trade, even in the face of economic and political decline.

America's attachment to a liberal trade policy—against strong social resistance—suggests that political behavior may be motivated by more than simple material interests. Yet the importance of ideas is downgraded in much contemporary work. Ideas are often viewed exclusively in instrumental terms—they legitimate the interests of the powerful but have no independent causal weight. My intent is to show the inadequacy of such an approach and to demonstrate that beliefs about the causal connections between interests and policies are at least as important as the nature of the interests themselves.

Even if analysts assume that political leaders fully understand their own interests, those of their constituents, and those of the nation as a whole, political actors still have to rely on an explicit (or implicit) theoretical model in making choices about policy strategies. In a world clouded with uncertainty, political entrepreneurs cannot predict with any assurance what policy or range of policies will lead to the outcomes they prefer. Thus I focus on causal ideas, explaining why some were selected over others at different times, analyzing the impact of the choice of economic models on the constitution of trading rules and procedures, and exploring the lasting effects of these institutions on trade politics.

I make two different arguments about ideas and economic policy making. The first involves a general understanding of the role of ideas in politics. Throughout history, political entrepreneurs have faced choices among competing policy options. In most cases, policy makers have incomplete information about their environment and thus must rely on causal models in making policy choices. Here ideas are like road maps, linking policies to a constellation of interests. But ideas also serve other purposes. Even when political entrepreneurs understand the effects of changes in market forces, they still depend on ideas about how to translate these forces into a political and economic program. It is not markets but ideas that establish the rules of the game, that demarcate for policy makers the proper form of new programs, that privilege particular constituencies.

This book also makes a longitudinal argument about the historical processes of policy change. Ideas not only condition the action of political leaders at one point in time but, through their incorporation into institutional structures, also affect the evolution of policy over time. To explain contemporary policy, we must begin our analysis with the historical origins of trade institutions and laws. Such an archaeological investigation is necessary because American trade policy has been very "sticky": the creation of rules and procedures to enforce a particular economic strategy at one point acts as a constraint not only on current behavior but also on the range of options available to future entrepreneurs.

The overall argument of this book has not been presented elsewhere, although the theoretical problem is explored in an article in *International Organization*, Winter 1988. Some of my research on American policy in the 1930s and 1940s appeared in *International Organization*, Winter 1989, and in John Ruggie, ed., *Multilateralism Matters* (New York: Columbia University Press, 1993).

My work has benefited greatly from the advice of friends and colleagues. I received invaluable assistance from Geoffrey Garrett, David Lake, Peter Katzenstein, and Robert O. Keohane, all of whom read earlier versions of the manuscript and offered sage advice on key theoretical and empirical issues. I also received help at various stages of my research from a host of individuals: David Abernathy, Daniel Drezner, John Ferejohn, Jeffry Frieden, Joanne Gowa, Nina Halpern, John Ikenberry, John Hall, Peter Hall, Stephen Krasner, Roger Noll,

R. Doug Rivers, Kathryn Sikkink, Barry Weingast, and the students in my 1990 graduate seminar Ideas and Politics. All deserve my thanks. Research assistance was ably provided by Orania Markau, Georgia Markau, Christopher Way, Jonathan Kaplan, Amy Searight, and Scott Wilson. I thank Roger Haydon at Cornell University Press for being so patient and generous with his time and Trudie Calvert for her editorial assistance.

While doing research, I benefited enormously from the support of three organizations. The Foreign Policy section of the Social Science Research Council provided both teaching release time and funding for two conferences on ideas and foreign policy. Summer support was given by the Smith Richardson Foundation and the Stanford Institute for International Studies.

JUDITH GOLDSTEIN

Stanford, California

*Ideas, Interests, and
American Trade Policy*

CHAPTER ONE

Ideas, Institutions, and the Politics of Protectionism

To social commentators and political analysts alike, American trade policy is an enigma. Since World War II, American executives have committed the United States to a "liberal" international trade regime. Through participation in multilateral tariff reductions and endorsement of the rules and norms of free trade, the United States facilitated the creation of an open trading system. And even in the face of increasing foreign competition, recent presidents have insisted that the American market remain open. But we can also find evidence of a very different American policy. Export restraint agreements, antidumping laws, and subsidy protections reveal an American government that shelters many industries from the pressures of the international market.

Neither position is wrong. The United States remains fundamentally committed to a liberal trade regime; at the same time, domestic policies restrain the movement of goods across America's borders. This seeming contradiction sparks lively debate over just what American policy is. It simultaneously creates an analytic problem for international relations scholars, particularly those who wish to understand American laws that regulate international trade. These myriad laws vary significantly in the protections of home market they offer, even to otherwise similarly situated industries. Producers who request relief from imports may find that protection of their market is not in the "national economic interest" under one law but can be achieved under a different statute. American behavior can look more or less liberal depending on the legal indicator chosen.

This book addresses the anomaly of concurrent, contradictory forms of trade policy in the United States. American policy is governed, I

1

suggest, by laws that are vestiges of old ideas about the appropriate conditions under which governments should offer protection. Nineteenth-century protectionist economic doctrine and the post–World War II belief in the efficacy of markets both have contemporary legal manifestations. These contradictory ideas—that the government should defend the home market against foreign producers and that it should take a laissez-faire aproach to foreign competition—coexist in American law as legitimate objectives for trade policy.

Because successive trade laws are layered one on top of another—outlasting the purposes for which they were originally created—explanation of American policy must look beyond purely interest-based arguments. In general, such analyses fail to consider adequately how interests translate into political outcomes. Although domestic and international interests are fundamental to economic policy making, the translation of interests into behavior is not straightforward. The choice from a range of possible strategies to realize economic interests may be as important, perhaps more important, in explaining political behavior than are "objective" material interests themselves. Political action is also influenced by existing institutional and legal structures and by the shared beliefs of political actors.

Thus it is not enough to study individual preferences over outcomes—what are commonly called *interests*—to explain behavior. Rather, analysis must focus on preferences over actions or the choice of *strategy*. Objectively "optimal" policies with which leaders can attain their political goals may exist, but their adoption is contingent on their being embedded in some politically salient theory or analysis. For example, the decision whether governments should adopt Keynesian policies in the 1930s or 1940s was not settled by objective facts. Classical economics had suggested that to stimulate employment during economic downturns, governments should not cushion the effects of recession. Keynes argued precisely the opposite, believing that government spending has desirable multiplier effects on aggregate demand. Each theory offered a clear but different causal relationship between government intervention and employment. Political leaders could not choose between the two on objective grounds; rather, their selection of policy was inherently political.[1] In the choice among plausible paths or strategies to attain one's interests, the political power of ideas about economic phenomena plays a critical role.

[1] On the cross-national adoption of Keynesian policies, see Peter Hall, ed., *The Political Power of Economic Ideas* (Princeton: Princeton University Press, 1989). Although Hall studies why an economic idea is adopted, he does not argue that the power of the idea itself explains its acceptance. Rather, the book showcases the considerable variation in the use of Keynesian theory across countries.

Moreover, ideas do not influence behavior simply at one moment in time. Once a set of beliefs has become encased in institutions, these ideas can influence policy even after the interests of their creators have changed. Whatever the explanation for the initial adoption of Keynesian policies, later economic policy was constrained by the multitude of actors who benefited from them. Similarly, American trade laws—often reflecting defunct economic theories—have had an enduring influence on the articulation and aggregation of social interests in protetionism. The legal institutionalization of economic ideas allows "old" rules to continue to influence the actions of individuals, firms, and political actors even though contemporary lawmakers share few concerns with those who originally drafted the statutes.

In sum, beliefs play a dual role in politics. First, at any given moment in time, ideas provide political entrepreneurs with strategies that suggest ways to maximize their interests. Ideas serve as focal points or road maps, providing guidance to leaders. If the ideas that are selected conform with or legitimate the interests of their supporters, they could be understood as mere "hooks."[2] But this notion significantly underestimates the role of beliefs. Political choice invariably occurs in conditions of uncertainty: entrepreneurs rarely know which policy idea will maximize their interests. Their choices are molded by the existing state of knowledge and by the political savvy of the supporters of particular economic policies. In such an environment, ideas themselves become predictors of the direction of policy at least as powerful as are simple calculations of interest.

This book also makes an intertemporal argument. Once a strategy or "policy idea" is selected by politicians, for whatever reason, it has long-term ramifications. Policy ideas leave vestiges; political rules and norms formed in response to and in support of an economic idea fundamentally influence the environment for future political choices. History matters. As policy makers select a particular course of action, they simultaneously constrain the choices of future politicians.

The agenda of this book is to demonstrate that ideas matter, both cross-sectionally and intertemporally, in American trade policy. I have organized it as a policy chronology to show how central decision makers become increasingly constrained by earlier economic policy choices. The book examines why particular economic policies were selected, how these economic choices were institutionalized in legal procedures,

---

[2] Kenneth A. Shepsle, "Comment," in Roger Noll, ed., *Regulatory Policy and the Social Sciences* (Berkeley: University of California Press, 1985), pp. 231–37.

and how these laws imposed constraints even after the close of the epoch in which the original ideas had guided policy.

THEORETICAL FOUNDATIONS

The Study of Trade Policy

Few political phenomena have been studied as thoroughly as tariff policy. Customs barriers provide the longitudinal and cross-national data that social scientists have long used to support different political theories.[3] Two approaches to trade protectionism are currently popular.

First, structural or neorealist approaches consider trade policy a component of overall foreign policy. Structuralists argue that a nation's stance on trade is determined by its relative power. Nations with preponderant power have an interest in pursuing liberal or open trade; less powerful states are more likely to resort to protectionism.[4] According to this argument, the United States provided the collective goods necessary for the creation of a liberal trade regime after World War II, both because of absolute economic gains from trade and because of reasons of international security. America's declining hegemony, structuralists argue, should have resulted in a policy shift: more protection of domestic markets, less interest in maintaining a liberal international trade regime.

The second approach applies a more general interest group or plu-

[3] See, for example, E. E. Schattschneider, *Politics, Pressures and the Tariff: A Study of Free Private Enterprise in Pressure Politics, as Shown in the* 1929–30 Revision of the Tariff (Englewood Cliffs, N.J.: Prentice-Hall, 1935); Raymond A. Bauer, Ithiel de Sola Pool, and Lewis A. Dexter, *American Business and Public Policy: The Politics of Foreign Trade* (Chicago: Aldine Atherton, 1972); Alexander Gerschenkron, *Bread and Democracy in Germany* (1943; Ithaca: Cornell University Press, 1989); Stephen D. Krasner, "United States Commercial Monetary Policy: Unraveling the Paradox of External Strength and Internal Weakness," in *Between Power and Plenty: Foreign Economic Policies of Advanced Industrial States*, ed. Peter J. Katzenstein (Madison: University of Wisconsin Press, 1977), pp. 51–87; Helen Milner, *Resisting Protectionism: Global Industries and the Politics of International Trade* (Princeton: Princeton University Press, 1988); Ronald Rogowski, *Commerce and Coalitions: How Trade Affects Domestic Political Alignments* (Princeton: Princeton University Press, 1989).
[4] See, for example, Stephen D. Krasner, "State Power and the Structure of International Trade," *World Politics* 28 (1976): 317–47; David Lake, *Power, Protection, and Free Trade: International Sources of U.S. Commercial Strategy, 1887–1939* (Ithaca: Cornell University Press, 1988); Joseph Grieco, *Cooperation among Nations: Europe, America and Non-Tariff Barriers to Trade* (Ithaca: Cornell University Press, 1990). The most succinct articulation of the theory is Robert Keohane, "The Theory of Hegemonic Stability and Changes in International Economic Regimes, 1967–1977," in *Change in the International System*, ed. Ole Holsti et al. (Boulder, Colo.: Westview, 1980).

ralist model of domestic politics to trade policy. Interests again are crucial, but the analytic focus is now on domestic political processes. From this perspective, what determines the course of trade policy is the interaction among parties, interest groups, businesses, unions, and other actors. Such bargaining is traditionally said to favor producers over consumers and to foster powerful protectionist pressures.[5] Producers' interests in protection are narrow and immediate; consumers' interests in free trade are diffuse and unorganized. When they want protection, well-organized and powerful producer groups should be able to get it.

Neither of these approaches satisfactorily explains the pattern of protectionism found in the United States. The postwar period has seen significant variations in the amount, timing, and form of protection granted by governments. But the variations are not what either approach predicts. For instance, today's overall tariff schedule is at a historically low level. But concurrently, recent American administrations have relied extensively on voluntary export restraints (VERs) to set quotas in response to the needs of particular industries. The most recent major piece of trade legislation, the Omnibus Trade Act of 1988, propelled American negotiators into new talks on trade liberalization. Simultaneously, however, Congress specified high import barriers on goods from two foreign companies, to punish them for selling technology to the Soviet Union.

The greatest analytic mystery, however, is the variation in government decisions on trade protectionism in cases that appear objectively identical. In the postwar period, companies that petitioned the International Trade Commission (ITC), the chief agency for administering trade aid, for "escape clause" exclusion from a trade agreement repeatedly found the agency unwilling to provide relief. Yet if they filed under an "unfair trade" statute, with no other change in conditions, the agency often gave them positive hearings.

In short, the issue analysts must address is not simply whether

---

[5] See, for example, Schattschneider, *Politics, Pressures;* Tom E. Terrill, *The Tariff Politics and American Foreign Policy, 1874–1901* (Westport, Conn.: Greenwood, 1973); Richard W. Thompson, *The History of Protective Tariff Laws* (New York: Garland, 1974); J. M. Dobson, *Two Centuries of Tariffs* (Washington: USGPO, 1976); Ernest Preeg, *Traders and Diplomats: An Analysis of the Kennedy Round of Negotiations under the General Agreement on Tariffs and Trade* (Washington, D.C.: Brookings Institutions, 1970); Robert Pastor, *Congress and the Politics of U.S. Foreign Economic Policy* (Berkeley: University of California Press, 1980); Jonathan J. Pincus, *Pressure Groups and Politics in Antebellum Tariffs* (New York: Columbia University Press, 1977); Timothy McKeown, "Firms and Tariff Change: Explaining the Demand for Protection," *World Politics* 36 (1984): 215–33; I. M. Destler, *American Trade Politics: System under Stress* (Washington, D.C.: Institute for International Studies, 1986); I. M. Destler and John S. Odell, *Antiprotectionism: Changing Forces in United States Trade Politics* (Washington, D.C.: Institute for International Studies, 1987).

groups in the United States have an interest in free trade or protection, or whether the international distribution of wealth has made closure a more appealing policy. Instead, it is why policy varies dramatically in the treatment of industries, even when we hold constant both international structural conditions and the needs and power of these industries.

Interest-based analyses, domestic and international, of trade policy are poorly equipped to address this question for two reasons. First, rationalist explanations—of which these are a subset—generally do not predict unique outcomes. Rather, strategic interactions between individuals, groups, or states often sustain a multitude of equilibria.[6] To explain a particular outcome, even game theorists must move beyond a simple model of interests to conventions, learned behavior, focal points, bounded rationality, and the like. Analysts of trade policy, too, must move beyond interests to understand, for example, how strategic actors decide on a particular policy, why suboptimal policies endure, and what conditions generate such outcomes.

Second, interest-based trade analyses pay too little attention to the institutional attributes of the system in which actors bargain and choose strategies. For example, economists and political scientists who investigate trade issues often argue that aberrations in liberal trade result from pressures exerted by noncompetitive but politically powerful economic groups. Openness is, they assume, optimal for aggregate social welfare. Free trade conditions become the baseline for analysis; deviations are caused by political (albeit economically motivated) phenomena. All protection is explained by the undue political influence of noncompetitive sectors. But since most trade economists are not interested in a positive theory of government, they give little thought to the processes by which interest-group pressures elicit government responses. The translation of interests into outcomes is assumed, and as

---

[6] Political science has inherited this dilemma with its increasing use of microeconomic methodology. Although economics may be more amenable to rationalist-based explanations than is politics, even economists confront the problem of multiple equilibria (the so-called folk theorem). For elaborations see David Kreps, *A Course in Microeconomic Theory* (Princeton: Princeton University Press, 1990). The need to go beyond simple "interests" is exemplified in the classic game, the "battle of the sexes." Here two people need to agree on some joint outing. Neither wants to go out alone, but each wants to go out to different places. The payoffs then are 0,0 on the off cells and 1,2 and 2,1 respectively on the other cells. Both nonzero cells are equilibria. Therefore to explain the decision of each player and the behavioral outcome, we need to add some other variable to the model. Shared beliefs coordinate behavior in that they lead each party to expect certain behavior from the other.

6

a result, there is often too much focus on the demand for assistance, too little on the institutional arena in which aid is allocated.[7]

Political and economic actors, however, do not live in a frictionless world. Rather, as institutionalists are quick to point out, individuals make choices in an environment that has established rules and norms of action. But institutionalists agree on little else. On key questions such as the function of institutions, the types of constraint institutions impose on self-interested behavior, and explanations for the choice of a particular set of rules and norms, those who otherwise identify themselves as institutionalists have little in common.[8]

Institutions are always present for rational choice analysts, who define politics as the action of individuals optimizing under a given set of constraints. But why *that* set of constraints? Analysts who are quick to agree that institutional structures shape individual behavior often assume those institutions are fixed and exogenous.[9] More recently, however, rational choice theorists have increasingly turned to an endogenous theory of institutions: instead of treating institutions as given, they have focused on the creation of rules and norms.

[7] See William A. Brock and Stephen P. Magee, "The Economics of Pork-Barrel Politics," Report 7511, Center for Mathematical Studies in Business and Economics, University of Chicago (February 1975); Brock and Magee, "The Economics of Special Interest Politics: The Case of the Tariff," *American Economic Review* 68 (1978): 246–50; Brock and Magee, "Tariff Formation in a Democracy," in *Current Issues in Commercial Policy and Diplomacy*, ed. John Black and Brian Hindley (New York: St. Martin's, 1980), pp. 1–9; Ronald Findlay and Stanislaus Wellisz, "Endogenous Tariffs, the Political Economy of Trade Restrictions and Welfare," in *Import Competition and Response*, ed. Jagdish Bhagwati (Chicago: University of Chicago Press, 1982), pp. 223–38; Magee, "Endogenous Tariff Theory: A Survey," in *Neoclassical Political Economy*, ed. D. C. Collander (Cambridge, Mass.: Ballinger, 1984), pp. 41–55; Magee and Brock, "A Model of Politics, Tariffs and Rent Seeking in General Equilibrium," in *Problems of Developed Countries and the International Economy: Human Resources, Employment, and Development*, vol. 3, ed. Burton Weisbrod and Helen Hughes (London: Macmillan, 1983), pp. 497–523.

[8] Institutionalism covers a wide spectrum of writings. On the sociological side see, for example, James March and Johan Olsen, *Rediscovering Institutions: The Organizational Basis of Politics* (New York: Free Press, 1989). For a less functionalist account of institutional formation and maintenance see Terry Moe, "Political Institutions: The Neglected Side of the Story," *Journal of Law, Economics and Organization* 6, Special Issue (1990): 213–53 and "The Politics of Structural Choice: Toward a Theory of Public Bureaucracy," in *Organization Theory: From Chester Barnard to the Present and Beyond*, ed. Oliver Williamson (New York: Oxford University Press, 1990). For examples of functionalist theories of institutions see Kenneth Shepsle, "Institutional Equilibrium and Equilibrium Institutions," in *Political Science: The Science of Politics*, ed. Herbert Weisberg (New York: Agathon, 1986), and Barry Weingast, "The Political Institutions of Representational Government," Working Paper in Political Science P-89-14, December 1989, Hoover Institution.

[9] For example, see Kenneth Shepsle and Barry Weingast, "Institutionalizing Majority Rule: A Social Choice Theory with Policy Implications," *American Economic Review* 73 (1983): 357–72.

Here, rationalists part company. For one group, rules mirror the interests of the powerful in society. There are well-specified reasons why actors may delegate power to a new organization as a rational response to future uncertainties over, for example, who will control government. Thus one party may protect its future stake in a policy by creating a bureaucracy that will pursue its interests even while the party is out of power. Existing rules and norms reflect the relative power of actors at the creation of an institution, not an optimal policy to solve problems of collective action.[10] According to this logic there is no reason why institutions should be functional from the perspective of society at large.

Many other rationalists, however, argue that institutions emerge as a functional response to problems of collective action, a means to reduce uncertainty and transaction costs.[11] At minimum, institutions provide and coordinate information about members.[12] Those who study international politics find this characterization appealing. In the absence of authoritative international courts and sanctions, international institutions assure that nations act in their "enlightened self-interest." It is logical that both individuals and nations would choose to sacrifice some degree of independence in order to obtain joint gains.[13]

Not all "institutionalists" share a rationalist epistemology. Rather than look at how institutions serve interests or constrain the optimization of preferences, many focus on institutions as part of shared intersubjective meanings in society. Cooperation, for example, may be seen as a by-product of shared cultural practices, not the outcome of reasoned thought.[14] It may be not that rules and norms constrain behavior but that the meanings and understandings of those rules influence

[10] Such an argument is made by Moe, "Politics of Structural Choice," on the domestic level. Similarly, on the international level, the power of nations has been suggested as the reason particular rules and norms have been incorporated into international regimes. See also Stephen Krasner, "Global Communications and National Power: Life on the Pareto Frontier," *World Politics* 43 (1991).

[11] See Robert Keohane, *After Hegemony: Cooperation and Discord in the World Political Economy* (Princeton: Princeton University Press, 1984).

[12] See Paul Milgrom, Douglass North, and Barry Weingast, "The Role of Institutions in the Revival of Trade: The Law Merchant, Private Judges, and the Champaign Fairs," *Economics and Politics* 2 (1990): 1–23.

[13] But in the domestic setting a legal system can enforce agreements between individuals. Under such conditions, individuals have a greater incentive to delegate authority and to establish institutions that do more than merely convey information about the behavior of members.

[14] For examples in international politics see Friedrich Kratochwil and John G. Ruggie, "International Organization: A State of the Art on an Art of the State," *International Organization* 40 (1986): 753–76; John G. Ruggie, "Continuity and Transformation in the World Polity: Toward a Neorealist Synthesis," in *Neorealism and Its Critics*, ed. R. O. Keohane (New York: Columbia University Press, 1986), pp. 131–57.

how individuals understand their interests. Institutions themselves may come to be valued not for what they can do for individuals but for the principles they embody. Shared rules and norms do not just allow actors to optimize their interest; they may become internalized in individuals' ethical codes and thus long outlast any functional purpose. Thus, as Robert Keohane notes, institutions may endure "that are not plausibly viewed as the product of human calculation and bargaining."[15]

This study of American trade laws concedes that functional needs generate incentives to create institutions, legal or otherwise. However, to explain particular outcomes, I go beyond the assumption that individuals are "self-seeking" to ask how rational actors go about furthering their interests. This explanation for behavior looks beyond material interests to beliefs about the efficacy of particular strategies for attaining these objectives. I do not want to argue about whether "objective" interests motivate trade policy; I assume they do. This book focuses, instead, on how those interests are conceived by those making policy decisions and on the strategies they believe are available to attain those interests. Further, the choice of an economic policy spawns unsuspected consequences. As many institutionalists suggest, policies can be maintained long after they cease to be functional responses to the needs of society or of its powerful members.[16] Economic choices are long-lasting, not only because their institutionalization influences future constellations of interests but also because, in part, individuals come to value the economic policy's rules and norms themselves.

The Role of Ideas and Their Institutionalization

The conventional rationalist assumes that government officials are either reelection maximizers or budget maximizers and that producers and consumers maximize profits and consumption, respectively. Such is the starting point for much contemporary political analysis of economic policy making. These assumptions may or may not be correct. Defenders are far more interested in their predictive power than in their truth.[17] I believe it is neither necessary nor productive to fight over the centrality of interests in political analysis. Rather, I argue that analyses of commercial policy based solely on interest calculations are

[15] Robert Keohane, "International Institutions: Two Approaches," *International Studies Quarterly* 32 (1988): 379–96.
[16] See Terry Moe, "Interests, Institutions and Positive Theory: The Politics of the NLRB," *Studies in American Political Development* 2 (1987): 236–99.
[17] Milton Friedman, "The Methodology of Positive Economics," in his *Essays in Positive Economics* (Chicago: University of Chicago Press, 1953).

insufficient because they do not provide sufficient explanation for numerous "idiosyncratic" outcomes.

Why? People may know exactly what they want but still rely on some set of beliefs (about the actions of others and the nature of the world) in order to select an appropriate strategy. In a world shrouded in uncertainty, interest maximization alone tells us little about the choice of a particular political activity. It is probably true that interests, broadly defined, motivate individual action. It is equally clear, however, that individuals face choices in the way they go about acting on those interests. Only in a world of complete information could interests be perfectly congruent with strategies.

Consider, for example, the difficulties of an American official who wants to maximize the probability of reelection when selecting a commercial policy. The policy chosen has a direct effect on the economic well-being of a wide array of consumers: if tariffs are too high, trade will stop. But the leader may rely on producer groups for funding to fight elections and hence must be attentive to their demands for protection. And, as a foreign policy tool, protectionism can affect the economic position of an ally or competitor. So the optimal commericial policy would serve the interests of relevant interest groups and the electorate at large and still protect American interests abroad. To derive this optimal policy, the official must predict long-term shifts in international markets, anticipate the probable behavior of trading partners, and foresee America's future productive capacity. Even if it were possible, the costs involved in such calculations would be huge, and the uncertainty introduced in implementation and by cheating or error makes the effort worthless.[18] It is no surprise that the history of tariff policy over the last two hundred years indicates that although many have sought optimal, rational solutions, institutional and ideational variables have had very powerful effects on policy.

Thus, I begin by rejecting two simple models of policy making. First, purely materialist analysis of individual choice is inadequate. Although interests motivate political action, uncertainty undermines the ability of interest-based models to predict specific outcomes. The explanation of commercial policy presented here suggests that ideas about the working of the economy may be as important as the material interests of voters and representatives.

Second, purely functional and noninstitutional accounts of public policies are insufficient. The history of trade policy in the United States

---

[18] These problems of uncertainty are further explored in John Kingdon, "Ideas, Politics and Public Policies," paper delivered at the 1988 annual meeting of the American Political Science Association.

points to the importance of past policy decisions; the initial choice among competing ideas constrains and shapes all future political responses.[19] On a macrohistorical level, political outcomes are path-dependent. As Stephen Jay Gould so aptly suggests, life is the result of the conjoining of innumerable small events into one of many possible patterns.[20] Policy conjunctures have a lasting impact through the development of institutions, either directly by a slow-changing legal system or indirectly through the development of enduring rules and norms. Institutions can reflect "extinct" ideas; they may not represent existing social preferences. And without consideration of the particular institutional context in which interests are articulated and aggregated, policy analysis is incomplete.

Ideas in Politics

In this book "ideas" are defined as shared beliefs.[21] The economic beliefs with which we are concerned are *shared causal beliefs*—beliefs about cause-effect relationships initially deriving authority from the status of their bearers. Causal ideas are tantamount to strategies: they are road maps showing actors how to maximize interests, whether those interests are material or ideational.[22] Because causal beliefs may be associated with deeply entrenched normative beliefs, they usually reflect underlying values. In general, however, many causal ideas could

[19] On path dependence see W. B. Arthur, "Competing Technologies and Economic Predictions," *Options*, April 1984; Arthur, "Competing Technologies, Increasing Returns and Lock-In by Historical Events," *Economic Journal* 99 (March 1989): 116–31; Arthur, "Industry Location Patterns and the Importance of History," Stanford University, Center for Economic Policy, Paper 84 (1986).

[20] Stephen J. Gould, *Wonderful Life: The Burgess Shale and the Nature of History* (New York: Norton, 1989).

[21] This definition and typology derive from Judith Goldstein and Robert Keohane, "Ideas and Foreign Policy: Beliefs, Institutions, and Political Change," in *Ideas and Foreign Policy*, ed. Goldstein and Keohane (Ithaca: Cornell University Press, 1993).

[22] Beliefs may not be only about causal relationships—they could be about far more fundamental or deeply ingrained values held by a polity. At a most fundamental level, ideas may be defined as worldviews—they are deeply embedded in culture, in people's conceptions of themselves, in modes of social interaction. A role for ideas at this level is suggested by Clifford Geertz, *Negara: The Theatre State in Nineteenth-Century Bali* (Princeton: Princeton University Press, 1980); Ruggie, "Continuity and Transformation," pp. 131–57; and Ernst B. Haas, *When Knowledge Is Power: Three Models of Change in International Organizations* (Berkeley: University of California Press, 1990).
Ideas may also be about norms but be more specific than worldviews. One class of such ideas specifies criteria for determining whether actions are right or wrong or good or bad—such ideas may be called shared principled beliefs. Shared principles are commonplace in politics; whether or not they can be separated from interests remains problematic. Thus we see ideas such as "slavery is wrong," "women are equal to men," and "abortion is murder" being both used and believed by political entrepreneurs.

function on a particular normative base. For example, commercial policy in the nineteenth century was premised on a set of causal ideas about the relationship between wages and trade. Those causal ideas were probably wrong; people abandoned them a century later on the assumption they were wrong. Although quite different, both sets of beliefs were compatible with American conceptions of the role of government. In general, ideas that do not "fit" with underlying social values are unlikely to find support among political entrepreneurs and the attentive public.[23]

Ideas are always present; they give meaning to action and prescribe legitimate individual and group claims for political and material goods. Beliefs are guides for action; hence we see their impact most clearly when issues of strategy are in dispute. At such moments ideas serve as the glue holding coalitions together—groups form around a vision of common interests or a justification for those interests. Most generally, as Max Weber suggests, ideas act as "switchmen" determining the "tracks along which action has been pushed by the dynamic of interest."[24]

How do beliefs make their way into the political process? It is helpful to imagine four stylized stages in the development of public policies. First, policy change is prefaced by a period of policy delegitimation. The status quo no longer meets the needs of political entrepreneurs, either because of exogenous economic change or because of endogenous political change. A policy window thereby opens: political entrepreneurs are willing to consider their present beliefs flawed. At these moments there will be an interest in policy change among policy makers and the public. Second, once there is an impetus for change, a period of "search" ensues and some alternative policy strategy is selected. Third, the choice of some new set of cause-effect relationships to guide policy stimulates a period of "experimentation," resulting either in a return to the status quo ante or in an agreement about the virtue of new policy. Last, in a period of institutionalization the ability of the policy to deliver on its promise affects the extent to which reinforcing rules and norms develop.

Movement through these stages is never preordained. For example, exogenous shocks will open a policy window only if existing institutions are unable to explain and respond to environmental change. Alterna-

---

[23] Perhaps the strongest example of how social values do not necessarily constrain beliefs—even principled beliefs—is the toleration and then rejection of slavery in Christian societies.

[24] Max Weber, "The Social Psychology of the World's Religions," in *From Max Weber: Essays in Sociology,* ed. H. H. Gerth and C. Wright Mills (New York: Oxford University Press, 1958), p. 280.

tively, a period of search can end with no options: no new ideas are generated, or those that exist lack political salience. The importance of Fortuna is also critical. In malevolent times the correct long-term policy can be rejected prematurely; a benevolent environment may lead political entrepreneurs to overvalue a minimally efficient policy.

Delegitimation and the Creation of Policy Windows

At some moments, politicians and the political process seem ripe for change; at others, innovation is ignored. What explains the demand for new ideas? In the case of economic policy making, three factors are of great importance: exogenous shocks, such as wars or international depressions, demographic changes, and the failure of current economic policies to generate desirable economic outcomes, all motivate political leaders to examine current policy. Fundamentally, it is the perception, whether warranted or not, of failure in current policy or political institutions or both that creates the incentive for political elites to change. Such moments create political space, windows of time, and political entrepreneurs begin to search out and try new policy prescriptions.[25]

Just about all significant changes in American trade policy have been prefaced by economic hard times. Slow growth or recession leads political entrepreneurs to question current policy and often allows newly elected elites to attempt policy reform.[26] Universally, political entrepreneurs will be motivated to change if present policy no longer meets their material needs, those of their constituents, or those of the nation.

---

[25] See, for example, Fred Block, "The Ruling Class Does Not Rule," *Socialist Revolution* 33 (1977): 6–28; Block, "Beyond Relative Autonomy: State Managers as Historical Subjects," *Socialist Register* 36 (1980): 227–42; Peter Gourevitch, *Politics in Hard Times* (Ithaca: Cornell University Press, 1986); Peter Hall, *Governing the Economy: The Politics of State Intervention in Britain and France* (Cambridge: Polity, 1986); John Kingdon, *Agendas, Alternatives and Public Policies* (Glenview, Ill.: Scott, Foresman, 1984); Theda Skocpol, "Political Response to Captialist Crisis: Neo-Marxist Theories of the State and the Case of the New Deal," *Politics and Society* 10 (1982): 151–201; Skocpol, "Bringing the State Back In: Strategies of Analysis in Current Research," in *Bringing the State Back In*, ed. Peter Evans et al. (New York: Cambridge University Press, 1985).

[26] Although it is true that economic decline most often motivates political action, such decline can be fairly particularistic. Thus demographic shifts can lead to the perception that current policy is failing new majorities, even if there are no other economic changes. This is probably the best explanation for the emergence of deregulation and supply-side economic strategies in the Reagan years. Although one could argue that the Reagan administration believed (given the depth of the depression in the early Reagan years) that economic programs were failing, it was more probably demographic shifts that favored the Republican party and the election of an ideologue that explain the demand for new economic policies.

Thus the perception of failed policy is a necessary, though not a sufficient, condition for fundamental change in economic policy.

Both epochal changes in American commercial policy detailed in this book were preceded by fundamental shocks to the economy. To explain, for example, the move in the 1930s away from protectionism, we must focus not only on growth in the supply of ideas such as "liberalism" but also on what explains variation in the demand for these new policy ideas. In this case, economic decline and its social dislocations forced political leaders to seek an explanation for and an answer to hard times. With the Depression came a change in control of both Congress and the presidency, bringing in individuals willing to adopt programs based on a different economic vision.[27] At that moment the demand for policy change was met by an alternative: trade liberalization.

But hard times are not always accompanied by policy change. A full model of policy making must consider which policy options are considered by policy elites.

Search for New Policies

For a change in policy to occur, "new" ideas must be available. They must be politically salient and carried by well-placed elites. But the right idea is not always present. Why do ideas vary in number and type across polities? And what is the relationship between this variation and selection for use by political entrepreneurs at any historical moment?

Functionalists have an easy response—ideas appear in response to social needs.[28] But as Richard Cooper has recently shown in the case of health care, ideas are not always available when they are needed, and even if found in one polity, they are often ignored in the next.[29] The Chinese invented gunpowder and the compass, yet they failed to build weapons either to expand abroad or to defend themselves. Thus we need to look further, at institutional, cultural, and other variables,

---

[27] This is consistent with Gourevitch's explanation in *Politics in Hard Times*. It differs only in the suggestion that the policy pursued by the political coalition was solely dictated by the "objective" interests of its members. I suggest that the existence of that coalition, as opposed to some other, and the programs it advocated both to attain power and once in office had as much to do with economic ideas prevalent in the 1920s as with materialist interests.

[28] For example, Marx argued that ideas reflect the underlying conditions of a society. Talcott Parsons suggested that they perform certain system goals. More recently, Douglass North argued that they reduce compliance costs. Most contemporary economists interpret ideas, when they see them, as responses to problems of signaling, contracting, or commitment.

[29] Richard Cooper, "International Cooperation in Public Health as a Prologue to Macroeconomic Cooperation," in *Can Nations Agree?* ed. Cooper et al. (Washington, D.C.: Brookings Institution, 1989).

to explain both the generation of new ideas—including scientific ideas—and their rate of diffusion through societies.[30]

But it is not only the content of an idea which influences whether or not it is "consumed"; the form of an idea—its complexity, its apparent fit with general values and other political issues, and its ability to be implemented—will determine whether it appeals to political entrepreneurs. Moreover, the status of the idea's bearer will be important.[31] For ideas to become politically salient they need to have sponsors, and those sponsors must either hold political power or influence those who do.

Liberal trade ideas, for example, arrived in the United States at about the same time, and were disseminated among an attentive public at about the same pace, as they were in Britain. Yet, in the United States they were virtually ignored for a century whereas in Britain they had a significant influence on policy by the mid-nineteenth century. The lack of salience of liberalism in the United States reflected both the limited status of those who held classical economic ideas and the inability of those people to present their beliefs in a manner that held political appeal. U.S. liberal trade ideas in the nineteenth century were too abstract and were built on a set of assumptions that seemed inappropriate for the American economy. In contrast, the argument for protection was more concrete and better developed as policy prescription. Only with the gradual expansion and professionalization of the discipline of economics, and the insistence by most major universities that all students have a grounding in classical economics, did individuals who believed in these ideas become able to translate them into a form usable for policy prescription.

Policy Experimentation

Once selected, some ideas have greater longevity than others. Why is this? Functionalists are again partially correct. In the realm of eco-

---

[30] On uses of science and technology, see Peter Haas, *Saving the Mediterranean: The Politics of International Environmental Cooperation* (New York: Columbia University Press, 1990), and Ernest Haas, *When Knowledge Is Power.* There is a distinction to be made between technological and other ideas. Although some of what is science becomes validated in a way other ideas, causal and normative, cannot be, scientific truths too rely upon agreement of a community of experts. Scientific communities often disagree and even when they agree, they are not always correct.

[31] It may be, as Cooper and P. Haas suggest, that entrepreneurs act on new ideas only if there is already a consensus among the professionals or carriers of the idea. See Cooper, "International Cooperation," and Peter Haas's work on epistemic communities as the bearers of new scientific knowledge. For domestic institutional and social variables see Hall, *Political Power of Economic Ideas.*

nomic ideas, it is critical whether the policy delivers on its promises. It is a rare policy indeed that can maintain the support of a political coalition without delivering benefits to its members. But although functionalists may be correct that ideas are usually abandoned when they no longer serve their intended purpose—whether the commonweal or the particularistic interests of political elites—they are wrong to assume that only optimal ideas become institutionalized. Often the environment in which an idea is tested, not the quality of the idea itself, determines perceptions of the policy's success.

The history of American trade policy makes it clear that when the economy flourishes there is little incentive to change policy, whatever the objective merits. If, in contrast, existing policy confronts hard times, it is abandoned, again regardless of its economic merits. Policy makers attend to the interaction of trade policy with the international economic environment, and so global market conditions and other structural variables play a critical role in the decision among policies. However, the international environment does not stipulate just one policy option; it may constrain the range of choices, but for large states the constraint is likely to be weak.

The distribution of economic power after World War II, for example, meant that several trade policies would have worked as well or better at the onset of the Depression. The Democrats could have returned to their pre-Depression advocacy of unilateral tariff cuts; the Republicans could have backed a proposal to liberalize trade in primary products but not trade in manufactured products. It is by no means clear that reciprocal trade liberalization in these years was the optimal policy— given America's dominant position in the world economy, *any* relatively more open trade policy would have led to increased growth. But American policy makers did not think about alternative policies. Rather, they became convinced that only one policy, that is, liberalization of trade through treaty, explained the expansion of postwar trade. This interpretation was crucial to the future development of American policy. The assumption that liberalism caused economic growth resulted in systematic discounting of new information that suggested American industries might need more government assistance in order to compete on world markets.

In short, the environments in which policies are tested and evaluated vary, and these differences matter. For even the best-laid plans, it may be Fortuna that decides whether feedback on the merits of a policy idea is positive. If policies are tested in a benign or benevolent environment, they will appear to meet the needs of their creators. In malevolent environments, however, even the best long-term solution to a problem may be abandoned prematurely. Even so, it is unlikely that any one policy will continue to be optimal over time; as the economic needs of a country change, so will its preferred policy. Yet policy shifts are more often abrupt than gradual. Individuals and political coalitions attach themselves to particular views of the world so that change is difficult. Most crucially, the actions of insitutions created to administer public policies serve to perpetuate those policies.

Policy Institutionalization

Institutions may perpetuate ideas in two ways. First, they may preserve political support even for a poorly functioning policy because they affect the ways and the extent to which elites respond to changes in the environment. Second, institutions influence individuals' incentives and can create new constituencies in support of particular public policies.

Once created, organizations are slow to change.[32] Institutions are legal vestiges of previous policy beliefs and are created to serve a particular mandated purpose. Mandates evolve from a political consensus that was generated to support a social need or a particular policy response by a government. Institutions, then, reflect a set of dominant ideas translated—often through legal mechanisms—into formal government organizations.

Today, most social scientists agree that government and administrative structures create differing incentives and opportunities for members of society. Rules, norms, expectations, and traditions establish constraints on individuals within the specific institution, on elected leaders outside these organizations, and on society in general. In the United States, both government institutions and civil society are bound by the rule of law. In fact, the elaborate set of legal rights and obligations encased in American law sets U.S. politics apart from those of many of its trading partners. In the United States, laws are established to protect a distrusting civil society from a potentially intrusive government. The rule of law, however, encourages a time lag between current political climate and current institutions. Because it is difficult to change an institution's governing legal status, U.S. organizations live long beyond the mandate that created them. Public organizations do change, but they change more slowly than the environment in which they operate. This legal constraint leads to the layering of institutions:

[32] See Marver H. Bernstein, *Regulating Business by Independent Commission* (Princeton: Princeton University Press, 1955); Anthony Downs, *Inside Bureaucracy* (Boston: Little, Brown, 1967); Herbert A. Simon, *Administrative Behavior: A Study of Decision-Making Processes in Administrative Organization* (New York: Macmillan, 1947); James G. March and Herbert A. Simon, *Organizations* (New York: Wiley, 1958).

creating anew is easier than removing the old. In short, both new and old policy ideas can have organizational manifestations simultaneously.

Once in place, institutions temper the influence of changes in domestic and international politics. Groups organize and interact with government within prevailing institutional constraints. Similarly, changes in market conditions are filtered through institutions. International forces are interpreted through institutional lenses that describe what changes are progressive, which do or do not affect national or particularistic interests, and what mechanisms government officials may use in response. Though elites constantly update in response to political and economic changes, both their perceptions of the importance of these shifts and what they see as legitimate responses are refracted through entrenched structures of belief.

THE STUDY OF AMERICAN COMMERCIAL POLICY

How have beliefs influenced American commercial policy? To understand both past and contemporary policy, first, we need to explain why some and not other economic ideas made their way into the political arena. Although the generation of ideas is beyond the scope of this work, characteristics of particular ideas explain their salience to political entrepreneurs. Second, as well as investigating the supply of ideas, we need to explore the demand for and the political process of selecting theoretical models by political entrepreneurs. And third, we need to investigate the impact of political institutions on how interests—international and domestic—are articulated and understood. If institutions are vestiges of defunct economic theories, they should be like old redwood trees whose rings provide visual evidence of the weight of the past.[33]

In a sense, this is an archaeological study, examining the origins of the legal institutions that determine contemporary U.S. trade policy. Variation in laws is seen as a reflection of conflicting ideas about the ends of commerical policy, as entrenched in the American legal system. I begin with the generation of trade theory in the United States. Moving through time, I concentrate on the availability of ideas about commercial policy, the demands for them by political entrepreneurs, and their transmission into the political arena. For convenience I have suggested analytic divisions between periods, but these divisions are not

---

[33] This metaphor was suggested by Robert Keohane, who pointed out that in their size and shape tree rings provide indexes of changes in environmental conditions.

meant to downplay the constant threads in trade policy; throughout American history, actions by politicians constrain future policy choices.

The next chapter examines the choice of economic policy in a relatively uninstitutionalized period, one moreover in which there was no hegemonic economic ideology. As a result, commercial policy in the first half of the nineteenth century shifted with changes in party control of government. Material interests provide a good explanation for the positions various groups and coalitions advocated; ideas played a role only in that economic discourse gave regional parties a rationale for the commercial policy they supported. This flexibility ended when the Republican party adopted protectionism, marking the beginning of the first of two trade eras. The Republican choice of high tariffs cannot be explained solely in terms of the material interests of their political constituencies. The new party contained a broad array of groups whose interests varied greatly. Just as critical as interests to the party's choice among economic positions was the way intellectuals "marketed" protectionist ideas.

Why was protectionism salient when economic liberalism—an idea that appeared in political debate around the turn of the nineteenth century—conformed as well, perhaps better, with general American values, institutions, and constituent demands? Free-trade ideas diffused broadly in the early decades of the century, but they were politically inert by midcentury. Essentially, the form in which they were offered was both too abstract for and irrelevant to what politicians saw as the American predicament. Most important, free-trade analysts had no theory about how increased trade would allow free labor to maintain high wages. When the Republican party sought to maximize the interests of its diverse constituency, it believed that only high tariffs could assure "free land, free labor, and free men." Such a vision did not start at the bottom—in fact, manufacturers were split on what kind of tariff would maximize their wealth. Rather, it was supplied by economists and appeared to be vindicated by the economic booms and declines that had accompanied previous changes in tariff levels.

Chapter 3 analyzes the consequences of the Republican party's decision to become the defender of protectionism. In the period of high tariffs from 1870 to 1930, this dominant economic vision constrained U.S. responses to changes in the world economy. With the completion of the transnational railroad, the United States could transport midwestern grain quickly and cheaply to market. By the last decade of the century, the United States had become the major manufacturing nation in the world. Both of these changes led domestic groups to demand that their government find new markets. Similarly, the growth of the American economy pointed clearly to the potential gains from trade.

Yet in a period when interest calculations would suggest the United States should have opened markets to world trade, leaders pursued the opposite policy, significantly increasing levels of protection.

Why did changes in interests not translate into corresponding changes in policy? The simple answer is that the protectionist vision and its accompanying institutions biased all political activity. Although constituents wanted policy that would meet their needs for trade expansion, the response of political entrepreneurs reflected the use of an economic model that was, given American economic advantage, far from optimal. Thus the explanation for policy stasis relies both on demand and on supply: congressional institutions and the absence of an alternative vision reinforced protectionist policies.

Protectionism may not have been an optimal policy, given America's place in world markets, but until the Great Depression it did not interfere with American growth. Protectionist ideas were maintained both as a "filter" interpreting interests and as a vision of how to reconcile vastly changing interests. Chapter 4 argues that the Depression dispelled any lingering beliefs in the virtues of closed markets. When the expanded Democratic party once again gained control of government, it had the opportunity to put in place a new economic program. But what program would the Democrats pursue?

In the midst of a worldwide depression, unilateral tariff reductions—the Democratic platform of the previous century—appeared the "sucker's payoff."[34] The administration thus embarked on a search for policy, settling on reciprocal trade only after attributing postwar abundance to the expansion of international trade. The Depression created an opportunity for change; the chosen path reflected the political savvy of those who had a particular vision of trade policy. Acceptance of this vision can be attributed to the rise of American hegemony, the rapid growth of the economy, and the association of affluence with liberal trade.

Although they advocated trade reform, the Democrats did not completely dismantle the extant protectionist legal system. Thus both protection and openness remained incorporated in American law. This coexistence became a problem only after the 1970s, when these old legal mechanisms forced now-liberal central decision makers to acquiesce to specific protections. To temper societal resistance to trade

---

[34] The policies of nations in the 1930s appear in line with the predictions of a harsh Prisoner's Dilemma game. In fact, competitive devaluations, rising tariffs, and general nationalism influenced the Democratic party's view of whether or not the United States would benefit from unilateral actions. Given the general behavior of nations, policy makers assumed that other nations would take advantage of an American policy of unilateral reductions.

policy, elected officials turned to symbolic forms of aid, most of which did not protect producers from market forces but, instead, served merely to redistribute the gains from trade.

Finally, the book addresses the consequences of institutionalization. Chapter 5 investigates the impact on contemporary policy outcomes of laws created over the preceding century. These laws have both constrained the choices of policy makers and influenced the behavior of labor and capital in soliciting trade assistance. Chapter 5 sets out to explain the paradox of contemporary American trade policy: the variation in the forms of protectionism that political leaders have advocated since World War II. In defending the explanation of policy based on its ideational history, the chapter looks at aggregate data on industry protectionism to assess the power of rival explanations.

Chapter 6 generalizes, from this account of the making of American commercial policy, four findings that should inform all studies of the role of ideas in politics. First, the mere existence of ideas inside or outside a polity in no way guarantees that political entrepreneurs will seek them. Both the form of the idea and the status of its bearers will determine whether even "good" ideas are noticed. Second, once cognitive models are in place, they may be adhered to even after they no longer maximize relevant interests. They remain in place because they operate as filters, systematically discounting information about the failures of existing theory. As interests diverge in times of flux, moreover, entrepreneurs rely more heavily on cognitive models as a guide to meeting constituent interests. Further, as policies become institutionalized, they shape and channel interests.

Third, the analytic key to explaining why some but not other ideas are incorporated into policy lies with political entrepreneurs. When elites seek new economic ideas, how do they select from among the possibilities? How do they become convinced that a particular choice will optimize their interests? In one sense the answer to both questions lies in whether political leaders perceive a strategy as maximizing their own, their constituencies', and the nation's interests. But clarity is rare in any of these three interest categories. Thus political entrepreneurs seek new solutions when old ones appear not to be working, either because of exogenous shocks or merely because voters are dissatisfied with the policies pursued by a previous party. Politicians select ideas they see as applicable to their larger interests. From the available pool, they will choose a policy with the most positive externalities, that is, a policy that answers the needs of as many of their interests as possible. Clearly, this says nothing about choosing an *economically* optimal policy, for such a policy may not be well articulated, may not be known, or may fit poorly with other policies to which the political entrepreneur is already committed.

Finally, how do politicians obtain feedback on the "correctness" of their strategies? Here, there is a large role for Fortuna. The right policy may be discounted because of the wrong application of the right solution. Conversely, a suboptimal policy may be adopted because outcomes are propelled by other events. What comes out most clearly from the case of U.S. trade, however, is that policy is path dependent: the world does not start anew at each decision point. Rather, history builds an ever-more-complex web of interests, ideas, and policies.

CHAPTER TWO

Generation and Selection: Antebellum
Ideas, Politics, and the Tariff

In the seventy-five years between the adoption of the Constitution and the Civil War, American commercial policy evolved from traditional mercantilism, to a quasi-liberal emphasis on free trade, and finally, following the war, to protectionism. This transformation did not result from objective shifts in America's national interest but, rather, reflected new beliefs about America's place in the world and altered perceptions about the efficacy of particular economic policies. In general, this period was characterized by the increasing legitimacy of protectionist ideas among the attentive public and government officials.

For those who follow contemporary debates on trade policy, discussions in the early nineteenth century are surprisingly familiar. Central then, as now, were three key issues: the costs of protectionism to the economy, the need to assure "fair" trade, and how best to adjust labor and capital to shifts in the direction of trade. The specific policy prescriptions associated with each of these issues have changed over time, but the theoretical core with which policy makers evaluate trade policy has not. The evolution of American trade policy since 1800 is a story not of the discovery of new knowledge but of changes in the political salience of economic theories and the uses to which they were put by political decision makers.

This chapter examines why liberalism—an idea that appeared in political debate around the turn of the nineteenth century—was abandoned in favor of protectionism. Common wisdom portrays early nineteenth-century America much as Alexis de Tocqueville did in the 1830s, as a society inherently imbued with "liberal" values. For the most part, the caricature was accurate; analyses of the evolution of American

23

culture and government policy rarely ignore the influence of liberal beliefs on political outcomes. The one area that resists such categorization is commercial policy. Although Americans became familiar with liberal trade ideas in the early nineteenth century and liberalism informed aspects of early tariff policy, these ideas were abandoned just when American products were becoming competitive on world markets.

I argue that interest-based analyses—whether emphasizing domestic politics or broad national interests—cannot adequately explain why protectionism proved so attractive to political entrepreneurs after 1860. Such analyses suggest that these ideas were embraced by the Republicans, the party of protection, because they served either the party's constituency or the nation as a whole better than possible alternatives. This is not the case. The Republican party adopted protectionism even though modified free trade would have served its diverse constituency and the nation as well or, looking ahead, even better.

In contrast, the behavior of political actors in the period before the Civil War can be explained on the basis of traditional interests. For the South, concerned mainly with trade in primary commodities, tariffs were anathema because they meant higher prices for secondary products. Similarly, northern commercial interests opposed tariffs, arguing that they were a disincentive for trade. Not surprisingly, manufacturers supported high tariffs. In this period, changing regional interests and, to a lesser extent, changes in party constituency explain the variations in congressional actions on the tariff.

The politics of tariff policy changed after midcentury. While southern Democrats continued to favor low tariffs, the new Republican party organized around the banner of "free labor" and the commercial policy that was believed to maximize the interests of nonslave workers. In the mid-nineteenth century, economic experts agreed on a proposition we now know to be a false, that is, that protectionism assures higher wages for labor than does free or modified free trade. The belief that protectionism would bolster the interests of free labor explains the Republican affinity to commercial closure. Rather than merely reflecting the old Whig economic program and constituency, the party platform reflected a particular causal association between government policies and economic outcomes. Once protection was adopted, the Republican party elevated it to a place on the national political agenda, thereby ending flexible tariff rates and moving the tariff floor substantially upward.

In this chapter I look first at the intellectual arguments surrounding the tariff issue and the creation of the policy of protectionism. Key to

24

the explanation of why liberal thought failed to influence policy after midcentury is the inability of its defenders satisfactorily to resolve three issues that were of central concern to political entrepreneurs: What role could and should commercial policy play in the development of the domestic economy? What is the responsibility of the state for correcting dislocations in labor and capital resulting from changes in market forces? How much control could and should states exert over markets? At midcentury, supporters of free trade argued that commercial policy should not be used to foster economic development, that government was not responsible for abrogating market dislocation, and that laissez-faire was the optimal government policy. I suggest that none of these ideas appealed to the new Republican party's leadership. The defense of protectionism, never as well specified as the free-trade alternative, was clear on certain points: protection maximized wages, assured a domestic market, and guarded the economy against changing international market forces. This causal "packaging" made protectionism—as compared with the liberal alternative—far more attractive to political entrepreneurs in the embryonic Republican party.

Second, the chapter looks at the process of setting tariffs in the antebellum period and assesses the degree to which economic thought influenced particular political outcomes. The general conclusion is that it is difficult to prove that economic ideas had an impact before midcentury. In this early period parties defended their constituents' interests, based on whether or not they would gain from increased international trade. In debate, representatives merely used contemporary economic thought to legitimate the trade policy preferences of their constituents. Although congressional debate revealed policy makers to have a good understanding of economic theory, their understanding of economic thought adds little to an interest-based model of political behavior. This is not the case for the analysis of politics later in the century. Although the "objective" interests of relevant actors—farmers, laborers, capitalists—changed little after midcentury, these groups and their representatives no longer lined up individually or in coalitions in defense of expected positions.[1]

After midcentury interests become indeterminate predictors of economic policy for two reasons. First, perhaps as a result of the diversification of the American economy, groups that had once been united on commercial policy began to diverge. Southern farmers continued

---

[1] A good guide to "objective" interests in trade is provided by Ronald Rogowski in *Commerce and Coalitions: How Trade Affects Domestic Political Alignments* (Princeton: Princeton University Press, 1989). Interests are determined by factor endowments. In the United States in the antebellum period, land was rich and labor and capital poor. Thus

to defend trade openness, but other groups, from commercial investors to industrial producers, increasingly spoke with different voices. Sometimes their motives were strategic. Southern intransigence, for example, made it impossible to defend high tariffs in the early 1850s, so alternative policies, such as reducing costs by lowering tariffs on primary products, explain the actions of industries such as woolens that were hurt by trade. But other groups were far less clear about what trade policy would maximize their interests. The economic analyses of the time proved a critical determinant of the political positions they ultimately defended.

Second, the Republican party was a conglomerate of divergent trade interests. Western farmers, New England merchants, and midwestern industrialists were all represented by one economic platform. For these groups' interests, protectionism was in no sense the only, or even the most obvious, position for the party to defend. The lack of clarity on economic platform made party elites uncertain about just what policy could and would serve to bind this coalition together. This uncertainty privileged economic thought as a guide for action.

THE AMERICAN DEFENSE OF PROTECTION

Tariff debate in the nineteenth century holds a unique place in American intellectual history. Few public policies have been advocated and opposed by so many great minds for such a sustained period of time. Although the theoretical basis for the positions individuals took is often unclear, supporters of free trade tended to follow the teachings of David Ricardo and the European classicists, while the advocates of protection traced their roots to the works of Alexander Hamilton, Daniel Raymond, and, ultimately, Henry Carey. In the nineteenth as in the twentieth century, a preference for free trade predominated in American colleges and universities. One should not, however, overstate the differences between intellectuals and laymen. Raymond and Carey, well-known protectionists, were brilliant economists well schooled in the European tradition. The great writers on both sides saw the tariff issue as part of a larger theoretical model of the American economy; and there were advocates on both sides who saw the issue

---

landowners should have wanted free trade; capitalists and labor should have endorsed closure.

in a single dimension, contributing little to the general state of economic analysis.[2]

The Influence of Early European Thought

In the seventeenth century, few colonists eschewed government controls over economic activity.[3] Reflecting the mercantilist view of commerce then dominant in Europe, the colonies sought a positive balance of trade so they could accumulate specie. To that end, government interference in economic matters was expected. The use of bounties, monopolies, prohibitions, and fines were accepted and, indeed, expected instruments of state power.[4] Such beliefs, however, were increasingly challenged in the eighteenth and early nineteenth centuries by new principles, which were far more individualistic than their predecessors and prescribed a far more limited role for the state in social and economic affairs.

In the last quarter of the eighteenth century, American intellectuals discovered Adam Smith. In his *Wealth of Nations,* published on the eve of the Revolution, Smith expanded upon the existing Physiocratic critique of mercantile doctrines. The French Physiocrats idealized agriculture and the economic freedom it allowed. As empiricists, the Physiocrats attempted to prove that only agricultural labor could lead to economic surplus and thus they advocated policies favoring agriculture over other sectors. Policies such as bounties, employed by governments in support of manufactures, were criticized because they penalized agriculture and slowed economic growth.[5]

Smith was far more systematic in his critique of mercantile doctrine than were the Physiocrats. The core of his analysis rested on an essentially different view of what motivated individuals in the market. Smith argued that man had a natural desire for consumer goods and a natural instinct for trade. No guiding hand was necessary to foster productivity and wealth. Good governments endeavored to keep order and protect property rights; intervention led to less productivity, not more. Smith recommended abandoning mercantile logic and policy in the

[2] Free traders and protectionists in this period were equally prolific, publishing similar amounts. See Paul Keith Conkin, *Prophets of Prosperity* (Bloomington: Indiana University Press, 1980), p. 172.

[3] On early economic policy see Carl William Kaiser, Jr., "History of the Academic Protectionist–Free Trade Controversy in America before 1860," diss., University of Pennsylvania, 1939.

[4] For early government policy see E. R. Johnson et al., *History of Domestic and Foreign Commerce in the United States,* Vol. 1 (Washington, D.C.: Carnegie Institute, 1922), p. 65.

[5] Conkin, *Prophets of Prosperity,* pp. 18–19.

belief that few forms of government intervention to develop a trade surplus made economic sense.

These ideas could not have found a more receptive audience than in the new states of the American republic.[6] They fit well with the dominant images Americans had of themselves and legitimated their criticisms of British commercial policy. By the turn of the nineteenth century, American society, far more than its European forebear, saw itself as the embodiment of Smith's logic. American workers aspired to be their own masters, and, far more than their European counterparts, they were owners of their land and the tools of their trade. Americans saw their distinctiveness as the result of the absence of the constraints of a class society and of their freedom to fulfill their economic potential. Thus developed the myth that an American worker was not only efficient but also free. Farm life was idealized, and free land symbolized America's economic uniqueness.[7]

If American values were compatible with both the Physiocratic celebration of agriculture and Smith's defense of laissez-faire, they had no such affinity with a third significant European school of thought: the dark side of economic progress, first portrayed in Thomas Malthus's *Essays on the Principles of Population* (1798). In an argument that was orthogonal to the American myth, Malthus concluded that mankind would ultimately be trapped by the limits of nature. Increases in agricultural productivity could not keep up with population growth, portending a future of misery and war.[8]

David Ricardo's interpretation of Smith, Malthus, and the Physiocrats was as important to nineteenth-century American economic the-

---

[6] Louis Hartz's interpretation of America as a "fragment" suggests that liberal ideas came with the settlers to the New World. At least in commercial policy, Americans did not already believe in liberal ideas. Rather, the views expressed by liberal philosophers fit well with their other beliefs and provided solutions to the particular problems they confronted. Thus liberalism was adopted because it appeared to explain reality better than did existing ideas, not because only liberals came to the New World. See Hartz, *The Liberal Tradition in American Political Thought since the Revolution* (New York: Harcourt, Brace, 1955).

[7] Only after midcentury did the "American" myth begin to deviate sharply from reality, at least for nonslaves. In 1776, 5 percent of the total population lived in cities. By 1830 only 9 percent had migrated to an urban setting, and by 1860 less than 20 percent was urbanized. In 1815, four out of five workers were still primarily engaged in agriculture. At the end of the Civil War one in two workers was still agriculturally based. Over 80 percent of white males in 1815 were self-employed. (These numbers are not exactly comparable with contemporary urban/rural data because in this period, categories commonly overlapped. For example, artisans kept chickens, hogs, and cows, and workers in rural areas engaged in nonagricultural tasks such as spinning, churning, weaving, sewing, smithing, milling, carpentry, and masonry.) See Conkin, *Prophets of Prosperity*, p. 6.

[8] Malthus's contributions were much greater and more complex, but the simple version of the "misery" hypothesis as a straw man had considerable influence on early American thought.

ory as were these schools of thought. Ricardo's work and its later clarifications by John Stuart Mill (1848) were to become the backbone of the orthodox or classical approach in American economics. Ricardo's contributions to economic thought were many, including the fundamental restructuring of the methodology employed in economics. Ricardo was far more systematic, rigorous, and "scientific" than earlier economists had been. As would become common practice in years after, Ricardo's theorizing began with an abstract model of the market; he derived his body of "laws" directly from this stipulated universe and from a defined set of actors and rules of economic intercourse. This rigor and abstraction were celebrated in scholarly circles and emulated in universities but ultimately rendered free-trade ideas more distant and foreign to both citizens and elected officials than was the alternative of protectionism.

In the course of two decades, the writings of the critics of state intervention became the basis of economic analysis in the classroom. Once translated, Jean Baptiste Say's textbook, *Treatise on Political Economy*, popularized the classic approach. Say accepted much of Smith's work, disagreeing with him and the Physiocrats only in their according agriculture a special place in an economy. Say is best remembered for suggesting that national economies need only increase output; demand, he insisted, would naturally follow. Say's emphasis on the harmony of all interests in society, his rejection of the sectoral and class-based comparisons found in both Smith and the Physiocrats, and his belief in the possibilities for economic cooperation among all interests in society made his text an American best-seller. As did most Americans, Say spurned the pessimism of Malthus, arguing instead that specialization and efficient production would assure growth and prosperity.

The Early American Writers on Economics

Nineteenth-century academics were not the only source of ideas on commercial policy. In colleges, Americans taught and expanded upon European free-trade ideas. But after the 1820s, extended treatises favoring protection were also produced by self-avowed "practical" professionals and laymen who were trenchantly critical of classical British thought. These individuals incorporated the insights of popular pamphleteers such as Franklin and Hamilton with elements of European liberal thought to create a uniquely American defense of protectionism.

Benjamin Franklin was one of the first and is probably still the most respected of American pamphleteers. His work in the last quarter of the eighteenth century reflected his reading of the French Physiocrats and, to a lesser extent, of Smith and David Hume, both of whom he knew personally.[9] Franklin glorified the American worker, who was free, well paid, and prosperous; his counterparts in industrial England were enslaved, underpaid, and impoverished. Franklin did not think the British model of industrialization was appropriate for the United States. Rather, he agreed with the Physiocrats that agriculture alone was "truly productive of new wealth."[10]

Because he advocated an agricultural economy, Franklin argued for an expansion of commerce to meet the growing needs for finished products as a substitute for the development of an indigenous manufacturing sector. Trade, he suggested, was mutually beneficial; protectionism was unjustified because it interfered with exchange, elicited retaliation, raised prices, reduced wealth, and encouraged smuggling.[11]

Franklin opposed manufacturing on both economic and moral grounds. Manufacturing would never prosper, he argued, even with government assistance. As long as workers could exit and gain a living from cheap land, wages would remain excessively high in the cities. Until all the land was settled and urban wages declined, Franklin argued, manufacturing would be an unnecessary drain on state revenues. Perhaps more fundamentally, he feared for the future of the American worker. He had seen the poverty and indifference of British labor and thought that these conditions were antithetical to the republican values of American society.

If Franklin was the intellectual forebear of the Jeffersonians, Hamilton was his most telling critic. Franklin espoused free-trade ideas for the same reasons that Hamilton argued in 1791 against liberal policies. Both saw a relationship between commercial policy and the future growth of manufactures in the United States. Franklin thought the colonies unsuited for manufactures; Hamilton saw manufacturing as America's future. Convinced of the necessity to promote nonagricultural production, Hamilton supported all mechanisms available to assure its development.

Hamilton's *Report on Manufactures* in 1791 is both a set of policy suggestions and a theory of trade relations. Like Franklin, Hamilton was famliar with the European theorists. Confronted with British refusal to make a commercial treaty with the new United States and French and Spanish discrimination, however, Hamilton presented a

[9] Kaiser, "History," p. 18.
[10] Lewis J. Carey, *Franklin's Economic Views* (New York: Doubleday, Doran, 1928), p. 142.
[11] Ibid., p. 19.

defensive prescription for economic development. Hamilton agreed with Smith on the advantages of an industrial future, but unlike Smith, he did not accord agriculture a privileged status. Rather, Hamilton advocated a policy in which manufacturing was the centerpiece. Comparatively, he saw agriculture as a primitive sector that could not contribute equal wealth to a nation. He argued that government bounties and tariffs were necessary if American industries were to survive their infancy.

Hamilton did more than defend manufactures against an American bias toward agriculture. He alleged that manufacturing bred specialization and thus possessed a unique advantage for society. Confronting opponents who idealized agriculture, he was forced to argue against the contemporary wisdom that manufactures could not survive in the United States because of a scarcity of labor, the "dearness" of American workers, and the lack of American capital.[12] Hamilton replied that where there was insufficient labor (some parts of the country were "pretty fully peopled," he is reputed to have said), manufacturing would bring women and children into the labor force, substitute machinery for labor, use people's leisure time, and promote immigration of skilled workers.[13] This increase in the labor force would naturally cause the price of labor to decline. Capital, he felt, would be attracted to the United States as needed.

Still, Hamilton needed to confront the new wisdom, that is, that capital and labor would find their most profitable place without government interference. Tariffs were said not only to discourage the profitable use of factors of production but to impose an inequitable tax on one section of the country and group of people for the benefit of another group or region. Hamilton's reply was that "unfair" trade was far more common than market-driven commerce. This reality necessitated an interventionist American response. Hamilton suggested that

> the influence of habit, the fear of failure, the inequalities existing between nations in point of industrial organization, the granting of aid to established industries by rival nations, and the concerted action of competitors through the media of dumping, underselling, extension of long-term credit and other devices might easily ruin or seriously hamper the existence of any newly established industry.[14]

Recognizing that duties would raise prices, Hamilton suggested that

[12] *The Works of Alexander Hamilton*, ed. Henry C. Lodge (New York: G. P. Putnam's Sons, 1904), 4: 107–8.
[13] Ibid., pp. 108–11.
[14] Kaiser, "History," p. 29.

the revenue they would generate outweighed this cost. The growth of productive enterprises would more than compensate for lost tariff revenue and higher prices. Hamilton did not deny that protection would divert labor and capital from one form of production to another, or that some regions and groups would benefit more than others. On the whole, however, he believed that "the aggregate prosperity of manufactures and the aggregate prosperity of agriculture are intimately connected."[15] A strong home market would elicit demand for agricultural products which would more than compensate the agricultural sector for government protection of manufactures. He suggested, as would protectionists throughout the next century, that the two sectors were intimately tied: manufacturing would assure a long-term demand for agriculture's surplus even if prices increased in the short term.

How would Hamilton protect manufactures? He suggested several policies in his 1791 report. The state could lay either protective or prohibitory duties, bar the export of material essential for manufactures, use bounties, exempt from duty raw materials essential for manufacturing, or use drawbacks. Hamilton preferred bounties. Duties did not facilitate exportation of finished products, and prohibitive duties made sense only in particular cases of intense competition. Bounties were more positive and direct; they did not lead to an increase in price, they did not contract supply, and they furnished the means of uniting agriculture and manufactures.[16] Bounties, he maintained, were legal under the general welfare clause of the Constitution. Bounties, however, required that there be a government to redistribute taxes. Because the United States lacked such a capacity, Hamilton defended customs duties, which were easy to collect and difficult to defraud; proceeds could then be converted into bounties and given to home manufacturers. According to his logic, duties were to be levied to maximize revenues; bounties were to be given to maximize the protection of infant industries.[17]

Compared with his intellectual descendants one hundred years later, Hamilton provided only a mild theoretical defense for tariff policy. Hamilton never defended autarky—protection was only a means to make a strong America, a temporary necessity, a political expedient that would eventually give way to a policy of free trade. Hamilton did defend a positive state; government could and should use its powers to promote its national economic interest. Government, he argued, can-

[15] Ibid., p. 31.
[16] Ibid., p. 35.
[17] Hamilton's defense of bounties is akin to contemporary economists' explanations for why subsidies are preferable to tariffs as a form of government intervention.

not rely on market forces alone to serve its interests. Not only would this not assure optimal developments, but the market was skewed by the actions of other nations.

Although a positive theory of tariff barriers had not developed by the turn of the century, the central parameters around which that debate would turn were established. Following the line of inquiry begun by the European liberals, the free traders developed a theoretical defense for free trade and a general critique of state intervention. Protectionists, by contrast, assumed that the federal government had a right and an obligation to direct economic development and argued instead about the optimal developmental strategy and the appropriate means of implementing it. By the early 1800s the central elements of the free trade–protection debate were set. The development of a labor force, the extent of autonomy of markets, and the responsibility of the federal government to organize economic development emerged as the focal points of discussions over trade policy for the next one hundred years.

Antebellum Economic Thought

Any observer of American thought in 1800 would have found scant evidence from which to predict that protection and not free trade would ultimately be the dominant approach to commercial policy throughout the century. It is hard to find a respectable defender of protectionism before the 1830s. Although some individuals had assimilated Hamilton's agenda and advocated the development of large-scale American manufacturing, they were no more successful than he was in affecting public policy. Gaining intellectual respectability for protection was an uphill battle. The works of Say, Ricardo, and John Ramsay McCulloch, professor at the London University and author of *The Principles of Political Economy*, only gave Smith's ideas increased legitimacy.[18]

America's first academic protectionist was Daniel Raymond, who, like his followers, oriented his work toward disputing Smith, Malthus, and Say.[19] Raymond's major treatise, published in 1820, was a systematic attack on Smith rather than a positive theory of protection. Raymond's writings reflect many of the problems Americans were having with free-trade ideas.

[18] In the 1820s, American universities taught almost all European texts. On the development of the field see A. D. H. Kaplan, *Henry Charles Carey: A Study in American Economic Thought* (Baltimore: Johns Hopkins University Press, 1931), pp. 17–18.

[19] In the introduction to his 1820 text, Daniel Raymond wrote that his prose was "an humble effort to break loose from the fetters of foreign authority—from foreign theories and systems of political economy, which from dissimilarity in the nature of the govern-

On a basic level, Raymond found fault with Smith's methodological individualism. According to Raymond, it was incorrect to identify the interests of the individual with those of the nation. "It is not possible in the multiplicity and diversity of human affairs that consumption should always just equal production," he argued.[20] Pursuing this logic, Raymond then asserted that "the great source of error . . . has been the confounding of national with individual wealth . . . no two things can be more different or distinct."[21] Foreshadowing Fredrick List's definition of national wealth as the "productive powers" of a nation, Raymond argued that factors unrelated to production such as type of government and the moral character of labor also influenced wealth. In Raymond's analysis, the government assures the prosperity of the nation, not the reverse. And no invisible hand would lead to a convergence of public and private interests: "The question, whether individuals should be permitted to sell, where they can sell dearest, and buy, where they can buy cheapest, ought not to be decided upon the narrow, contemptible principles of private interest, but upon the more expanded and noble principles of public interests."[22]

Smith's notion of universal truths was likewise rejected. As would the protectionist economists who followed, Raymond believed in American exceptionalism. The interests of all nations and individuals within nations were not identical. Rather, he argued that nations possess different interests, and those interests change over time, making it impossible to generate universal theories about optimal policy.

Like Hamilton, Raymond found fault with the Physiocratic notions inherent in Smith's work. Raymond could find no theoretical grounds for granting agriculture privileged status but believed that nations needed to balance their economies among agriculture, commerce, and manufacturing. But Raymond agreed with the Physiocrats and other early American writers that agricultural workers were a "superior class of men to manufacturers," healthier, courageous, and less corrupt.[23] And too, he said, a thriving agricultural sector would provide self-sufficiency and thus national autonomy. Even so, he maintained that whether governments should subsidize agriculture depended on the more general interests of the nation, not on the inherent superiority of one sector.

---

ments, renders them altogether unsuited to our country." Daniel Raymond, *Thoughts on Political Economy* (Baltimore: Fielding Lucas, Jr., 1820), pp. v–vi.

[20] Daniel Raymond, *The Elements of Political Economy* (New York: A. M. Kelley, 1964), 1: 123.

[21] Raymond, *Thoughts*, p. 26.

[22] Raymond, *Elements*, 1:149–50, 126, 219–21.

[23] Gary Hull, "The Prospect for Man in Early American Economic Thought," diss., University of Maryland, 1969, p. 68.

We should not interpret Raymond's ideas as a return to seventeenth-century principles; clear differences distinguish his protectionist logic from previous mercantilist thought. He agreed with Smith and other free traders that it was unjustified to use tariffs to obtain a favorable balance of trade or to accumulate gold or specie. Yet protection was justified if in the national interest. For Raymond, the employment of labor was key. Government should pursue protection if workers were idle or inefficiently employed. Under these conditions, tariffs served to increase demand for the services of labor, thereby adding to the total productive capacity of the nation. If labor was working at full capacity, however, only national military or diplomatic goals would justify protection. Thus Raymond did not provide a general economic defense of protection, and he disagreed with Hamilton that tariffs should be used to protect the burgeoning commercial class.

Raymond's work was a call for social solidarity and government responsibility. Although agreeing with Smith and Say that liberal trade might be the optimal policy for the United States, he argued that such a commercial policy would be possible only through overt government action. Free trade would never occur on its own.[24] But his assessment of America's economic needs and political infrastructure led Raymond to favor a policy of protection. He argued that protective duties would prevent British dumping of surpluses in the United States, guarantee a home market for American markets, and assure employment for labor.

Raymond's later works explicitly defended protectionism against its critics. In particular, he addressed the central thrust of the free-trade critique of protectionism, that is, that tariffs increased consumer prices. Raymond denied that tariffs significantly increase prices, insisting that changes in demand more than offset potential changes in cost. Import duties served to change consumption patterns, he argued, causing substitution to alternative products. Such a change in buying habits increased inventories and forced prices downward. Duties affected prices in relationship to the amount of home production: the greater the home production, the less the duty would increase prices. In short, he suggested that tariffs were not only compensated by price changes but ultimately led to an overall decline in prices.[25]

In the 1830s and 1840s, others took up the study of commercial

---

[24] Ibid., p. 70.

[25] "There is . . . no danger that high duties will ever prevent the importation of foreign products, to the full amount of our exports." See Daniel Raymond, "The President's Message and the Report of the Secretary of the Treasury, *American Review: A Whig Journal Devoted to Politics and Literature* 7 (April 1848): 388, 391–92. Raymond did not differentiate between the elasticity of demand among products or the price effects on products without substitutes.

policy.[26] J. Newton Cardozo, Thomas Cooper, Thomas B. Dew, and John McVickar spoke in the defense of free trade; Alexander Everett, Willard Phillips, John Rae, Calvin Colton, and Henry Carey defended protection.[27] Pamphleteers such as Hezekiah Niles and Matthew Carey, the editor of a Philadelphia paper that had long extolled the virtues of protection, were no less important though they contributed less to the general theoretical debate on commercial policy.

In general, the protectionists spent far more effort disputing the writings of the free traders than in developing a positive defense for protectionism. Three themes appear in all their texts. First, they all challenged the individualist epistemology of the European writers. Only Everett accepted the general principle that national and individual interests might converge. Most believed that divergent interests were as probable as harmony. Second, all reveled in the glory of the American social system and its free laborer. They envisioned trade liberalization as leading to the impoverishment of workers and the degradation of life in America. And third, all defended the uniqueness of the American case; the universal laws of Malthus, Smith, and Ricardo which, Colton argued, were a "vast British conspiracy to dominate the rest of the world," simply did not apply to the United States.[28]

The specific arguments used to support these propositions varied slightly from author to author. Everett, Rae, and Phillips stressed the importance of protecting the United States against the more advanced British economy.[29] Phillips, like Hamilton, saw tariffs as necessary for American self-sufficiency. He argued that laissez-faire made sense neither in international nor in domestic politics. In trade, laissez-faire would lead the United States into a position of subservience in international markets. Further, Phillips suggested that because free traders

[26] The impetus for the renewal of interest was tariff policy itself. The passage of relatively more protective tariffs in 1824 and 1828 and a decrease in tariffs in 1832 led to a widespread perception that the affluence of the 1820s and decline in the 1830s were owing to tariff policy.
[27] Cardozo edited and published the Charleston, S.C., *Evening News*. He also wrote *Notes on Political Economy*. Cooper, president of South Carolina College, wrote *Elements of Political Economy*. Dew taught at the College of William and Mary and wrote *Lectures on the Restrictive System*. McVickar, of Columbia College, wrote *Outlines of Political Economy*. Phillips practiced law but also tutored at Harvard for four years. Everett, a distinguished diplomat and editor of the *North American Review*, authored *New Ideas on Population*. Rae was a practicing physician who never taught political economy. Colton edited and wrote for the Washington, D.C., *True Whig*.
[28] Conkin, *Prophets of Prosperity*, p. 190.
[29] A. H. Everett, *America* (New York: Garland, 1974), pp. 138–41, 155, 175–76; Willard Phillips, *A Manual of Political Economy* (New York: A. M. Kelley, 1968), pp. 184–87; John Rae, *Statement of Some New Principles on the Subject of Political Economy, Exposing the Fallacies of the System of Free Trade and of Some Other Doctrines Maintained in the Wealth of Nations* (Boston: Hilliard, Gray, 1834), pp. 158–59.

favored agriculture over manufacturing, it was absurd to call free trade "neutral" for it so penalized American laborers as to be "wicked, calamitous, and ruinous."[30]

Similar themes appear in Colton's 1848 text. Colton argued that open and free competiton always favors the more established and more developed countries, allowing the rich to get richer while retarding the growth of younger and more dependent nations. Great Britain favored free trade only for reasons of economic self-interest, he suggested. And because they already enjoyed a competitive advantage, the British were exporting free-trade ideas as a mechanism to control potential competitors.[31]

Otherwise committed Ricardian scholars could not dispute that protection was the economically expedient policy for the United States. Cooper and McVickar agreed that American growth after the War of 1812 and the behavior of Britain before she repealed the Corn Laws and the Navigation Acts required some form of protection for newly developing industries. The large inflow of British goods that followed the War of 1812 left little doubt that American industries were threatened by competition and that their demise would not serve national interests.

Closely related to the argument for protection on grounds of political expediency was the version of the infant-industry hypothesis that was expounded in the second and third decades of the nineteeth century. Following a line of thought first advanced by Hamilton, protectionists defended tariffs to assure a diversified and growing economy. Colton's treatise, for example, argued that proponents of agriculture should support tariffs on manufactured goods because a large proportion of the inputs to a manufactured item were primary products produced by farmers. Exports of a manufactured product that used inputs of domestic farmers granted those farmers some of the value added of the manufacturing produce. Manufacturing, then, could be considered a form of agricultural labor, and imported manufactures from England camouflaged competition from British farmers. Thus tariffs against manufactures ultimately protected farmers from unfair competition. Colton estimated that Britain exported eight times more camou-

---

[30] Conkin, *Prophets of Prosperity*, p. 185.

[31] Colton argued that Great Britain had developed a successful manufacturing sector through 150 years of protection and adopted free-trade principles only late in its history. "It is never true that the strong want protection against the weak; but it is always true that the weak want protection against the strong. . . . The manufacturing [country] will be in favor of free trade, because, in that way, it can make the other [countries] dependent for those fine things, which will be wanted as soon as they are seen, but which can not be produced at home." Calvin Colton, *Public Economy for the United States* (New York: A. S. Barnes, 1853), pp. 61–62, 69–71, 90–97.

flaged agricultural products to America than she imported and that a continuation of this pattern would undermine farm prices.[32] Further, the United States should not continue to provide Britain with cheap raw materials but rather develop its own indigenous production. Even cotton would benefit far more from expanded manufacturers than from its continued export to other nations, he suggested.

As had Raymond, later protectionists denied that protective tariffs would levy an unfair tax on consumers. Raymond had claimed that over the long term domestic competition would dampen the inflationary effect of tariffs. Others found it less difficult to accept that tariffs would affect prices but still argued about who *should* and actually *did* bear those costs. Colton said that free trade was a form of foreign taxation that could be remedied by protection. Free entry of foreign goods, he argued, also freed foreign producers from paying taxes to the United States, gave them inordinately high earnings, and ultimately underwrote their repressive governments. Likewise, the importation of the products of cheap foreign laborers concealed an income tax on American workers that far exceeded any sales tax on consumer goods. Such trade would affect workers either through lower wages or unemployment.[33]

By far the most influential of the nineteenth-century protectionist economists was Henry Carey. Carey's work was the preeminent critique of Ricardo. Carey agreed with Ricardo that universal economic laws did exist; he simply believed that Ricardo had got them all wrong. From this general assumption, Carey built a distinctively American theory of political economy. His disposition toward protectionism grew in relation to his disenchantment with the European economists. His first text, *Essays on the Rate of Wages*, actually defended free-trade policy. In 1835 he argued:

> It is a disgrace to our age to see two such nations as those of Great Britain and France each hedging round its commerce by restrictions that limit their exchanges to a million of two pounds per annum, thus doing all in their power to frustrate the designs of a Deity, who, in giving to different parts of the earth different powers of production, paved the way for that intercourse which is most beneficial to mankind.[34]

The economic problems the country faced after 1837 led Carey to

---

[32] Conkin, *Prophets of Prosperity*, p. 195.

[33] Ibid., pp. 195–96. Colton, *Public Economy*, pp. 351–53, 356–59, 387–88.

[34] Henry Carey, *Essay on the Rate of Wages: With an Examination of the Causes of the Differences in the Condition of the Labouring Population Throughout the World* (Philadelphia, Carcy, Lea & Branchard, 1835), p. 14.

wonder why prosperity existed in the periods of protective tariffs while depressions corresponded with periods of free trade.[35] His answer was that protective tariffs served the nation's welfare. His works in the 1840s and 1850s reflect this change of mind. Commenting on the tariff of 1842 he argued, "Scarcely had it become a law, when confidence began to reappear, and commerce to revive—the first steps toward the restoration of the whole country, in the briefest period, to a state of prosperity the like of which had never before been known.[36] In contrast to earlier economists who argued that America's unique economic position justified the use of tariffs, Carey suggested that protective tariffs made economic sense for all nations. He commented that "the protected communities advanced steadily in wealth and strength, while those which were unprotected were as steadily declining toward anarchy and ruin."[37]

In *Past, Present and Future* Carey attacked Ricardo's notion of diminishing returns, substituting a model in which increasing human association led to both increasing power over nature and increased wealth. Carey accepted neither Malthusian nor Ricardian analyses of scarcity, class conflict, or developmental problems. Rather, Carey celebrated mankind's unquestionable ingenuity and ability to master nature.

The key to Carey's approach lay in the need for association. Any policy that promoted the cohesion of individuals, he argued, would work to promote general economic welfare. Carey accepted the need for commerce but not for trade. Commerce, he argued, was an exchange of equivalents which developed local association; trade, on the other hand, led to increasing distances between producers and consumers, rapid price changes, and profits at the expense of social welfare.[38]

For Carey, protection offered a means to develop home markets, to the benefit of both agricultural and manufacturing interests. For farmers, free trade meant they could not set their own price and would have to pay transportation costs to reach markets abroad. Carey's answer, not unlike Hamilton's, was to develop an internal market: "The meadow land of Pennsylvania is not worth the clearing, because the market for its products has no existence; and until the consumer shall place him-

---

[35] Carey's own personal fortune was adversely affected by the crisis of 1837, especially his investments in a paper mill and a coal mine. Kaplan suggests that Carey's conversion was owing to his conviction that protection would lessen British capital's almost total control over American industry and finance and would intensify internal commercial exchange among the states furthering the unity of the United States. See Kaplan, *Henry Charles Carey*, pp. 46–47.
[36] Henry Carey, *Principles of Social Science* (Philadelphia: J. B. Lippincott, 1888), 1: xii.
[37] Ibid., p. xiii.
[38] Kaiser, "History," p. 128.

self side by side with the producer, it can have none. Place him there, and nothing will be lost."[39] The home market, he argued, was less erratic and more profitable than foreign trade. Farmers could raise more varied products because the distance to market was not great; no profits would be sacrificed to high transportation costs. High rates of return for agricultural goods would lead directly to higher values for land.

In the *Principles of Social Science*, Carey developed his defense of the tariff based on the interests of labor.

> Commerce looks homeward-seeking to promote domestic intercourse. . . . Trade . . . looks altogether outward. . . . Commerce seeks to make a rich people, with a cheap, and therefore strong, government. Trade makes a splendid and wasteful, and therefore weak, government. The periods of protection have been those of economy and rapidly growing strength. Those of free trade . . . have been those of greatest splendor, waste, and weakness. Commerce, by promoting the development of individuality, furnishes employment for every variety of human faculty. Trade—forbidding that development—limits the range of employment, and compels whole populations to employ themselves in scratching the earth.[40]

Carey's explanation of the benefits to workers was not much different than those of earlier protectionists. Just as a closed market would yield higher prices for agricultural products and thus higher agricultural wages, those employed in manufacturing would benefit in a like manner. Immigration patterns in times of high tariffs served as empirical proof of this theory. Europeans were flocking to the United States, he argued, not to escape political problems at home but in search of high wages and employment opportunities. Carey could not dispute that price hikes would accompany tariffs. His response, however, was that short-term price hikes reflected dumping by British merchants who used low prices to maintain their monopoly in the American market. Anyway, he argued, higher prices were not a bad thing; they would stimulate new capital accumulation and more work.[41]

Believing that political and economic forces were inseparable, Carey attacked Ricardo for postulating arguments that rationalized a world economy controlled by England. Ricardo, he suggested, had objectified man and made him a commodity. Such an approach lent support for Britain's use of slave labor, its monopolization of technology and ma-

---

[39] *American Whig Review*, 7:303 (New York: G. H. Colton, 1848), quoted in Kaplan, *Henry Charles Carey*, p. 51.
[40] Carey, *Principles of Social Science*, 2:241–42.
[41] Conkin, *Prophets of Prosperity*, p. 289.

chinery, and its imperial domination. In 1776, the United States had taken but a first step in its quest for freedom from Britain. The United States had attained political freedom but was still under Britain's economic sway. Free trade would provide the means for continued economic control. As an alternative, Carey advocated equal exchange among nations. Given Britain's dominance in the world economy, free trade was exploitation; it could exist only among nations at similar levels of development. Thus he did not preclude eventual trade between the United States and England, but such openness would need to wait until the American economy had matured to self-sufficiency.[42]

Carey did not believe his work was critical of Smithian arguments. Rather, he blamed Ricardo and Malthus for turning academic economists down the wrong path. Countering their suggestion that political economy led "to the production of discord among men and nations,"[43] Carey argued that his notion of association was the correct extension of Smithian ideas.

> The object of protection among ourselves . . . is to carry into effect the system advocated by the great author of *The Wealth of Nations*, while aiding in the annihilation of a system that has ruined Ireland, India, Portugal, Turkey, and all other countries subject to it; . . . [protection] operates . . . [to] promot[e] . . . the prosperity of, and harmony among, the various portions of society; . . . it is that *the true, the profitable, and the only means of attaining perfect freedom of trade,* is to be found in that efficient protection which shall fully and completely carry out the doctrine of Dr. Smith in bringing the loom and the anvil to take their natural places by the side of the plough and the harrow.[44]

With the work of Henry Carey, protectionist ideas came of age in the United States. By midcentury political decision makers were presented with two opposing trade policy options. Free traders developed a defense for laissez-faire that centered on the relation between prices and tariffs. By contrast, protectionists argued that political intervention was necessary to combat British imperialism, assure economic development through a home market, and, most important, encourage high wages. Protectionists agreed that tariffs could affect prices; but instead of disproving this analysis they turned instead to the relationship between wages and tariffs. America was unique, they argued, in that industrialization was possible without the hardships found in Britain. Malthusian

[42] Ibid., pp. 287–88.
[43] Henry Carey, *Harmony of Interests, Agricultural, Manufacturing and Commercial* (New York: M. Finch, 1852), p. iv.
[44] Ibid.

41

logic, said protectionists, made no sense in the United States, which had unlimited land and resources. The key to this prosperity, however, was wages—if wages were to decline, the United States would start down the British path to a destitute and impoverished work force.

This analytic focus was critical in the development of the political salience of protectionist ideas. By midcentury, the central political problem facing decision makers was slavery. Because of their interest in the relationship between free and slave labor, political entrepreneurs were far more interested in the relationship between trade and employment than any other aspect of the free trade–protection debate. Free traders admitted that trade competition would lower wages. Low wages, protectionists countered, were a British disease. Thus the only available option for political policy makers interested in promoting a working class that was neither slave nor impoverished was protectionism.

Throughout this period, both America's intellectuals and elected officials were repeatedly challenged to explain and respond to the rapid changes occurring in the nation. In the first six decades of the nineteenth century, gross output in constant dollars increased 537 percent. In this same period, trade, as measured by the number of vessels coming to American ports, increased 451 percent. In these years the population density of the United States almost doubled. In 1800 there was one city of over fifty thousand. On the eve of the Civil War there were eighteen, two of which had populations over five hundred thousand. Still, in 1860, 80 percent of the population remained rural.[45] To be certain, the United States was on the eve of industrialization. But neither the increase in the numbers and wealth of the manufacturing sector nor increased reliance on world trade alone can explain the shifts that occurred in American policy after the Civil War.

CONGRESSIONAL POLITICS

On the question of the relationship beween economic ideas and tariff policy, congressional politics may be divided into two periods.[46] In the years before the Civil War, there was no consensus among congressional representatives even on the basic purposes of commercial policy. In the antebellum period the significant differences among representatives, reflected in debate and votes, were more regional than partisan. In this

---

[45] Defined as places of less than 2,500 people.

[46] Between 1816 and the Civil War, eleven significant revisions in the tariff schedule occurred. Between 1794 and 1816, by comparison, twenty-four new acts modified the duty on foreign imports.

early period, tariff policy reflected not only the electoral fortunes of the two main parties but a changing debate within each party over the general direction it should take on economic development and what economic doctrine maximized its interests. After the Civil War, both parties developed far more consistent economic defenses of the ends and means of commercial policy. Throughout, the arguments of representatives in defense of their preferred trade positions closely followed the theoretical positions enumerated by contemporary academics and lay economists.

The critical turning point in the politics of protectionism occurred with the creation of the Republican party, which thrust protectionist ideas onto the federal agenda. This critical event—the incorporation of protectionist ideas into a party philosophy—is not explicable through the examination of constituent interests alone. The decision of elites to organize the party around a pro-protection platform reflected dominant though inaccurate beliefs about the workings of the world economy suggested by economic theorists of the time.

Early Congressional Policy

The Constitution granted Congress the power "to lay and collect taxes, duties, imposts and excises, to pay debts and provide for the common defense" and general welfare. During most of its first half-century, Congress used tariffs for just that purpose. The tariff was the chief source of revenue to pay off war debts and to fund the building of infrastructure for the new nation. But from the start, many leaders saw the tariff also as a tool with which government could manipulate the economy. In its opening session, the First Congress considered motions for using the tariff to "encourage ... production ... and protect our infant manufactures."[47] The response that would be echoed for the next two hundred years was also stated in 1789 by James Madison: "However much we may be disposed to promote domestic manufactures, we ought to pay some regard to the present policy of obtaining revenue"; tariffs were an instrument to raise revenue, not elements of an industrial policy.[48] Debate over revenue and the industrial purposes of protectionism was joined to a third issue. Some thought the federal government should assume some responsibility for adjusting labor and capital to market forces. And the tariff was the natural instrument for that purpose because so few economic instru-

[47] Thomas FitzSimons (F-Pa.), quoted in R. W. Thompson, *The History of Protective Tariff Laws* (New York: Garland, 1974), p. 52.
[48] Madison quoted ibid., p. 54.

ments were available to the federal government. As Madison argued in 1789:

> Duties laid on imported articles may have an effect which comes within the idea of national prudence. It may happen that materials for manufactures may grow up without any encouragement for that purpose. It has been the case in some of the States, but in others regulations have been provided, and have succeeded in producing some establishments which ought not to be allowed to perish from the alteration which has taken place; it would be cruel to neglect them and direct their industry to other channels; for it is not possible for the hand of man to shift from one employment to another without being injured by the change.[49]

These three issues—industrialization, the need for revenue, and public responsibility for dislocation caused by market forces—dominated nineteenth-century congressional debates about economic policy. The revenue argument tended to be advanced by those who did not believe in the protection of labor and capital. By the century's end, such an argument would be closely associated with the Democratic party's position on the tariff. The other two arguments were carried by different political agents during the ensuing century. In the early part of the nineteenth century, Whig congressmen repeatedly used infant industries and later the home market to defend a high-tariff policy. The Whig and later Republican party position was that protected markets did not benefit industry alone. All groups benefited from lower prices, full employment, a high standard of living, and freedom from the exigencies of a trading system in which the foreign policies of commercial partners could well imperil the consistent availability of goods.[50] The issue of the right and obligation of the government to obtain revenues and ameliorate adjustment costs was part of a larger debate on the constitutionality of tariffs. The Democratic party until the 1930s would critique protectionism as an unconstitutional use of government powers. Later, the Republicans would advocate the tariff as a legitimate instrument of state power.

The Tariff Debate of 1816

By 1816, few observers could ignore the relationship between industrialization and economic closure. Indeed, it was hard not to witness

---

[49] Ibid.
[50] The benefits of autarky were consistently extolled throughout the century. For instance, Daniel Morrell (R-Pa.) argued in 1870: "A community relying upon one branch of manufactures, though surrounded by a grain- and cattle-producing country, is subject to severe fluctuations; but when these branches are largely multiplied, the unprosperous

how the absence of competition resulting from the Napoleonic War abroad and the War of 1812 at home had allowed American industry to prosper. Imports averaged $140 million a year between 1805 and 1807; in the next four years, they dropped to $70 million.[51] Correspondingly, before 1808 the United States had only fifteen cotton mills; by the close of 1809, eighty-nine new mills were in operation. By 1811, there were eighty thousand cotton spindles in operation, a tenfold increase in only three years.[52] The woolen industry, whose voice would be heard repeatedly in tariff debates over the next two decades, barely existed before this period; its birth was a direct result of the lack of British cloth on the market.

The coming of peace in 1815 abruptly ended America's economic isolation. The American market was deluged by foreign products, primarily from Britain. Imports for the year ending in September 1814 were valued at about $13 million. The following February, peace was ratified, which allowed half a year of "normal" commerce. In that half-year alone, imports increased to $113 million, reaching $147 million the following year.[53] Price changes were felt throughout the economy (see Table 2.1). The restoration of peace and freedom of the seas led the United States to eliminate war levies on foreign vessels at American ports; instead of reciprocating, Britain added new restrictions on shipped goods.[54]

The ill effects of the revival of British trade were not ignored. For many, economic decline seemed to vindicate Hamilton's message; only if the United States protected infant industries would industrialization occur. This message was heard both in and out of Congress. Hezekiah

---

manufacturers form only the exception and not the rule." *Congressional Globe*, 41st Cong. 2d sess., p. 3291.

[51] U.S. Bureau of the Census, *Historical Statistics of the United States from Colonial Times to 1970* (Washington: USGPO, 1975), Series U 1–25.

[52] Douglass North, *The Economic Growth of the United States, 1790–1860* (New York: Norton, 1966), p. 57.

[53] Edward Stanwood, *American Tariff Controversies in the Nineteenth Century*, vol. 1 (Boston: Houghton Miffin, 1903), p. 131.

[54] Much evidence was available that British policies of the period were aimed at undercutting new U.S. industries. For instance, Lord Brougham, in a speech before Parliament in April 1816, makes it clear that postwar exports to the United States were strategically aimed at the new industries. "The peace with America has produced somewhat of a similar effect [to that on the Continent], though I am very far from placing the vast exports which it occasioned upon the same footing with those to the European market the year before; both because ultimately the Americans will pay, which the exhausted state of the continent renders very unlikely, and because it was well worthwhile to incur a loss upon the first exportation in order by the glut to stifle in the cradle those rising manufactures in the United States which the war had forced into existence contrary to the usual course of things." Quoted ibid., pp. 167–68.

Table 2.1. Price changes, 1800–1820

Year	Consumer Price Index[a]
1800	51
1801	50
1802	43
1803	45
1804	45
1805	45
1806	47
1807	44
1808	48
1809	47
1810	47
1811	50
1812	51
1813	58
1814	63
1815	55
1816	51
1817	48
1818	46
1819	46
1820	42

Source: U.S. Bureau of the Census, *Historical Statistics of the United States from Colonial Times to 1970* (Washington: USGPO, 1975), Series E 135-166, Series U 207–212.
[a]Based on Consumer Price Indexes for all items (1967 = 100).

Niles, the editor of the economic journal *Niles' Weekly Register,* explained in 1816 why protection was necessary:

> There is certainly not much *profit* in raising children—a woman might earn more money if instead of nursing her infant and nourishing it as she ought, she were to cast it on the ground and apply herself to labor. But what would we think of a calculation like that? . . . I consider that the manufacturers of the United States stand to the government in the precise relation of an infant to its mother—if they are cherished they will repay, in the future peace and prosperity of the country, all that is done for them.[55]

But Congress remained unwilling to use tariffs or taxes to support specific industries. In its first draft, the 1816 act followed almost to the letter Hamilton's advice in his *Report on Manufactures.* Three classes of products were granted different rates of duties depending on whether they were produced domestically. Rates ranged from deliberately prohibitory to purely revenue-producing, thus accommodating both the

[55] *Niles' Weekly Register* 9 (1816): 2.

protective and revenue needs of the country. Congress then cut all the suggested rates and, in addition, limited the life of the tariffs. In the end, the tariff rates established in 1816 increased by about 42 percent from their prewar levels, a decline of 29 percent from the tariff legislated to fund the war. Because this tariff reduced rates in the face of competition, it cannot be considered protective. Neither arguments in defense of the new industries nor the idea of protectionism carried sufficient weight to supersede sectional interests.[56]

In 1816, regionalism was the critical dimension ruling debate; the division of interests in the United States favored mercantile groups over the new manufacturers. As might be expected, New England representatives were lukewarm toward protectionist amendments compared to the support given by those from the more industrial Middle Atlantic states. Voting was governed by regional loyalty. In debate, many representatives revealed an unwillingness to tolerate expenditures for other regions. Thus the North rejected protection for raw sugar and the South voted against duties on cotton textiles. This sectional bias was particularly potent in the coalition that developed between the North and South, causing the defeat of duties on iron products produced in the Middle Atlantic states.

An oddity of the 1816 debate that also appeared later was a significant disjuncture between the attention and support granted by speakers to the protectionist position and votes in support of the original pro-protection legislation. A majority of the speakers agreed on the need to support the new industries, acknowledging that the federal government should act to abrogate market forces, protect workers and producers, and counteract predatory British practices. In 1816, however, these arguments did not translate into votes.

The tariff of 1816 did little to resolve the key economic questions of the time. It neither protected manufactures nor provided a sufficient source of government revenues.[57] Between 1810 and 1820, the federal budget increased 167 percent (see Table 2.2). In the wake of the tariff act, the federal government acquired its first peacetime foreign loan. To meet its fiscal obligations, Congress voted in 1818 to raise money through a tariff on iron products and the extension of duties on cotton

---

[56] The debate revealed a continuing disagreement not only over tariffs but over whether the United States should industrialize. For example, John Ross (D-Pa.) argued that manufacturing "had a tendency to degrade and debase the human mind. [Manufacturing outside of the home was] destructive to the liberties of this republic." *Annals of the United States Congress,* 14th Cong., 1st sess., pp. 1272–73.

[57] After 1817, the government turned almost exclusively to the tariff as the source of public funds. That year, it annulled most internal taxes, including excise taxes, which left the government dependent on import taxes and the sale of public lands.

Table 2.2. Growth of the federal budget, 1810–1820

Year	Government outlays[a] (in millions of dollars)
1810	$4.2
1812	4.5
1814	7.1
1816	10.7
1818	11.2
1820	11.2

Source: U.S. Bureau of the Census, Historical Statistics of the United States from Colonial Times to 1970 (Washington: USGPO, 1975), Series Y 457–465.
[a] Figures are current dollar outlays of the federal government, not including those to the Army and Navy departments.

and wool products beyond their original three years. By 1820, fiscal pressures had led the House to undertake a full revision of the tariff; that bill was later defeated in the Senate.

During the next thirty years tariff policy was debated almost continuously in Congress; its preeminence on the political agenda was not displaced until the sectional controversies of the 1850s. Significant tariffs were passed in 1824, 1828, 1832, 1833, 1842, 1846, and 1857. Tariffs were relatively more protectionist between 1816 and 1833, although the compromise act of 1833 set timetables for a reduction which was completed by 1842. By 1842, duties were lower than they had been in 1816 (see Table 2.3).

Table 2.3. Average tariff rates, 1821–1857

Years	Duties as a percentage of all dutiable imports[a]
1821–1824	44.62
1825–1828	50.29
1829–1832	51.55
1833–1842	35.06
1843–1846	33.22
1847–1857	26.22

Source: U.S. Bureau of the Census, Historical Statistics of the United States from Colonial Times to 1970 (Washington: USGPO, 1975), Series U 207–212.
[a] Percentages are averages over the years indicated.

The structure of the tariff measures changed radically in this period. The issues of the minimum, of ad valorem versus specific tariffs, of warehousing versus immediate payment of duties upon arrival of goods into the United States, and of the general structure of tariffs all solidified in this period. Most remain features of contemporary tariff policy.[58]

High-Tariff Acts: 1824–1833

By the 1820s, participants in tariff debates commonly cited the writings of Smith and Ricardo to defend low tariffs. This emphasis contributed to an increasing sophistication in tariff discussions. Proponents on both sides displayed knowledge not only of Adam Smith but of a host of other economic writers. In general, free traders were more rigid and doctrinaire; protectionists were amenable to incorporating a range of positions into their policy prescriptions. Protectionists benefited from a working knowledge of classical thought and their ability to show how small modifications in liberal analysis would lead to radically different outcomes.

As in 1816, debate in these years turned on differing opinions on both state goals and what role commercial policy could and should play in meeting such goals. Thus discussions over whether the government had a right or responsibility to protect infant industry from British competition, assure the development of a large home market, maintain employment at high wages, and ameliorate market dislocations were juxtaposed with arguments about the right means to achieve those goals. The main argument put forth by advocates of low tariffs was that economic closure would keep the United States from benefiting from the international division of labor. As Lewis Williams (D-N.C.) observed: "With the labor of ten days, I can buy a piece of cloth manufactured in England; whereas, the same sort of cloth, manufactured in the United States, would cost me twelve or thirteen days labor, or a value equivalent to that."[59] Free traders argued that market forces could better judge how resources should be allocated than the government. Representatives increasingly accepted the protectionists' position that industrialization and high levels of employment were a state policy goal; free traders, however, now argued that the market and not the government could better set the appropriate wage rates that would guarantee full employment and industrialization.[60]

[58] One of the more contentious issues in the period was that of valuation. Valuation entailed not only the concept of the minimum or a protectionist floor for industry goods but a debate on the virtues of an ad valorem system, that is, tariffs as a percent of value against one of fixed rates, that is, a tariff set by the quantity of an item entering the United States.

[59] *Annals of Congress*, 19th Cong., 1st sess., p. 2111.

[60] For a comprehensive analysis of the economic arguments offered in the 1824 and 1894 tariff debates, see Richard Edwards, "Economic Sophistication in Nineteenth Century Congressional Tariff Debates," *Journal of Economic History*, 30 (December 1970): 802–38.

49

As in 1816, talk was a poor predictor of political outcomes in this period. Voting more often than not divided on regional lines with a consistent bloc of southern votes resisting protectionist legislation (see

Table 2.4. House votes on major tariff legislation, 1816–1842

Year	For	Against
1816	88 [a]	54
1824	107	102
1828	105	94
1832	132	65
1833	119	85
1842	116	104

Source: The data in this table are courtesy of Keith Poole and the Inter-University Consortium for Political and Social Research.
[a] The votes are final roll calls on House bills, not the House-Senate conference versions.

Table 2.4).[61] But again, representatives from neither the South nor the North spoke with one voice. New England congressmen maintained a free-trade position favoring their commercial interests well into the century; southern border states such as Kentucky and Maryland often cast votes for protection.

Societal, institutional, and economic changes prefaced the shift in tariff policy after 1824. Beginning in the 1820s, pro-tariff interest groups arose that were not solely industry-specific. In key industrial cities, special societies were organized to advocate high tariffs. Especially in New York and Philadelphia, these societies had a large, prestigious, and active membership. These groups and their conventions did much to keep protectionism on the political agenda. By the end of the decade, both *Niles' Register* and Matthew Carey's publications had significant followings. Major pro-protection conventions took place in Harrisburg, Philadelphia, and other cities. The message to Congress was not one-sided: advocates of protection quickly engendered organized opposition throughout the country. Free-trade newspapers in both the North and South embraced the cause and, after the 1828 act, actively promoted a campaign to "sell" free trade to the public. Free traders relied heavily on county or district meetings at which they adopted free-trade memorials to Congress. These memorials were circulated in communities and often became local political platforms. Such antiprotection appeals were not regionally based but came from

---

[61] As a measure of legislative behavior, I report here and in subsequent chapters just House votes. These votes are more prone to particularistic pressures than are Senate votes and are thus better measures of the extent of interest-based voting.

all parts of the country. For example, Henry Lee of Boston published such an appeal in a pamphlet which became one of the most widely circulated critiques of protection.[62] Even Niles later admitted that he could find few errors in Lee's argument.

Social changes alone, however, explain neither the form, extent, nor timing of protectionist legislation. The partisan division in government between 1816 and 1841 gave the Democrats the votes to pursue their policy of choice. Yet tariffs were relatively high until the late 1830s and were thereafter reduced, even when the Whig party was politically

Table 2.5. Partisan control of the House, Senate, and presidency, 1815–1860

Year	Congress	House	Senate	President
1815–1817	14th	DRa	DR	DR (Madison)
1817–1819	15th	DR	DR	DR (Monroe)
1819–1821	16th	DR	DR	DR (Monroe)
1821–1823	17th	DR	DR	DR (Monroe)
1823–1825	18th	DR	DR	DR (Monroe)
1825–1827	19th	AD	AD	C (Adams)
1827–1829	20th	J	J	C (Adams)
1829–1831	21st	D	D	D (Jackson)
1831–1833	22d	D	D	D (Jackson)
1833–1835	23d	D	D	D (Jackson)
1835–1837	24th	D	D	D (Jackson)
1837–1839	25th	D	D	D (Van Buren)
1839–1841	26th	D	D	D (Van Buren)
1841–1843	27th	W	W	W (Tyler)
1843–1845	28th	D	W	W (Tyler)
1845–1847	29th	D	D	D (Polk)
1847–1849	30th	W	D	D (Polk)
1849–1851	31st	D	D	W (Fillmore)
1851–1853	32d	D	D	W (Fillmore)
1853–1855	33d	D	D	D (Pierce)
1855–1857	34th	R	D	D (Pierce)
1857–1859	35th	D	D	D (Buchanan)
1859–1861	36th	R	D	D (Buchanan)

Source: U.S. Bureau of the Census, *Historical Statistics of the United States from Colonial Times to 1970* (Washington: USGPO, 1975), Series Y 204–210.

aAbbreviations indicate majority party in each chamber: AD = Administration; C = Coalition; D = Democratic; DR = Democratic-Republican; J = Jacksonian; R = Republican; W = Whig.

competitive (see Table 2.5). Two institutional changes in Congress better explain the policy shift toward high tariffs in this period. First, the reapportionment that followed the census of 1820 favored protectionism; demographic shifts created twenty-three new House seats from

[62] *Report of a Committee of the Citizens of Boston and Vicinity Opposed to a Further Increase of Duties on Importations* (Boston, 1827).

high-tariff states. The resultant change in the composition of the House facilitated the creation of a pro-protection coalition of Middle Atlantic and western representatives. Not only did protectionists benefit from increased numbers of representatives from industrial areas, but a reorganization of House committees in 1819, creating the Committee on Manufactures, allowed protectionist forces to coalesce within one standing committee.

Last, we must consider the economic changes in the period. While southern cotton and tobacco prospered, both agriculture and industry in the North continued to suffer under a depression that deepened in the closing years of the decade. By one estimate, nine-tenths of manufacturers were in debt by 1824.[63] These economic problems created the incentive while congressional memberships and structures created the ability to act on the demands of new articulate groups demanding protectionism.

Tariff Debate in the 1820s

In James Monroe's second annual message to Congress in 1818, he recommended a review of the tariff "for the purpose of affording such additional protection to those articles which we are prepared to manufacture, or which are more immediately connected with the defense and independence of the country."[64] The bill the House ultimately reported out of the Committee on Manufactures to be debated for two months in the House and two weeks in the Senate was an attempt to do just that. On the floor, opponents argued that the high tariffs in the act would ultimately undermine the revenue base of the country. Defenders of the act stressed its merit as a protector of industry; they were less concerned with its potential fiscal impact.[65] Proponents blamed the depressed state of the economy on insufficient aid to manufactures and, in particular, the absence of a home market. Those speaking to the question seemed knowledgeable about events in England and the growing British interest in free-trade doctrine. To counteract any suggestion that the United States should pursue the same course, the bill's supporters argued that regardless of current theoretical opinions on the folly of tariffs, Britain's protective policy

[63] John Tod (D-Pa.) made this estimate during a House debate on the 1824 act.

[64] Stanwood, *American Tariff Controversies*, 1:201.

[65] John Barbour (SRD-Va.) argued that "the exigencies of the Treasury do not call for an increase in revenues," while Churchill Cambreleng (D-N.Y.) argued that "our revenue system will be seriously injured by the measure." Henry Clay (D-Ky.) responded that even resorting to excise was preferable to a future without protection. *Annals of Congress*, 18th Cong., 1st sess., pp. 1983–85, 1575.

was still in full-scale operation.[66] As Henry Clay so aptly stated:[67] "In England [protection] has accomplished its purpose, fulfilled its end. She may safely challenge the most unshackled competition in exchanges. It is upon this very ground that many of her writers recommend an abandonment of the prohibitory system."[68]

Proponents defended tariffs much as they had in 1816. First, they argued for the need to develop a home market. As Clay explained: "The greatest want of civilized society is a market for the sale and exchange of the surplus of the produce of the labor of its members. This market may exist at home or abroad, or both. . . . But, with respect to their relative superiority, I cannot entertain a doubt. The home market is first in order, and paramount in importance. . . . Foreign nations cannot, if they would, take our surplus produce."[69] Not all agreed with these principles. Christopher Rankin (D-Miss.) replied: "The idea of a home market for either our produce or manufactures to any considerable extent, is most fallacious; it has no foundation in reason or truth, but is calculated to delude and deceive the people."[70]

Second, although wages remained an issue in 1820's, debate concentrated far more on the relation between tariffs and full employment than on high wages. In 1824, Silas Wood (D-N.Y.) suggested that "the interference of Government to procure employment for the surplus population is required to increase the wealth of the nation."[71] He then summed up what tariff supporters saw as a key problem which tariff policy should address: "Production exceeds consumption, and a portion of the people are without occupation, for want of employment."[72]

Following on the writings of early protectionists, representatives created a logic for economic closure based on employment. Most representatives assumed that employment was associated with the ability of producers to find markets for their goods. To what markets would Americans send their goods? Recent history had shown that foreign markets were either unavailable or at best erratic. If the United States wanted to assure employment for its workers it would need a thriving home market. And in the 1820s, the strategy to which representatives repeatedly returned to meet that goal was the use of tariffs. As stated

---

[66] See, for example, statements by Representative Tod, ibid., pp. 2229–32.

[67] Clay was not alone in his criticism of the British. Henry Martindale (W-N.Y.) argued: "To be sure, we get an equivalent for our money [in trade], and perhaps more, but we consume it, when we might make it. England gets our money, and she does not consume it. This is the secret of her wealth and of our poverty." Ibid., p. 1655.

[68] Ibid., p. 1990.

[69] Ibid., p. 1966.

[70] Ibid., p. 2010.

[71] Ibid., p. 2074.

[72] Ibid., p. 2073.

by Silas Wood (D-N.Y.): "If a farmer has no market for his surplus productions, the supply of his own wants will be the measure of his exertions; and if there be no foreign demand for the surplus produce of the country, the industry of the nation will be limited to the supply of the nation. The want of a market for surplus productions . . . effectually limits the exertions of industry."[73] Further, it was suggested that a strong home market would not only help industry but lead to prosperity in all parts of the American economy. John C. Calhoun (DR-S.C.) argued:

> Neither agriculture nor manufacturing nor commerce, taken separately, is the cause of wealth. It flows from the three combined and cannot exist without each. . . . When our manufactures are grown to a certain perfection, as they soon will be under the fostering care of the government . . . the farmer will find a ready market for his produce, and what is almost of equal consequence, a certain and cheap supply of all he wants. His prosperity will diffuse itself to every class in the community.[74]

Third, proponents were now forced to defend the constitutionality of protection as opponents openly questioned the legality of tariffs. For instance, P. P. Barbour (D-Va.) argued: "[This] bill does violate the spirit of the Constitution. [Tariff] power . . . was given to us for the purpose of raising revenue, which revenue is to be applied to the ends pointed out in the Constitution. Now, sir, as far as, by this bill, it is proposed to encourage manufactures or any other department of industry, we shall be using this power not only not for the purpose for which it was given, but for another and a different one."[75] Clay led the opposition: "The gentleman from Virginia has, however, entirely mistaken the clause of the Constitution on which we rely. It is that which gives to Congress the power to regulate commerce with foreign nations. The grant is plenary, without any limitations whatever, and includes the whole power of regulation of which the subject to be regulated is susceptible."[76]

Unlike the previous tariff vote in 1816, the 1824 bill passed without a strong North-South sectional bias. Men with strongly divergent views—James Buchanan (D-Pa.), Louis McLane (F-Del.), Samuel Houston (D-Tex.), Andrew Jackson (D-Tenn.), Martin Van Buren (D-N.Y.), and Richard Johnson (D-Ky.)—supported the act. A majority of both New England and southern congressmen cast their votes against it, but the

---

[73] Ibid.
[74] John C. Calhoun, *The Works of John C. Calhoun* (New York: D. Appleton, 1881), 2:166.
[75] *Annals of Congress*, 18th Cong., 1st sess., p. 1918.
[76] Ibid., p. 2121.

bill passed with strong support from the middle Atlantic states and the West. Not all were satisfied. In an almost prescient comment, Robert Hayne (D-S.C.) told the Senate: "Considering this scheme of promoting certain employments at the expense of others as unequal, oppressive, and unjust, viewing prohibition as the means and the destruction of all foreign commerce the end of this policy, I take this occasion to declare that we shall feel ourselves justified in embracing the very first opportunity of repealing all such laws as may be passed for the promotion of these objects."[77]

Four years later, Congress was debating a new tariff. Neither issues nor arguments had changed much. The constitutional issue was more heated; by now strict constructionists were opposing not only tariffs but all government-sponsored internal improvements. Overall, however, the supporters of tariffs had the upper hand with increasing numbers speaking of the desirability of a large home market for both consumption and production. Adjustment issues were also clearly articulated—many congressmen feared that lowering tariffs would shift market forces to the detriment of already employed workers and capital.

The industry that complained most bitterly about the tariff of 1824, woolens, played a crucial role in bringing the tariff issue to the floor of Congress in 1828. The woolen industry faced a specific problem: until 1816, wool had been duty-free. The 1816 act placed a 15 percent duty on raw wool. In 1824 the tariff was further increased, to 30 percent (to be effective after 1826). The economic effects of the duty on the industry as a whole were mixed. Although protection helped grazing interests, it undercut what little protection the finished woolens industry gained under either law. And although the duty on certain woolen goods jumped from 25 to 33.3 percent in 1824, this hike could not compensate for the increase in prices for raw materials. By 1826, half the machinery in the New England woolen factories lay idle.[78] According to manufacturers, their problems stemmed not only from a skewed tariff structure but from a lack of competitiveness against cheap British wool and finished goods. The latter, they claimed, were produced with considerably lower labor costs and, because of the ad valorem method of assessing duties, entered the country with an artificially low price tag. Thus in debate over the aborted 1827 tariff, the industry position was to request not an increase in duties (given the

---

[77] Ibid., p. 649.

[78] Historians do not agree on the cause of the decline. Taussig argues that the economic problems were not caused by the structure of duties; Stanwood contests that Taussig provides no data to support his claim. See F. W. Taussig, *The Tariff History of the United States* (New York: G. P. Putnam, 1914); Stanwood, *American Tariff Controversies.*

structure, such an increase was likely to add to its burden), but rather specific duties and the adoption of a "minimum" principle.[79] Though somewhat successful in the Committee on Manufacturers, the ill-fated bill proposed a tariff system with both ad valorem and minimum rates.

The next year, in the Twentieth Congress, protectionists did not control the key Committee on Manufactures. Yet when the dust settled, Congress had legislated the most protectionist tariff to date. The Speaker of the House, Andrew Stevenson of Virginia, purposely appointed to the committee representatives who were hostile to the Harrisburg convention. Still, the bill they reported followed, in most details, the plan the convention had proposed. In one of the stranger episodes of political maneuvering, the committee, aligned with free traders on the floor, decided to construct a bill so onerous that it would be guaranteed defeat even by supporters of protection. Thus the committee bill set high duties on many industries that protectionists cared little about and denied it to those they did. Most egregious of all, the committee specifically denied aid to finished woolens. Outside of Congress, the bill was universally criticized.

Congressional debate echoed that of 1824. In the economic discussion, the only new element in the public discourse centered on the causes of the woolen industry's depression and the role played by British tariff policy. Protectionists contended that changes in the structure of British tariffs had created the prevailing economic malaise in the industry; free traders responded that this assertion lacked proof.

In the House, the bill passed over southern and New England opposition. On the floor, Senate amendments further increased duties and led Daniel Webster to his ultimate claim that this was a "bill of abominations," reinforcing John Randolph's (D-Va.) comment that "the bill referred to manufactures of no sort or kind except the manufacture of a President of the United States."[80] The vote in the Senate was sectional. New England voted to support woolens and thus the total bill; the South, except for eight votes, opposed. President John Quincy Adams signed the bill and it became law.

In the end, no one took credit for the act. Even Niles would not associate himself and the "real" protectionists with this piece of legislation. The South was uniformly aghast at the bill's passage. Flags flew at half-mast as those involved in commerce foresaw in this act the death knell for America's trading future. No one had expected the bill to

---

[79] The industry would pursue the opposite strategy in the 1850s, arguing not for new or higher duties on finished products but for inclusion of primary wool on the free list.
[80] Stanwood, *American Tariff Controversies*, 1:290.

pass.[81] But as the South pondered the right of government to set tariffs, the rest of the country prospered under its "abominations." Horace Greeley reports in the first volume of *Hunt's Merchants' Magazine* that, considering the ten years when protectionist policy was predominant, from 1824 to 1834, "its friends may defy its opponents to show any ten successive years when commerce was so uniformly, generally and inwardly prosperous."[82]

Greeley was right. The economy was on an upswing, although there is little evidence that the cause was the 1828 tariff. Imports increased, confounding the predictions of those who said that high duties cut revenues and inhibit sales. As Raymond had predicted, prices declined, even though free traders argued this was impossible. Even commercial groups, who defended free trade, noticed that the prices of protected products were considerably lower than they had been without protection. Manufacturers prospered; the country had full employment at high wages. Such economic times did not go unnoticed; many firms sent affidavits to Congress confirming their impression that the tariff was the reason for the economic upswing, and protection's supporters chronicled the connection between the high-tariff years and prosperity. Thus Clay, supporting a tariff resolution in 1832, could remark: "If the term of seven years were to be selected of the greatest prosperity which this people have enjoyed since the establishment of their present constitution, it would be exactly that period of seven years which followed the passage of the tariff of 1824."[83]

The times supported protection. Even if the passage of the 1828 act owed more to serendipitous factors than to the power of the high-tariff coalition, the concordance of high tariffs and general prosperity allowed protectionists to argue persuasively that it was the tariff that had caused the affluence. Even though free traders found other causes for the price decline and claimed the prosperity of the West resulted far more from natural resources than political decisions, the protectionists responded that the country was merely reaping the benefits of a large home market. Later, when the financial crisis of 1837 followed a tariff reduction, this widespread belief that the peak of duties was associated with economic prosperity led to the immediate call for tariff revision in Congress.

But though protectionism had shown itself to be an economically viable policy, its success created a problem Congress could not ignore.

---

[81] One measure illustrates how unlikely its passage was thought to be: before all other tariff legislation, importers, anticipating a hike in duties, rushed in inventory under the old rates to get a windfall after the new rates were set. In 1828, no such rush occurred.

[82] Stanwood, *American Tariff Controversies*, 1:350.

[83] U.S. Congress, *Register of Debates*, 22d Cong., 1st sess., vol. 8, p. 1, pt. 258.

The affluence of the 1820s had led to budget surpluses in the 1830s. Until this time the defense of protection was based on the need to keep American manufacturers competitive; it was not intended to swell government revenues, nor could any protectionist say it should. In the South, the tariff was already seen as a form of redistribution used by the North to fund expensive internal improvements. With the growth of budget surpluses, free traders found themselves the lucky recipients of a new, politically salient critique of high-tariff policy. Making the argument that the tariff was unconstitutional and led to excess government spending, free traders attracted enough northern allies to give them a majority of seats in Congress. Thus Congress began the new decade by agreeing to reduce revenue duties. The targeted products, however, coffee, tea, cocoa, molasses, and salt—products not made in the United States—indicate resistance to undoing the protectionist net that had gone up in the previous years.

Nullification and the 1830s

President Jackson, in his message to the Twenty-second Congress, urged tariff reform. Although protectionists agreed that the general duty level deserved reduction, they differed with their opponents over how that should occur. Hayne (D-S.C.), arguing for the free traders, proposed that after a period of phased reductions, no industry should be protected much above the mean. Clay, in the name of the protectionist coalition, reasoned that Congress should uphold the system of protection but eliminate duties on products that no longer needed them or that were not produced in this country. But the protectionist forces had a problem: Clay's proposal was estimated to be insufficient to rid the treasury of its surplus.

Protectionists' interests fared poorly after they lost control of the Committee on Manufactures. Although John Quincy Adams, who headed the Committee on Manufactures, issued a report in 1832 in which he expressed his personal view that protection was historically justified and necessary, his bill was not supported by others in the committee. On the politically problematic wool issue, the committee bill eliminated the system of minimums in the woolen schedules and cut the overall duty on them. The bill did no better once it reached the floor. Under pressure, the protectionist coalition deteriorated. In amendments, Massachusetts voted against Pennsylvania's iron duties, and in response, Pennsylvania voted against duties on textiles. Members crossed party lines to vote regional interests. In the Senate, changes in the bill tended to increase levels of protection, but most of these additions were removed in conference.

In the end the act substantially changed the tariff schedule, but not all in the expected direction. More items were allowed in without duty: in 1828, 49 articles were on the free list, in 1832, that number rose to 180. Wool received some reductions, but cotton, iron, and glass maintained a fair degree of protection. The duty on sugar dropped, mostly as a means for southerners to punish Louisiana's adhesion to protection. But sterling was revalued, which, in effect, increased tariff protection. Most radical perhaps was that in the name of trade liberalization, a system that had existed since 1789—adding 10 percent to the cost as declared on an invoice—was repealed.

The 1832 act had a short history. Although the act had reduced many duties, South Carolina maintained that it legitimated the policy and principle of protection. South Carolina was not alone in this thought: after passage, the protectionist coalition also found in the act a confirmation of American adhesion to protectionist principles. In the midst of the controversy President Jackson offered a compromise scheme for tariff revision. He suggested that two factors should set future tariff levels: the amount of foreign trade regulation and the production of goods essential during war. If levels existed beyond that dictated by these needs, they should be reduced but with the caveat that the new levels should not undermine either the revenue needs of the government or domestic investments.

But in January 1833 protectionists argued that it would be political blackmail to reconsider the tariff issue before the 1832 act even took effect. Rufus Choate (W-Mass.) claimed that "it would be mere affectation in me to pretend not to see that this bill is introduced because South Carolina had prospectively nullified the law."[84] Daniel Jenifer (NR-Md.) concurred: the bill "might appear to some to be the result of a combination to preserve particular interests without regard to the sacrifices of others, or a political maneuver to ensure the balance of power."[85] Nathan Appleton (W-Mass.) commented that "the only ground after all on which the immediate and hurried action of this House can be justified is that it is necessary to the preservation of the Union."[86] But as protectionists quickly noted, they still could do little to stop tariff revision: it was politics, not economics, that was driving Congress. And though the protectionists successfully showed that the 1832 bill would do little to change the revenue situation (because lowering rates would increase imports) this message carried no political

---

[84] *Register of Debates*, 22d Cong., 2d sess., vol. 9, pt. 1, p. 974.
[85] Ibid., p. 1063.
[86] Ibid., p. 1204.

weight. Meanwhile, Clay and the Senate had devised a compromise: a nine-year gradual reduction down to a revenue tariff. His bill would not abandon protection, he argued, but only suspend it temporarily. And by 1842, he pointed out, manufacturers would get free raw materials.

The dwindling protectionist coalition outlined its main objections to Clay's bill. The notion of equal reductions for all products, the lack of discrimination in choosing tariff aid, the decision to measure tariff need by revenues (and not by the needs of manufacturers), and Congress's promise to relinquish its right to impose duties were all targeted in pointed criticism on the floor.

Although supported by the South, Clay's bill was not entirely opposed to the interests of manufacturers. The bill required that starting in 1842, duties be paid immediately and in cash. The much-disputed system of valuation would also change. After 1842, "duties [would be] assessed upon the value thereof at the port where the same shall be entered, under such regulation as may be prescribed by law."[87] The home market system of valuation, so open to fraud, was finally eliminated. Further, under the proposed system, freight and insurance would be added to the amount on which the duty was set.

The House passed the Senate bill virtually unaltered. Again in debate protectionists protested what Clay was asking of them. Asher Robbins (W) of Rhode Island declared: "It has been said that [the act] preserves the principle of protection. What signifies it to preserve the principle of protection if protection itself is not preserved?"[88] But even in the House the South had the votes to pass the bill.

Not until 1842, when the new revenue system was scheduled to take force, did the tariff again elicit political controversy. The staged tariff reductions began, and the act ushered in four years of economic prosperity for the American economy. Prosperity, however, was to be short-lived.

In sum, political debate in the first third of the century revolved around but did not solve three central economic issues. The role commercial policy should play in economic management, the extent of responsibility held by government for aiding in the adjustment of labor and capital to market forces, and the extent to which economic forces could be harnessed for foreign policy or other political purposes remained contested political issues. As opposed to later periods, Congress at this time was still debating the fundamental goals of commercial policy. Some claimed a need to use tariffs to develop manufactures; others saw tariffs as undercutting their view of American development,

[87] Ibid., p. 404.
[88] Ibid., p. 787.

60

which lay in production of agricultural commodities. Many in Congress spoke of a responsibility to assure high employment and of the legitimacy of using tariff policy to regulate labor's dislocation. Questions of constitutionality on this issue were raised over what means were actually in the legal purview of Congress. The South would eventually use the constitutional argument to defend regional interests in low tariffs.

Also in this period began the increasingly divisive debate over whether markets can and should be controlled through political means. Throughout this debate elected officials alluded to the British manipulation of international markets. Serious debate also occurred over whether markets or governments should set prices. In general, however, whether true of not, the ability to control the market was in far less dispute in the 1820s as compared to 150 years later than was whether that control served a social purpose.

Although Congress did not resolve any of these fundamental questions of political economy, the manner in which the debate was posed would influence outcomes for the rest of the century. The arguments that the tariff was a domestic and not purely a foreign policy instrument (even in the face of observations about British predatory practices), that employment depended on control of the home market, and that budget surpluses were fashioned to be illegal set the parameters of later discussion. In the 1820s, as in the 1940s, the exigencies of the market led people to associate economic affluence with a particular tariff level. In the 1820s and early 1830s, protectionism coexisted with growth. One hundred years later, the free traders observed the opposite relationship. In both periods, affluence was overdetermined.

Although the form of the free trade–protection debate influenced politics later in the century, in this period, the interests of participants explain particular affinities to economic arguments. Thus the South heralded the free-trade ideas of the classical theorists while early midwestern industrializers used Hamilton to defend their desire for state intervention. Regionalism, constituents' economic interests, and changes in both the placement of congressional seats and the committee system were far more critical elements of policy setting. To a great extent, all these factors were associated with changing demographic patterns and the uneven growth of industry. Later, ideas about the appropriate strategies for representing changing constituent interests would become of equal importance.

Low-Tariff Acts: 1842 to the Civil War

In many ways, the period from 1837 to 1843 resembled the Great Depression of the 1930s. The earlier depression was long and deep, with declines in both domestic and export prices, a cessation of capital imports, and the defaulting on government securities by individual states. The depression hit hardest in the South and West. As the price for cotton continued to decline and production shrank, it became apparent that cotton would never regain a dominant position in the American economy.

The financial crisis of 1837 did not cause an immediate renewal of the tariff debate. The tariff reductions of the 1833 compromise held. Rates found to be protective—that is, any in excess of 20 percent ad valorem in the 1832 bill—decreased 10 percent every other year until 1841. By 1842, rates for these protected industries had declined by 50 percent to the agreed 20 percent standard duty.

The final rate, however, remained in effect for only a few months. Not surprisingly, the intensity of the depression led to a shortfall in the treasury and a change in party control in Congress, with the Democrats becoming the minority party for the first time in two decades. Partisan control and the continuing economic dislocation from the depression supplied the impetus for the tariff act of 1842.

The 1842 tariff act was the most complex Congress had yet passed. The tariff schedule was far more specific, making the bill itself about three times as long as previous tariff acts. In addition, the act abandoned the home valuation principle and upheld cash payments of duties. In general, duties returned to their 1832 levels. The bill assessed an average 30 percent duty on most imports for purposes of revenue, with higher rates for protected industries and lower duties on their raw materials.

Only two years after the bill was enacted, the Democrats regained control of government. Newly elected President James K. Polk appointed as his secretary of the treasury a fellow southerner, Robert Walker, one of the more adamant free traders of the period. Walker and Polk immediately declared the need to revamp the tariff system.[89] In his annual address, Polk appeared less doctrinaire than his appointee, but he nevertheless warned Congress that it "may undoubtedly, in the exercise of a sound discretion, discriminate in arranging the rates of duty on different articles, but the discriminations should be within the revenue standard and be made with the view to raise money for the support of government."[90] In general, he argued, no duty should be raised to a level that would cut imports; all rates must be set to assure a balanced budget.

---

[89] Polk's selection of Walker clarified his tariff position. Needing Pennsylvania to carry the election, he had selected George M. Dallas, a loyal protectionist, for his vice-presidential candidate. Throughout the state, the slogan "Polk, Dallas and the Tariff of 1842" was used to draw votes.

[90] Stanwood, *American Tariff Controversies*, 2:42.

In his first annual treasury report to Congress, Walker summarized the antebellum free-trade position. He argued that, in considering tariffs, government should adhere to six principles:

1. That no more money should be collected than is necessary for the wants of the government, economically administrated.
2. That no duty should be imposed upon any article above the lowest rate that will yield the largest amount of revenue.
3. That below such rate, discrimination may be made, descending in the scale of duties; or, for imperative reasons, the article may be placed in the list of those free from all duties.
4. That the maximum revenue duty should be imposed on luxuries.
5. That all minimums, and all specific duties, should be abolished; and ad valorem duties substituted in their place—care being taken to guard against fraudulent invoices and undervaluation, and to assess the duty upon the actual market value.
6. That the duty should be so imposed as to operate as equally as possible throughout the Union, discriminating neither for nor against any class or region.[91]

Along with other free-traders, Walker acknowledged that a 20 percent average duty would probably yield the necessary revenue.[92] If this were not enough, removing items from the free list would yield any needed additional revenue. On the controversial constitutional question, Walker argued that the Constitution gave Congress the power to set tariffs only for the purpose of raising revenue. If tariffs were so high that they stemmed the flow of imports and cut revenues, Congress was not fulfilling its constitutional mandate.

Walker made what would become, in the twentieth century, the conventional economic critique of tariffs. He argued that the only fair tariff was on luxury items, whether or not they were domestically produced; anything else discriminated against the poor. Such discrimination occurred, he said, because tariffs increased prices, despite what others had claimed. He believed that when the prices of imports rise, so do those of their domestic rivals, "for being like articles their price must be the same in the same market." Higher prices, he continued, did not benefit workers by increasing demand for their services. Rather, protection rewarded only capital: "A protective tariff is a question regarding the enhancement of the profits of capital. That is its object, and not to augment the wages of labor, which would reduce

---

[91] *Report from the Secretary of the Treasury,* December 3, 1845, 29th Cong., 1st sess., p. 4.
[92] Ibid., p. 5. He argued against a horizontal duty structure because "such a scale would be a refusal to discriminate for revenue, and might sink that revenue below the wants of governments" (p. 4).

those profits." Further, "it discriminates in favor of manufacturers and against agriculture by imposing many higher duties upon the manufactured fabric than upon the agricultural product out of which it is made." Walker refuted claims that the tariff hikes of the 1820s had lowered prices. He argued instead that "improved machinery, diminished prices of the raw material, or other causes" were responsible. To those who said that tariffs equalized differences between foreign and domestic wages, he answered that this rendered "the duty a tax on all consumers for the benefit of the protected classes." He likened the situation to a hypothetical one, in which the federal government sent a marshal to collect taxes from the entire population, then handed the funds to manufacturing capitalists so that they could sustain their business or realize a larger profit. "Capitalists," he said, "should not expect exorbitant profits. Under revenue duties it is believed they would still receive a reasonable profit—equal to that realized by those engaged in other pursuits; and it is thought they should desire no more, at least through the agency of governmental power."[93]

Clearly Walker believed that market forces, not the government, should decide the extent and direction of trade. Reciprocal free trade, he said, "would best advance the interest of all." Refuting the contention that the United States should "meet the tariffs of other nations by countervailing restrictions," he argued that increasing duties at home would not lead to "a reduction of foreign tariffs, but the reverse, by furnishing the protected classes there with the identical argument used by the protected classes here against reduction. By countervailing restrictions we injure our own fellow citizens much more than the foreign nations at whom we propose to aim their force. . . . Let our commerce be as free as our political institutions. Let us, with revenue duties only, open our ports to all the world; and nation after nation will soon follow our example."[94]

Walker believed the United States should follow England and liberalize trade. He claimed that duties were hurting, not helping, the majority of Americans; the protective system was inept, especially in its impact on farmers. "The farmer and planter," he argued, "are to a great extent forbidden to buy in the foreign market and confined to the domestic articles enhanced in price by the duties. The tariff is thus a double benefit to the manufacturer and a double loss to the farmer and planter. . . . We have more fertile lands than any other nation, can raise a greater variety of products, and, it may be said, could feed and clothe the people of nearly all the world. The home market of itself is

[93] Ibid., pp. 4–15.
[94] Ibid.

wholly inadequate for such products. They must have the foreign market; or a large surplus, accompanied by great depression in price, must be the result."[95]

Oiled by Walker's logic and a Democratic majority, the 1846 act moved quickly through Congress. Once passed, it remained in force for eleven years. The act established eight classes of goods, ranging from duty-free to 75 percent tariffs. The highest rates were reserved for revenue items, most notably liquors. Iron and cotton, in the second highest category, received a 30 percent duty; wool was placed in Schedule C, which received a 25 percent duty. All specific duties and minimums were abolished. Any item not listed was to get a 20 percent duty that, as Webster and John Niles (D-Conn.) pointed out, imposed as high a duty on raw materials as on manufactured products—in some cases even higher.

The Walker tariff was by no means universally applauded. Between its passage and the Civil War, both Whig and other anti-Democratic forces attempted tariff reform. But they repeatedly failed to muster a sufficient coalition to change the status quo. Perhaps because the economy was doing well before the 1857 financial panic, or because the slavery issue overwhelmed the political community, protectionism was not a preeminent issue in Congress during the 1850s. The 1848 election brought the Whigs once again to power and, although they renewed their call for protection, they did little about it. The next tariff to be legislated—six months before the 1857 crisis—was again relatively liberal, structured much like Walker's act. Its support derived neither from party nor region, although the West was the area most opposed to it; traditionally free-trade and traditionally protectionist regions united in a coalition that included such strange bedfellows as New England, Pennsylvania, and New Jersey.

It took the worst panic in twenty years, combined with the lowest tariff in the nineteenth century, to rally protectionist opposition. The prosperity of the mid-1840s to mid-1850s was akin to that of the 1920s. Expectations were high, speculation rampant, and little thought given to what was causing financial growth. Growth, however, had been spurred for specific, time-bound reasons. The war with Mexico, discovery of gold in California, the European revolutions of 1848, poor harvests in Europe, and, ultimately, the Crimean War had all benefited the American economy.

In this period of low tariffs and economic growth, the counterarguments of congressional protectionists shifted substantially. Although never straying far from Hamilton's original formulation, their defense

[95] Ibid.

of infant industry gave way to a defense of America's high wages. The nationalistic element of that argument—that is, that the interests of producers in their home market should take priority over the interests of any foreign producers, or, for that matter, other foreign or economic objectives—merged with a general defense of any policy that promised to maintain high wages for workers. American wages had always been high as a result of labor scarcity. In the early part of the century, many feared that these high wages would prevent industrialization. But once it became apparent that the United States was industrializing neverthe-less—and without the workers' impoverishment that had occurred in Britain—policy makers universally proclaimed themselves the defend-ers of high wages. And because protectionism remained the best of the few tools available for government manipulation of the economy, it was the instrument of choice for purposes as diverse as assuring high wages and increasing national wealth or welfare.

As in the previous high-tariff period, the division of constituent in-terests explains much of the variation in American tariff policy. In the second third of the century, the need to placate southern opposition made free-trade logic convenient for many in both parties. Walker's exposition of the logic of free trade also enhanced the status of free-trade ideas. Even when the Whigs held majorities, they could not mus-ter a defense against the logic Walker used to move debate away from the issue of wages to that of prices and revenues. Indicatively, few indus-tries attempted to fight southern opposition. Manufacturers in this period, such as wool producers, found it far more expedient to ask for a reduction in the tariff on primary inputs than to attempt to increase aid to finished products.

Thereafter, however, the free-trade position weakened, but for more reasons than the fall of the South. As the Republican party gathered together its new and very diverse constituency, it found free traders unable to supply an economic vision of how the party was to meet the interests of this new coalition.

Supplying the Republican Party's Vision

When the Republican party emerged as a conglomerate of old Whigs, disenchanted Democrats, and fringe third parties, its leaders were con-fronted with a range of issues that crosscut the interests of their broad constituency. To make matters worse, there remained no consensus, even among experts, on the basic economic effect of protection on wages, production, and prices. How would American wages—higher than any found in Europe—fare without protection? Just what was the empirical relationship between tariff levels and economic growth? Was protection, as a foreign policy issue, in the national interest or did it detract from American power and welfare?[96] Did protection deny trade opportunities and thereby aid particular classes, groups, or regions at the expense of others, or did it provide a home market and thus strengthen America's place in the world? Or was it true, as Walker had argued, that tariffs would never serve the interests of workers because they raised the general price of consumer items—or were protectionists correct in asserting that economic closure was in the interest of producers, consumers, and laborers?

The party's tariff platform reflected then contemporary understanding of these key questions. Free-trade logic was discounted, not because of its southern heritage but because supporters were unable to prove that trade would keep wages high, guarantee economic growth of both labor and capital, and prevent foreign exploitation. Free traders had always been at a disadvantage to defend America's economic autonomy and high wages. Thus they had avoided discussing wages, instead arguing from their strengths, that is, the effect of duties on prices and the need to balance the budget. But when slavery and, inadvertently, wage questions became the central issue of national politics, this strategy pushed the new Republican party into the protectionist camp.

Wages

Between 1820 and the Civil War, commonly held views on labor, as articulated in Congress, changed. In the early 1820s, Malthusian logic and a general conviction that labor wages were too high held sway. For example, Christopher Rankin (D-Miss.) in 1824 argued: "This state of things [high wages] will pass away when our population becomes too dense to be supported by the cultivation of the best soil, and to be employed in commerce. We are then and not until then prepared for manufacturing."[97] With the development of industry, this position became anachronistic; it was replaced by a sense of the value of independent laborers as citizens and as producers of wealth. Except in the South,

---

[96] Daniel Morrell (R-Pa.) argued with insight in 1870 about British policy: "If, however, free trade is really so beneficial, why is it that Great Britain is so discontented with her apparent monopoly of the theory? Can it be pure philanthropy that makes her statesmen and philosophers so eager to have others share its blessings? Their fanatical laudation of free trade wears a sinister look." (*Congressional Globe*, 41st Cong., 2d sess., p. 3292). "The repeal of the corn laws by Great Britain in 1847, was in fact one of the largest measures of protection to British manufacturers ever achieved. It was a victory of cheap bread, won by workingmen and manufacturers, by Cobden and Bright, over hereditary land-owners, and without which any increase of English operatives or extension of British manufactures had become impossible" (ibid., p. 3293).

[97] *Annals of Congress*, 18th Cong., 1st sess., 42:2010.

Malthusian logic was rejected in favor of a new respect for labor and a fear for workers' pauperization.

With a growing regard for the economic rights of the working class came questions about how American laborers would fare if foreign trade increased. Most were pessimistic. An 1831 convention of protectionists in New York declared: "It is to rescue the labor of the American people from an inferiority—a subjection at once dishonorable and burdensome, at once degrading to its character while it increases its toils— that those [protective] laws were originally passed, have all along continued and now exist."[98] In Congress, Webster concurred, declaring in 1833 that "a just and a leading object in the whole [protective] system is the encouragement and protection of American manual labor."[99] In debate, he went further, arguing that "the free labor of the United States deserves to be protected. The true way to protect the poor is to protect their labor."[100]

The theoretical connection between wages and protectionism took many forms. One was to see the tariff as a method to forestall western migration. The Convention of Friends of American Industry noted: "The establishment of domestic manufacturers had the effect of restraining emigration from the settled to the unsettled parts of the country . . . protective policy . . . enable[d] men to invest their capital and labor in manufactures at home instead of being compelled to emigrate and to occupy themselves in clearing."[101] More often, protection was said to assure American goods a market or to ensure that competition with pauper labor would not force owners to lower wages.

The inability to prove an empirical relationship between wages and tariffs fueled the already contested issue in Congress. In 1832, John Bell (W-Tenn.) argued convincingly that the South and Southeast received none of the benefits of protection, either in higher wages or profits, and instead had to pay increased prices for the products bought from "tariff" states. In his speech on the "American System," Clay had countered by reasoning that a protective tariff would increase the price of labor throughout the country, although he could give no proof. George McDuffie (D-S.C.) in 1830 represented a middle position, arguing that the price of labor had fallen in the South but had increased in the North.

By midcentury a repeated theme of speakers in Congress was that

---

[98] George Benjamin Mangold, "The Labor Argument in the American Protective Tariff Discussion," *Bulletin of the University of Wisconsin Economics and Political Science Series,* vol 5. no. 2, p. 71.
[99] Daniel Webster, *Works* (Boston: Little, Brown, 1851), 1:283.
[100] Mangold, "Labor Argument," p. 72.
[101] Ibid., p. 61.

tariffs defend the wages of American workers by taxing the products made by poorly paid workers in foreign countries. For example, John Davis (W-Mass.) argued in 1837:

> The poor only ask of you that you would pursue toward them an American policy—a policy which will give them good wages for their labor—and they will take care of themselves. They entreat of you not to reduce them to the deplorable condition of the miserable population of foreign countries, by reducing their wages to the same standard. . . . Break down the business in which it is employed by subjecting it to direct competition with foreign pauperism; lessen the demand for labor by introducing foreign productions, and . . . you will then have as poor and wretched a population.[102]

Not surprisingly, representatives from the northern states were most apt to support tariffs on these grounds. Thus James Buchanan (D-Pa.) said that it was cruel and unjust to neglect workers for the benefit of foreign labor, and Webster pointed out that the Constitution extended protection not only to capital but to labor. In 1828, Isaac Bates (W-Mass.) argued:

> If you hope . . . to maintain our system of Government, you must maintain the people at the elevated standard of living, and, as entirely dependent upon it, of moral and intellectual culture which they now hold. This they cannot do if you bring the day laborer, who must earn his $.75 to feed, to clothe, and to school his children, into contact and competition with him who will work for six pence sterling, because he wants and cares for none of these things and because six pence will answer all his purposes.[103]

The truth notwithstanding, by the 1840s, congressmen in both parties were legitimating the government's policy on protection by tying high wages to economic closure. The Whigs promoted the dual slogans in Pennsylvania of "No reduction of wages" and "A protective tariff." Societies such as the Friends of Protection lobbied extensively for aid on behalf of those employed in manufacturing. Home League meetings picked up the labor theme. Practices of other countries—from

---

[102] Ibid., pp. 89–90.
[103] *Congressional Debates*, 20th Cong., 1st sess., vol. 4, pt. 2, p. 2014.

paying low wages to bounties—were used as evidence of what a future of low tariffs would bring to the United States.[104]

The Economy

If "pauper labor" was the first concern around which the opponents of free trade rallied, the second targeted the free traders' "faulty reasoning" on the operation of market forces. Throughout the nineteenth century, both sides claimed that their tariff position was responsible for good economic times. For example, Greeley reputedly wrote in the *Whig Almanac* for 1846:

> The three years of low duties, as in the two former periods of relatively free trade, had been years of general depression, of numerous bankruptcies, of labor widely destitute of employment, of enormous and harassing commercial indebtedness abroad, and of stagnation or feeble progress in improvement and wealth at home. The three years' existence of the present tariff have been years of reviving energy and confidence, of increasing and prosperous industry, of extensive and varied improvement by building, establishing new branches of productive labor, etc., and of healthful trade.[105]

Not surprisingly, the goal of both sides was the economic growth of their constituents. But the road to that goal remained unmapped. With little fear of factual contradiction, protectionists could claim the economic vitality after 1828 and then point to the 1857 depression as a result of the low tariff of that year; for their part, the free traders claimed the ten years of affluence following the Walker tariff. In retrospect, such arguments had far more psychological weight than truth. The actual sources of these periods of economic decline and prosperity were more complex. Nonetheless, these causes and effects were re-

---

[104] Whigs were not alone in endorsing protectionism in the name of labor. In 1842, northern Democrats often cited the protection of labor to defend the tariff. For example, James Buchanan argued in the Senate: "The price of mechanical labor is much cheaper in Europe than in this country; and, therefore, if you impose no higher rate of duty upon the made-up article, than upon the material of which it is composed, you must destroy their business. . . . Because, notwithstanding your duty, their labor comes into equal and direct competition with the pauper labor of foreign countries." In response to the free-trade idea of the equity of uniform rates of duties, he responded: "[They] would be severely oppressive to the poor: because it would impose the same ad valorem tax, in all cases, upon the luxuries and the necessaries of life, upon the costly wines used by the rich, and upon the coarse woolen garment necessary to protect the poor from the piercing cold of the northern blast." *Congressional Globe*, 27th Cong., 2d sess., 2:950–51.

[105] Stanwood, *American Tariff Controversies*, 2:32–33.

peatedly linked as government officials attempted to describe the workings of the market.

Foreign Policy

A third dimension of the trade debate—foreign policy—was equally
important on the eve of the Civil War. Clearly, many who addressed
the issue feared that free trade would guarantee the United States a
"sucker's payoff." Clay expressed this concern in 1842: "If free trade
could be made universal [I] would subscribe to it at once; but as long
as other nations act on the protective system, [I will] continue in favor
of this country taking care of its own industry in preference to foster-
ing that of foreign nations." As evidence, Clay pointed to the excessively
discriminatory duties England imposed on imports to protect its manufacturers. He also cited Britain's Corn Laws, which protected its agriculture and excluded, by a new sliding scale, the breadstuffs that the
United States needed to exchange with others on favorable terms of
free trade.[106]

Free traders took an aggressive position in this debate. The South
was dependent on foreign trade. The defense of low trade barriers was
associated with the South's fear that protectionism would foreclose
trade and raise prices of needed finished products. Dixon Lewis (D-
Ala.) was said to have argued in Congress in 1842

> that there must be a proper reciprocity between the seller and the buyer
> in order to produce a healthy state of trade. The life of business [is]
> competition. . . . Unless we [seek] the markets of the world for our pro-
> ductions, we [can] claim no advantage over the savage. What [are] the
> benefits of civilization, except that by the aid of machinery it enables
> the inhabitants to have clothing or other conveniences which the savage
> could not.[107]

In a similar vein, Robert Hunter (D-Va.) argued in 1842 that he was

> astonish[ed] that, in this enlightened age, the exploded doctrines of a high
> protective tariff should be revived, when other nations were advancing
> with the progressive spirit of the times, and laying down their restrictive
> armor, this country was asked to revive a policy that would better become
> the empire of Mehemet Ali, than such a nation as ours.[108]

---

[106] *Congressional Globe*, 27th Cong., 2d sess., 2:348.
[107] Ibid., p. 742.
[108] Ibid., p. 743.

George McDuffie (D-S.C.), in 1844, concurred:

> That foreign trade should increase by high and prohibitory duties on foreign imports, is one of these wonderful "facts" which constitute the manufacturing theory . . . [in what] appears to me an incomprehensible confusion of ideas, he [George Evans] maintains that high duties reduce prices by increasing competition! That is, you exclude the competitor who can sell cheapest, and precisely because he does sell cheapest, in order to reduce prices by increasing competition! Why, sir, the very genius of paradox can go no further.[109]

Protectionists, however, were not deterred by these arguments. When confronted by Walker's free-trade vision, Andrew Stewart (W-Pa.) declared that the debate over trade policy was in reality "a contest for the American market. Foreigners, and especially the British, [are] the parties on the one side, and the Americans, on the other; and the only question [is], which side should we take? By adopting free trade, we give our markets and our money to foreigners; by adhering to protection, we secure both to our own people." He also pointed out that protection was not necessarily a tax on society undermining social welfare by foreclosing purchase of the cheapest item. Rather, he said: "Duties levied for revenue on articles we cannot produce, generally increase prices; whilst protective duties, levied on articles we can and do produce, always, in the end, diminish prices. The truth of both these propositions [is] proved by undeniable facts, and by all experience."[110] The real tax on society, he asserted, resulted from a lack of duties, which had "established a monopoly by checking competition."[111]

Each side stigmatized the other as anti-American. Stewart declared his fellow protectionists to be the nationalists. His adversaries (in particular he mentioned the "gentleman from Alabama") were characterized as friends of the British who wanted to open ports to the manufacturers of all the world. They would, he contended, allow a flood of goods produced by the paupers of Great Britain to sweep away the rising prosperity of poor but industrious Americans. "They [want to] crush American enterprise; grind down American labor, and put their countrymen on a footing with the very sweepings of the poorhouses of Europe."[112]

The collapse of one of the two major parties created a rare opportu-

---

[109] *Congressional Globe*, 28th Cong., 1st sess., Appendix, p. 143.
[110] *Congressional Globe*, 29th Cong., 1st sess., Appendix, p. 936.
[111] Ibid.
[112] Ibid., p. 940.

nity for reorganizing political coalitions into new political structures. The birth of the Republican party, then, marked a critical turning point in the history of U.S. protectionism. Although the tariff issue did not play a crucial role in the shift in party membership in the 1850s, the concurrent intellectual debate on commercial policy explains why the party eventually endorsed high tariffs. The Republicans did not simply adopt the Whig position on tariffs. Rather, high tariffs were ultimately defended in a way that enabled all elements of the new coalition—from old northern Democrats, who were involved in commerce, to western farmers, who needed a market for their surplus production—to accept protectionism as a strategy serving their long-term interests.

THE REPUBLICAN PARTY AND THE TARIFF

Between 1860 and 1875, the Republican party controlled American government. With the exception of a limited period in the 1870s when the reform movement challenged its leadership, the party pursued protectionist policies when in power. The tariffs that were enacted, first to increase revenues for the war and later as part of the party's economic program, helped to assure high levels of protection for the next seventy years. After 1875, the Democrats regained control of the House. Yet by then, protectionist ideas were so widely endorsed both in and out of government that even Democratic reform tariffs were doomed to be far less liberal than those in the antebellum period.

The call of the new Republican party—"free soil, free labor, free men"—could not have been more tailored to the protectionists' analysis of the economy in the 1850s. At the heart of Republican ideology lay a belief in the dignity and rights of labor. In their critique of southern slave labor, the Republicans extolled the superiority of the capitalist system, which enabled the average laboring man to prosper. In this decade, Abraham Lincoln declared that "labor is prior to, and independent of capital . . . in fact, capital is the fruit of labor."[113] Free labor meant labor with economic choices, in particular, the choice to rise to ownership and out of the working class.

By the mid-1850s, policy makers confronted two competing interpretations of the economic benefits of tariff policy. The free-trade argument generally appealed to Democrats, who scorned any government involvement in social, developmental, or commercial rela-

---

[113] Eric Foner, *Free Soil, Free Labor, Free Men: The Ideology of the Republican Party before the Civil War* (New York: Oxford University Press, 1970), p. 12.

73

tions. The second developed as a critique of the first; thus it was more flexible, less defined, and more appealing to the diverse groups in the Republican party. Protectionists suggested that free trade did little to secure the fruits of industrialization and potentially threatened the standard of living of the new working class. Tariffs, they argued, kept cheap foreign products off the market and eliminated unfair labor competition. Further, protectionists suggested that emancipation rested on commercial policy, for only tariff duties would protect free labor from foreign "slavery."[114] As an 1860 newspaper editorial implored, "We ask that the free laborers of the country shall be protected from competition with laborers who are bought and sold."[115]

The idea that high tariffs served Republican constituent interests was promoted by the party elite. In particular, Henry Carey was crucial in molding protection into the party's social agenda as an economic policy. Carey had long argued for a natural harmony among classes. He refuted the notion of the Jacksonian Democrats that social antagonism was inevitable and thus could defend the tariff and industrialization as in the interests of all social classes even though, in fact, it was northern society that was Carey's exemplar. Only in the North did social mobility and economic independence offer workers the promise of eventual self-employment. He agreed with Lincoln that in the North there was no class that was "always to remain laborers."[116] Thus the form of industrialization Carey and the party envisioned was exemplified in the New England of the 1850s. Measured against this model, southern society was fundamentally flawed, setting up an "irrepressible conflict" between the free and slaveholding societies.

But the tariff became central to party politics for reasons other than regional economic differences. Although it is commonly said that high tariffs were meant to lure Pennsylvania voters, such analysis belies the intellectual basis behind the party platform. The policy certainly did not unite the material interests of all party members, especially the large numbers of Democrats and new western voters who supported the Republicans on the eve of the Civil War. Rather, Republicans walked

[114] Tariffs also appealed to some within the antislavery coalition, who deplored the ethic of competition. Some religious groups claimed that such a philosophy, which endorsed lowering costs by reducing wages, was ethically unchristian.

[115] Quoted in James L. Huston, "A Political Response to Industrialism: The Republican Embrace of Protectionist Labor Doctrines," *Journal of American History* 70 (June 1983): 53.

[116] Foner, *Free Soil*, pp. 30–33. Despite the ideology of social mobility, prospects of workers or farm laborers leaving their class declined after 1860. Also, the people who could take advantage of free land were not wage earners from the crowded cities but eastern farmers. The introduction of farm machinery in the 1850s made it more expensive and thus more difficult for farm laborers to become independent yeomen.

a fine line between the antislavery issue, which united otherwise divergent voters, including disenchanted Democrats, and the issues brought in by the former Whigs.[117] Other important elements in the new party included New York Barnburners, Free Soilers, and Know-Nothing nativists. All were united in their rejection of the Kansas and Nebraska compromise; they differed, however, on their economic programs. Thus the Whig platform on economic development, which included the tariff, internal improvements, and regulation of currency, was modified by the other groups' traditions of strict construction of the Constitution, opposition to government involvement in the economy, and hostility to tariffs, corporations, banks, and monopolies.[118] For example, the Barnburners had fought against the Erie Canal, endorsed Jackson's views on hard money, and supported Van Buren, while the Democratic Free Soilers opposed all aspects of the traditional Whig economic program. Consequently, early Republican state party platforms contained few explicit statements of an economic program.

As the 1850s drew to a close, many traditional elements of each group's economic platform disappeared. Internal development rendered earlier debates on building canals and roads obsolete. Corporations flourished; although views on regulatory law differed, the original resistance to corporate development faded. Democrats still favored hard money, but within the new party they came to accept both coin and paper currency.

Tariffs became part of the Republican party's economic platform incrementally. In 1856, the national party platform did not mention tariffs. (In state elections, however, both parties in Pennsylvania supported protection for iron interests, even though the Democratic party platform of 1856 had proclaimed "progressive free trade throughout the world."[119] Two years later, the platform advocated a revenue tariff with incidental protection.[120] That proposal, tested among Pennsylvania voters in 1858, was thought to have been responsible for reducing the number of the state's Democrats in Congress from fourteen to four.

Still, ambiguity clouded the economic platform. The 1860 platform, written by John A. Kasson, a free-soil Democrat, was vague on the issue, never once mentioning the word "protection." Yet the program it discussed was embryonic of the one the party would hold for the

[117] The Republican party was far more than the old Whigs renamed. Half of Lincoln's cabinet were former Democrats. At least eight former Democrats served as Republican senators. The House also had a contingent of these former Democrats between 1854 and 1860.
[118] Foner, *Free Soil*, p. 168.
[119] Ibid., p. 116.
[120] Ibid., p. 175.

ensuing century. The plank called in general for "an adjustment of . . . imports . . . to encourage the development of the industrial interests of the whole country."[121] Ambiguity served the party's purpose: it allowed the members of the Pennsylvania delegation to say that they had received what they wanted and the *New York Evening Post* to claim that the party had come out in favor of free trade.

The Panic of 1857 however, had extinguished what little faith members of the party had had for liberal trade. The remaining Whigs— traditionally associated with banking interests—conceded that banks contributed to the depth of the crisis. Many erstwhile Whigs accepted the criticism leveled by former Democrats that banks had issued too much paper money and had failed to confront currency issues. Meanwhile, the Whigs' traditional fear of low tariffs seemed vindicated. The ensuing depression mobilized workers. Unemployment meetings became arenas to vent anger. Bread riots gave rise to the fear that the United States might not be immune to the dire predictions of Malthus and Ricardo. Then, in 1859, the trade union movement, which had been stymied by the recession, went through a radical resurgence of organizing. The Republican party needed a response to the working-class crisis; its answer was a high-tariff policy. The party suggested that the problem plaguing workers was low tariffs, not industrialization. Protectionism, as a strategy to protect workers' wages and correct the economy, was simple and comparatively easy to effect.

To further their point, the Republicans claimed that the relatively low tariffs then in force had exacerbated the panic. The 1857 act essentially followed the principles of the Walker tariff, adding even more goods to the free list. But coinciding as it did with the conclusion of the California gold rush, it was destined to fail. As government revenues fell, even President Buchanan moderated his views on liberal tariffs. In his first annual message in 1857, Buchanan acknowledged the shortfall in the treasury but urged a continuation of the current tariff policy because it had "been in operation for so short a period of time." A year later, he urged "that the incidental protection thus afforded by a revenue tariff would, at the present moment, to some extent, increase the confidence of the manufacturing interests, and give a fresh impulse

[121] The platform further stated "that while providing revenue for the support of the general government by duties upon imports, sound policy requires such an adjustment of these imports as to encourage the development of the industrial interests of the whole country; and we commend that policy of national exchanges which secures to the workingmen liberal wages, to agriculture remunerating prices, to mechanics and manufacturers an adequate reward for their skill, labor, and enterprise, and to the nation commercial prosperity and independence." Stanwood, *American Tariff Controversies*, 2: 117.

to our reviving business."[122] Later in the address he argued for specific duties and not the ad valorem system because the former was more advantageous to manufacturers. By the time of his fourth annual address, he was arguing for the specific duties proposed in the pending Morrill tariff bill.

The firing on Fort Sumter and the ensuing economic crisis boosted a budding interventionist economic program into general party ideology. The passage of the Morrill bill in 1861 was made possible largely by the secession of the southern block of free-trade votes, not unity within the party. When passage appeared assured, a host of new groups came forth to solicit aid, and most gained the concessions they sought. (The Senate had added 156 amendments to the bill passed by the House in the previous session. The House agreed to all except the duty on coffee and tea.) The bill was enacted, and the war came.

Congress, in emergency sessions, repeatedly turned to the tariff to provide revenues.[123] Even Salmon P. Chase, the former Democrat who now headed the Treasury Department, abandoned his free-trade position and agreed that tariff hikes were necessary. War tariffs were placed on a range of goods, including sugar, molasses, tea, and coffee. The free list dwindled. Under the Morrill Act, 182 items were on the free list; by 1862, only 99 items remained. By 1864, hardly any items, except the crudest of raw materials used by manufacturers, were still on the list. The war was not a one-sided boon for manufacturers, however. War taxes were high and, in many respects, the tariff merely compensated producers by guaranteeing them a home market.[124] In 1865, protection was further increased when ad valorem duties were added to the existing specific duties. Trade suffered dramatically in this period, not only from high domestic duties but from the virtual cessation of the cotton trade.

Postwar Policy

At the end of the Civil War, support for protectionist legislation splintered and the party's tariff position came under increased scrutiny. Not only tariffs were criticized; the enormous array of import, income,

---

[122] *The Works of James Buchanan,* ed. John B. Moore (Philadelphia: J. B. Lippincott, 1910), 10:158, 265.

[123] Prices rose so dramatically during the Civil War relative to prices in Europe that even if Congress had not needed revenues, it would have had to enact barriers to trade or foreign goods would have flooded the market.

[124] In 1864, a report issued by Commissioner of the Revenue David A. Wells found that taxes varied between 8 and 15 percent. John Dobson, *Two Centuries of Tariffs: The Background and Emergence of the United States Trade Commission* (Washington: USGPO, 1976), p. 16.

and excise taxes enacted to fuel the war effort and pay the government debt seemed onerous now that the fighting was over. As a result, most internal taxes were dropped, but import fees remained at over 40 percent. The economy boomed; the tariff was neither halting an influx of foreign goods nor decreasing government revenues. Members from northern industrial districts had no reason to doubt tariff policy. But others in the Republican coalition, who had not objected to artificially high tariffs during the war, suggested that tariffs should be treated like other taxes, especially in a time of budget surpluses. In the West, agricultural groups failed to see how duties served their interests. (In the following years, tariff aid would be extended to agriculture, but in the 1870s the controversy only fueled Republican party problems.) Spearheading the drive for reform was David Wells, the chairman of a revenue commission created by the Internal Revenue Act of 1865. While on the commission, Wells underwent a dramatic conversion on the issue of tariff policy. Initially a supporter of tariffs, he became a crusader for free trade, writing extensively and campaigning tirelessly for trade reform. Perhaps because of excess revenues, or perhaps simply because, as members of the party often commented, "times were changing," the Republicans did not push more protectionist legislation through Congress and instead supported mild tariff reductions. In 1870, duties were dropped on tea, coffee, wines, sugar, and molasses. But duties on products made at home were retained, indicating that protection was not to be undone. Even when the party splintered over corruption in the Grant administration, Republicans attempted to control criticism by lowering the overall rate of protection rather than undoing the protective system itself.[125] Thus the 1872 act reduced tariff levels by a flat 10 percent. That reduction was short-lived. A year later the economy went into decline, causing such a great drop in revenues that, just before a strong Democratic majority returned to the House in 1875, wartime tariff rates were resumed. Thus the Republicans left the new Democratic administration with a high tariff, establishing commercial policy as a central issue of party politics for the next fifty years.

CONCLUSION

The antebellum years were critical ones in the history of American tariff policy. In these years, the interests and power of groups within

[125] The liberal Republicans ultimately broke from the party and ran their own presidential candidate. The candidate, however, who was also supported by the Democratic party, was Horace Greeley, the most well-known protectionist of the period.

the United States rapidly changed in conjunction with changes in America's position in world markets. Three sets of interests vied over trade policy. Southern and western agricultural producers favored low tariffs. Budding northern manufacturers, who often encountered predatory competition from Britain, argued for the opposite. Northern commercial interests most often sided with the South. Tariffs in this period were relatively volatile. High tariffs existed into the 1830s and were subsequently lowered as the power of southern Democrats in Congress increased.

Two contradictory theories of what tariff level would maximize American growth also developed in this period. The first advocated low tariffs and a noninterventionist state; the second argued for high tariffs as a means for the state both to assure industrialization and to ameliorate market-imposed social dislocation. In the first half of the century, as measured by congressional debate, liberal trade ideas prevailed; thereafter, they lost their political salience to the alternative.

For most of the period reviewed in this chapter, tariff policy can be explained without resort to these economic ideas. Regionalism, industrialization, and pork-barrel politics all motivated elected officials. These officials were not much unlike their counterparts in later years. Although less likely to be professional politicians, once in Congress they attempted to benefit their constituents' interests. Representatives from Pennsylvania wanted to assure growth in the coal and iron industry; southern planters wanted to assure strong demand for cotton. Each side propounded the economic views that appeared to vindicate its preferred position.

But whereas ideas may have merely legitimated the interests of groups in the first half of the century, economic theory in the 1850s was critical to the position ultimately advocated by the new Republican party. As the interests of regions became increasingly crosscutting, less clarity existed as to what actions would serve specific purposes. Manufacturers began to speak with different voices. Producers making goods at dissimilar levels of specialization did not have the same interests; a tariff on a primary or secondary product did not serve the interests of the producer of finished goods. But even interests that should have been obvious often did not appear so. For instance, in retrospect, western farmers would have been as well or better off with low tariffs. Instead, the West ultimately defended closure. Increasingly, the politics of commercial policy depended on the interplay of interests with ideas about exactly which economic policy served which constituency.

Why did the Republicans become the party of protection? Looking ahead, we can imagine that the party of business would want to keep the state from interfering with market forces. Yet that idea did not dominate in the 1850s and 1860s. Rather, party entrepreneurs who represented business, who wanted to establish the United States as a great market and sought to keep workers' wages high, thought that protection was the best means to that end. They came to that conclusion because the economic debate in the 1850s suggested it. Of course, once established as policy, protection itself created interests and, by the 1880s and 1890s, it would have been politically costly to dismantle the protectionist regime. But such was not the case in this early period. Protection was chosen as an option because the party, and not constituents, thought it appropriate. Interest-group activity cannot explain the timing and content of the Republican party plan; the party could as well have adopted a milder policy of protection or a policy of a revenue tariff with protection for special groups.

This chapter has pointed to several variables that explain the party's logic. Clearly, both academic and popular analyses of wages led the free-labor party to assume that protection was the policy of choice. But the timing of economic booms and declines was also critical. The Panic of 1857 was the last in a series of economic fluctuations that showed how the opening of American borders to foreign goods could cause great economic upheaval. Although tariff policy had little to do with these economic declines, a widespread perception that tariffs were causal led to a revision in policy. Here, as elsewhere, we must always ask not only what objective constraints political entrepreneurs faced, but what they believed the causes of these constraints to be.

In sum, the tariff debates in the antebellum period show the importance of both talk and entrepreneurship in political analysis. Politics was always part and parcel of every tariff act. The specifics of who got what once the act entered Congress were influenced by logrolling, the savvy of representatives, and, of course, partisanship. But just as important was the development of theory on how tariffs would or would not maximize constituents' interests. In this period, academic and lay analysts generated a set of ideas about economic phenomena. Political entrepreneurs in both parties used these ideas to build and cement coalitions. But, as we will see in the next chapter, the decision of the Republican party to glue a coalition around a high-tariff policy had a far more fundamental influence on politics than was understood at the time.

CHAPTER THREE

Institutionalization: Putting
Protectionism in Place, 1870–1930

In the Gilded Age, America's industrial, commercial, and agricultural economy diversified, establishing the United States as one of the giants on the world scene. It was during this period of increasing American competitiveness and relatively more open European markets that the United States moved to institutionalize trade protections.[1] Ironically, policy during this period ran counter to America's apparent interests; as the United States became increasingly competitive on world markets and more interested in world trade, American policy became increasingly more autarkic. In this chapter I ask why, as the United States acquired a greater comparative advantage in a range of industrial and farm products, did policy makers spurn liberalization even though they acknowledged the need for increasing foreign trade?

In many respects, modern American economic history begins with the Civil War. The year 1869 was the last in which the value of American farm output exceeded that of nonfarm production.[2] Changes in the distribution of wealth allowed the new industrial centers to outstrip landed interests in the battle for control of the American economy. The signs of industrialization were everywhere. In 1860, the nation had 31,000 miles of railways; fifty years later, 240,000 miles of railways linked towns and villages into one transporation system.[3] In 1860 the

[1] Tariffs in Europe varied in the second half of the century. There was a radical reduction in tariff levels throughout Europe in the 1860s and 1870s. Then, except in England, levels began to rise. Even at their peak, Europeans protected few products at American levels.

[2] U.S. Bureau of the Census, *Historical Statistics of the United States from Colonial Times to 1970* (Washington: USGPO, 1975), Series F 238-249.

[3] Ibid., Series Q43, Q44-72.

United States produced just thirteen tons of raw steel; by 1901, over one thousand times that much was produced annually.[4] The period witnessed the rise of big business, the triumph of a policy favoring industrialization, the closing of the frontier, and America's first imperialistic adventure at the close of the Spanish-American War. The United States was thrust onto the world scene by World War I and emerged an economic giant. Along with a change in economic base, the class constitution of American society shifted. A new and diverse middle class eventually predominated in both urban and rural settings, and the southern plantation society declined. The growth of cities created new white-collar jobs and a new urban bourgeoisie; blue-collar workers obtained increasingly higher wages and ultimately unionized. Together, these were the precursors of American economic hegemony.

What is counterintuitive about American behavior, from the perspective of those who study international politics, is that these social and economic changes failed to produce expected changes in foreign economic policy. Industrial expansion increasingly led groups to look abroad for new markets.[5] Increased pressure on elected officials further politicized the already partisan tariff issue. Yet policy makers ignored both classical economic theories and British application of those theories, turning instead to the home-grown concept of protectionism. The result of the political debate on trade in particular and the national economic interest in general led Congress repeatedly to enact higher, rather than lower, barriers to international commerce. With the exception of Woodrow Wilson's 1913 act, even when the relatively free-trade Democratic party gained control of government—twice on a tariff-reform platform—it accepted the basic tenets of the Republican protectionist program. The Democrats' trade liberalization stance fifty years later should not be confused with their tariff reform platform of the nineteenth century.[6] Instead of liberalization, the most radical changes in American commercial policy in the period reinforced protectionism: the McKinley Tariff in 1890, the Dingley Tariff of 1897, and Smoot-Hawley in 1929–30 all led to record high national tariffs. In short, this period witnessed a new consensus on the merits of protectionism, even though the economic rationale for such a policy vanished.

---

[4] Ibid., Series P231-300.

[5] American exports increased rapidly in the period after 1870. Total growth in preceding decade was: 1880—148 percent; 1890—15 percent; 1900—75 percent; 1910—14 percent; 1920—111 percent. Ibid., Series E135-166 and U 187-200.

[6] The Democratic party did not seek a tariff solely to raise revenue. While the Democrats controlled government, tariffs were set at rates well above levels that would meet expected revenue needs. This suggests that although a partial explanation, it was more than merely the enactment of an income tax in 1913 that explains the change in Democratic party position in the 1930s.

This chapter examines the disjuncture in American policy between national need and foreign policy. I argue that analyses of interests, whether domestic or international, cannot explain the form or extent of the Americn market closure. Rather, I suggest that the entrenchment of the protectionist vision conditioned how leaders interpreted changes in domestic group interests and the place of America in the world economy; this vision led central decision makers and the attentive public to ignore feasible alternative policies. Throughout the period and especially after 1890, constituents pressured political leaders to devise a policy that would meet their needs for trade expansion.[7] But rather than engendering policy makers to question the efficacy of present policy, this pressure on government officials led to a reinforcement of protectionist doctrine. Thus pressures alone cannot explain the pattern of policy. As important were the economic strategies selected by political leaders in response to societal demands.

To demonstrate the importance of the choice of economic strategy, this chapter is divided into three parts. First, as in the last chapter, the status of economic ideas in this period is reviewed. Although liberal thought was triumphing in economic debates in colleges, the protectionist vision dominated policy prescription throughout this era. Second, tariff debates and policy outcomes are scrutinized. As opposed to the earlier period in which both the protectionist and free-trade positions were echoed in Congress, after midcentury protectionist ideas dominated debate. With the exception of the ill-fated 1913 Democratic act, policy makers ignored evidence of potential benefits from opening markets and instead repeatedly legislated high tariffs. Third, the chapter examines how politics were affected by the interplay of changing academic ideas on the virtues of open markets, increased American involvement in world trade, and changing social demands for access to foreign markets.

ECONOMIC THOUGHT IN THE SECOND HALF OF THE NINETEENTH CENTURY

Writing about the closing years of the nineteenth century, V. L. Parrington describes the philosophical changes that accomplished the industrialization of the American economy:

In the years following the war, exploitation for the first time was provided

---

[7] One of the best works on this period which attempts to chronicle how America's changing international interests influenced domestic politics is David Lake's *Power, Protec-*

with adequate resources and a competent technique, and busy prospectors were daily uncovering new sources of wealth. The coal and oil of Pennsylvania and Ohio, the copper and iron ore of upper Michigan, the gold and silver, lumber and fisheries of the Pacific coast provided limitless raw materials for the rising industrialism. . . . A free people had put away all aristocratic privileges and, conscious of its power, went forth to possess the last frontier. Its social philosophy, which it found adequate to its needs, was summed up in three words: preemption, exploitation, progress. . . . Preemption meant exploitation and exploitation meant progress. It was a simple philosophy and it suited the simple individualism of the times. The Gilded Age knew nothing of the Enlightenment; it recognized only the acquisitive instinct. That much at least the frontier had taught the great American democracy; and in applying to the resources of a continent the lesson it had so well taught, the Gilded Age wrote a profoundly characteristic chapter of American history.[8]

For both the social commentator and the economic analyst, the second half of the nineteenth century presented a host of complex new economic dilemmas. The Civil War had pointed to inherent conflicts in America's system of production and distribution. Almost simultaneously, the rise of big business forced analysts to confront the fundamental problems of economic organization. Although these issues plagued elected officials, their debate was scarcely influenced by the growing academic sector. Economic theorists of the day responded to the changing American economy by developing increasingly sophisticated normative and analytic models, which could have done much, but did little in this period, to inform political action.

Political entrepreneurs' lack of understanding and interest in the field of economics did not go unnoticed. Charles Dunbar, a noted nineteenth-century economist and author, placed the blame squarely on his own profession, explaining that "the United States have, thus far, done nothing towards developing the theory of political economy, notwithstanding their vast and immediate interest in its practical applications."[9] According to Dunbar, "down to the year 1820 no American produced any treatices on political economy which the world has cared to remember."[10] Furthermore, he suggests, "the years which followed from 1840 down to the war for the Union were . . . much less prolific

tion, and Free Trade: International Sources of U.S. Commercial Strategy, 1887–1930 (Ithaca: Cornell University Press, 1988).

[8] V. L. Parrington, Main Currents in American Thought, vol. 3 (New York: Harcourt, Brace, 1930), pp. 9–10.

[9] Charles Dunbar, "Economic Science in America, 1776–1876," North American Review 122 (January 1876): 140.

[10] Ibid., p. 134.

of works on political economy than the period [before]."[11] Sidney Sherwood, professor of political economy at the Johns Hopkins University, agreed that the history of economic analysis in the United States was remarkably sparse, noting in 1897 that "much of our economic literature, like Caesar's commentaries, has been written on the march."[12] Richard T. Ely, one of the founders of the American Economic Association, concurred: "Throughout the first half of the nineteenth century, our forebears were, generally speaking, too much engaged in the stupendous task of 'subduing a continent' to reflect deeply on their activities."[13]

Such observations reflect nineteenth-century self-perceptions far more than a true rendering of the field of economics. In reality, by the 1820s American political economists were participating in and were influenced by European economic debates. After the Civil War, the field of political economy grew rapidly into a major academic discipline. Indicatively, the required number of economics classes in the top sixty American colleges increased more than six times between 1870 and 1890.[14] By the close of the century, three-fourths of American colleges taught economics, most requiring all students to complete at least one introductory course.[15] The basic assigned texts included American as well as British authors; Arthur Lathan Perry's *Elements of Political Economy*, published in 1866, remained the major text for most of the latter nineteenth century.

This blossoming of theoretical economics in the academic sector, however, had little effect on a political sector that was seemingly in search of new ideas to help it cope with a changing America. Events in the United States were in marked contrast to those in Britain in that the American debate over trade policy that occurred outside of academia actually contradicted theories promulgated within the class-

[11] Ibid., p. 136.

[12] Sidney Sherwood, *Tendencies in American Economic Thought* (Baltimore: Johns Hopkins University Press, 1897), p. 7.

[13] Richard T. Ely, *Ground under Our Feet* (New York: Macmillan, 1938), p. 121. T. E. Cliffe Leslie argued in "Political Economy in the United States," *Fortnightly Review*, (28 [October 1880]: 492), that the field of economics could not help but be affected by American abundance: "The free trade controversy in England grew out of dear bread, depressed trade, low wages, and low profits; and it gave political economy most of its importance in English estimation during the last generation. Had Great Britain been as large, as fertile, and as underpeopled as the United States, Mr. Mill might have made a fortune in a counting-house instead of a reputation as a political economist."

[14] J. Laurence Laughlin, "The Study of Political Economy in the United States," *Journal of Political Economy*, (December 1892): 4.

[15] L. C. Marshall et al., "Teaching of Economics in the United States," *Journal of Political of Economy* 19 (May 1911): 777. The authors estimate that about 18,400 students were taking at least an elementary class in economics by the turn of the century.

room. Although American economists were willing to take on the major economic issues of the time, they were unable to influence the political process. In good part, their impotence was self-imposed. As the economics field became increasingly professional after 1880, academics distanced themselves from the political process and scholarship became increasingly less intelligible to the lay audience.

Idiosyncracies in American Economic Thought

Along with, and partially explaining, their distinct, overall effects on policy, the American and British disciplines differed in at least four ways.[16] All four speak to the relative insularity of economic thought in the United States in the last quarter of the century.

First, unlike their European counterparts, American economists were nearly unanimous in rejecting Malthus's theory that a population will eventually outstrip its means of subsistence. Virtually everyone contributing to the debate on general principles of economics in the United States—protectionists and free traders alike—rejected this doctrine. Henry Carey, William Ellis Thompson, Peshine Smith, and Francis Bowen, the chief protectionists of the period, agreed on this point with Amasa Walker and Arthur Latham Perry, writers of free-trade textbooks, whose work was the backbone of nearly all U.S. college courses. Together, they agreed that "American exceptionalism" made this component of European scholarship inapplicable. The rapid industrialization of the U.S. economy eventually diminished this notion.[17] But until that time, American exceptionalism cast a spell of skepticism over other elements of classical thought.

Second, in the United States, theological considerations were an active component of economic thought until the turn of the century in the writings of both protectionists and free traders. Whereas British and German economists had separated themselves from their theological bases, many U.S. economists were ministers, and the economics field remained wedded quite late to religious thought. European ideas such

[16] Leslie, in "Political Economy in the United States," pp. 493–99, suggests these differences. Protectionist ideas were not buried forever in Britain. But although there was a revival of interest in protectionist logic in the early twentieth century as a response to the decline of the empire, these protective ideas met as recalcitrant a political liberal vision as liberal ideas met America's protective vision.

[17] The eventual adherence to classical ideas covaried with the growing professionalism of the discipline. As well, obvious changes in the American economy made these ideas more acceptable. Although in 1820 the notion that there would exist in America a permanent working class—at times enslaved by a factory system—was impossible to comprehend, industrialization revealed that the United States was no better at avoiding such problems than Europe had been.

as the "harmony of economic interests" and the existence of the "invisible hand" made their way into American scholarship as examples of divine will. For example, Perry's book—the best-selling American text—suggests that one of the main purposes of economics is the "examination of the providential arrangements, physical and social, by which it appears that exchanges were designed by God for the welfare of men." Similarly, his theory of value and rent is based on the proposition that "God is a giver," and not a seller and that "God never takes pay for anything, and has not authorized anybody to take pay in his behalf; what's paid for is the service of man, and not the bounty of nature."[18]

American scholarship differed from its European counterpart in two additional ways. In England, theory was based on an assumption that competition would equalize wages and profits across occupations and locations. Such an assumption was ignored or rejected by most nineteenth-century American theorists, who, for much of the century, had little aversion to government intervention in economic matters. Thus it was difficult, if not impossible, to criticize the fundamental assumptions of protectionist doctrine.

A last dissimilarity between American and European economic thought is intrinsically tied to the history of the trade policy debate. While free-trade ideas dominated British classrooms by the start of the nineteenth century and the political arena shortly thereafter, protectionism was still taught in U.S. colleges as scientific doctrine. In the 1870s, only one European professor of economics, Isaac Butt of the University of Dublin, still taught protectionist ideas. In Germany, only one well-known academic, Gustav Friedrich von Schmoller of the University of Strasburg, supported high tariffs. No textbook in England or on the Continent advocated protection as public policy.[19] Comparatively, in the United States, protectionist ideas were considered as seriously as were classical economic arguments. To the consternation of the majority of classically leaning economists, university administrators declared that the presentation of economic doctrine should be balanced by introducing both perspectives into the analysis of trade policy. Thus the arguments of protectionist thinkers such as Carey, Thompson, Smith, Bowen, Julian Monson Sturtevant, and Marcius Wilson were well represented, though not always believed, by American instructors. To blame only administrators for the inclusion of protectionist logic in course requirements would be unfair. By continuing to legitimize

---

[18] Arthur Latham Perry, *Elements of Political Economy* (New York: Charles Scribner, 1866), pp. 1, 58–59.
[19] Leslie, "Political Economy in the United States," p. 499.

government intervention in economic development, the economics community itself could do little but accept that, in fairness, such a policy could support either openness or closure. In America, all four factors—the rejection of Malthusian doctrine, the continued view that American exceptionalism was associated with God's will, the reliance on government intervention rather than market forces, and the continued legitimacy of protectionist ideas—guaranteed that no clear vision of the virtues of a free-trade policy emanated from the economics community.

These distinctly American views, dominating academia in the last half of the nineteenth century, had all but vanished by World War I. Believers in classical economic theory and Smithian trade ideas dominated academic discourse by the century's end. Only a few of Henry Carey's disciples remained to defend protectionist doctrine, and even their authority had waned. By the dawn of the twentieth century, only pockets of protectionism remained in American academia. No supporter of free trade could be appointed to a chair, or for that matter attract enough students to make up a class, in any school in Pennsylvania. Harvard still had a protectionist chair, but the endowment was later shared with a free trader. Charles F. Dunbar, teaching at Harvard, was considered a mild protectionist; Cornell still had one professor, Marcius Wilson, who had published a protectionist treatise; and the president of Illinois College, Julian Monson Sturtevant, had at least one protectionist article on his vita. Only one respectable protectionist book, by Simon Patten of the Wharton School at the University of Pennsylvania, was produced in their period.[20] By the turn of the century, the presentation of protectionist doctrine was left to the popular press and lay pamphleteers. Yet this change among academics carried no political weight. At the same time that free-trade ideas eclipsed alternatives in the work of professional economists, the opposite vision increasingly dominated debate in political quarters.

The Economics Profession

Much of the blame for the inability of academic free-trade ideas to influence political discourse can be laid at the feet of American scholars themselves. Early on, fundamental divisions in the economics field undermined the potential that their policy recommendations might carry political weight. And later, after the field consolidated, economics became increasingly abstract and distanced from policy prescription.

The American Economic Association developed as a reaction to dissent among academics. In the last quarter of the century, the key intel-

[20] Simon Patten, *The Economic Basis of Protection* (Philadelphia: J. B. Lippincott, 1890).

lectual division in academia was between devotees of classical British economic theory and economists who subscribed to "historicism," brought to America by students who had visited German universities.[21] These historicists, in an attempt to fight mainstream American economics, created the American Economic Association in 1885. "While we appreciate the work of former economists," the organization's statement of principles read, "we look not so much to speculation, as to historical and statistical study of actual conditions of economic life as the backbone of the discipline of economics."[22] Reacting to the British defense of laissez-faire, the founders of the association declared themselves in favor of state intervention: "We regard the state as an educational and ethical agency whose positive aid is an indispensable condition of human progress. While we recognize the necessity of individual initiative in industrial life, we hold that the doctrine of laissez-faire is unsafe in politics and unsound in morals."[23] Francis Walker, the only member of the group who was a university professor, served as its first president. All other established economists, including James Laurence Laughlin, William Graham Sumner, and Frank William Taussig, avoided the new association. Within a decade, however, the association was controlled by the very classical thinkers its founders had shunned. Within another decade, the association had become the center of professional academic economic thought in the United States.[24]

[21] Historicism was based on the belief that the history of law and institutions must be studied to know the origin and the proper developmental sequence of a nation's conception of law. Historicists argued that modern writers overemphasized the role of science in economics. They claimed that contemporary economic knowledge was too abstract and its conclusions stated in too absolute a form. Laughlin, "Study of Political Economy," pp. 1–19.

[22] J. K. Normano, *The Spirit of American Economics* (New York: John Day, 1943), pp. 135–36.

[23] Normano, *American Economics*, p. 136.

[24] The intensity of debate between the two schools of thought is evident in articles in *Science* in 1886. Writing for one side, Sumner, Taussig, and Arthur T. Hadley decried state intervention in the economy. Sumner argued that "it is a complete mistake to interpret the course of things which we see as moving toward more regulation." Hadley argued that "the danger of believing that economics can be interfered with by human effort is ten times greater than the danger of extreme belief in laissez-faire." Taussig argued that economic science had little to do with the functions of the state. On the other side, Erwin Seligman defended what was then known as the "new economics": "The modern school holds that the economic theories of any generation must be regarded primarily as the outgrowth of the peculiar condition of time, place, and nationality, under which the doctrines were evolved, and that no particular set of tenets can arrogate to itself the claim of immutable truth, or the assumption of universal applicability to all countries or epochs. We do not wish to disparage the work of previous economists; but, just because of our belief in the relativity and continuity of economic doctrine, we are compelled to regard much of what was at that time comparatively correct and feasible, as today positively erroneous and misleading." Quoted in Normano, *American Economics*, pp. 136–37.

Ironically, professionalization of the field coincided with the virtual death in the United States of the historical movement that had founded the association.

Although professionalization resolved the problem of discord in economists' public policy voice, it did little to make economics more accessible to politicians. Instead of contributing to the ongoing political debate, academics increasingly left the job of explaining and understanding the "real" needs of the American economy to lay economists. As the century drew to a close, the chasm between the two groups widened. Academic economics became increasingly organized, homogenous, and oriented to fundamental theoretical issues. Economic analysis began to rely heavily on statistical and ultimately formal techniques. In the university classroom, teachers increasingly based their courses on McCulloch and Mill, straying little from the English classics. The few who did consider the uniqueness of America's economy, especially those studying commercial policy, found their theories ignored in the ongoing academic debate.[25] And as academic thought became increasingly isolated from the protectionist debate, it was the pamphleteers who provided policy prescriptions consistent with political practice. No better testament to the political impotence of free-trade ideas can be found than in the tariff debates after 1880, in which protagonists demonstrated a far less sophisticated understanding of economic policy than they had in the 1820s.

The academic sector further distanced itself from political discourse through a gradual shift in the topics studied. Although the key economic issue confronting politicians was trade policy, scholars migrated toward issues concerning money, land, labor, and social reform. Few economists in major universities wrote any new analyses supporting free-trade commercial policy.[26] The only work of consequence in this period, Simon Patten's *Economic Basis of Protection* in 1890, defended a high-tariff policy. Patten noted his isolation from mainstream economics. In 1912 he declared: "American economics has done everything but what was expected of it. It was supposed that this new group of thinkers would be historical, but no historical work has been done. The unexpected was the rise of the school of deductive theorists—the very

[25] Charles Dunbar wrote in 1891 of "the singular derogation from scientific methods implied in the demands frequently made in the last few years in the United States for some different and special treatment of the burning question of protection or free trade." "The Academic Study of Political Economy," *Quarterly Journal of Economics* 5 (July 1891): 403.

[26] The one great work that appeared was a history of tariff policy. The first edition of Taussig's classic *The Tariff History of the United States* (New York; G. P. Putnam) was published in 1892 as a compilation of his earlier essays. The book went through many editions as Taussig added analyses of later tariff acts.

thing the formation of the American Economic Association was designed to prevent."[27]

Arguments stipulating the appropriate conditions for state intervention into the economy existed only in the works of the few enduring advocates of protection. Patten himself openly rejected competition as an inefficient method for industrial regulation and growth. Like Henry Carey before him, he argued for cooperation rather than competition as the basis of an economic system. Interventionists' government programs, from the tariff to explicit social planning, might, he argued, be necessary public policy.[28]

For other academics, the debate over commercial policy was subsumed within a larger debate on the benefits of laissez-faire. The logical extension of theories preached in university classrooms was the idea that government intervention should occur only if it enforced competition. Government was justified and, in fact, obligated to intervene to maintain a smooth-running market only where monopolies existed. Economists argued that the government protected competition by enforcing the rules of the market, not by direct intervention. As is indicated in the next section, this faith in the free market stood in stark contrast to the protectionist ideas advocated by elected officials throughout much of the century. The position defended repeatedly in congressional debate was that a reduction of duties would lead to a similar reduction in the wages of the laboring class, not to the more equitable use of resources.

CONGRESSIONAL TARIFF POLICY

Both congressional debate and public policy in this era reflected the weight of protectionist ideas in the minds of elected officials. The public discourse reveals that elected officials were concerned with the same issues as were classical economists, yet when mixed with particularistic interests of their constituents, an inability to understand the rapid changes in the American economy, and protectionist ideology, the congressional voice had more affinities with theology than with scientific analysis.

Although thousands of pages of debate prove that the trade issue loomed large on the political agenda, there was little in congressional

[27] Simon Patten, "The Reconstruction of Economic Theory," in Patten, *Essays in Economic Theory*, ed. Rexford Guy Tugwell (New York: Knopf, 1924), p. 275.
[28] Patten was not the only dissenter of the period. Henry George and Brooks Adams, among others, also disagreed with much contemporary analysis.

debate to show that representatives knew or understood the works of the great economists. And if they were aware of the great strides in statistical analysis since the Civil War, few attempted to use statistics to present a cogent case for either of the party positions. Both sides sought to raise the standard of living for the American worker. Both sides understood well that economic growth and their electoral fortunes hinged on the correct tariff level. But at the end of the nineteenth century, the process of finding that correct tariff resembled alchemy more than science.

In this period, Republicans contended that continuing the protections granted during the Civil War was an economic necessity. Their key argument was that the tariff compensated for lower foreign wages. As Nelson Dingley of Maine explained in 1894, "A tariff should be a duty which covers the difference of the money costs of production and distribution here and abroad of an article which can be produced or made here substantially to the extent of our wants without natural disadvantage."[29] Ignoring that productivity varied across nations, Republicans were able to show that American wages—and thus prices—exceeded those of our trading partners.

Democrats, however, cannot be characterized as defenders of free trade during the period. Although they advocated lowering tariff barriers, in no way did they dispute the general economic model presented by the Republicans. Few defended a general tariff level below 30 percent, and it was only when tariffs crept over 40 percent for particular commodities that the Democrats cried privilege and balance. Budget surpluses, they maintained, were the only valid indicator of whether tariffs were excessive; for most of the period, surpluses were seen as a signal that the tariff no longer served its economic purpose. Democrats agreed that the tariff should protect workers' wages, but they argued that reform to encourage cheap primary products was a better way than the tariff to protect wages. As William Lyne Wilson, the Democratic representative from West Virginia, explained: "wages depend on the products of [the worker's] labor. Whatever goes as a tax into the material he uses is a diminution of the wages of the laboring man. As you cheapen his materials . . . you enable him to put his finished products on the market at prices that will rapidly and indefinitely increase [his wages]."[30]

If the first dimension of debate in Congress was wages, the second was the benefits of reciprocity. As defined by an economist of the pe-

---

[29] Quoted in Richard Edwards, "Economic Sophistication in Nineteenth Century Congressional Tariff Debates," *Journal of Economic History* 30 (1970): 827.
[30] Ibid., p. 830.

riod, reciprocity was "the granting by one nation of certain commercial privileges to another, whereby the citizens of both are placed upon an equal basis in certain branches of commerce."[31]

Although in modern times the idea of reciprocity has been used as a strategy to lower barriers to trade, reciprocity in the Republican platform was a form of retaliation. The United States threatened a "stick" of higher rates while failing to offer the "carrot" of preferential access to the American market. Consequently, Congress's resorting to "reciprocity" legislation should not be viewed as an indication of its interest in trade liberalization.[32] Reciprocity was used as a tool for international bargaining, to be employed by negotiators only as a means to gain more favorable treatment for American exports. The protection of American producers was never negotiable. In the United States, reciprocity meant that foreign nations could be punished by an even higher American tariff if they failed to give American exports access to their markets.

Republicans who advocated reciprocal trade agreements argued that they would increase demand for American products and enable Americans to buy from cheaper, non-British manufacturers. With this logic in mind, the United States had negotiated its first explicitly reciprocal trade agreement in 1844 with the German Zollverein; this treaty, like most of its successors, was rejected by the Senate on the grounds that the president held no constitutional right to enter into commercial agreements with other nations. Only Congress could initiate revenue measures. But it was not only questions of executive prerogative that forestalled passage of these treaties; debate in both houses revealed a deep suspicion of the principle of reciprocity. These fears date to early in the century. For example, Daniel Webster had argued: "I do, gentlemen, entertain the strongest belief that the principle of reciprocity acted upon the government is wrong, a mistake from the beginning, and injurious to the great interests of the country."[33] But as the century progressed and the American economy became increasingly involved in world trade, the idea of reciprocity gained popularity as a means

---

[31] J. Laurence Laughlin and H. Parker Willis, *Reciprocity* (New York: Baker and Taylor, 1903), p. 2. Laughlin details the evolution of the idea of reciprocity from British maritime law into trade agreements.

[32] I disagree with Scott and Lake that the Canadian Reciprocity Treaty of 1854 heralded a "new era of trade liberalization." Rather, reciprocity was an extension of protectionist logic. See Scott C. James and David A. Lake, "The Second Face of Hegemony: Britain's Repeal of the Corn Laws and the American Walker Tariff of 1846," *International Organization* (Winter 1989): 11.

[33] Henry Rice, "Reciprocity Treaties and Commerical Intercourse with British Colonies," *Merchant Magazine and Commerical Review* (March 1845): 263.

both to maintain protection at home and to gain access to markets abroad (see Table 3.1).

Table 3.1. Growth in GNP, imports, and exports, 1810–1930 (in percent)

Year	GNP	Imports	Exports
1810–1820	24.9[a]	0.0	37.5
1820–1830	86.9	0.0	38.8
1830–1840	91.2	80.0	90.3
1840–1850	85.6	122.2	38.2
1850–1860	37.5	85.0	143.7
1870–1880	87.2	91.2	147.8
1880–1890	33.9	30.8	14.6
1890–1900	54.2	17.6	74.6
1900–1910	68.5	65.0	14.3
1910–1920	20.9	44.8	110.7
1920–1930	18.6	− 30.5	− 44.4

Sources: Thomas Berry, *Revised Annual Estimates of American Gross National Product* (Richmond, Va.: Bostwick Press, 1978); Brian Mitchell, *International Historical Statistics* (Detroit: Gale Research, 1983); U.S. Bureau of the Census, *Historical Statistics of the United States from Colonial Times to 1970* (Washington: USGPO, 1975), Series U 187–200, E 135–166, Y 204–210; U.S. Department of Commerce, *Statistical Abstract of the United States* (Washington: USGPO, 1990), No. 762.
[a] Figures reflect change in constant dollars (1967 = 100).

While debate in this era centered on the two issues of reciprocity and wages, policy outcomes had three general characteristics. First, the height, form, and structure of barriers kept American tariffs above those of other nations (see Table 3.2). Second, although the tariff became increasingly politicized in this period, the tariff policies of both parties were far more similar to each other than to what would be policy in the next century. The one exception is the 1913 Wilson tariff, which in many senses was a preview of the ideas that would guide commercial policy after World War II. And third, over time, group interests become an increasingly poor predictor of political support for tariff legislation. Western farmers, eastern manufacturers, and big business stayed within the Republican party fold and supported high tariffs, even though a policy of economic openness at home and abroad would have better served their intrinsic interests.

The Politics of Setting Tariffs

Between the Civil War and the election of Franklin Roosevelt, fifteen men were elected president of the United States. Only three were Democrats. Still, until the turn of the century, there was intense competition between the parties. Between 1870 and 1896, Democrats con-

Table 3.2. European tariff rates, 1875 and 1913 (average percent on manufactures)

Country	1875	1913
Austria	17.5	18
Belgium	9.5	9
Denmark	17.5	14
France	13.5	20
Germany	5.0	13
Italy	9.0	18
Holland	4.0	4
Spain	17.5	41
Sweden	4.0	20
Switzerland	5.0	9
United Kingdom	0	0
Unweighted average	9.32	15.09

Source: Paul Bairoch, *Commerce extérieur et developpement économique de l'Europe au XIX siècle* (Paris: Mouton, 1976).

Note: Averages for 1875 were computed using the middle of the given range.

trolled the House 62 percent and the Senate 15 percent of the time. Thereafter, the Democratic party fractured and, except for the House between 1910 and 1918, Republicans controlled government until the Great Depression. The tariff remained the key partisan issue throughout the period. Even so, with the exception of Wilson's tariff in 1913, duties remained above their post-1830s antebellum rates (see Tables 3.3 and 3.4).

Table 3.3. Average tariff rates, 1870–1929

Years	Duties as a percentage of all dutiable imports
1870–1872	44.2
1873–1883	42.3
1884–1890	45.3
1891–1894	48.9
1895–1897	41.6
1898–1909	47.3
1910–1913	40.8
1914–1922	28.3
1923–1929	38.2

Source: U.S. Bureau of the Census, *Historical Statistics of the United States from Colonial Times to 1970* (Washington: USGPO, 1975), Series U 207–212.

After 1870, the cyclical character of antebellum tariff policy gave way to solid support for protection. This is not to suggest that tariff

Table 3.4. Partisan control of the House, Senate, and presidency in years of major trade legislation, 1870–1929

Year	Congress	House	Senate	President
1870	41st	R[a]	R	R (Grant)
1872	42d	R	R	R (Grant)
1883	47th/	R	R	R (Arthur)
	48th	D	R	R (Arthur)
1890	51st	R	R	R (Harrison)
1894	53d	D	D	D (Cleveland)
1897	54th/	R	R	D (Cleveland)
	55th	R	R	R (McKinley)
1909	60th/	R	R	R (Roosevelt)
	61st	R	R	R (Taft)
1913	62d/	D	R	R (Taft)
	63d	D	D	D (Wilson)
1922	67th	R	R	R (Harding)
1929	70th/	R	R	R (Coolidge)
	71st	R	R	R (Hoover)

Source: U.S. Bureau of the Census, Historical Statistics of the United States from Colonial Times to 1970 (Washington: USGPO, 1975), Series Y 204–210.
[a] Abbreviations indicate majority party in each chamber: D = Democratic; R = Republican.

reformists were silent after 1870: on the contrary, the reformist coalition survived and included a growing number of intellectuals and politicians who were continually fine-tuning their appeal. But on the whole, this group was of marginal importance. Instead, pro-tariff interest-group influence on the legislative process peaked in these years, reaching its highest point in the first quarter of the twentieth century.

In the years after the Civil War, events began to alter the political and economic environment facing political decision makers. These years witnessed the gradual demise of the party state and the introduction of the civil service. Government expanded in size, and leaders gained the ability, and sometimes even the willingness, to engage in international matters. Within Congress, the era ended with two fundamental changes in political structures. First, the Ways and Means Committee, always a key actor in tariff policy making, trounced the Speaker of the House in a skirmish over congressional rules and norms. There followed a consolidation of power, which awarded Ways and Means, for the next half-century, legislative control of tariff setting. Second, a federal income tax was passed in 1913. As the federal budget grew, it became apparent that tariffs, even with reform, would not supply enough revenue. The passage of the income tax was not a surrogate for tariff reform, but by providing an alternative source of government revenues, it was a necessary prerequisite for that reform.

Taking Positions on the Tariff: 1870s and 1883 Acts

Congress in the 1870s, as opposed to legislatures of the 1880s and 1890s, was relatively conciliatory toward tariff reform. With the end of the war and a return to normalcy, Republican leadership faced growing numbers who argued that high wartime tariffs were no longer necessary. The Republican party acceded to such demands, carefully choosing the areas of trade legislation open for reform.[34] But as Taussig noted, the Fortieth Congress, nervous about eroding public support for high tariff levels, did much to conceal the actual height of protection; the resulting tariff was so complex that domestic producers did not know exactly how much they were protected. "Duties that plainly levied taxes of 60, 80, and 100 percent would hardly have been suffered by public opinion or enacted by the legislature," he explains.[35] Anti-tariff feeling was so pronounced that even the protectionist Speaker of the House found it prudent to appoint a Ways and Means Committee favorable to tariff reform when the Forty-first Congress opened in 1869.

Reformist sentiment did not lead to tariff reductions, but it does explain the oddities in the structure of the 1870, 1872, and 1875 tariffs. In the 1870 act, duties on tea, coffee, sugar, spices, and pig iron figured prominently. At the same time, Congress felt compelled to expand the free list from 20 to 130 goods. This combination encouraged trade, led to a big budget surplus, and further fueled critics who now insisted that the government rid itself of excess revenues. As in the 1840s, the Democrats were not the only ones to condemn budget surpluses; the Republican party divided on the issue. Liberal Republicans, splintering from the party in disputes about spending and corruption in the Grant administration, joined Democrats in calling for reform on a range of issues, including tariffs.

In response, the 1872 tariff, initiated in the Senate, reduced tariffs

---

[34] For instance, Senator John Sherman of Ohio, commenting on the 1872 tariff act, which lowered tariffs 10 percent, said the bill was necessary to preserve the protectionist movement: "I believe it is for their interest [protectionists in the House] to have this reduction of ten percent made, because their interest is so connected with the general interest of the subject-matter, with the maintenance of the protective system, that I believe it would be a misfortune to them if this concession to the consumer of the country should now be refused." *Congressional Globe*, 42d Cong., 2d sess., pt. 3, p. 2017.

[35] Taussig, *Tariff History of United States*, p. 215.

on many manufactured items by 10 percent and further enlarged the free list.[36] The bill passed despite a protest in the House that the Senate had overstepped its constitutional prerogative by initiating what the House considered a revenue bill. But again, it was clear that the bill's passage was greased by fears of potential reformist opposition at the upcoming Republican convention. In debate, few in the party supported even this modest reform.

It was fortuitous that the Panic of 1873 came on the heels of the 1872 tariff. As the economy declined, all but the most ideological members of the reformist coalition dropped tariff reduction from their agendas. As a result, the 1872 reductions were repealed in 1875 and the tariff increased, most notably on tobacco, liquor, molasses, and sugar.

From 1875 to 1883, the tariff held even though the issue increasingly divided the parties.[37] The Democrats stressed that the tariff should not "protect one class of citizens by plundering another."[38] The Republicans maintained that the tariff was the only means available to guarantee both high wages and economic prosperity.[39] The tariff dominated presidential campaigns, and within the House, divisions became so unbreachable that Ways and Means handed responsibility for preparing tariff legislation to a subcommittee that consisted solely of members from the majority party.

In this setting, neither party could ignore the large government surplus that had accumulated after 1880 (see Table 3.5). Thus before beginning work on a new tariff act, the Republican president, Chester Arthur, in an attempt to temper reform efforts, recommended the creation of a noncongressional committee to study the tariff question. Congress acceded in 1882 by legislating America's first Tariff Commis-

[36] Senator Sherman said that the tea and coffee provisions of the 1872 law cost the government an estimated $16 million in lost revenues. Enlarging the free list was estimated to cost a little more than $2.5 million. The more general 10 percent reduction was estimated as an $11 million loss in government revenues. *Congressional Globe*, 42d Cong., 2d sess., pt. 5, p. 4215.

[37] The only change to the tariff schedule between 1875 and 1883 was the addition of salt and quinine to the free list.

[38] The Democratic convention in 1876 declared: "Reform is necessary in the sum and mould of Federal taxation, to the end that capital may be set free from distrust and labor lightly burdened. We denounce the present tariff, levied upon nearly four thousand articles, as a masterpiece of injustice, inequality, and false pretence." Donald B. Johnson and Kirk H. Porter, *National Party Platforms, 1840–1972* (Urbana: University of Illinois Press, 1973), p. 50.

[39] The Republican national platform for 1876 declared: "The revenue necessary for current expenditures and the obligations of the public debt must be largely derived from duties upon importations which, so far as possible, should be so adjusted to promote the interests of American labor and advance the prosperity of the whole country." Four years later, the Republican platform declared: "Duties levied for the purpose of labor should so discriminate as to favor American labor." Ibid., pp. 54, 61.

Table 3.5. Budget surplus/deficit, 1870–1930

Year	Surplus or deficit (in millions of dollars)[a]
1870	$101.6
1875	13.4
1880	65.9
1885	63.5
1890	85.0
1895	−31.5
1900	46.4
1905	−23.0
1910	−18.1
1915	−62.7
1920	291.2
1925	717.0
1930	737.7

Source: U.S. Bureau of the Census, *Historical Statistics of the United States from Colonial Times to 1970* (Washington: USGPO, 1975), Series Y 335–338.
[a] Negative signs indicate deficits.

sion.[40] Once empowered, the commission solicited and received testimony from over six hundred witnesses in twenty-nine communities, the majority speaking of how they would be adversely affected if tariff levels dropped. Although the commission's final report did recommend reform, it supported the Republican position of an immutable relationship between tariff level and wages. It recommended that some tariffs drop as much as 25 percent, but that rates on manufactured goods increase in proportion to the amount of labor entailed in the production of the good.[41]

When passed into law, the 1883 tariff followed the commission's recommendations only in that some rates rose and others fell. Contention over the tariff heightened in both chambers, and the strong protectionist bias in the House gave the conference committee much latitude in writing the final bill; the partisan composition of the conference led few to think that anything but a highly protective bill would be forthcoming. Not surprisingly, then, the conference report raised many tar-

[40] Such a commission was first suggested by Senate Democrats in the 1879–80 session. Nevertheless, the commission was finally formed by a Republican majority over Democratic opposition. Arthur appointed John Hayes, the secretary of the Wool Manufacturers' Association, as president of the commission. Arthur had a hard time finding others to serve—at least five on his initial list refused the invitation—perhaps because the association was perceived to be biased toward protection, more probably because it was perceived to be impotent.
[41] Stanwood, *American Tariff Controversies*, 2:206.

iff rates over those proposed in either the House or Senate versions. The final tariff created only minor changes in customs revenues. Revenues did decline slightly in the next few years, but the primary cause was general economic conditions rather than any specific change in tariff policy.

Between 1883 and 1890, Congress considered several bills; none succeeded in gaining majority support. Even when the Democratic party held large majorities in the House no new legislation was passed. In good part, this situation reflected the party's inability to agree on more than a general platform of tariff reform. The official party position favored horizontal reductions, with exceptions, and increased numbers of goods on the free list. The appeal of a comprehensive horizontal tariff cut was limited, however, especially among eastern Democrats. The notion of exceptionalism was just as problematic, for many argued that it allowed logrolling abuses. Thus in key votes, Democrats could not count on support from many within their own party who remained wedded to protectionist ideas. For instance, in the 1884 fight over naming a Speaker of the House, the issue of tariff reform dominated the proceedings. The eventual loser, by a scant number of votes, was a Pennsylvania Democrat who supported existing tariff levels.

When the Democrats wrote their 1894 platform, their statement on the tariff was far more ambivalent than a decade earlier. The platform did not introduce the old principle of a tariff for revenue only but instead outlined a policy of tariff reduction within the general principles of protection:

> Knowing full well that legislation affecting the occupations of the people should be cautious and conservative in method, not in advance of public opinion, but responsive to its demands, the Democratic party is pledged to revise the tariff in a spirit of fairness to all interests. But in making reduction in taxes it is not proposed to injure any domestic industries, but rather to promote their healthy growth. . . . Many industries have come to rely upon legislation for successful continuance, so that any change of law must be at every step regardful of the labor and capital thus involved. . . . The necessary reduction in taxation can and must be effected without depriving American labor of the ability to compete successfully with foreign labor, and without imposing lower rates of duty than will be ample to cover any increased cost of production which may exist in consequence of higher rate of wages prevailing in this country.[42]

The Republicans in the 1880s were equally unsuccessful in building

---

[42] Johnson and Porter, *National Party Platforms*, p. 66.

a coalition around reducing the revenue surplus. Republican leaders advocated the removal of the internal taxes legislated during the Civil War on tobacco, cigars, snuff, fruit, brandies, and liquors; they agreed that some limited reductions in customs duties were necessary as well. But this mild program failed to gain the assent of a majority because even when party and regional differences could be reconciled, problems with forecasting revenues allowed any minority to question the utility of suggested tariff reductions.[43]

Fueling High Tariffs: 1890 and 1894 Acts

The tariff issue did not slumber. As the new decade began, the tariff assumed an unprecedented importance as an instrument of party politics. In the previous decades the Democrats and Republicans, if not existing in happy harmony, at least had a tacit agreement about the judiciousness of radical changes in customs duties, but such agreement dissipated when each party turned to customs policies to distinguish itself from the opposition. Grover Cleveland's decision to actively pursue tariff reform while president did much to invigorate debate;[44] his defeat in 1888, rightly or wrongly taken as evidence of popular support for high tariffs, led the Republicans to champion all that Cleveland had fought against.

One can only speculate on why the tariff assumed such proportions in the late 1880s. It is unlikely that shifts in public opinion drew leaders to this issue. Public opinion was divided yet not polarized and far too amorphous to galvanize such action. It is also unlikely that politicians were swayed by new arguments from the popular press. Hundreds of pamphlets were published on both sides of the issues, but this level of activity had been going on for many years. Leaders were not merely reacting to these publications; they were far less sophisticated and, in many senses, less radical in their prescriptions than commentators on

[43] For a more thorough history of legislation between 1883 and 1890 see O. H. Perry, "Proposed Tariff Legislation since 1883," *Quarterly Journal of Economics* 2 (October 1887): 69–79.
[44] In his third annual message at the opening of the fiftieth Congress, Cleveland explained why he had targeted tariff reform: "Under our present laws, more than 4,000 articles are subject to duty. Many of these do not in any way compete with our own manufactures, and many are hardly worth attention as subjects of revenue. . . . The radical reduction of the duties imposed upon raw material used in manufactures, or its free importation, is . . . an important factor in any effort to reduce the price of these necessaries. . . . [thereby] our people might have the opportunity of extending their sales beyond the limits of home consumption, saving them from the depression, interruption in business, and loss caused by a glutted domestic market." Fred L. Israel, ed., *The State of the Union Messages of the Presidents*, 1790–1966 (New York: Chelsea House/Robert Hector Publishers, 1966), 2:1595–96.

either side. Perhaps, as one scholar suggests, the issue appeared simply because no others existed.[45] The southern issue was dead. Both parties sought administrative reform. Trade, more than any other issue, was a reliable way to distinguish among groups. Whatever its political convenience, however, the politicization of the tariff issue led policy makers further away from considerations of foreign economic interest.

In their quest to gain voter support for their tariff position, both parties argued that their particular vision served the interests of the working class. Republicans claims that high tariffs protected American wages. Free trade, they argued, would swamp the U.S. market with goods produced by cheap but impoverished foreign labor. Unequal competition would close factories and lead to unemployment, poverty, or, worst of all, the duplication of terrible foreign working conditions in the United States. The Democrats took the opposite line. Protection, they declared, had little to do with wages. The tariff was merely a tax on goods produced. The tariff supported monopolies, hurt consumers, destroyed competition, and thus reinforced trusts, which directly led to the degradation of American labor. Despite this claim, Democrats never advocated removing tariffs on all protected items; rather, they agreed that tariffs were necessary on at least some products. Which items could legitimately be taxed was the issue. As prone to particularistic concerns as was the opposition, Democrats tended not to lower rates on goods produced in Democratic districts. They targeted goods not produced at home or products necessary for the manufacture of finished goods.

In hindsight, neither side presented a position that made much economic sense. None of the radical changes American industry, labor, and farm producers were undergoing could be easily fixed by tariff reform. Yet both parties suggested that altered tariffs would remedy all the deleterious consequences of change. The potency of the tariff as a cure for these ills was, and remains, severely limited.

The opening shots in the fight over the 1890 McKinley Tariff were fired in 1888 when the Ways and Means Committee marked up a tariff bill. The committee, appointed by the Democratic leadership, included only one representative from a manufacturing state. As was the custom, the majority party framed the bill—if contemporary rumors were true—with the help of members of the Treasury Department. The committee neither asked for nor received advice from manufacturing interests, hardly surprising because the party held that the common good had been sacrificed to those interests. This first Democratic effort,

---

[45] Tom E. Terrill, *The Tariff, Politics, and American Foreign Policy, 1874–1901* (Westport, Conn.: Greenwood Press, 1973), p. 8.

known as the Mills Bill, placed all raw materials on the free list, substituted ad valorem for specific rates of duty, and proposed a general reduction for a specific group of protective duties. Two-fifths of the revenue reductions were to come from the expanded free list, the rest from reductions in tariff rates. In addition, the bill abolished the specific schedules of duties and substituted a general provision for classes of goods. The measure passed in the House on a strong partisan vote and went to the Republican Senate. The Senate's Committee on Finance, finding these measures not particularly onerous, revamped the bill but did not raise the overall tariff level. The committee reduced the duty on sugar by 50 percent and raised duties on only a few specific items. These few increases, they argued, would help prevent imports from increasing so drastically that revenues would not decline sufficiently. The 1888 election took place in the midst of this debate. The Republicans returned to the White House and regained a majority in the House of Representatives. Although it had already returned to the House, the Mills Bill was dead.

President Benjamin Harrison's immediate call to Congress for tariff revision indicated that he viewed his election, and that of his party, as a mandate to increase protection. Now that the Republicans controlled the White House and both houses of Congress, they certainly had the power to do so. In his tariff message, he stressed the need not only to protect the home market but also to address inequalities in the law, especially any differences in treatment between farm and industrial goods. He agreed that revenues needed to be reduced, but tariff rates could not be set "by fixing our eyes on the public treasury alone. [Duties] have a direct relation to home production, to work, to wages, and to the commercial independence of our country."[46]

Following Harrison's call, Congress moved first on administrative reform. Legislation passed in June 1890 created a Board of General Appraisers whose responsibility was to determine the classification and value of all imported goods. In the past, the courts repeatedly had been forced to arbitrate on specific valuation decisions in the frequent disputes between importers and the Customs Bureau. This legislation attempted to take that power away from the courts.

The McKinley Tariff of 1890 specifically addressed tariff levels. Following what had become Republican party custom, the committee heard testimony from a broad range of groups, although manufacturing interests were clearly overrepresented. On the House floor, few voters deviated from their party's position. In the Senate, the Committee on Finance held more hearings, which, together with action on the

---

[46] *Congressional Record*, 51st Cong., 1st sess., vol. 21, pt. 1, p. 86.

floor, led to the addition of 496 amendments to the House bill. The conference committee reconciled the two versions, favoring the Senate (only 51 of the Senate amendments were dropped), and it became law in October 1890.

The McKinley Tariff marks a turning point in American commercial policy history for several reasons. First, in 1890, for the first time, the tariff schedule specified rates for both agricultural and nonagricultural products—a change of great importance to the Republican party's farm constituency, which had repeatedly claimed that it was being ignored in the tariff-setting process. These tariffs cemented the party's relationship with agricultural producers, bringing farming interests squarely into the protectionist coalition.

Second, in this act Congress explicitly legitimated the use of bounties to aid industries. The key case was that of imported sugar, which for the previous hundred years had provided the bulk of revenues for the state coffers. This act placed sugar on the free list, reducing its cost by a third—a move designed to provide relief for consumers.[47] This cut, however, threatened to bankrupt the far less efficient American growers, who in 1890 controlled about an eighth of the domestic market. The answer was state subsidization. Once sugar was granted the subsidy, John Steward of Vermont claimed the same right for producers of maple sugar and sorghum, a claim supported in the Senate version of the act. (The courts upheld subsidies soon after by refusing to be explicit on the question of bounties in a related suit.)

Third, with aid to the tin-plate industry, Congress broadened the definition and use of infant-industry protection for the purposes of import substitution. Against the outcry of the manufacturers of tinware, the act doubled the duty on tin plate, a product not manufactured in the United States, not represented by any organized interest, and used as a primary product in the manufacture of other goods. Republicans said that this move would encourage the growth of the industry; Democrats called the idea ludicrous, arguing that no manufacturer showed any interest in producing tin plate and that attempts to produce tin plate outside Wales had failed. In other words, they said, consumers would pay higher prices for products made with tin plate. To

[47] The Republicans made a tactical mistake, however, in the final draft of the act. Upon passage, all increases in the tariff schedule went into effect at once. For sugar, however, the rate decreases were postponed for six months until after the midterm elections. Whether or not this was the reason, the McKinley Tariff was extremely unpopular and the Republicans lost six seats in the Senate and eighty-nine seats in the House.

protectionists, this was a small extension of the notion of protection of existing industry; to the opposition, it was economic nonsense.[48]

Finally, the 1890 act was the first legislation that explicitly incorporated the idea of reciprocity into American trade policy. For the preceding one hundred years, American policy makers had considered commercial policy an exclusively domestic issue. This is hardly surprising given that American manufacturers could hardly saturate their home market, let alone worry about extensive access to foreign markets.[49] The situation changed in the closing years of the nineteenth century as increases in efficiency led to trade surpluses and a new

Table 3.6. Growth of U.S. productivity, 1870–1930

Year	Output of all commodities (1899 = 100)		Real hourly earnings (1900 = 100)
	Total	Per man-hour	
1870	31	61	59
1880	46	67	73
1890	71	82	90
1900	100	100	100
1910	143	125	116
1920	186	151	113
1930	281	243	134

Source: Adapted from Seymour E. Harris, *American Economic History* (New York: McGraw-Hill, 1961), p. 72.

interest in foreign markets[50] (see Table 3.6). At the same time, agricultural producers—worried about surpluses—found themselves increasingly unable to find an outlet for their products other than England (a result of continental European and South American restrictions on American products). When Congress explicitly took up this issue in

[48] To placate opposition, Congress inserted a sunset clause into the act stating that the duty would cease if the industry did not, by 1897, have a production level equal to one-third of the foreign competitors' imports in any year after 1890. The duties, however, served their intended purpose.

[49] This is clearly not true of primary product exports. For example, the United States exported 298 million pounds of cotton, grown almost exclusively in the South, in 1830. Exports of cotton grew steadily until reaching almost 2.5 billion pounds, worth $251 million, in 1890. Likewise, U.S. exports of tobacco, another crop grown almost exclusively in the South, grew from 84 million pounds, worth $6 million, in 1830, to 244 million pounds, worth $21 million, in 1890. U.S. Bureau of the Census, *Historical Statistics of the United States, Colonial Times to 1970* (Washington: USGPO, 1975), Series U274-294.

[50] Productivity increases were dramatic toward the end of the century. Productivity rose minimally between 1870 and 1880, but it rose 36 percent between 1889 and 1901. Ibid., p. 948.

1889–90, the representatives revealed clear limitations in both their knowledge of, and concern with, the basic elements of classical trade theory. In debate, no one suggested that the United States lower tariffs either as an incentive for reciprocal lowering of foreign trade barriers or as a means for foreign countries to gain American currency with which to buy American goods. Even Democrats failed to mention what had been said fifty years earlier, that U.S. tariff policy might lead to the loss of markets for southern cotton. Rather, products covered under the protective umbrella were considered non-negotiable; reciprocity was envisioned as a stick, not a carrot. Congress believed the role of the president was to use this stick in a timely manner: he would increase tariffs between periods of congressional tariff-setting whenever nations did not respond to American demands that they lower trade barriers on specified items.

More important than anyone else in bringing forward the issue of reciprocity was Secretary of State James G. Blaine. Returning from the International American Conference, Blaine reported to President Harrison that there was great potential for expanded trade with Latin America. He suggested that the United States negotiate some kind of customs union through which its trading partners would lower barriers to American products. Blaine convinced Harrison that trade patterns between the United States and Latin America were unequal and that Latin American protection was at fault. Harrison used these arguments in a letter to Congress in which he suggested that an attempt be made to expand trade with Latin America. He noted that more than 87 percent of Latin American products were admitted duty-free into the United States whereas U.S. products met high trade barriers.[51] Harrison added that the United Stated had given Latin America additional access with the passage of the recent House bill that placed sugar on the free list but had received scant reciprocal treatment.

The quick legislative response indicates that Congress found Harrison's arguments persuasive. In answer to constituents' demands for new markets, Senator Eugene Hale of Maine proposed an amendment to the trade act authorizing the president to "declare the ports of the United States free and open to all the products of any nation of the American hemisphere upon which no export duties are imposed" for a specified list of American exports.[52] This version of the proposal, however, was not adopted. Blaine, an ardent protectionist, never considered significantly lowering duties. Free trade with South America was never an option. Such trade would have endangered American wool

---

[51] *Congressional Record*, 51st Cong., 1st sess., vol. 21, pt. 7, p. 6256.
[52] Ibid., p. 6259.

growers, among other producers. Furthermore, the potential of increased agricultural imports from Canada made the idea of allowing all the Western Hemisphere free access to American markets even less appealing. The alternate version that the Senate Finance Committee devised was much more in the spirit of the protectionist coalition. This amendment empowered the president to increase the tariff on a number of articles if, in the subsequent two years, the nations supplying these products had not lowered their duties on American goods.

The chief criticism of reciprocity in Senate debate concerned its constitutionality, not its ostensible purpose. The Democrats argued that the reciprocity amendment gave the president taxing rights that belonged exclusively to Congress. Even a few prominent Republicans suggested that the president should merely recommend changes to Congress, which would then amend the tariff act. Most Republicans, however, argued that Congress had already set tariffs by passing the act; the president, they claimed, was merely implementing congressional decisions. This power, they reasoned, was no different from powers the Supreme Court had upheld.

In the end, the McKinley Tariff, like all tariffs in the decade, reflected the partisan composition of Congress. The act raised average rates to 46.5 percent and extended coverage to many products never before listed on the tariff schedule. Along with increased rates, the adjunct bill streamlined the administrative process, reducing cheating by importers and allowing more efficient collection of customs duties.

With passage of the McKinley Tariff, trade politics took on a predictability that would hold through the Great Depression. The Democratic party became the tariff reform party. When a clear party position was stated, protectionism was characterized, not as unjustified but as misused, causing high prices, unequal wages, and budget surpluses that drained the economy. In the 1890s, the Republicans would continue to champion high tariffs. But though political lines were firmly drawn, debate on the floor and in committee continued as if each side was open to persuasion. Controversy surrounded every aspect of the schedule, from wool, to glass, to lumber.

The passage of the McKinley Tariff did not bring bad fortune to the Democrats. In midterm elections, the party successfully played on public fears of price increases and gained a majority. Even so, the Democrats could do little but suggest legislation, targeting a range of products for tariff reduction, including wool, binding twine, and tin plate. Partly their impotence was political: in the fifty-second Congress, they controlled only the House. Even in the fifty-third Congress, after they had swept both houses, they still did little to substantially reform the tariff, largely because they had no ready alternative to high tariffs.

In 1876 and 1880, Democractic platforms had defended a tariff for revenue only. After their defeat in 1880, the 1884 and 1888 platforms reflected a less drastic approach to tariff reduction, stressing the need to keep afloat industries that depended on protective tariffs. Only in 1892, in a 564 to 342 vote, did the Democratic convention renounce this position, instead stating:[53] "Republican protection [is] a fraud, a robbery of the great majority of the American people . . . the federal government has no constitutional power to impose and collect tariff duties, except for the purposes of revenue only . . . the McKinley tariff law [is] the culminating atrocity of class legislation."[54] But the party was still far from united on what constituted a revenue tariff. During the presidential campaign of 1892, Cleveland argued that tariffs were promoted by special interests and were unconstitutional. But Cleveland himself was far less radical than the platform on which he campaigned. He defended not free but freer raw materials; not free trade but a fair distribution of the tariff burden.

Even if the Democrats had not interpreted victory as a mandate for tariff reform, they would have had to address the issue of trade policy. By fiscal 1893–94, the year Cleveland reassumed the presidency, the government budget had fallen into deficit (see Table 3.5). The cause was on the spending side—there was neither a decrease in tariff revenues nor a decline in overall levels of imports. In defense of their 1890 bill, the Republicans could justly claim that it did not boost prices; prices that had risen in anticipation of the new duties began a ten-year decline after the tariff went into effect (see Table 3.7).

After highlighting tariff issues in the campaign, the Democrats turned almost immediately to recasting tariff policy. The resulting legislation, however, never realized the hopes of its supporters. Rather, the history of the passage of the 1894 act and its specific content reflect just how hard it was at this time to alter economic policy.[55] The House

[53] The conservatives who dominated the platform trade committee reported a resolution that was a far cry from a free-trade position: "And we demand such a revision of the tariff laws as will remove their iniquitous inequalities, lighten their oppression, and put them on a constitutional and equitable basis. *But in making reduction in taxes it is not proposed to injure any domestic industries, but rather to promote their healthy growth. . . . Many industries have come to rely upon legislation for successful continuance, so that any change of law must be at every step regardful of the labor and capital thus involved.*" Quoted in Stanwood, *American Tariff Controversies,* 2: 313.

[54] Johnson and Porter, *National Party Platforms,* p. 87.

[55] At the time, commentators blamed the Senate for the height of the 1894 tariff act, but there is little reason to suppose that the tariff should have been anything other than protective. The House version, written by someone then considered a free trader, did not lower tariffs below their 1883 rates. Further, Senate debate echoed controversies over the Democratic platform. There was simply no consensus on a trade liberalization strategy even within the free-trade party. This interpretation varies from the one offered by

Table 3.7. Price changes, 1870–1930

Year	Consumer Price Index[a]
1870	38
1880	29
1890	27
1900	25
1910	28
1920	60
1930	50

Source: U.S. Bureau of the Census, *Historical Statistics of the United States from Colonial Times to 1970* (Washington: USGPO, 1975), Series E 135–166.
[a] Based on Consumer Price Indexes for all items (1967 = 100).

version of the Wilson bill illustrates very clearly what the radical reformers in the late nineteenth century envisioned as a legitimate tariff. William Wilson, chair of the Ways and Means Committee, proposed a tariff that reflected his deep-seated beliefs in the efficacy of free trade as well as his limited experience in the practice of Democratic politics. His background was in academia, and upon retiring from politics he returned to a college presidency. He was well schooled in the English classics, and his views reflected the liberal bias recently triumphant among American academic economists. Wilson's zeal was reinforced by his interpretation of the last election as a mandate from the American people for tariff reform. His report to the House reduced most duties on manufactured items and placed all raw materials on the free list. Not surprisingly, it was criticized by reformers as inadequate and lambasted by protectionists as undisguised free trade even though the act retained at a slightly lower level the protectionist structure of the McKinley Tariff. More radical was the length of the free list and the inclusion of wool. Overall, in Wilson's original version, few of the industries that had been protected in past decades were left outside the government's protective umbrella, and tariffs did not drop much below their 1883 levels.

The bill made its way through the House with few hitches. No one bothered to represent the act as a revenue measure because everyone knew it would draw less money than the McKinley Tariff had. Those who said they feared continued budget deficits were reminded of the

---

Taussig, *Tariff History* (1914 ed.), pp. 284–320, which sees the dissent in the Senate as merely reflecting old problems and squabbles with President Cleveland. On other issues, however, including the contentious silver question, Cleveland was able to control his own party.

history of increased revenue under the Walker tariff. To garner the votes of Populist representatives, an amendment legislating an income tax was placed on as a rider to eliminate the need for either duties or bounties on sugar.[56] The bill passed without one Republican voting in its favor and with seventeen Democrats dissenting.

The Senate was far less sanguine than had been the House about Wilson's bill. Even though the Senate was controlled by Democrats, many of them were less interested in tariff reform than were those in the House. The senators from New York, for example, opposed any act that contained an income tax; senators from Louisiana stated that they would oppose any bill that did not include duties on sugar. As many as twelve of the forty-four Democratic senators were on record as opposing some portion of the House bill. Along with the thirty-seven Senate Republicans, this opposition formed a sizable coalition. The bill faced other problems; as it moved into the Senate, the economy fell into a steady decline, making state needs for revenue more pressing and spurring popular opposition through petitions and demonstrations.

The Senate's version of the Wilson bill, written by a subcommittee of the Finance Committee, reflected strategic, not ideological, considerations.[57] Almost all changes restored the status quo. The exception was sugar, which was to be taxed a hefty 40 percent, with an additional duty on refined sugar. Most items came off the free list (except wool and lumber), specific duties were replaced by ad valorem duties, and many compound duties were reintroduced. Debate was long and sometimes acrimonious as the Democratic leadership tried hard to keep its members united. This was no easy task. Although the House bill had made concessions to certain industries that would clearly be jeopardized if tariff aid were removed, the Senate version expanded that category to include just about all important constituencies. It had little systematic adherence to the Democratic party's plan for revenue-only tariffs, or even its position on the constitutional prohibition banning protective duties. On the floor, only one Democrat voted against the final act. In all, 634 amendments had been added in the Senate. When the bill returned to the House, the Ways and Means Committee opposed each one. Wilson's condemnation was sweeping but unavailing: "The bill comes back to the House with these two great fundamental principles of just taxation and these two great fundamental principles

[56] The tax was later ruled unconstitutional by the courts.
[57] An earlier version, which had further lowered tariffs, was written by Senators George G. Vest (D-Mo.) and Roger Q. Mills (D-Tex.). But when the caucus learned of this, it took the bill out of the hands of these senators and gave it to the subcommittee, with instructions to report a bill that met the needs of 51 percent of the Senate.

of Democratic policy [ad valorem duties and free raw materials] in a large measure overridden and neglected."[58] The result was a series of conferences and compromises, each moving the House closer to the Senate version of the bill. The final bill became law without Cleveland's signature.

Those who promised economic gains from trade liberalization would have found 1894 a better year for passing protectionist legislation. The declining economy did not turn up when Wilson's act became law, and its critics were fast to capitalize on the tariff's failure either to raise revenues or to spur economic growth. Indeed, the times were ill-fated not only because of the downturn in the economy but because the tariff issue was tied to both the silver issue and the growing affinity between the Democratic and Populist parties. In 1894 the people returned a Republican majority to the House and a Republican plurality to the Senate. Two years later, Republicans gained a majority in the Senate and the Republican William McKinley was elected president. Once in control of the government, the Republicans finessed the silver issue and turned instead toward erasing the budget deficit, enacting the highest and most comprehensive set of tariff barriers yet legislated. The economy flourished although the new legislation was not responsible. The tariff issue thereafter slumbered into the next century.

The Dingley Tariff of 1897

Compared to earlier tariffs, the legislative history of the Dingley act of 1897 was surprisingly uncomplicated. President McKinley, elected on an antisilver stand, chose to concentrate first on the more familiar tariff question. In a message to a special session of Congress, he asked for legislation that would increase revenues, preserve the home market, revive and increase manufactures, and encourage agriculture. The House responded by quickly making moderate changes to tariffs. Nelson Dingley of Maine, chair of the House Ways and Means Committee and an ardent advocate of protectionist doctrine, orchestrated the bill through committee and onto the House floor. The bill began in the House as a very moderate revision of the Wilson act; it reinstated the wool schedule but kept tariffs at their 1894 levels on many other items. On the floor of the House, few representatives offered amendments to the committee report.[59] The bill passed quickly to the Senate, where

---

[58] *Congressional Record*, 53d Cong., 2d sess., vol. 27, pt. 27, p. 7191.

[59] The majority party was able to constrain floor discussion by passing a five-day rule giving the introducing committee first right to suggest amendments. The discussion of the bill itself began with an unimportant part of the tariff schedule that nonetheless fueled two days of floor discussion. The Ways and Means Committee took up the bulk

its debate absorbed a substantially greater amount of time. When the Finance Committee released the altered bill to the full Senate, it had revised the existing schedule slightly downward.[60] All the amendments added on the floor, however, favored higher duties, even those from the Finance Committee. In all, over 870 new amendments were added to the original House version, four-fifths of which were accepted in conference. Both houses easily agreed to the final version, and when the president signed the bill he enacted the highest average rate of customs duties yet imposed. Once again, the final bill was more protectionist than either its House or Senate versions.

The Dingley act did more than raise tariffs; it returned reciprocity to the centerpiece of tariff policy. In 1894, the reciprocal provisions of the McKinley act had been repealed. Then, in 1896, the Republican platform had pledged a return to these principles:

> We believe the repeal of the reciprocity arrangements negotiated by the last Republican Administration was a National calamity, and demand their renewal and extension on such terms as will equalize our trade with other nations, remove the restrictions which now obstruct the sale of American products in the ports of other countries and secure enlarged markets for the products of our farms, forests and factories. Protection and Reciprocity are twin measures of American policy and go hand in hand.[61]

In keeping with this promise, the Dingley act authorized the president to negotiate reciprocal trade treaties and to retaliate against countries found to be discriminating against American exports. The later action did not need Senate approval; the former needed the approval of both houses. As in 1890, the president could respond to duties he felt were "reciprocally unequal and unreasonable" by suspending the free admission of tea, coffee, tonka beans, and vanilla beans. Sugar and hides, which received similar treatment in 1890, were now subject to a tariff and thus could not be used to induce foreign cooperation. The president was also given the power to reduce duties on a select group of

---

of the remaining debate time with its amendments, leaving almost no time for admissible amendments on the heart of the tariff act.

[60] The feeling in committee had been to leave the tariff unaltered until more pressing economic issues were resolved. In particular, Nelson Aldrich, the head of the Senate Finance Committee, and other Republican leaders in the Senate (with the approval of President McKinley) were making plans for an international bimetallism agreement with France and England as the means to reunite the two wings of the Republican party. Discussions with France tied such an agreement to the enactment of more favorable import duties for such French products as wine, silk, woolens, and gloves. See Lawrence Chamberlain, *The President, Congress and Legislation* (New York: Columbia University Press, 1946), pp. 97–98.

[61] Johnson and Porter, *National Party Platforms*, p. 107.

items. On crude tartar, brandies, champagne, wines, and artwork, for example, the president could, "after securing reciprocal and reasonable concessions," institute controlled tariff reductions on his own. This new provision was fashioned after a system inaugurated in France in 1892 in which the government legislated a system of maximum and minimum duties.

The act reflected the contemporary application of the idea of reciprocity only in that it expanded presidential authority to negotiate to reduce tariffs up to 20 percent. This provision, however, which was inserted by the Senate, was so circumscribed that it assured no such treaties would ever come into existence: treaties needed to be made within two years, they could be in a force a maximum of five years, and they needed the approval of both houses.[62]

Because the idea of reciprocity was interpreted through the lenses of the prevailing system of beliefs about protectionism, American discussions and use of reciprocity deviated sharply from those in other European countries. The United States did not ignore the policies of its trading rivals; in fact, the move to reciprocity was partially in response to actions abroad. But Americans understood reciprocity far differently than did the British. Albert Hopkins, Republican from Illinois, nicely summed up the Republican view: "Reciprocity is scientific protection and is adapted to our improved commercial conditions and civilization. . . . It has been found to work admirably in [European] countries. It has given them the control of the markets of the world on many of the articles specified in these commercial or reciprocal agreements."[63] Nor did the majority of Democratic reformers associate reciprocity with trade liberalization. As Albert Todd of Missouri argued: "A like inequity exists in the so-called 'reciprocity' features of this bill. . . . Who derived any benefit from the practical operation of the reciprocity clause of the McKinley law but the pork-packing, and the beef-packing,

---

[62] The general trend in American commercial policy since the Civil War made it almost impossible to negotiate any of the treaties that were mandated in the Dingley act. Kasson of Iowa, who was appointed a special commissioner for the negotiation of reciprocity treaties, later reported: "The condition of commercial feeling in Europe as I found very soon after undertaking these duties, was exceedingly hostile to the United States. The Dingley bill had produced an effect all over the continent of Europe of exasperation throughout the commercial world, and among the governments as well, to such an extent that one high officer—the Premier of the Austria-Hungarian Government—has openly proposed a union of official action against the United States commerce as their only means of protecting their own commerical interests. In that state of feeling, at first, there seemed no disposition anywhere on the continent of Europe or in the Governments of South America to take any steps under the reciprocity clauses of the bill." Quoted in Laughlin and Willis, *Reciprocity*, p. 300.

[63] *Congressional Record*, 55th Cong., 1st sess., vol. 30, pt. 1, p. 135.

the milling and the sugar trusts?"[64] But not all Democrats failed to see that the principle of reciprocity could be used in support of policies they had advocated. John C. Bell of Colorado noted in debate:

> When the Democrats put an article on the free list, the Republican party shouts "Democratic free trade," while at the same time, when the Republican wants to put it on the free list, he has a little scheme which he calls "reciprocity," but which is simple free trade in its most cunning form under another name, under which the Republicans sometimes even bribe other countries to join in free trade with us. Our friends talk as if they had just discovered reciprocity. Why, sir, it has been a principle of every political party.[65]

And W. Jasper Talbert of South Carolina repeated that "our Republican brethren say that they will pry open the foreign markets by their "reciprocity" provision. . . . So, after all, the great Republican party is trying to steal our Democratic ideas away from us by calling it by a different name. They are trying to take our free trade robe off of us, and don it themselves and parade it before the country as 'reciprocity.'"[66]

But reciprocity was not a liberal idea in 1897 or in 1890. For American statesmen, it was a means to get at foreign markets. In the great mercantilist tradition, it was also a means to increase wealth by increasing the flow of specie into the United States. To sell more goods, the United States needed more markets. Reciprocity was a way to pry open new markets for manufacturers who were already secure in their own territory. No one intended the United States to negotiate away current barriers protecting goods produced at home. Rather, policy makers wished to mitigate, perhaps even eliminate, increased consumer prices for a small range of goods that had no competitors in the home market. Indicatively, what became Section 5 of the Dingley act was simply a way to impose retaliatory duties upon the goods of all countries that encouraged exports to the United States. By statute, the secretary of the treasury could counter a bounty from a foreign nation by increasing the duty on that product upon importation. This was the basis of twentieth-century countervailing duty laws, not the forebear of reciprocal reductions in tariffs. Only later did the Senate agree to include a House amendment allowing the United States to conclude any agreement in which tariffs could potentially be lowered.

In any event, America's attempt to conclude reciprocal trade agree-

[64] Ibid., p. 340.
[65] Ibid., p. 137.
[66] Ibid., pp. 268–69.

Table 3.8. Growth in GNP, agriculture, and industry, 1869–1929

Year	Per capita GNP (1947 dollars)	Indices of output (1899 = 100)	
		Agriculture	Manufacturing
1869	$370	43	25
1879	570	63	36
1889	630	79	66
1899	800	100	100
1909	920	115	158
1919	1,100	126	222
1929	1,040	145	364

Source: Adapted from Seymour E. Harris, *American Economic History* (New York: McGraw-Hill, 1961), p. 70.

ments were doomed to fail. While the Dingley Tariff was in force, seventeen reciprocity treaties were negotiated. Thirteen went to Congress for approval, but none passed into law. Four—with Italy, Portugal, Germany, and France—did not require a congressional vote, and, although enacted, they had little economic impact. As explained by J. Laurence Laughlin of the University of Chicago and H. Parker Willis, of Washington and Lee University, the United States failed because we were "neither willing to present our reciprocity agreements to the world at large upon equal terms, as does France by its maximum and minimum system, nor do we stand ready to extend to all the benefits gained by any one country which enters into a process of bargaining with us, as is done by Germany. We offer no tariff concessions, save to those countries which we believe may be induced to grant us concessions that are more than equivalent."[67]

The Dingley act had legislated the highest average tariff rate of the nineteenth century and would stay in force for the next twelve years. The ensuing hiatus in tariff politics had both economic and political roots. Throughout the period the Republican party retained control of government and found its concerns for commerical policy dwarfed by other problems. But more important, the United States experienced strong economic growth, suggesting no reason for legislators to tinker with tariff policy (see Table 3.8).

The Beginnings of Reform: 1909 and 1913 Acts

As the 1908 elections approached, the tariff reappeared as a political issue. Many associated the problem of trusts with overly protective tar-

---

[67] Laughlin and Willis, *Reciprocity*, p. 29.

iffs. Others criticized the tariff for causing prices to rise, cutting into the real income gains of workers and farmers. America's commercial policy was further blamed for causing economic panics in 1904 and 1907, although these claims were of dubious validity. Most problematic for the Republican party, however, was criticism from previous supporters of the Dingley act. Notable among these progressive critics were President Theodore Roosevelt's secretary of state, Elihu Root, and his secretary of war, William Howard Taft, both of whom argued that the time had come for tariff reform.

Still, mainstream Republicans were slow to abandon a tariff policy that had been successful for the preceding three decades. In 1904, the Republican platform had stressed that "the measure of protection should always *at least* equal the difference in cost of production at home and abroad." Four years later, the Republicans conceded that, although there was a need to "equaliz(e) the cost of production at home and abroad," "the true principle of protection is best maintained by the imposition of such duties *as will equal* the difference between the cost of production at home and abroad" (emphasis added).[68] Although the change from "at least" in 1904 to "as will equal" in 1908 seems minor in retrospect, this alteration represented what the party considered a concession to critics: the party dropped the notion that preference should be given to domestic industries in competition with foreign producers. But it still failed to accept the legitimacy of fair competition between foreign and home producers in the American market. By keying tariffs to the cost of production, the party assured domestic preference. As in the past, concern remained focused on keeping American wages high and stopping potential pauperism, not on what was produced, per unit of cost.[69]

Shifting with the mood of the country, President Taft demanded tariff reductions in 1909. But as had become common, by the time it left the legislature, the 1909 act did little to alter tariff policy. As reported from the House, the act lowered the average duty by decreasing rates on raw materials, but it maintained or increased tariffs on finished goods. Iron ore, coal, hides, petroleum, and other products were placed on the free list; wool and cotton goods remained protected. The bill, a product of a Ways and Means Committee led by a staunch protectionist,

---

[68] Johnson and Porter, *National Party Platforms*, p. 158. Taussig erroneously says that this concept was new. Taussig, *Tariff History*, p. 363.

[69] Taussig quotes Senator Aldrich: "Assuming that the price fixed by the reports is the correct one, if it costs 10 cents to produce a razor in Germany and 20 cents in the United States, it will require 100 percent duty to equalize the conditions in the two countries. . . . And so far as I am concerned, I shall have no hesitancy in voting for a duty which will equalize the conditions." *Tariff History*, pp. 364–65.

Sereno Payne of New York, was supported by a broad coalition. The price of this support was extensive compromises on features of Taft and Payne's original bill, which, although less protective than its predecessor, retained high duties. The bill was changed little on the floor and passed with a 217 to 161 vote.

The Senate altered both the spirit and the sense of the act. The committee reported the bill out only two days after the House passed it, adding an astonishing 847 new amendments, more than half of which increased rates significantly. Moreover, previous duties were restored on almost all the goods placed on the free list by the House; many ad valorem rates, which the House had used routinely, were replaced by specific duties—not because fixed rates yielded more income but because they were perceived as a more efficient way to protect industry. These changes were championed by Nelson Aldrich, an uncompromising defender of tariffs, who sat as chair of the Finance Committee. Critics of the House version seemed to be everywhere, and many used the issue as a platform from which to fight the Republican leadership. Further, drawing a special message of condemnation from President Taft, an income tax was once again added on the Senate floor. After eleven weeks of debate, the Senate bill was approved by a vote of 45 to 34. In conference committee, the president attempted to pressure Senate members into support of the House rates. He was unsuccessful, and the final act did little more than nudge policy in the direction of the Republican party's new tariff platform.

The vast differences between this bill and its Democratic successor reflect the political confusion of the period engendered by fundamental changes in America's place in the world. The radical growth of the economy had made international trade increasingly attractive to American producers. But from the perspective of Congress and the president, the key foreign economic policy issue was not increasing world trade but how best to combat discrimination against American products abroad. Given America's high tariff rates, this discrimination was not necessarily unfair. But the Republicans chose not to focus on the reciprocal relationship between American and foreign rates. In fact, in 1909, the reciprocity sections of the Dingley act of 1897 were repealed and the president was instructed to cancel any existing agreements. In its place, the 1909 Payne-Aldrich act granted the executive even more far-reaching rights to retaliate against purportedly unfair trade. Instead of passing one set of rates, Congress authorized two: a minimum and maximum tariff schedule. The bill Taft signed contained minimum rates; if justified, the president could increase these rates by adding a 25 percent tax on the value of an import from a country that was "unduly discriminatory" to American products. Discrimination was broadly defined as either high foreign tariffs or export incentives such as bounties. Further, the president was instructed to use maximum rates after March 1910 unless he was satisfied that countries were not so discriminating. Whether or not discrimination was a problem, Taft never chose to raise rates above their minimum levels.

As an aid in determining whether tariffs were sufficient to meet foreign unfair trade practices, the Tariff Commission was re-created. Congressional intent in 1909 was to create a board that would do no more than gather information to help the president in applying the minimum-maximum principle. The attempt to make the board an arm of Congress, which would have given it authority in the preparation of tariffs, was rejected.

Problems in the Republican party finally boiled over and, after decades of political hegemony, a period of Democratic control was ushered in. The Republicans suffered their first decisive defeat in the midterm elections of 1910, a year in which tariff policy was a watershed campaign issue. Significantly, the economy had continued the downward slide that began with the 1907 panic. Having touted themselves as the "party of prosperity," the Republicans were now condemned for not carrying out their economic platform.[70] Following an aggressive Democratic campaign, they lost control of the House and suffered a great reduction of their majority in the Senate. Two years later, Woodrow Wilson was elected president, the first Democrat to hold the office since Grover Cleveland. Wilson's ability to mobilize the electorate on the tariff issue and his skill in showing Taft to be less of a reformist than he had claimed to be during his 1908 campaign were key to the Democratic success. During Wilson's tenure, Congress passed the most liberal act since the Walker tariff. The bill lowered tariff levels, mandated an income tax, and expropriated the Republicans' reciprocity issue by giving the president the right to negotiate reciprocal trade agreements, subject to congressional ratification.[71] Although in many respects this act presaged postwar American policy, it was doomed to failure.

The liberalization of the tariff in 1913 was no political surprise. Wilson was a confirmed tariff reformer, having described the Payne-Aldrich Tariff as "miscellaneously wrong in detail and radically wrong in

[70] Once again the Democratic party argued that poor economic times were caused by the high tariffs. And again, evidence was scant. In the first decade of the century, all nations experienced a rise in prices, most probably because of the increased supply of gold. U.S. inflation, which the Democrats also blamed on duties, was better explained by poor agricultural output and the decline in available arable land.

[71] By 1910, the idea of reciprocity was becoming problematic for the extreme protectionist wing of the Republican party. Taft's treaty with Canada in which certain agricultural products entered duty-free barely passed Congress, even with the Republican majority. The treaty was rejected in Canada.

principle."[72] Furthermore, Wilson began his term with majorities in both houses and was in a position to carry out his campaign pledge. Throughout the previous two years, the Democratic majority in the House had written a number of ill-fated reformist bills, signaling its intent to overhaul existing tariffs. So by the time Wilson arrived in the White House, Oscar Underwood's Ways and Means Committee had already written a new tariff bill. The bill met with great party unanimity, much of the credit going to Wilson, who played a key role throughout the process. Wilson kept in daily contact with party leaders on the progress of the bill. In an unprecedented move, he came to Capitol Hill and spoke in favor of tariff reform. He served as his own congressional liaison, repeatedly writing letters to solicit bipartisan support. His personal interventions led, among other things, to the expansion of the free list to include the bastions of protection, wool and sugar. Although some party members thought the bill more radical than necessary, voting was nevertheless touted as a symbol of party unity. In the House, only five Democrats voted against passage.

Although the bill faced a greater battle in the Senate, Wilson's intervention and organizing strategy succeeded in keeping it intact. Again, he made the issue a test of party loyalty, forcing a Democratic caucus to take a stand for its passage. He further pressured senators by going to the public and mobilizing opinion for reform. Because the Democrats had a majority of only seven in the Senate, he knew that any defections would be costly. Wilson's work paid off; the bill that was reported from the Finance Committee was even more liberal than its House counterpart. During the two months of debate on the floor, all the amendments that affected tariff rates lowered duties. When the final measure came to a vote, only two Democrats (both from sugar states) voted against the measure, while two Republicans crossed party lines to vote with the majority. Small differences were resolved in conference, and the president signed the Underwood Tariff Act of 1913.

In retrospect, the 1913 act was a low-tariff act in a protectionist era. If World War I had not come on the heels of its passage, it might well be remembered as America's opening to international trade. Many reasons suggest, however, that the 1913 act should simply be noted as a manifestation of the economic uncertainty of these times, not as a harbinger of change. At the time of its passage, commentators far more often saw the Underwood Tariff as an extension of the protectionist tradition than as an acceptance of liberal trade principles. Taussig, writing a summary of the act for the *Quarterly Journal of Economics* a

---

[72] Woodrow Wilson, "The Tariff Make-Believe," *North American Review* 190 (October 1909): 535.

year after its passage, suggests that its appearance as a major revision in the theoretical basis of tariff formation was incorrect. Rather, he argued, the act rested on the fundamental principles of the era. The Republican demand for equalization of the cost of production had indeed been replaced by the new notion of a "competitive tariff," which protected only "legitimate" industries. But, said Taussig, the differences between the two approaches were far more rhetorical than real. Both maintained that domestic producers should always compete with foreign producers on "equal" terms. And, even more than the Republicans had, the Democrats held the state responsible for assuring this equality, despite the uneven distribution of factors of production. The Democratic party platform had argued not that protection was unnecessary but that it was overly burdensome. Tariffs, mainstream Democrats believed, should not exceed whatever level was needed to assure the viability of domestic industries and thus competition on the American market. Thus both parties agreed that duties should favor American industries that were operating less efficiently than their foreign competitors, or operating with some disadvantage such as higher labor costs. Neither party accepted the free-trade position that the market and not governments should set cost and production patterns.[73]

Writing in 1914, Taussig suggested that each party's catchwords, though similar in denotation, had different connotations among the electorate. The Republicans wanted to be seen as friends of domestic industry, fighting for tariffs high enough to protect domestic producers from cheap imports. The Democrats, on the other hand, wanted to be seen as friends of the consumer, fighting for tariffs low enough to assure a competitive market. Yet despite their ostensible desire for competition, the Democrats were more than willing to fix duties without supporting data on the level that would assure such competition. Indicatively, they refused to allocate money to continue the Tariff Commission, the one logical candidate for devising a "scientific" tariff schedule. As a result, few good data were available to establish appropriate tariff levels. Statistics supplied in testimony were suspect; those computed by committees revealed the inability of Congress to meet the task of preparing a tariff. Like the Republican tariff process, the Democratic process was inherently political. Democrats refused to cre-

---

[73] One of the stranger parts of the Democratic argument was the defense of protection only for legitimate industries. Because legitimacy did not mean that the industry could compete in a free market, it is unclear just how one would know at what point it was overly subsidized and had become "illegitimate." F. W. Taussig, "The Tariff Act of 1913," *Quarterly Journal of Economics* 28 (1914): 1–30.

ate a regulatory institution, seeing it as a Republican issue.[74] Instead, the committees haphazardly recast the old specific rates into ad valorem rates.

Hardest to reconcile in the tariff of 1913 was the addition of wool and sugar to the free list. The additions make sense only as political symbols because they were poor extensions of the new Democratic philosophy on commercial policy. The new status of sugar made no sense given the spirit of the tariff; the sugar market had long been competitive, and so, even by Democratic party standards, should have received legitimate protection.[75] The tariff level on wool was an issue that had haunted the Democrats since 1894. In 1913, the original House report had kept a 20 percent duty; Wilson pushed for no duty at all. By Democratic party logic, the wool market should have appeared competitive because the duty had not been high enough to constrain imports. But for the Democrats, the issue was not just free wool but the abolition of the compensating duty on wool goods.[76] Woolens had duties of over 50 percent, sometimes as much as 150 percent. To keep protection on woolens, Congress attempted to discover what the real duty on woolens needed to be if wool came in free. The only previous time when cost equalization had been attempted for the industry—by the 1882 Tariff Commission—had resulted in the finding that variations in the conditions of production across the United States made such calculation nearly impossible. Despite these problems, Congress took data collected by the Tariff Commission, placed wool on the free list, and voted to give woolens a 35 percent tariff, the computed difference between U.S. and foreign expenses.

As had Republican tariffs, the Democrats' 1913 act protected "fair trade." Indicatively, the 1913 law did not change the 1909 antidumping provisions. In addition, although it eliminated executive power to set

[74] Even Taussig, who was critical of all aspects of the Republican tariff program, commented that the Tariff Commission had been composed of experts who had attempted in the best manner to bring scientific reasoning and information to bear on setting tariff levels. Using a commission, he suggests, was a far superior means of setting rates than within the legislature. He notes that the reports prepared by the commission were even used by the Democrats, and it was only because the commission was cast in partisan terms that it was disbanded in 1912.

[75] The sugar industry, however, was one of the most long-standing, visible, and disliked trusts, making it a likely target both for Democratic and Republican reform. As it happened, the duty-free provision was never enacted. To allow the sugar industry and the federal treasury, which relied heavily on sugar revenues, a period of adjustment, sugar was to retain its previous duty until 1916. In 1914, the Democratic losses in Congress ushered in a period of factional disputes, one of which led in 1916 to the relegislation of the sugar duty.

[76] The Republican system had allowed intermediate and finished goods a compensatory duty for tariffs on primary products used in production. The form of this compensatory duty was usually specific, with an ad valorem rate then added.

the minimum and maximum duty, Congress authorized the secretary of the treasury to impose additional duties on any product that was priced too low because of a foreign government grant or bounty. Along with antidumping protections, this principle underpinned both Democratic and Republican fair-trade legislation. Imposing such a principle, however, had proved far more difficult than writing the law. Since the 1890s, administrative provisions to determine unfair trade had become progressively more complex and difficult to adjudicate. This situation was somewhat ameliorated in 1890 with the creation of the Board of Apraisers. Then, in 1909, the Court of Customs Appeals was created to deal with the growing number of trade issues that were still in dispute. An attempt further to deter fraud in valuation and collections motivated Congress in 1913 to give the secretary of the treasury authority to impose an additional 15 percent duty on importers who refused to submit their books for review.

In retrospect, the changes in the 1913 tariff were large in relative terms although the new tariff schedule did little to alter American production patterns. In 1914, Taussig wrote that history's judgment of the success or failure of the 1913 tariff would have little to do with the tariff itself. The comment proved to be prescient. "Though we are much in the dark, concerning the causes of the periodic alternations of activity with depression," he wrote, "every competent observer will agree that among these causes tariff legislation is of the least import."[77]

A year after passage of the 1913 act, war broke out in Europe. In the spring of 1917, the United States joined the conflict. The war brought the American government into daily economic decision making as never before. The new income tax was used as a fund-raising mechanism, and the War Industries Board manipulated prices and supply far better than customs duties ever had. American production was spurred by the joint phenomena of increasing demands for exports to allies and isolation from the fighting itself. Not only did the traditional industries expand, but a new set of manufacturing "war babies" were born from the lack of European competition. At war's end, the nation's sense of its self-sufficiency had grown, a new set of infant industries was endangered by resurging competition, and the agricultural economy faced a severe depression. Such was the backdrop for the writing of the last of American protectionist laws.

The Last High Tariffs: 1922 and 1929

The Republicans regained control of both houses in 1918. Almost immediately, they began to revise tariffs. In December 1920, they at-

[77] Taussig, "Tariff Act of 1913," pp. 29–30.

tempted to restore duties to their pre-1913 levels; Wilson twice vetoed such bills. The sentiment for increased tariffs, however, was widespread. In 1920, Republican Warren G. Harding was elected to the presidency on the promise that he would lead the nation back to "normalcy," including a return to the "old" tariff system.

The 1922 Fordney-McCumber Tariff presaged its more famous sibling, Smoot-Hawley, in process and content. Hearings were long and arduous. Committees sat for months deliberating on the particulars of the schedule. The Senate Finance Committee alone sat for six months in hearings. Interest groups, too, played an important role in the process, but few voices spoke for either moderation or liberalization. All compromises leaned toward more protection. The Senate added over two thousand amendments—all tariff hikes—to an already protectionist House bill. On the floor of the Senate, the bill was debated for almost four months. Controversy raged over a number of provisions, including the protection of chemicals and the system of valuation known as the "American selling price."[78] The only consensus was over the need for higher tariffs. After making two trips to a conference committee, the bill passed in both houses in September 1922.[79]

In response to changing demands, both international and domestic, the Republican party had devised what it considered an adequate response to American interests in world trade. But keeping changes within the protectionist tradition led to a strange hybrid of reforms. Essentially, the Fordney-McCumber act mandated a significant increase in presidential autonomy over tariffs. But this flexibility was circumscribed by the act's two central concepts: the president could change tariffs only if American goods were subjected to discrimination or to guarantee American and foreign "cost equalization."

Section 315, the intellectual heir of minimum-maximum duties, again empowered the executive to increase tariffs when American products faced foreign discrimination. Following the suggestion of William Culbertson, vice-chair of the Tariff Commission, Harding asked in his annual message for "a way . . . to make for flexibility and elasticity, so that rates may be adjusted to meet unusual and changing conditions which can not be accurately anticipated."[80] This flexibility gave Harding the right to increase the tariff in cases of discrimination against Ameri-

---

[78] Under this system the value of certain imported goods was appraised not by their foreign price or their domestic price but by the price of a "comparable and competitive" American good.

[79] The first conference report returned the bill with a dye embargo, an attempt—allegedly orchestrated by DuPont—to protect its new manufacturing interests. Both houses had rejected the embargo in their original bills; when the conferees returned the bill with the embargo restored, the House voted to recommit the report, with all but four Democrats in agreement.

[80] *Congressional Record*, 67th Cong., 2d sess., p. 37.

can products. The 1922 act also gave the president some discretion to lower rates. Specifically, the act stipulated that "in order . . . to put into force and effect the policy of the Congress . . . whenever the President . . . shall find it shown that the duties fixed in the Act do not equalize the differences in costs of production in the United States and the competing foreign countries," he may raise or lower duties for the purpose of equalizing these costs.[81] He was limited only by a 50 percent cap. The new Tariff Commission was to provide the data to help determine appropriate tariff levels.[82]

The years following the passage of the Fordney-McCumber act were prosperous ones for all sectors of the American economy, with the exception of agriculture. By 1929, the flow of U.S. goods and services had reached an all-time high; industrial production had risen 50 percent over the level of the preceding decade.[83] The agricultural sector, however, quickly declined after its post–World War I boom. In the 1920s, agricultural prices fell dramatically.[84] Various remedies were suggested for the agricultural malaise; the most uncontested was increasing agricultural tariffs. Thus in 1928, presidential candidate Herbert Hoover declared his intention, if elected, of legislating new agricultural tariffs.

In January 1929, the Ways and Means Committee announced that it would begin hearings for a limited revision of the tariff. Although nonagricultural products had not been in Hoover's original plan, the committee chose to consider them as well. Thus began tariff legislation that was to demonstrate conclusively the deficiency of the American policy-making process.

In hearings, representation of private interests was one-sided, organized, and vocal. More than eleven hundred people attempted to give testimony before the House Ways and Means Committee. Even with a

---

[81] F. W. Taussig, "The Tariff Act of 1922," *Quarterly Journal of Economics* 37 (November 1922): 19.

[82] Although the old Tariff Commission had not been reauthorized in 1912, Wilson unexpectedly changed his mind in 1916 and asked Congress to create a bipartisan board with broad powers to investigate the administration and the fiscal and industrial effects of the tariff laws. Characteristically, Wilson made his request with little prior communication to Congress. Authorization for the board was slipped into a general revenue bill and, under presidential pressure, passed into law.

[83] Ross Robertson and Gary Walton, *The History of the American Economy* (New York: Harcourt Brace Jovanovich, 1955), p. 405.

[84] Between 1850 and 1920, the value of farmland increased every year; between 1920 and 1935, it fell by over 50 percent. Indicatively, the parity ratio, that is, the ratio of prices received by farmers to prices paid, including interest, taxes, and wages, considered to be 101 in 1913, fell to 80 by 1921. Another way to measure the depth of the farm depression is by acreage of farmland: between 1850 and 1950 the total acreage of U.S. farmland rose every year except from 1920 to 1925. U.S. Bureau of the Census, *Historical Statistics of the United States,* pp. 461–62, 489.

time limitation of two minutes per witness, almost eleven thousand pages of testimony were heard, almost all of it arguing for more protection. Similarly, the Senate Finance Committee was besieged by groups interested in testifying for higher tariffs. The Finance Committee split into four bipartisan hearing groups, producing testimony that ran over nine thousand pages.

On the floor, representatives of both parties were unconstrained in adding amendments to the committee bill. The original bill was moderate, the work of the fifteen Republican members of the subcommittee of the House Ways and Means Committee. But in the complete committee and on the floor of the House, amendments made the act far more protectionist. The Senate showed no consideration for the work completed in the House. Sectional controversy between manufacturing and agricultural regions led to months of fighting in committee over the content of the bill to be introduced onto the floor. When it was reported out of committee, 431 changes had been made to the House bill.[85] On the floor, a coalition of agrarian Republicans and Democrats attempted to increase rates on raw materials and lower rates on manufactured products; after almost four months of debate, they compromised on rate increases for both primary and finished products. In all, the Senate had amended the House bill over one thousand five hundred times. When the Smoot-Hawley Tariff was signed into law in 1930, it had raised the average ad valorem rates on dutiable imports to 52.8 percent.

Although some proponents claimed that Smoot-Hawley would assure economic prosperity, many others—including all academic economists—disparaged both the act and the process of its passage. Ten years later, the freshman senator Arthur Vandenberg would label the act an atrocity and claim: "It lack[ed] any element of economic science or validity. I suspect that the 10 members of the Senate, including myself, who struggled through the 11 months it took to write the last congressional tariff act, would join me in resigning before they would be willing to tackle another general congressional tariff revision.[86] Within two months of passage, major trading partners began to raise tariffs. By 1931, twenty-six countries had quantitative restrictions and exchange controls. In 1932, the United Kingdom abandoned the remnants of its free-trade policy for preferential trading blocs.

[85] Only 177 of the changes were increases, 254 of the alterations suggested rates lower than those in the House bill. Many of the latter changes, however, were in unimportant areas of production.

[86] Harry C. Hawkins and Janet L. Norwood, "The Legislative Basis of United States Commercial Policy," in William B. Kelly, *Studies in United States Commercial Policy* (Chapel Hill: University of North Carolina Press, 1963), p. 78.

The concurrent depression was America's worst. Some would later say it was a fitting accompaniment to the highest tariff of the century. Between 1929 and 1933, the American economy crumbled. U.S. Gross National Product in current prices declined 46 percent, from $104.4 billion to $56 billion. Prices, in constant dollars, declined 31 percent; industrial production declined by more than one-half; wholesale prices dropped one-third, and consumer prices declined by one-quarter.[87] Employment fell almost 20 percent, and unemployment rose from 1.5 million to over 13 million. Between one-quarter and one-third of the civilian work force was unemployed. This depression was longer and deeper than any of its predecessors. In 1920–21, the decline had been sharp (43 percent of output), but the nation had recovered in less than two years. In this case, not until 1939 would output again exceed its 1929 level.[88]

In sum, the Fordney-McCumber act, like its successor Smoot-Hawley, was typical of post–Civil War tariff acts. Neither shifts in the international environment nor growth in producers' economic efficiency were reflected in these bills. Rather, they were premised on the belief that America could increase its exports abroad without deregulating the home market. Although many understood the logic of free trade, they viewed protection with export expansion as economically superior. Their rationale was that although the United States had suffered sporadic periods of decline, the post–Civil war years had seen great economic advances. In the case of industries that did suffer because of their inability to gain access to foreign markets, the government threatened a policy of negative reciprocity: if foreign markets would not open to the United States, then America would further close her own.

Although much was contested about the form and height of tariffs, the parties agreed on many other aspects of tariff making. Both sides saw tariffs as part of a national agenda. The Democrats opposed overly high rates because they detracted from national welfare, not because the groups did not have a right to protection. Many found fault with the political process of setting tariffs. Both parties agreed that protectionism was legitimate when it provided a "fair" market for American producers. It was illegitimate when it was an overt intrusion into the marketplace. As the tariff schedule became increasingly complex in response to America's expanding production, tariff making fell prey to particularism, logrolling, and excesses in legislative time and effort (the latter more because of the legislative process than any real difference in philosophical position). The result was exceedingly high tariffs.

[87] Robertson and Walton, *History of the American Economy*, p. 404.
[88] Ibid.

As alternatives, policy makers considered having a congressional tariff commission, or an executive agency, or even the president set levels. Most of these ideas, however, conflicted with both parties' interpretation of congressional rights as set in the Constitution. Thus free-trader Taussig could lament in 1922 that "the country can adjust itself to extreme protection or high protection or moderate protection or even to free trade, and can go on prosperously under any one of them," as long as some tariff level was maintained. "Constant vacillations are a great evil," he explained, "for the simple reason that the influence of the protective system on our industrial system, whether good or ill, is not so far-reaching as most people think. But an influence it has, and that influence is particularly bad in so far as it is inconstant and incalculable."[89] Taussig was not alone in recognizing that the political nature of the process was becoming ever more dangerous. As industrial production became more complex and Congress less willing to delegate decisions on particular products, tariff revisions not only became more time-consuming, but they also affected more sectors of the economy, often in painful ways. When the fourth major revision in two decades led to a further increase in protection, neither party was happy. When Smoot-Hawley was followed by depression and a change in party control, the seeds were sown for a change in the traditional congressional role in commercial policy makings.

IDEAS AND THE INSTITUTIONALIZATION OF PROTECTION

Ideas about economics, about politics, and about the workings of the international economy all influenced trade policy making in this period. In particular, two ideational changes that occurred in the ensuing years exemplify the importance of particular beliefs in this period. First, in the years discussed in this chapter, one economic vision dominated the setting of commercial policy. While antebellum tariff policy reflected differing and usually partisan visions of trade relations, the economic strategy of high tariffs and, later, negative reciprocity eclipsed all alternative policies. Second, throughout this period there was an unquestioned belief in both parties that the legislature had the ability and the right to grant tariffs as political "pork." The ideas of protectionism as economic policy and tariffs as "pork" would be soundly repudiated by both parties in the years after World War II. Just as the benefits of trade openness and an executive-centered trade policy are rarely questioned in the contemporary liberal era, in the

[89] Taussig, "Tariff Act of 1922," pp. 27–28.

protectionist epoch, high barriers to trade and a logrolled tariff were ideas that were taken for granted.

High Tariffs and Negative Reciprocity

Most social scientists who focus on late nineteenth-century politics look to tariff disputes as a means of distinguishing party position. Although tariff differences were central to each party's identity, nineteenth-century parties still argued within one general economic paradigm. Even the most liberal Democrats agreed with their Republican opponents that free trade was not in the national interest, that America had to be protected against cheap "pauper labor," that the idea of free trade was a manifestation of British imperialism, and that the notion of a home market was sound. Both sides looked to the tariff as a panacea for economic problems. Their causal model, that is, which direction to take tariffs after providing a protectionist floor, varied in what now appear as inconsequential ways. One can look at the debates in Congress and at the legislated tariffs as indicators of the continuity in this period. Except for the 1913 act, tariff levels remained remarkably stable and high no matter which party wrote the tariff act.[90]

During the period, both parties came to agree that governments needed to resolve the problems posed by rapid economic expansion and production surplus. In earlier years, Republicans were more comfortable with rapid industrialization and active government involvement in the economy; by century's end, Democrats also represented industry and commerce. Thus powerful Democrats such as Abram Hewitt of New York claimed as loudly as his opponents did that his party's position on the tariff best supported the interests of his industrial constituency. Compared with ethnic and regional differences, philosophical differences over commercial policy were small.[91] The Republican party advocated a program of reciprocity, and the Democrats tacitly accepted its underlying logic. Both parties shared a bilateral "barter" theory of export expansion. Instead of accepting the basic

[90] There was more fluctuation when both free and dutiable items are considered. When expansion of the free list is considered, the 1922 and 1930 tariffs look less exclusively protectionist than does the McKinley Tariff of 1890. However, use of the dutiable index is the better measure of protection of finished as opposed to primary products (many of which had no American competitor). Although fights over free wool and especially sugar were key to coalition formation over specific tariffs, the right to set tariffs on American industry threatened by either cheaper manufacturing labor or unfair competition is the dimension of tariff policy better reflected in the dutiable list.

[91] Terrill argues that the lack of deep cleavages on the tariff was a reason it became the issue of party differences in the second half of the nineteenth century. *Tariffs, Politics and American Foreign Policy.*

notion of comparative advantage, the parties maintained a more mercantilist view of trade. To expand U.S. trade with a country, Americans thought they had only to provide a specific product with access to the U.S. market. The reciprocity agreements reached by Blaine in the Garfield adminstration or by the Arthur administration were resisted far more for constitutional, procedural, and symbolic reasons than for philosophical reasons. The radicals in the period were more likely to be on the conservative side. For example, William Kelly of Pennsylvania never relinquished his belief that the United States could exist in splendid isolation and self-sufficiency. No political coalition advocated what we now call neoclassical economic theory, even though it was taught in universities and practiced by our trading partners.[92]

The preceding review of congressional speeches and policies reveals the hub of the nineteenth- and early twentieth-century debates. The protectionists never strayed far from the ideas of Hamilton and Jackson on the American system. They declared themselves to be economic nationalists, endorsing an activist, protective policy that would advance peace and the public welfare. Furthermore, they played on latent hostilities toward the Old World, which had long been a dimension of American political thought; their nationalism hinted at Anglophobia and anti-Europeanism. American industry had to defend itself, they argued, against Europe's tactics and cheap goods. The Democrats' counterpoint rested on the means, not aims, of foreign economic policy. Their key defense was that protectionism may have reaped the economic wealth claimed by Republicans, but at the cost of great inequalities. High tariffs, they said, disrupted the flow of goods, favored certain sectors over others, and increased consumer prices. Republicans claimed that protection would bring wealth and social harmony; Democrats that it increased prices to benefit the privileged few. Both sides made a special appeal to the farmer: Republicans claimed that foreign competition threatened American farmers; Democrats that the protective system skewed tariffs in favor of finished products and so did little

---

[92] Even David Wells accepted some protection as necessary for fiscal and industrial reasons. In the pamphlet entitled *A Primer for Tariff Reform,* Wells argues pointedly for the adoption of a free-trade posture. Yet he defines free trade as "an adjustment of taxes on imports as will cause no diversion of capital from any channel into which it would otherwise flow, into any channel opened or favored by the legislation which enacts the customs." He argues that free trade "does not mean the abolition of custom houses. Nor does it mean the substitution of direct for indirect taxation, as a few American disciples of the school have supposed." To Wells, protection for revenue needs was healthy and legitimate. It was pernicious only when it redirected the flow of land, labor, and capital into those industries in which the United States could not potentially hold a comparative advantage. David Wells, *A Primer for Tariff Reform* (New York: New York State Revenue Reform League, 1884), pp. 3–4.

to help them. Democrats reasoned that lower tariffs would not only instigate the freer flow of American goods into foreign markets but would also lower the price of products in the United States. (The goods in question were either not produced at home or "illegitimately" protected.) Republicans countered that farmers' prosperity depended on a strong demand for their products at home and that demand was based on industrial growth, which, in turn, hinged on the protection of industry.

By the 1880s, both parties agreed that export expansion was in America's interest. But it was the Republicans who were able to find a road between the American system and growing sentiment that America's future lay in expanded export trade. They popularized the concept of reciprocity, heralded protections against export subsidies and foreign dumping, and pioneered a more flexible tariff system. All these responses to America's changing role in the world economy were crafted not to challenge the existing ideological structure but to mesh with current values. Reciprocity did not have to be a Republican issue. As the subsequent decades would reveal, it was to become the basic tenet of a multilateral move toward free trade. Later, Democrats would incorporate it into their post–World War II platform. In this period, however, the Republicans massaged the idea and turned it into a symbol of protectionism.

The Republican trade ideas—the combination of protection and reciprocity—appear almost impossible to reconcile given contemporary thought on trade policy. Yet the party was successful just because it was able to capitalize on the strong, chaotic undercurrent of belief in the American population. The strange mix of ideas is perhaps best captured in the inaugural meeting of the National Association of Manufacturers. The organization recognized at its first meeting in 1895, as it still does, that its interests lay in export expansion. That members chose as their keynote speaker William McKinley, champion of protection, is no stranger than the warm reception they gave to one speaker who called on the convention "to find some escape and salvation from governmental policies which are injurious to the business community." McKinley argued that government protection of the home market was a "plain and natural right." He continued:

> The moral of our present situation is that the prostration of manufactures is the downfall of all other business interests. We want our own markets for our manufactures and agricultural products; we want a foreign market for our surplus products which will not surrender our markets and will not degrade our labor to hold our markets. We want a reciprocity which will give us foreign markets for our surplus products and in turn that

will open our markets to foreigners *for those products which they produce and which we do not.* (Emphasis added)[93]

The proceedings of this 1895 convention again show the dominance of protective ideas in this era. The cause-and-effect relations posited by speakers and members would be meaningless after World War II. Everyone at the convention wanted export expansion. Speaker after speaker made this point straightforwardly. Yet no one remarked on the interplay between export and import expansion, supplying American specie to foreign buyers, and comparative advantage. Instead, markets were referred to as "belong[ing] to us" when speaking of areas south of the border, or else reciprocity was simply hailed as a mechanism that would open markets without injury to American producers or loss of American control of the market.[94]

The response of policy makers to changes in the American economy after World War I also reflects the hegemony of the protectionist vision. The passage of the 1913 tariff is intuitive. Given the growth of the American economy, the increase in relative American power, and changes in the relative importance of domestic producers, congressional action to increase trade would be expected. But if that act can be explained by the changing constitution of interests in the United States, the return to high tariffs in the 1920s—a policy incongruent with emergence of America as a world power—can only be explained by the power of the idea of protectionism. Even as central decision makers faced new problems, they remained wedded to an economic strategy that deviated markedly from one that would maximize economic prosperity.

Thus from 1870 to 1934, U.S. policy was inherently protectionist, no matter which party was in control of Congress. When the nation envisioned a future of trade expansion in the 1880s, export growth was seen through mercantilistic or fair-trade lenses. Instead of opening

[93] Albert K. Steigerwalt, *The National Association of Manufacturers, 1895–1914* (Ann Arbor: University of Michigan, Graduate School of Business Administration, 1964), pp. 20–21.

[94] Business interests and the Republican party's economic platform did not mesh well at the gathering. The convention could agree only on the right of government to control the home market, but not on the tariff level necessary to do this. The diversity of industries represented caused disagreements, as did the inability to arrive at a technical formula with any degree of accuracy. The lack of consensus on tariff height pushed delegates to stress what did unite them—that is, the benefits of reciprocity. Even so, some castigated the existing Republican reciprocity programs. Participants thought the United States should emulate the structure embodied in the tariff of 1890, which gave the president, not Congress, the right to change tariff levels. The form of reciprocity in the 1897 act, which returned control to Congress, was condemned by the association. See ibid., pp. 63–65.

up American markets, policy makers threatened to further close them if treated unfairly by other nations. Instead of maximizing the efficiency of American industries, central decision makers worried about other nations cheating through export subsidies or dumping on the American market. All trade legislation in this period reflected this bias. Policy makers cared little about the effects of American legislation on general foreign policy goals. Their attention centered instead on the willingness of other nations to exploit American high wages for access to the large U.S. market. The legislature's job was to establish procedures to protect producers. And those procedures, once enacted into law, did much as their creators imagined.

Professionalization of Tariff Making

The notion that the protection of the home market was an efficient economic policy was implemented through a political process that made tariffs "pork" to be distributed by legislators in both parties. In the years following the Civil War, no one questioned the hegemony of Congress to set tariffs in this manner. By the turn of the century some policy makers suggested that the executive needed to be more involved. Forty years later, few members of the legislature or the public believed in or defended the virtue of having Congress set tariffs.

In retrospect, it is easy to reconstruct the path to the professionalization or depoliticization of tariff policy making. As early as 1866, Congress recognized the need for expert advice and created the Office of the Commissioner of Revenue. In 1882, Congress created another commission to prepare for the upcoming general tariff revision. Like later congressional committees, this commission held hearings and gathered information, even if appointments biased the selection of its experts and witnesses. Then, in 1888, the Department of Labor set up a cost-of-production study to improve methods of tariff making. (Later, in 1912 after the Tariff Commission's funding was discontinued, the Bureau of Foreign and Domestic Commerce again conducted cost-of-production studies to help determine optimal tariffs.) In 1909, the first formal attempt to establish a permanent board of experts was legislated. Although vague, the act authorized the president "to employ such persons as may be required" to assist him in administering the maximum and minimum provisions of the tariff act. Finally, in 1917, the present organizational structure was authorized, giving the board broad investigative powers to help Congress set rates. Although Congress came to see the utility of using experts to provide information, it still refused to give up control over rates. Authority was delegated only to the Treasury Department, which ruled on customs violations and countervailing and antidumping cases. The key change occurred only in the 1930s, when Congress invested the executive office with the right to fix rates.

Analysts often look at the growing complexity and size of the tariff schedule to support a functional explanation for the loss of congressional power. But although executive office involvement in trade policy did increase after the 1890s, in no sense do the data above suggest that congressional delegation was inevitable. At least two other scenarios were possible. As is argued in the next chapter, Congress could have vested power to set tariffs with an independent commission and used its oversight powers to control the general direction of policy. Liberalization or continued protection could have occurred through procedures similar to those found in the areas of securities, labor, communication, or budgeting. Alternatively, Congress could have retained control, even of this complex area, through an enlargement of committee responsibility. A tariff committee similar to the Agricultural Committee could have developed the expertise necessary to structure reform. Tariffs and agricultural subsidies are akin in complexity, reliance on economic data and forecasting, and interest-group involvement. Given how little independent authority was granted to the Tariff Commission and the president in this period, it would be hard to defend an evolutionary process ending with congressional abandonment of tariff control. Rather, as is argued in the next chapter, two ideational reasons explain the shift in control. First, a popular association between Smoot-Hawley, depression, and interest-group involvement made congressional representatives believe that control of tariffs could undermine their ability to get reelected. Second, general acceptance of the idea of reciprocity precluded explicit legislative involvement. When the Congress moved to reform tariffs, the method chosen was not unilateral reductions, a method employed by the British. Rather, policy makers relied on the more familiar notion of reciprocity. Reciprocity, however, required international negotiations, an arena in which the executive, and not Congress, held the constitutional prerogative.

CONCLUSION

In much of the period covered in this chapter, American needs and economic ideas were out of sync. In retrospect, we know that the answer to America's growing demand for trade lay with the reciprocal opening of foreign and domestic markets. We also know that competition, both at home and abroad, does not necessarily lower wages, impoverish workers, or create social chaos. Actually, it provides cheaper consumer goods and more efficient industries. By the turn of the century the "objective" interests of the United States and of the major constituencies within the dominant Republican party required the deregulation of trade. But policy makers systematically ignored classical trade theory in this period, despite the advocacy of many. Why? Three reasons emerge from this review.

First, even economists of this period admitted that they were poor carriers of their own message. In 1924, Simon Patten is reputed to have noted that his fellow economists were "a hybrid product of bookworms and hair-splitters." Richard Ely warned in 1900:

> Let us take care that we are not crushed by our own learning! Much that has been laboriously gathered together will be swept aside before we reach 1909, and will be thrown on the rubbish-heap of ingenious but fruitless speculation. I think it may be said that the theoretical work of the decade has as a rule lacked sufficient boldness. We have been too timid, and hence in some cases spent much time in petty refinements while essentials have been overlooked.[95]

And Thorstein Veblen described "certified economists" as having minds that were "like old music-box[es], full of tender echoes and quaint fancies."[96] American economists, disinterested in political affairs, were busy in this period creating a discipline whose beauty was its abstraction and often its irrelevance for particular policy questions.[97] The success of these deductivists was hard won. Alternative policy-oriented revolts occurred twice among the disciples, in the 1870s by the historicists and in the 1920s by the institutionalists. Both attempts failed to unseat the major academic figures in universities. This discord did little to enhance the status of the bearers of these ideas. Contempt for professional economists flavored this period. We need look no further than the writings of Edward Bellamy and the social utopians at the turn of the century to see a strong dislike for the field.[98] Disdain

---

[95] Richard Ely, "A Decade of Economic Theory," *Annals of the American Academy of Political and Social Science* 15 (March 1900): 111.

[96] George Santayana, "The Genteel Tradition in American Philosophy," in *Winds of Doctrine* (New York: Charles Scribner's Sons, 1913) p. 192.

[97] As late as the onset of World War I, the American Economic Association distinguished itself from groups such as the American Historical Association by refusing to organize a professional body for patriotic service. When asked, the association is reported to have "decided that it was not best to do anything as an organization," having been "influenced to no little degree by the constitutional provision prohibiting the Association from going on record in controverted matters." Carol Gruber, *Mars and Minerva: World War I and the Uses of the Higher Learning in America* (Baton Rouge: Louisiana State University Press, 1975), p. 121.

[98] See, for example, Edward Bellamy, *Equality* (New York: Appleton, 1897).

for academics tinged the debates on trade issues. Only later, when economics classes became incorporated into the core curriculum on university campuses, were students universally educated in classical ideas. Concerned with public policy, these students popularized economic ideas and made them available for political entrepreneurs and policy makers seeking alternatives to protection.

A second, equally fundamental reason explains American antipathy to the ideas of British classicists. European theories appeared out of step with the realities in the United States. It was the laymen, not the theoretical economists, who understood the realities of the New World. In an often-quoted remark, List said, "When . . . I visited the United States I cast all books aside—they would only have tended to mislead me. The best work on Political Economy which one can read in that modern land is actual life."[99] Several factors separated America from the model that prevailed in British thought: the availability of free land, the acceptance of government as integral to civilizing the wilderness and the attendant rejection of laissez-faire, and the depth of the American people's belief in social harmony. These differences evaporated during the twentieth century. Class differences, the closing of the frontier, scarcity, and problems with capitalism worried many who had believed that the United States was to be spared the problems of Europe. When the United States entered World War I, political isolationism was not the only casualty. More fundamentally, entrance into the world economy meant the end of the marginalization of classical economic thought.

But it is not enough to argue that America's failure to adopt classical trade theory rests either with economists or with their models. Just as critical was the political counterpart of the hegemony of protectionist ideas. Once the parties associated themselves with protectionism, they found themselves stuck. The constraints were coalitional as well as cognitive. High tariffs united an otherwise diverse Republican party; for the Democrats, the protectionist status quo became a filter, causing them to interpret demands for change, domestic and international, through a colored lens. Especially after both parties realized that the recovery from the 1873 depression was fueled by rising exports, particularly wheat, the constraints imposed by a history of protection are evident. We know that many at the time, including David Wells, argued that U.S. producers would need to seek foreign markets to prosper.[100]

---

[99] Normano, *Spirit of American Economics*, p. 197.

[100] Unlike the Republican party and even opinion leaders in his own Democratic party, Wells accepted the tenets of free trade and argued that America would gain access to essential markets only through lower tariffs. The majority of Democratic reformers fo-

But the mainstream response, the promotion of high tariffs and reciprocity, makes sense only when we consider the prevailing economic models. Instead of changes in interests creating space for new policy ideas, old ideas and an institutional structure that promoted particularistic gains from tariff policy led policy makers to ignore available solutions to the problems posed by America's new place in the world.

Policy makers did not ignore interests; rather, they responded to them as they had in the past. Change was incremental, never straying far from the fundamental model used since the creation of the Republican party. This is not to say that leaders acted irrationally—this economic policy had accompanied a period of rapid economic growth. Rather, many policies could have led to some growth; the one chosen, however, became increasingly dysfunctional over time. Even so, it would take a great shock, in the form of the Great Depression, and an electoral realignment to shake up the institutional and cognitive constraints created by what, at the time, was a small decision by the Republican party to endorse high tariffs.

---

cused instead on cheap raw materials to reduce the cost of manufacturing and boost the competitiveness of American products, and lower, not low, tariffs.

CHAPTER FOUR

Reforming Institutions: The Liberalization of Trade Policy

The passage of a trade act in 1934 marks a dramatic shift in American trade policy history. With its enactment, institutional control over commercial policy left Congress and moved to the executive branch, which, with this new flexibility, slowly but systematically lowered American barriers to trade. Inquiry into this era centers around two questions. First, what is the relationship between these institutional changes and the incorporation of liberal ideas into American trade policy? And second, what explains the pattern of protectionism in this liberal era?

As in the previous chapter, American policy in this period cannot be explained exclusively through the study of interests. Market incentives for liberalization existed, as they had for the previous fifty years, but were only a necessary, not a sufficient, cause for the change in domestic policy in the 1930s. Similarly, the pattern of aid in this period is not simply a function of either the power of groups seeking protection or changing economic or security goals. Rather, both trade openness and the pattern of industrial exceptions from liberalization reflect institutional structures and the ideational beliefs of elected officials.

The explanation for the role of ideas in policy making in this period runs parallel to that suggested in the previous chapter. In the preceding chapter I argued that at a critical juncture, the creation of the Republican party, political entrepreneurs built a coalition around a particular economic policy. After a period of experimentation, characterized by some fluctuation in tariff rates, high tariffs increasingly became institutionalized. The proof that protectionist ideas and resultant institutional structures constrained political leaders was a marked deviation in actual policy from that predicted from the objective interests of powerful groups and the country as a whole.

This chapter and the next focus on the role played by liberalizing ideas and resultant liberal institutions in the formation and maintenance of commercial policy. By the early 1930s, both the economic model and the policy process associated with high tariffs were in disrepute. This national mood created a policy window, allowing those critical of high-tariff policy to restructure tariff-making institutions to facilitate tariff reform. The shock of the Great Depression then created an opportunity for political entrepreneurs to restructure trade institutions so as to preclude what had occurred in the previous era: the use of tariffs for particularistic benefits.

The outcome was a radical change in policy. Although few political leaders agreed with classical economists on the eve of the Great Depression, few disputed their analytic model in the wake of World War II. Whereas earlier Congresses had encouraged interest-group participation in creating tariffs, the new system foreclosed such involvement. Nineteenth-century protectionism prospered with a party system that encouraged the distribution of tariff benefits, but the institutional structures enacted in the 1930s favored a market-driven trade policy.

These changes were not launched because free traders obtained control of Congress; although many were critical of protectionist doctrine in the midst of the Great Depression, the majority had not yet defined and promoted an alternative policy. Change occurred because of a favorable trading environment and institutional structures that made liberal ideas palatable. Generalized support for free trade developed much as had support for protectionism—slowly and only after the trade program delivered the economic growth its supporters had promised.

But policy change did not occur tabula rasa. Rather, the new rules and norms were created on top of old structures, incorporating aspects of previous trade policy. Liberal trade policy in the United States was never as thoroughly institutionalized as was its British predecessor. Although the beliefs of those who made policy in the nineteenth century were thoroughly discredited, the institutions, in particular the laws created to carry out the protectionist vision, were never dismantled. The result was an institutional hybrid; the legal basis upon which government administered its trade policy in the period after World War II was a mix of new liberal and old protectionist laws.

In sum, this and the next chapter argue that ideational change in this period occurred because free traders took advantage of institutional reforms so as to facilitate trade liberalization. Because of the association between wealth, peace, and liberalism, political elites came to agree with these liberal ideas. But as America's relative position in the world eroded, trade openness became increasingly problematic for elected officials. In this later period, liberal institutional structures allowed these officials to sustain their preferred open trade policy even in the face of strong domestic resistance. American laws did not uphold "textbook" free trade, however, but a uniquely American policy that defended both "free and fair" trade.

To demonstrate the interactive effects of ideas and institutions since the Great Depression, this chapter progresses as follows: first, the origin of the ideas that became central to the structuring and passage of the 1934 act are examined. The key change in the ideational beliefs of the majority in this period was not centered on economics; although the Depression clearly showed protectionism to be detrimental to economic growth, critics first looked to the organization of government itself as the source of economic problems. To demonstrate that liberal policies were far from hegemonic in this early period, this section juxtaposes the 1934 act to farm legislation which encouraged quite opposite trade behavior. Second, as in previous chapters, specific legislation is surveyed to assess whether or not laws reflect particular ideational patterns. Evidence suggests that legislation in this period was far more liberal than expected given earlier congressional conduct. And third, the chapter examines the resurgence of unfair trade beliefs in reaction to American economic decline. As opposed to the previous century, when unfair trade legislation was a guise for economic closure, in this period, elected officials turned to unfair trade laws as a means to enforce free-trade rules abroad.

THE ORIGINS OF ECONOMIC OPENNESS

When U.S. industry precipitously declined in the 1930s, policy makers were divided about how to effect recovery. In the early days of his administration, Franklin D. Roosevelt encouraged members of his administration, Cordell Hull, Rexford Tugwell, and George Peek—all of whom held radically different views on public policy—to devise responses to America's economic problems. The outcome was a trade policy based on vastly different philosophies. The administration acted unilaterally, devalued the dollar (the equivalent of a 50 percent increase in tariffs), abstained from international attempts to stabilize currencies, and initiated programs that forestalled trade liberalization. The Agricultural Adjustment Act (AAA) and the National Industrial Recovery Act (NIRA), central to the new policies, explicitly argued for higher, not lower, levels of import restrictions.[1] Simultaneously, however, the

[1] Section 3(e) of the NIRA gave the president broad powers over imports so that the United States would not "render ineffective or seriously . . . endanger the maintenance

administration pursued programs that had the potential for expanding trade. Following on the president's first-year promise that a new trade program was imminent, a trade reform act was passed in 1934.

Although not appreciated at the time, this legislation fundamentally altered American trade policy. In particular, two institutional innovations set the parameters of future American trade liberalization. First, the act granted the executive rather than Congress or an appointed commission, such as the International Trade Commission, the power to negotiate tariff levels. Second, the act mandated that tariff levels would be a response to reciprocal agreements with trading partners. Any reductions, however, would extend to all other parties granted "most-favored-nation" (MFN) status. Although these changes did not mandate the lowering of tariff levels, they created the opportunity for free traders to implement their particular vision of economic policy. Thus in mid-decade, after the National Recovery Administration (NRA) was ruled unconstitutional, Hull and others turned to the administrative structures legislated in 1934 to pursue trade liberalization actively. These institutional choices, which led to a uniquely American set of interrelationships within the trade administration, are explicable only by examining the beliefs of political entrepreneurs in these years.

Congressional Delegation to the President for Setting Tariffs

No one was surprised when Roosevelt's secretary of state, Cordell Hull, submitted a bill that lowered American tariffs. As early as 1907, Hull had gone on record as a free trader, and Roosevelt had supported tariff reductions before his election.[2] Because of the Democratic majority in Congress, many analysts assume that the 1934 act was nothing

---

of any code or agreement." The AAA in Section 22 established that imports ought not to "render ineffective, tend to render ineffective or materially interfere with" AAA programs; Section 32 authorized the secretary of agriculture to set aside 30 percent of annual customs revenues to subsidize exports.

[2] Elliot A. Rosen, *Hoover, Roosevelt, and the Brain Trust* (New York: Columbia University Press, 1977), pp. 106–7. It is doubtful, however, that the choice of Hull reflected a deep-seated commitment to trade reform on the part of the administration. During the campaign, Roosevelt had argued that, although Smoot-Hawley was overly isolationist, he still would extend protection to industry and agriculture. We know that Hull had little support within the Brain Trust during the 1932 campaign. Rosen, *Hoover*, p. 343. Men such as George Peek, who agreed with Hull on little, were much closer in philosophy to members of Roosevelt's entourage. It is clear from Hull's memoirs, however, that Hull thought he and Roosevelt had consonant trade policies: "We did not discuss foreign affairs to see whether we agreed in our attitudes toward them. Neither of us felt the need to do so." Cordell Hull, *The Memoirs of Cordell Hull* (New York: Macmillan, 1948), p. 159.

more than a typical reformist tariff. But such analyses overlook a simple point: the Democrats did not lower rates after their assumption of power as they had done in the past. In fact, the 1934 act was not a tariff revision at all—it was an amendment to Smoot-Hawley, authorizing a new set of procedures for reducing tariffs. From this perspective, the act more closely resembles its Republican predecessors than traditional Democratic measures.

Up through 1913, the Democratic party had advocated unilateral reductions in tariff levels. In 1932, the party pursued a different course. In part, this reflected an erosion of unity within the party on economic policy. In the years following World War I, many within and outside the party had begun to express skepticism about the worth of foreign trade. As the party increasingly found its electoral support among blue-collar labor, the fear that trade would undermine labor's economic position—the long-standing Republican anxiety—reappeared in policy debate.[3] But also, the traditionally liberal banking community had become increasingly unsure about trade policy. The prominent Chicago banker Walter Liechtenstein expressed a popular sentiment when he said, in 1925, that one could support free trade in theory but find it unworkable in practice "because the country's economic system was built on the theory of protection."[4]

This is not to suggest that the Democratic party was pro-protection. Roosevelt and most members of his administration criticized Smoot-Hawley and attributed economic decline in part to excessively high tariffs. But by the early 1930s, criticizing high tariffs was not uniquely Democratic sport.[5] Perhaps as a result of the growing dominance of equilibrium analysis among economists, or more probably because the aftershocks of Smoot-Hawley reinforced the predictions of reformists and undermined industrial confidence in using tariffs, both parties

[3] In the early days, Roosevelt was more committed to domestic labor and work standards than to trade, which was not inconsistent with the recommendations of a number of economists writing after World War I. See Joseph Dorfman, *The Economic Mind in American Civilization*, vol. 4 (New York: Viking, 1959), p. 6. On local support for protection, see Power Yung-Chao Chu, "A History of the Hull Trade Program, 1934–1939," diss., Columbia University, 1957, p. 112.

[4] Dorfman, *Economic Mind*, pp. 45–46.

[5] Hoover argued during the 1932 campaign: "Congressional [tariff] revisions are not only disturbing to business, but, with all their necessary collateral surroundings in lobbies, logrolling, and the activities of group interests, are disturbing to public confidence." Quoted in Robert Pastor, *Congress and the Politics of U.S. Foreign Economic Policy* (Berkeley: University of California Press, 1980), p. 69. Had he been reelected, Hoover probably would have considered tariff revision. In fact, many of the new administrative changes had their origins in Republican tariffs—not only reciprocity but the idea of executive control was associated with Republican, and not Democratic, policies. Thus the Democratic majority may explain the ease with which the bill passed Congress but not the important innovations it contained.

acknowledged that there was probably a relationship between American policy on imports and access to export markets. But a radical policy alternative like free trade was not then and never had been a Democratic doctrine. Democrats were interested in reform, not sharp departures from current policy.

Roosevelt himself was no clearer than was his party about his trade preferences. Although associating himself with Wilsonian internationalism, Roosevelt hedged on all issues that were potentially unpopular. Most members of his Brain Trust did not advocate liberal policies. Influential advisers such as Raymond Moley and Rexford B. Tugwell were far more interested in national than international solutions to world problems. All members of the president's entourage criticized Hull's suggestion to cut tariffs unilaterally by 10 percent, a suggestion that would have been far less problematic one hundred years earlier. Hugh Johnson, for instance, argued that "the world's high tariff system constituted a formidable economic reality. There could be no assurance that reductions in our own tariff structure would have a favorable impact on world trade or yield us any measurable economic benefit."[6] Thus Moley, reviewing commerical policy, noted that "nothing with which we have been dealing has been subject to such wide differences of opinion."[7]

Given these disagreements, even among the party elite, it is no surprise that by 1932 Roosevelt's campaign pledge was for only moderate changes in commerical policy. He argued that the United States should have "a tariff program based on profitable exchange for each nation, with benefit to each nation, but never at the expense of a violent and general shake-up in business."[8] Although he stated that current tariffs were generally too high, Roosevelt never responded to Hoover's challenge about which duties he would lower. By the close of the campaign, Roosevelt had pledged continued protection for the industrial sector and a tariff policy that would protect the domestic marketplace for American farmers.[9]

Roosevelt's election did not preordain trade liberalization. In an early report on the future of trade, the Department of Commerce concluded that there were two trade reform strategies that the administration could pursue. Department economists argued that the tariff could become a tool for improving industrial productivity. The administration could rate industries and refuse to protect those that were inefficient.

---

[6] Rosen, *Hoover*, p. 344.
[7] Ibid., p. 345.
[8] Ibid., p. 346.
[9] Ibid., p. 347.

In many ways, this road was the one Democrats had followed in 1913. The Commerce Department's other alternative was to recognize that trade was a two-way street and that, therefore, reciprocal tariff cuts would be appropriate. Either alternative could have become law. The second path was consonant with the views of Secretary of State Cordell Hull.[10]

But to give Hull's free-trade ideas all the credit for the trade reform program would be as analytically misleading as to credit the Democratic party with finally achieving its hundred-year-old platform. Hull was successful at trade liberalization only because his ideas were consonant with the new institutional structures. In retrospect, his support of executive delegation was probably more critical to the history of the trade reform program than was his commitment to liberalism. Testifying at the House Ways and Means Committee hearings, Hull defended the central innovation in the act: the delegation of power to the executive. He argued that the new law merely gave the president powers similar to those held by leaders in the vast majority of nations:

> It is manifest that unless the Executive is given authority to deal with the existing great emergency somewhat on a parity with that exercised by the executive departments of so many other governments for purposes of negotiating and carrying into effect trade agreements, it will not be practical or possible for the United States to pursue with any degree of success the proposed policy of restoring our lost international trade.[11]

But Hull had been arguing this position consistently since he arrived in Congress. Before the Depression, his views were in the minority among party members.

Hull's position became salient in the 1930s because, on the eve of the Depression, both the content and the method of setting tariffs faced broad-based criticism. Before the Depression, many had argued that the legislature could no longer oversee the increasing number of American products on the tariff schedule. It was repeatedly suggested that the lack of a scientific basis for setting tariffs was the cause of

[10] Although Hull consistently defended liberal trade, he had a limited understanding of why liberalization was in America's interest. William Allen, in a study of Hull's trade philosophy, finds that although Hull's conclusions were generally correct, they were often correct for the wrong reasons. Allen, "The International Trade Philosophy of Cordell Hull, 1907–1933," *American Economic Review* 43 (March 1953): 116.

[11] U.S. Congress, House of Representatives, *Hearings on Reciprocal Trade Agreements*, 73d Cong., 2d sess., pp. 5–6. Hull was essentially correct. By 1934, with only a few exceptions, the major commercial countries of Europe and Latin America had moved to a system whereby their heads of state could enter into reciprocal trade agreements with other countries.

constant tariff revisions and the resultant economic uncertainty.[12] Men across the political spectrum, from Andrew Carnegie to Frank Taussig, agreed on this point.[13] Not only inefficiency in procedures drew criticism. Many believed that the institutions themselves were essentially corrupt. Tariff policy was wrangled behind closed doors and tailored for particular groups and powerful lobbies. In short, critics claimed that the traditional means of setting tariffs, which involved months of tedious hearings in which unreliable information about the economy was pitted against partisan pressures, was outdated.[14]

The highest tariff in America's history had been legislated against this backdrop. The Depression brought immediate and wide-ranging recriminations against congressional tariff setting. The electorate soundly punished the party in control, reminding both parties that hard times resulted in electoral defeat. Few congressional representatives disagreed on the need for trade reform. At the beginning of the Great Depression, reform ideas centered on two ways to change the tariff-setting process. Both entailed the delegation of congressional power, either to the executive or to an independent agency. If one knew little of the history of thought on tariffs, one might assume that the latter option would have been chosen and the Tariff Commission (TC)

[12] The tariff acts of 1890, 1894, and 1897 each comprised about sixty pages of statutes. By 1922, tariff acts were over one hundred pages long. Congress's increasing difficulties were reflected in the comment of Representative Halvor Steenerson (R-Minn.), in 1909, who described congressional "embarrassment for lack of reliable information in the work of tariff revision." See Daniel Tarullo, "Law and Politics in Twentieth Century Tariff History," *UCLA Law Review* 34 (December 1986): 292–95.

[13] Ibid., p. 294.

[14] By 1934, accounts of the effects of private interests on the political process were well-known. See, for example, Arthur Bentley, *The Process of Government* (Bloomington: Principia Press, 1908); Edward Herring, *Group Representation before Congress* (Baltimore: Johns Hopkins University Press, 1929); Peter Odegard, *Pressure Politics; The Story of the Anti-Saloon League* (New York: Columbia University Press, 1928). As early as 1911, Ida Tarbell writes of "the shock and disgust . . . in the discovery that our tariffs are not good and bad applications of the principles of protection, but that they are good or bad bargains." Tarbell, *The Tariff in Our Times* (New York: Macmillan, 1911), pp. 363–64. In 1935, E. E. Schattschneider would explain: "In tariff making, perhaps more than in any other kind of legislation, Congress writes bills which no one intended. All policies are defected and warped in being reduced to statute, but where the difficulties of the process are great, the original design may be battered beyond recognition and the policy utterly confused. This is especially true in tariff legislation because law making in this field is beset with incomparable embarrassments and perplexities, and the labor in evolving the statute is great to the point of agony." *Politics, Pressures and the Tariff: A Study of Free Enterprise in Pressure Politics* (New York: Prentice-Hall, 1935), pp. 9–10. Even Senator Reed Smoot (R-Utah), champion of protection, saw problems with the system: "It is the desire of all parties that the tariff shall be equitable to the producer and consumer alike and that it shall not unnecessarily burden our foreign commerce. But to achieve this result under world conditions existing today frequent modifications of rates are necessary. Present conditions can be met in a far better way through administrative action than by legislative enactment." *Congressional Record*, 67th Cong., 2d sess., p. 5875.

granted primary responsibility for tariff setting. Following the example of the Interstate Commerce Commission (ICC), the TC's power could easily have been expanded to include setting tariffs. After all, in the 1920s, the TC had been indispensable in providing information and guidance to those representatives who sought its advice.

Nevertheless, the Democratic party spurned this solution, for in 1934 it assumed that the TC was an instrument of Republican trade policy. In the 1920s and 1930s, the Republican party's response to reformers had been to enlarge the TC's responsibility. Although a Democratic president had created a bipartisan Tariff Commission, the Republican party in the 1920s had used the commission as an agent of its high-tariff policy. For example, in 1922, the Republican majority had expanded the commission's mandate by empowering it to join the president in adjusting tariffs in line with congressional criteria.[15] Again in 1930, the Republican majority turned to the TC to rule on which industries might need tariff hikes to equalize production costs.[16] Its findings were then reported to the president, who could respond only by choosing between the TC-recommended rate and the existing rate.

Since the Democrats never seriously considered the TC option, the second alternative—delegating power to the president—was inherently more appealing, especially given a Democratic president.[17] Roosevelt also had good reason to believe that the courts would not question expanding his authority into the trade arena. The key problem with such delegation in the past had been the lack of judicial approval. But the Supreme Court had ruled differently on the constitutionality of Section 315 of the 1922 act. In *J. W. Hampton Jr. and Co.* v. *United States,*

[15] Of the five hundred applications for tariff review received between 1922 and 1928, the TC rejected over half after preliminary consideration. Of the one hundred that were investigated by 1928, the president changed tariffs in twenty-six. All but two were duty hikes.

[16] In 1922, Congress gave discretionary powers to the executive with the minimum-maximum provision while simultaneously expanding the TC's powers of investigation. Between 1922 and 1930, when the commission's role was reexamined, Congress and the president battled over who had what rights. The president maintained that he had the right to supervise investigations as well as make final decisions on changing tariffs. Members of the commission disagreed. In spring 1923 liberal members of the TC attempted to set the tariff agenda by choosing their own subjects for investigation (in this case, determining cost-of-production figures). The courts and Congress upheld the rights of the president; ultimately the problem was solved with the removal of the remaining liberal Wilson appointees. For a more thorough analysis of the period, see John Day Larkin, *The President's Control of the Tariff* (Cambridge, Mass.: Harvard University Press, 1936), pp. 8–30.

[17] The partisan constitution of government was a necessary but not a sufficient explanation for party action. Ex ante, no one could have guessed that a long period of Democratic party hegemony had begun. This is not to argue that party control did not matter. In all previous attempts by the Republican party to expand executive discretion, the Democrats had been vociferous opponents on constitutional grounds.

the court compared tariff making with railroad regulation and argued that if "Congress were to be required to fix every rate, it would be impossible to exercise the power at all." In this case, the court suggested, the executive was merely executing the law, not making it.[18] Clearly, granting the executive such discreation fit well within Roosevelt's general political strategy of executive aggrandizement.[19]

Further, the overwhelming agreement that unilateral tariff cuts were no longer an appropriate way to reduce tariffs reinforced the logic of executive power. As Assistant Secretary of State Francis Sayre explained, if the United States pursued a unilateral strategy, "we would not thereby gain immediate reduction of foreign trade barriers, nor would we thereby secure ourselves against discrimination on the part of foreign nations against American goods."[20] But if the United States were to cut duties only upon a negotiated agreement, the president held the constitutional authority to enter into such negotiations with foreign governments. If Congress wanted tariff reductions through negotiated trade agreements, it would need to invest the executive with the appropriate powers. This was the logic that the administration offered and Congress accepted.

In sum, the 1934 congressional delegation to the executive office was an unusual moment in congressional history. Until Roosevelt, Congress often gave an administrative agency the power to implement its acts but retained oversight, appointment, and budget authority. Here, Congress not only gave up administrative rights, it also relinquished policy and oversight control to the president. Congress set tariff policy after 1934 only in the broadest sense. The president was authorized to lower tariffs to a specified limit for a specified time period. He could set individual tariffs, cutting the current rates substantially. Congress could have mandated that it ratify all treaties negotiated by the president. Instead, its members specifically denied themselves even this au-

---

[18] Tarullo points to a contradiction in the *Hampton* ruling. Under the flexible clause, the president did not have to start an investigation. This allowed him, if he wanted, to ignore Congress's cost-of-production principle and decide independently under what situations he would begin an investigation. "Law and Politics," p. 321. This discretion was noted by the opposition in the Senate. Senator Irvine Lenroot (R-Wisc.) complained that "Congress has no power to delegate power to the President to consider freight rates in one case and disregard them in the other. He cannot constitutionally be given such option." *Congressional Record*, 67th Cong., 2d sess., p. 11217. The president could also determine how to compute the cost of production, thus rationalizing almost any tariff rate. This, too, was pointed out in testimony. See statement by Senator Wesley Jones (R-Wash.). Ibid., p. 11043–44.

[19] On the logic of delegation in this period see Judith Goldstein and Barry Weingast, "The Origins of American Trade Policy: Rules, Coalitions and International Politics," unpublished paper, 1993.

[20] Francis B. Sayre, *America Must Act* (Boston: World Peace Foundation, 1936), p. 34.

thority. After 1934, treaties that were within the reductions specified, ex ante, by Congress were enacted and implemented through executive order.

Three factors explain the form of congressional delegation in 1934. First, the reason for congressional delegation explains the lack of oversight. As Assistant Secretary of State Henry Grady noted during hearings on the 1940 reauthorization of executive tariff authority, "When the question of Senate ratification is discussed, I cannot help but wonder if what is not desired is Senate non-ratification . . . ratification is tantamount to repeal."[21] Congress's interpretation of the dire economic impact of Smoot-Hawley led it to fear all aspects of tariff setting, including agreeing to trade treaties. Second, the lack of an administrative solution to the tariff problem is best explained by the perception of a close association between the TC and the Republican tariff program. And third, the enfranchisement of the executive was made possible by new court decisions that granted the executive rights in this area and motivated by the belief that negotiated reductions could not occur without presidential involvement. As an administrative representative explained during hearings in the House, "national and international economic conditions make broad executive discretion powers imperative."[22]

But delegation alone cannot explain the opening of American markets. Although the Democrats condemned Smoot-Hawley, the alternative was not necessarily liberal trade. As late as 1930, Jacob Viner could remark that "the contrast is striking between the almost undisputed sway which the protectionist doctrine has over the minds of statesmen and its almost complete failure to receive credentials of intellectual respectability from the economists."[23] But protectionism was an idea whose time was over. Because of this disenchantment, the Hull alternative became increasingly appealing. By the mid-1920s, many analysts had pointed to foreign policy problems which derived from America's high tariffs. John Larkin, writing in 1926, articulated a popular sentiment:

Any tariff law framed solely upon the basis of the difference in cost of production has and can have but one object in view; that is, the granting of aid to domestic industry and totally ignoring whatever effect such action would have upon the Federal revenues . . . [and] our international

---

[21] *Extension of Reciprocal Trade Agreements Act: Hearings before the House Committee on Ways and Means on H.R.J. Res. 407*, 76th Cong., 3d sess., p. 726.

[22] Henry Tasca, *Reciprocal Trade Policy of the United States* (Philadelphia: University of Pennsylvania Press, 1938), p. 33.

[23] Jacob Viner, *International Economics* (Glencoe, Ill.: Free Press, 1951), p. 109.

trade. . . . [These] are such important factors in our present economic life that they cannot be ignored without baneful results to our future welfare and prosperity.[24]

Protectionism not only spelled disaster for the American economy but it bred political disaffection and electoral punishment. The message of Smoot-Hawley was all too clear to the new freshman Democratic class: tariff politics and high tariffs breed economic and political decline. But liberalization could have taken many forms. The path chosen reflected contemporary beliefs about the way tariffs should and should not be reformed.

Reciprocity and Most-Favored-Nation Status

Delegation of authority made liberalization possible. The legislated manner of trade liberalization reflected ideas about the optimal form and general benefits of international trade treaties. In this period, the reconceptualization of two old policies—the extension of most-favored-nation status and reciprocity—explains much of the trade liberalization program that was to follow. But as suggested below, neither of these policies was inherently liberal; depending on how they were implemented by political leaders, they could either encourage or discourage trade.

By accepting an unconditional MFN principle, a country promises that it will give all importing nations the lowest tariff barrier it had negotiated with any one of them. This principle was not universally accepted in the United States before the 1920s. Until that time, the United States negotiated agreements based on conditionality, or the provision that tariff concessions would be extended only to countries that gave the United States the same concessions. Such a proviso led to discriminatory agreements among parties. If all nations cannot benefit from a tariff reduction, then the agreement, by definition, is discriminatory.

From February 1778, when the United States concluded a trade treaty with France, until the 1920s, just about all American treaties held the same qualification found in the first treaty: "The most Christian King and the United States engage mutually not to grant any particular favor to other nations, in respect of commerce and navigation, which shall not immediately become common to the other party, who shall enjoy the same favor *freely if the concession was freely made, or on allowing the same compensation if the concession was conditional* (emphasis

---

[24] Larkin, *President's Control of the Tariff*, pp. 4–5.

added).[25] The italicized phrase guaranteed that third parties did not get the same treatment as the signer of the agreement unless a specific concession was made to the United States.

The United States formally adopted the principle of unconditional MFN status in 1923. American acceptance of the principle was celebrated with little fanfare or understanding of the impact this small procedural change would have on future trade relations. The move to unconditionality developed out of a controversy over differing interpretations of the powers granted in the flexible tariff provision of the tariff act of 1922. As understood at the time of its passage, flexibility was supposed to stop discrimination against U.S. exports in the tradition of earlier reciprocity clauses. Its inclusion was championed by Senator Reed Smoot (of later Smoot-Hawley fame). Congress gave no hint in its discussion that it interpreted this section to mean that, in the future, the United States should avoid discriminatory agreements. One member of the Tariff Commission, a proponent of unconditionality, however, understood the legal implications of the wording of the section. After passage, William Culbertson wrote to Secretary of State Charles Evans Hughes explaining that if the intent of Congress were to be followed, all discriminatory agreements had to be eliminated.[26] According to Culbertson, Congress had mandated that the United States increase duties in all cases in which a nation did not give U.S. exports the same preferential treatment it gave to those of another country. This meant that the president must increase the tariff on the goods of all nations that were party to a tariff agreement without the United States. Culbertson went on to argue that Congress could not have intended Section 317 to be used in this fashion. To fulfill the will of Congress, the United States would need to render all treaties unconditional. Secretary Hughes communicated this to President Harding, who, with little thought, approved it as a new policy. In August, it was announced that all future treaties would contain an unconditional MFN clause.

There was no mandate to lower tariffs in the 1920s, and the issue of unconditionality was moot. It would be important only when tariffs became negotiable in 1934. By then, however, the United States had negotiated such treaties for a decade.[27] Did Congress intend to liberal-

---

[25] Richard Carlton Snyder, *The Most-Favored-Nation Clause* (New York: Kings Crown Press, 1948), p. 29.

[26] William J. Culbertson, *Reciprocity* (New York: McGraw-Hill, 1937), pp. 244–58.

[27] At the time of passage of the 1934 act, the United States had already moved to negotiate unconditional treaties with ten countries which represented 12 percent of total American exports. There were an additional seventeen unconditional executive agreements covering another 10 percent of total exports. Still in force were thirteen

ize trade in the 1920s and did Section 317 indicate that intent? Some scholars, including Culbertson, argue that this is the case.[28] In Congress, however, no one had argued that Section 317 mandated a change in MFN status. In fact, the bill's sponsors resolved the debate by assuring senators that Section 317 in no way was to be interpreted to eliminate conditional MFN treaties. It is implausible to insist that Congress intended such an interpretation. But whether knowingly or not, the United States had backed into a more liberal trade posture.[29]

Not only did sentiment about the efficacy of MFN agreements change in this period, but even more fundamental was a change in the interpretation and use of the term "reciprocity." As argued in the previous chapter, reciprocity was a policy closely associated with Republican high tariffs. Reciprocity legislation in the nineteenth century gave the executive authority to punish other nations that did not give American exporters "fair" access to their markets. As early as 1883, President Arthur had asked Congress whether it would be "advisable to provide some measure of equitable retaliation in our relations with governments which discriminate against our own."[30] Again in 1890, the idea appeared in Section 3 of the trade act, which provided penalty duties on items imported from countries whose duties on American products were, in the opinion of the president, "unequal and unreasonable." Reciprocity was a way to penalize other countries—not a carrot to liberalize world trade but a stick to use if foreign nations discriminated against American products. This form of reciprocity was substantive bilateralism: the United States negotiated to give and gain equal concessions.[31] At a time when the United States granted only conditional

conditional treaties and conditional executive agreements covering 34 percent of exports. Previous to the change in policy in 1923, the United States had signed only three unconditional treaties, in 1850, 1871, and 1881, all recognized at the time as exceptions to policy. Percy W. Bidwell, "Tariff Policy of the United States: A Study of Recent Experience," Report to the Second International Studies Conference on the State and Economic Life (New York: Council on Foreign Relations, 1933), pp. 4, 5, 8.

[28] Culbertson, *Reciprocity*, p. 69; and Tasca, *Reciprocal Trade Policy*, pp. 116–21.

[29] There were sound, functional reasons for a shift from conditional to unconditional MFN policies after World War I. William Kelly, *Studies in U.S. Commerical Policy* (Chapel Hill: University of North Carolina Press, 1963), pp. 44–94, argues that the United States enjoyed relative immunity from discrimination before the war because few U.S. actions before 1890 might have inspired foreign retaliation; the United States benefited from the unconditional treaties of other nations (particularly European treaties); and noncompetitive agricultural goods dominated American exports. But increasingly hostile trade, the necessity for new treaties, growing reliance on manufactured goods, and the shift from debtor to creditor made the United States vulnerable to discrimination after World War I.

[30] Quoted in Larkin, *President's Control of the Tariff*, p. 48.

[31] Tasca, *Reciprocal Trade Policy*, p. 6.

MFN status, such negotiations were discriminatory by definition and were difficult to expand multilaterally.

Such an approach was challenged by the supporters of liberalization, who spoke of reciprocity in terms of "formal bilateralism," that is, bilateral action with multilateral implications.[32] Put more simply, negotiations are conducted between countries whose import-export mix gives them the incentive to grant each other a trade concession (presumably with the low-cost producer). Once a concession is granted to the principal supplier, other nations are also granted that new tariff. In the United States, those who argued for formal bilateralism were, in effect, arguing for negotiations based on unconditional MFN principles, because as long as the United States maintained a single-column tariff system, a change in a tariff resulting from a bilateral agreement would benefit any importer of that product.

Thinking on reciprocity changed gradually. In 1919, the TC issued a report on the history of American reciprocity. The report concluded that the "policy of special arrangements, such as the United States has followed in recent decades, leads to troublesome complications."[33] But a return of Republican control of government brought a return to isolation and little interest in using international bargains to maximize America's economic interests. In response to the quickly failing economy, the Democrats backed a bill at the start of the seventy-second Congress, in 1931, which included, among other features, a call for reciprocal trade agreements "under a policy of mutual concessions." Although Hoover vetoed this bill, its reciprocity proposal appeared in the tariff plank of the Democratic national platform and was endorsed by then governor Roosevelt as well as exporting interests and key academics.[34]

But ambiguity remained in the Democratic party's position on trade negotiations and the implications for trade of the 1934 endorsement of both reciprocity and unconditional MFN treaties. Most still accepted the contradictory visions of reciprocity as retaliation and the idea of unconditional MFN agreements. Even the State Department's interpretation of the Trade Agreements Act of 1934 failed to absorb the new meaning of reciprocity, contending that the act "provides that the duties . . . shall be extended to all countries but provided that they may be confined to such countries as do not discriminate against American commerce."[35] The State Department's press release argued that such

---

[32] Ibid.
[33] Bidwell, "Tariff Policy," p. 52.
[34] Ibid., pp. 57–59.
[35] Quoted in Larkin, *President's Control of the Tariff*, p. 54.

ability to punish is, in fact, "wholly in accord with the unconditional MFN principle."[36] Different members of the administration voiced similar misunderstandings. Hull, who saw the 1934 act as a doorway to liberalization, saw no contradiction between the 1922 and 1930 acts, which legislated retaliatory provisions through the maximum and minimum provision, and the 1923 decision to conclude only unconditional MFN agreements. He argued that if the United States signed with the principal low-cost producer, no industry would be hurt by secondary importers. This view was not universally shared. The more common view was represented by George Peek, the special adviser for foreign trade, who argued that the ideas of reciprocity and unconditional MFN principles were not compatible.[37] He continued to advocate negotiations on a country-by-country basis. In the short term, Peek's exit from government allowed Hull to orchestrate multilateral trade agreements. In the long term, the successful culmination of trade agreements and the ensuing rapid recovery assured an internationalist meaning for reciprocity.

The 1934 Act

In all respects the 1934 act differed from previous legislation. Politically, in the House, where Smoot-Hawley had elicited eleven thousand pages of testimony in forty-three days, the 1934 act had fourteen witnesses, six of whom were from the administration.[38] For the first time in years, the minority was permitted to help formulate the bill and amend the act on the floor.[39] The week-long Senate committee hearings were brief, but on the floor there was considerably more discussion.[40] The chief controversy surrounded the delegation of authority to the executive. In the end, this amendment to the 1930 act passed both houses with a nearly perfect partisan vote. The bill enabled the president to reduce rates up to 50 percent from Smoot-Hawley levels. Henceforth, he would also be able to conclude trade agreements without further congressional action. Commenting on the loss of this traditional congressional power, the minority report stated that the bill "places in the hands of the President and those to whom he may dele-

[36] Ibid.

[37] Ibid., p. 55.

[38] Lawrence Chamberlain, *President, Congress and Legislation* (New York: Columbia University Press, 1946), p. 133. All but two of the nonadministration witnesses opposed the bill, although all supported the general objective of increasing trade.

[39] The act came to the floor without a closed rule but with a large enough majority to ensure rejection of all opposition amendments.

[40] Hearings ran from April 26 through May 1. Sixty-five witnesses either appeared or filed briefs. Chamberlain, *President, Congress and Legislation*, p. 135.

gate authority the absolute power of life and death over every industry dependent on tariff protection."[41]

More fundamentally, the 1934 law legislated into force new ideas on tariff administration and bargaining. No longer would the United States have a single-column tariff system. New trade agreements would bring lower rates for all countries with MFN status while others would be subject to the higher Smoot-Hawley rates. Private parties, once so influential in setting their own rates, would have their hearing but in an arena tangential to tariff setting. If interest groups were the big losers, the big winner was the president, who now had power over tariff classification and reclassification, control of valuation procedures, and the statutory right to reduce rates.

To fulfill the mandate of the 1934 act, new institutional structures were created and populated by individuals whose professional and personal interests lay in tariff reductions. Within the Department of State, three committees now focused exclusively on the foreign policy aspects of trade. First, the Executive Commercial Policy Committee was created in November 1933 to coordinate American commerical policy "with a view to centralizing in the hands of one agency supervision of all government action affecting our imports and export trade."[42] Members were high officials from various government departments. Second, the Trade Agreements Committee, created to help instigate and conduct oversight of trade treaties, included representatives from the Departments of State, Agriculture, Treasury, and Commerce. A third group, the Committee for Reciprocity Information, was created to assure Roosevelt's promise that "no sound and important American interest [would] be injuriously disturbed" by the trade agreements program.[43] Its chief activity was to hold public hearings. Over the ensuing few years, members of all three committees became convinced of the value of trade liberalization. Functionally, they diverted attention from Congress; professionally, they saw their jobs as assuring the continuation of the liberalization program.[44]

No greater change was felt with the law's passage than in Congress, which abdicated direct tariff-making responsibility and adopted a new

---

[41] Quoted in Schattschneider, *Politics, Pressures and the Tariff,* p. 145.

[42] Tasca, *Reciprocal Trade Policy,* p. 29.

[43] John Day Larkin, *Trade Agreements: A Study in Democratic Methods* (New York: Columbia University Press, 1940), p. 69.

[44] For a thorough explanation of the initial state groups charged with trade liberalization, see Tasca, *Reciprocal Trade Policy,* pp. 45–73. The Trade Agreements Committee continued to exist until 1962, when it was replaced by the cabinet-level Trade Information Committee. The committee was to be chaired by the special trade representative, a new position in the executive office of the president, whose chief job was to be chief U.S. negotiator and the central coordinator and adviser on trade issues.

role in the making of policy. Henceforth, Congress would act as a "balancer" and a broker; Congress would assure the passage of a "fair" trade bill that supplied mechanisms to safeguard America's interests at home and abroad and, although eschewing direct protectionism as bad economic policy, relied on executive actions to aid particular constituents. But as is argued below, a liberal trade policy was in no way guaranteed by the passage of this legislation.

Agricultural Trade Policy and the Idea of Parity

The path to trade liberalization—from the 1923 decision on MFN agreements, to the 1934 act, and ultimately to the creation of a multilateral trade organization—was only one side of American trade policy. On the other side were events that occurred simultaneously in the area of agricultural trade.

If the 1934 trade act set the United States down a path of reducing barriers to manufacturing trade, the 1933 Agricultural Adjustment Act accomplished just the opposite for farm products. While liberalization in nonagricultural goods was guided by the twin assumptions of reciprocity and MFN agreements, agriculture policy was far more influenced by the idea of parity. Whereas the former concepts granted a place for international markets to regulate the demand and price of American products, the latter idea forced government to regulate just about all aspects of production.

The notion of a parity price developed in the 1920s. In essence, it implied that the agricultural sector should garner prices and profits akin to those found in industrial production, or at minimum, at a time when the agricultural sector was relatively prosperous. Legislative guarantees of a parity price were to be unrelated to economic factors such as the world price for a particular commodity. Once parity was established as the backbone of agricultural policy, competing notions that prices should be set by world supply and demand conditions were ignored.[45] The policy implication of guaranteed parity was problematic

[45] In the Agricultural Adjustment Act of 1933, prices were to be set so as "to reestablish prices to farmers at a level that will give agricultural commodities a purchasing power with respect to articles that farmers buy, equivalent to the purchasing power of agricultural commodities in the basic period [i.e., 1909–14]." In the Soil Conservation and Domestic Allotment Act of 1936, the parity goal shifted from price equality of agricultural commodities and the prices of things farmers purchased to income equality between farm and nonfarm populations. In 1938, the act moved back to an emphasis on agricultural incomes and the products farmers consume by providing for direct parity payments to producers of the basic crops equal to the difference between the market price and the fair exchange value. As one commentator noted in 1938, "The congressmen did not want to hear any more nonsense about equalizing incomes—what they wanted was a

from the perspective of those who advocated open trade borders: the parity price maintained farm prices in the United States above those found on world markets, thereby creating an incentive for producers in other nations to export farm products to the United States. Without explicit import controls, government-set prices would be undermined.

Farm Legislation

Legislators well understood that increased competition in the home market held the potential for undermining agricultural supports. The response was to enact trade restrictions. Thus Congress included in the original and subsequent authorizations on farm subsidies the right both to set import quotas and to give export subsidies if necessary to maintain prices. The ideological underpinning of trade liberalization— that is, that government should rely on markets to set price and quantity—was never accepted as a tenet of agricultural policy.

The 1933 act, which revolutionized American farm policy, was the last of a series of attempts to deal with an agricultural depression that began at the end of World War I.[46] The Agricultural Adjustment Administration in the Department of Agriculture, created by the 1933 act, was given the authority to reduce production and to increase prices for seven basic crops—wheat, cotton, corn, hogs, rice, tobacco, and milk and its products. In subsequent acts, other commodities were added and other means were given to the administration to elevate farm prices. The focus of government activity was an attempt to reduce supply; ultimately, direct cash payments were used as an incentive for farmers to stop production. Between 1934 and the outbreak of the war, the government paid about $4.4 billion to producers in return for their not bringing crops to market.[47]

From the start, farm groups had little interest in and much apprehension about the reciprocal trade agreements program. In testimony, the Grange—one of the best-organized of the farm groups—opposed all forms of trade liberalization and the Farm Bureau argued that only industrial tariffs should be lowered. Their attempt to exclude agriculture from the program lost by a relatively small margin (54 to 33) in

proper price for their cotton and corn. If they got that, income would take care of itself." John Black, *Parity, Parity, Parity* (Cambridge, Mass.: Harvard University Committee on Research in the Social Sciences, 1942), p. 57.

[46] See Judith Goldstein, "The Impact of Ideas on Trade Policy: The Origins of U.S. Agricultural and Manufacturing Policies," *International Organization* 43 (Winter 1989): 31–72.

[47] Allan Rau, *Agricultural Policy and Trade Liberalization in the United States, 1934–1956* (Geneva: E. Droz, 1957), p. 66.

the Senate in 1934. Farm opposition, however, did not disappear with the passage of the 1934 act. As late as the 1945 extension of the Reciprocal Trade Agreements Act, wool, cattle, sugar, and dairy interests, among others, opposed the extension in testimony before the House.

In retrospect, these groups had little to fear. The Roosevelt administration showed itself willing to protect agricultural products if necessary to maintain farm incomes. On the heels of the 1934 trade act, Congress passed, and Roosevelt signed, the Jones-Costigan Act, explicitly mandating sugar import quotas. Further, under section 22 of the AAA, the administration authorized import quotas on wheat and wheat products, butter, milk products, cheese, oats, barley, rye, rye flour, peanuts, wheat, wheat flour, cotton, and cotton waste. The administration also limited imports of filberts, almonds, flax seed, linseed oil, and peanut oil through import fees. Import licenses were deemed necessary for other products, including butter and apples. Wheat, wheat flour, cotton, and cotton waste imports were allocated by country, in direct conflict with the equal treatment concept that was to become a central norm of the General Agreement on Tariffs and Trade (GATT).

But it was more than the use of import quotas which revealed fundamental conflict between free-trade ideas and American policy. Under Section 32 of the AAA, the U.S. government was authorized to use export subsidies for agricultural exports. Under the 1935 version of the law, the secretary of agriculture was granted the right to use up to 30 percent of gross customs receipts to increase farm exports "by the payment of benefits . . . or of indemnities for losses incurred in connection with such exportation." In his January 1936 budget message to Congress, Roosevelt publicly acknowledged the contradictions in his legislative proposals. His public response was explicit support for liberalization. Roosevelt requested that export subsidy provisions be repealed. But indicative of sentiment at the time, he was ignored by Congress. Thus in 1944, when Roosevelt's State Department declared America's intention to assure a multilateral and liberal future for world trade, the Agriculture Department allocated $118 million to subsidize exports of wheat, cotton, corn, tobacco, fruits, tree nuts, and dairy and meat products.[48]

On the whole, increased domestic and foreign demand for American farm products during World War II made prewar agricultural programs inoperative. After the Lend-Lease Act passed Congress in 1941, agricultural products were shipped abroad in ever-increasing amounts. By the end of 1944, $5 billion worth of agricultural products had been exported under the program's provisions. Cotton export subsidies were

[48] Ibid., p. 80.

stopped in 1942; wheat export subsidies ended in 1943.[49] Although price supports were in effect for 166 different agricultural goods in 1945, the policy was cheap; the war kept market prices at about their price-support level. The result was that at the close of the war, the agricultural sector had expanded by 20 percent. Prices paid to farmers were about 200 percent above their prewar levels.[50]

To encourage war production and assuage the fear of drastic price declines at the close of the war, the Steagall Amendment to the extension of the Commodity Credit Corporation in July 1941 increased government supports not only for the original group of protected products but also for expanded supports to other agricultural goods. Few forgot what increased output in World War I had done; government officials assumed and promised that at the end of the current war, price and production controls would be used to avert a second agricultural depression. Yet counter to these predictions, the war's end did not herald a slump in prices. The demand for American products actually rose, leading to even higher farm prices. Output reached unprecedented levels. By 1947, the average prices received by farmers were 25 percent above those received the year before. This meant that the provisions established by the Steagall Amendment remained dormant. Only in a few products—potatoes, eggs, butter, dried milk, wool, and turkey—did the government employ price-support programs.

Even so, as American negotiators moved ahead on the trade regime, they found that agricultural supports and farm protections were difficult, if not impossible, to overturn. In the 1945 renewal of the trade act, Congressman Stephen Pace of Georgia had offered an amendment to safeguard further the farm program from trade treaties. Though the amendment did not pass, it was clear that Congress's commitment to liberalization did not extend to the removal of protections for agriculture. When in 1948 the demand for agricultural goods finally fell, price-support programs went immediately into force. The Steagall Amendment, which was set to expire, was replaced by similar and more permanent protections in the Agricultural Act of 1948. And in 1951, the extension of the trade act formally stated that trade agreements could not be concluded in violation of existing agricultural programs.

In sum, as the United States embarked on the creation of a new liberal international trade regime, its own domestic policy was mired with inconsistencies. Although the State Department was unequivocal on the benefits of multilateral trade liberalization for the American

---

[49] Under the Surplus Property Act of 1940, export subsidies for cotton were begun again in 1944.

[50] Rau, *Agricultural Policy,* p. 88.

economy, the Department of Agriculture declared simultaneously that under no conditions could the United States delegate control over import protections for farm products. It was not that the intrinsic interests of the agricultural sector were orthagonal to trade liberalization. By the late 1940s, the prosperity of American agriculture was clearly associated with exports: the United States was supplying 39 percent of the world's wheat, 41 percent of the tobacco, and 49 percent of the cotton. Few could ignore the importance of agriculture to America's export economy. Yet both farm groups and elected officials were politically wedded to government controls on price and supply. It would take twenty years for producers and political leaders to realize the costs of this strategy.

Constructing an International Trade Regime

During World War I, Cordell Hull proposed in a resolution to the House of Representatives that the United States establish a multilateral trade organization. Although dismissed at the time, the idea reappeared in State Department discussions as early as 1939. By that time, suggests Richard Gardner, postwar planning was infused by a common interest in assuring that unlike after the last war, there would not be "inadequate handling of economic problems. Consequently, [planners] placed great emphasis on economics in drawing blue-prints for a better world."[51]

Early in the war State Department officials began formal and informal meetings with British and Canadian officials to discuss postwar trade issues. In these talks and from ensuing policies, America's support for applying liberal principles to commercial policy became increasingly apparent. In the Atlantic Charter in August 1941, in Article VII of the Master Lend-Lease agreement in 1942, at Bretton Woods in 1944, and at the San Francisco conference to establish the United Nations, there were declarations of a causal relationship between open commercial policies and peaceful relations among states. Then two documents—the *Proposals for Expansion of World Trade and Employment*, completed by State Department officials in December 1945, and the *Suggested Charter for an International Trade Organization of the United Nations*, released in September of the following year—revealed specific plans for a trade regime that was liberal, multilateral, and nondiscriminatory. Both the GATT, which came into formal existence on the first of January 1948, and the International Trade Organization (ITO)

---

[51] Richard N. Gardner, *Sterling-Dollar Diplomacy* (New York: McGraw-Hill, 1969), p. 4.

Charter, ratified in the fall of 1947 in Havana, have their intellectual origins in these American documents.

In moving from their blueprints, State Department officials confronted numerous problems. Perhaps most fundamental was that nations agreed only abstractly with American principles for building a new trade regime. The variation in national objectives was most visible in talks between the two key negotiating nations: Britain and the United States. The British argued that the goal of trade policy was full employment; trade liberalization was an acceptable strategy only to the extent that it met this goal. State Department negotiators, however, agreed only that changes in trade policy should not be at the cost of the economic vitality of particular sectors or producers. They, as opposed to the U.S. Department of Agriculture, never agreed that the trade regime should be created to meet domestic political goals.

The general position of the United States was outlined in the original American *Proposal:* "What is needed is a broad and yet detailed agreement among many nations, dealing at one time with many different sorts of government restrictions upon trade, reducing all of them at once on a balanced and equitable basis, and stating rules and principles within which the restrictions permitted to remain should be administered."[52] Later, in 1946, the American policy was further clarified by Clair Wilcox, the head of the American delegation in London negotiating with the British on the ITO: "Every nation stands to gain from the widest possible movement of goods and services. . . . That international trade should be abundant, that it should be multilateral, that it should be non-discriminatory, that stabilization policies and trade policies should be consistent—these are propositions on which all nations, whatever their forms of economic organization, can agree."[53]

Comparatively, while American negotiators argued that the primary principle of a trade organization was to reduce barriers to trade,

[52] Quoted in Edna Wilgress, *A New Attempt at Internationalism* (Paris: Société d'Edition d'Enseignmement Superieur, 1949), p. 12.

[53] Quoted in Gardner, *Sterling-Dollar Diplomacy*, p. 270. In a speech during the London conference, Wilcox further clarified what he meant by multilateral trade: "International trade should be multilateral rather than bilateral. Particular transactions, of course, are always bilateral. One seller deals with one buyer. But under multilateralism, the pattern of trade is, in general, many-sided. Sellers are not compelled to confine their sales to buyers who will deliver them equivalent values in other goods. Buyers are not required to find sellers who will accept payment in goods that buyers have produced. Traders sell where they please, exchanging goods for money, and buy where they please, exchanging money for goods. Bilateralism, by contrast, is akin to barter. Under this system, you may sell for money but you cannot use your money where you please. . . . Imports are directly tied to exports and each country must balance its accounts, not only with the world as a whole but separately, with every other country with whom it deals." Wilgress, *New Attempt at Internationalism*, pp. 37–38.

Stafford Cripps, representing the British, suggested that the prime object was to "achieve an agreement as to the manner in which the nations can co-operate for the promotion of the highest level of employment and the maintenance of demand and can bring some degree of regulation into world trade and commerce."[54] Such a position made little sense to American negotiators. The Americans doubted that nations could or should ask others to participate in domestic policies to maintain full employment. Employment, it was argued, could not be "as absolute as in the case of other matters which lie entirely within the volition and control of nations."[55] But it was not only the right of a multilateral organization to set domestic employment goals which sat poorly with the American delegation. As well, they differed on what the national employment objective should be. In 1945, the Full Employment Act had been rejected by Congress; its alternative in 1946 was far closer to the American conception of the responsibility of government, that is, ambiguity on both what constituted full employment and executive discretion over the use of economic tools to meet employment goals. The Americans would concede only that nations should not use "measures likely to create unemployment in other countries."[56]

The outcome was a series of compromises in the ITO charter. The heart of the settlement involved exceptions to rules under specific conditions relating to balance-of-payments adjustments. In London, the British got the assurance that "in case of a fundamental disequilibrium in their balance of payments involving other countries in persistent balance of payments difficulties, which handicap them in maintaining employment, [nations] will make their full contribution to action designed to correct the maladjustment."[57] Among actions to be taken, countries could, when necessary, resort to quantitative restrictions.

In many respects, the fundamental issue of the time was quantitative restrictions. When the gold standard collapsed in 1931, competitive devaluations made tariffs an insufficient mechanism for the protection of the economy. Nations then moved to explicit quantitative controls as a means to shelter domestic industry. From the perspective of the State Department, quotas, unlike tariffs, not only were inherently discriminatory but also were associated with the economic nationalism of the interwar period. As early as 1933, the State Department pointed to quotas as the more onerous form of trade restriction, explaining that at least tariffs were potentially open to reciprocal bargaining.

---

[54] Gardner, *Sterling-Dollar Diplomacy*, p. 271.
[55] Ibid.
[56] Ibid., p. 272.
[57] Ibid., p. 276.

Although the trade regime ultimately allowed quotas, both British and American negotiators shared a general distaste for quantitative restrictions. But confronted with domestic political pressures, both agreed that that principle could be ignored under special circumstances. To accommodate both parties, these exceptions grew to include a range of situations, from postwar transition to balance-of-payment disequilibrium and domestic support programs.

This last category was introduced by the American delegation. Before the war ended, American negotiators had informally indicated that they could sign no agreement that did not award special consideration to American agriculture. They argued that quantitative restrictions to protect either an international commodity agreement or a domestic commodity program were legitimate extensions of previous principles. Then, in line with its own needs, the United States proposed that restrictions be allowed only for domestic programs that controlled output. And when used, quotas and other restrictions would operate in such a way "as would reduce imports relatively to domestic production as compared with the proportion prevailing in a previous representative period."[58]

In the spring of 1947, the United States further clarified its position to the fifty-six participating nations at the United Nations Conference on Trade and Employment in Geneva. Now, American acceptance of a trade regime was contingent upon four exceptions. First, in 1946 the United States had included a new safeguard in its trade treaty with Mexico which allowed for portions of that agreement to be rescinded under specific conditions. Now the United States asked that such an escape clause—allowing suspension or withdrawal of tariff agreements if serious injury occurred to a domestic producer—be included in all its future agreements. Second, although GATT and the ITO were to forbid quantitative restrictions, such restrictions were to be allowed for the protection of agricultural commodities under specified conditions. Third, agricultural exports were to be an exception to any general pledge against export subsidization.[59] And fourth, if necessary to protect essential security interests, any obligation specified in the charter could be abrogated.[60] These exceptions were not negotiable. Thus the United States vetoed a motion by China to extend the exceptions to

[58] Ibid., p. 150.
[59] The proposal specified that members who were paying export subsidies on agricultural commodites cooperate in negotiations of commodity agreements. If no agreement was reached, export subsidies would be allowed provided they did not increase the product's share of the world market relative to a past representative period.
[60] The elasticity of this proposal was quickly recognized when the United States used the security release to justify import restrictions on cheese and wool.

include manufactured goods; likewise, it refused a motion by China, India, and the Netherlands to allow quantitative restrictions to apply to all domestic price stabilization measures.[61]

But the inclusion of these exceptions was still insufficient to garner domestic approval.[62] By the time Congress considered the final ITO charter, almost every important group was lined up against ratification. Some groups argued with the National Foreign Trade Council that the employment provisions "would operate inexorably to transform the free enterprise system of this country into a . . . planned economy . . . and threat[en] the free institutions and liberties of the American people."[63] Others suggested that the ITO would allow countries to pursue inflationary policies and still maintain quantitative restrictions against American exports. The sanctioning of restrictions for balance-of-payments reasons and rules on foreign direct investment, argued business groups, were inconsistent with their interpretation of the purpose of the multilateral trade regime.[64]

The demise of the ITO did not end the multilateral trade regime. The commercial policy provisions of Chapter V of the ITO charter, the heart of what America wanted in a trade regime, were incorporated into Part II of the GATT. This new document codified America's preferences on trading relations as stated at the start of the negotiating process. Like the ITO, the GATT was multilateral. Control of the organization was shared by all members, all agreed to give others MFN status, and nondiscrimination was a central norm. But in operation, the GATT was a network of simultaneous bilateral reciprocal agreements. Unlike the ITO, the GATT did not aspire to be a multilateral mechanism for the formal control of all aspects of trade.[65] In this way, the United States finessed demands by other nations to specify policy guidelines for the new regime. But this limited purpose was an asset;

---

[61] Rau, *Agricultural Policy*, pp. 111–12.

[62] See Gardner, *Sterling-Dollar Diplomacy*, pp. 348–81.

[63] Ibid., p. 376.

[64] The condemnation by the International Chamber of Commerce was sweeping. "It [ITO charter] is a dangerous document because it accepts practically all of the policies of economic nationalism; because it jeopardizes the free enterprise system by giving priority to centralized national governmental planning of foreign trade; because it leaves a wide scope to discrimination, accepts the principle of economic insulation and in effect commits all members of the ITO to state planning for full employment." Ibid., p. 377.

[65] Because of its more minimalist task, the GATT was authorized through presidential decree under rights given by the trade agreements program instead of through congressional assent. In practice, this meant that its legal basis was somewhat unclear. It was not until 1968 that the president asked Congress for and received permanent authorization for contributions to the running of the organization. Previously, American contributions were buried in a State Department line item entitled "international conferences and contingencies." Ibid., p. xxxiv.

even while the ITO charter was being discussed in national capitals, the GATT had initiated its first round of trade talks. These talks, called in 1947, were the first of eight major bargaining sessions which GATT would sponsor.[66]

LIBERAL TRADE POLICY

New international trade structures and an executive willing to enter into multilateral talks brought changes in both American barriers to trade and levels of trade flows. Whereas in 1934 trade duties were still at 46.7 percent, by 1962 they were at 12 percent. These changes were felt throughout the world. World trade increased from $97 trillion at the war's end to $270 trillion at the time of the 1962 act.[67] This trend would continue. By the 1990s average duties stood at about 5 percent. American import growth ran consistently ahead of GNP (see Table 4.1).

Table 4.1. Average tariff rates compared with changes in GNP and imports, 1934–1991

Years	Average tariff rate[a]	Percent change in GNP	Percent change in imports
1934–1958	23.8	201.1	233.2
1958–1962	12.0	20.5	21.1
1962–1974	10.5	51.7	311.8
1974–1979	6.0	17.0	39.6
1979–1984	5.6	9.7	9.6
1984–1988	5.4	14.9	18.9
1988–1991	5.2	2.8	6.0

Sources: U.S. Department of Commerce, *National Income and Product Account of the United States, 1929–1982* (Washington: USGPO, 1983); U.S. Department of Commerce, *Survey of Current Business,* July 1987; U.S. Department of Commerce, *Statistical Abstract of the United States* (Washington in USGPO, 1990), Nos. 690, 762, 1412; U.S. Bureau of the Census, *Historical Statistics of the United States from Colonial Times to 1970* (Washington: USGPO, 1975), Series E 135–166, U 187–200, U 207–212.
[a] Average tariff rate is based on duties collected as a percentage of all dutiable imports for each year in the period.

After 1934, the Reciprocal Trade Agreements Act was extended by Congress in 1937, 1940, and 1943. By 1945 almost all of the 50 percent

[66] The other talks were the Annecy in 1949, Torquay in 1951, Geneva, 1956, the Dillon Round, 1960–61, Kennedy Round, 1964–67, the Tokyo Round concluded in 1979, and the ongoing Uruguay Round.
[67] Statistical Office of the United Nations Department of Economic Affairs, *Statistical Yearbook, 1953* (New York: United Nations Publications, 1953), pp. 368, 369; ibid., 1963, pp. 450–51.

limit on negotiating authority had been exhausted in twenty-eight reciprocal trade agreements. To extend the program, the 1945 act granted the president the authority to reduce rates another 50 percent. Trade authority was granted again in 1948, 1949, 1951, 1954, 1955, and 1958; the last renewal inaugurated the Dillon Round of trade talks. Only in 1962 did President John F. Kennedy introduce trade legislation that was for the first time not an adjunct to the 1934 act.[68]

Between 1947 and 1962, the entire complexion of the trade issue changed. Trade policy lost much of its partisan character. Even those who still opposed aspects of the liberalization program eschewed "old-line" protectionism.[69] As early as 1948, the critics of legislation expanding trade were branded as isolationists—a universally criticized foreign policy stance. As the Cold War intensified, the administration repeatedly argued that a vote against open trade was a vote against the "free world." Repeatedly, domestic welfare was juxtaposed to American foreign economic policy. The result was that liberal legislation was increasingly passed by both Republican and Democratic administrations[70] (see Table 4.2).

Although few in this period criticized the general effort to increase world trade, both Republicans and Democrats opposed aspects of liberal administrative procedures. Before 1934, critics could undercut tariff legislation, but by the late 1950s, only certain abridgments were politically feasible. Dissent centered on such issues as the use of a peril point, the wording of escape clause conditions, and the particulars of bargaining arrangements. No one questioned the mandate to enter into multilateral negotiations to lower tariffs and nontariff barriers. No one advocated a return to the old protectionist regime or to congressional preeminence over tariffs. Starting in the 1960s, America showed a willingness to negotiate away even agricultural protections; by the 1980s, liberalization of farm trade became a central element on the U.S. negotiating agenda. Each time legislation was renewed, restrictions were

[68] For a review of congressional policy see Pastor, *Congress.* On the 1962 act, see Ernest H. Preeg, *Traders and Diplomats* (Washington, D.C.: Brookings Institution, 1973); and John W. Evans, *The Kennedy Round in American Trade Policy* (Cambridge, Mass.: Harvard University Press, 1971).

[69] Few pro-protection interest groups remained. The most active in the 1950s was the Old Protective Tariff League. Founded in 1885, it had changed its name in the 1920s to the American Tariff League and, after 1958, to the American Trade Council. It, the Nation-Wide Committee on Import-Export Policy (founded in 1953), and the Liberty Lobby (founded in 1955) were the only organized ideological resisters to liberalization. See Pastor, *Congress,* p. 111.

[70] Under Wilbur Mills, free-trade views were a prerequisite for membership on the prestigious House Ways and Means Committee. See John Manley, *The Politics of Finance: The House Committee on Ways and Means* (Boston: Little, Brown, 1978).

Table 4.2. Partisan control of the House, Senate, and presidency, and House votes on liberal trade legislation, 1934–1988

Year	Congress	House[a]	Senate	President	Percent Yes
1933–1934	73d	D	D	D (FDR)	71
1957–1959	85th	D	D	R (Eisenhower)	76
1961–1963	87th	D	D	D (Kennedy)	70
1973–1975	93d	D	D	R (Nixon)	66
1977–1979	95th	D	D	D (Carter)	98
1983–1985	98th	D	R	R (Reagan)	90
1987–1989	100th	D	D	R (Reagan)	68

Sources: Robert A. Pastor, *Congress and the Politics of U.S. Foreign Economic Policy* (Berkeley: University of California Press, 1980), p. 197; *Congressional Quarterly Almanac,* 1979, 1983, 1984, 1987, 1988; Eric Austin, *Political Facts of the United States* (New York: Columbia University Press, 1986), pp. 50–58.

[a] The votes are final roll calls on House bills, not the House-Senate conference versions.

placed on the executive. Some were substantive, most were symbolic.[71] But to focus only on these restrictions and the congressional battles they spawned is to overlook the high degree of continuity in postwar American trade history.

The election of Dwight D. Eisenhower to the presidency and his subsequent trade policy were key tests of America's commitment to free trade. Although liberalization had thrived in the long period of Democratic rule, trade barriers remained high in 1952. Once again in power, Republicans could have turned back the clock but did not. Instead, during the eight years of the Eisenhower presidency, Republican leaders did little more than slow down the liberalization process, even when they controlled both houses of Congress.[72] Eisenhower's blue ribbon commission mandated to review trade policy was headed by Clarence Randall, chairman of Inland Steel Corporation and a known

[71] It was often hard at the time for legislators to see the implications of small changes in laws and thus to impute intent from action. For instance, the 1962 act excluded the peril point. Congressional leaders convinced skeptics that the protections would remain because Congress required the Tariff Commission to advise the president of the effect of tariff reductions on particular industries. But the peril point had given opponents of protection control of the agenda. It mandated that the TC define a limit beyond which executive branch negotiators could no longer offer concessions. Fear of giving away too much protection of a particular industry was the fundamental reason for congressional support for only item-by-item and not horizontal negotiations. Comparatively, the escape clause gave control of the agenda to the executive branch, which decides what industries would be opened for concessions and only afterward, if industries met specific criteria, could they petition for an increase in duty up to the prenegotiated level.

[72] In his memoirs, Eisenhower said that some members of Congress, to his surprise, still disagreed with him on the need for low tariffs. See Dwight D. Eisenhower, *Mandate for Change, 1953–56* (Garden City: Doubleday, 1963), pp. 194–95.

advocate of free trade. It was no surprise when the commission recommended an extension of the trade liberalization program.[73]

Eisenhower in 1958—as would Kennedy in 1962 and Richard Nixon in 1974—worked assiduously to assure congressional passage of a trade bill that would allow him to negotiate further tariff reductions. For the most part, they were successful.[74] In 1958 the president launched the Dillon Round of trade talks with authorization to lower rates up to 20 percent; in 1962 a 50 percent negotiating authority was granted, and in 1974 the authorization was to lower tariffs up to 60 percent and to eliminate those under 5 percent. Although the Dillon Round had limited success, the Kennedy Round of negotiations rivaled earlier talks in both scope and depth of reductions. The average cut for all industrial products was about 35 percent, which, although it represented only a quarter of world trade, was 80 percent of the trade of those products still regulated by tariffs.[75] This success was repeated in the Tokyo Round following passage of the 1974 act. The Tokyo talks dealt with tariff and nontariff barriers, proposed codes on subsidies and countervailing duties, customs valuation, technical barriers and standards, government procurement, and import licensing procedures. Furthermore,

---

[73] The establishment of the Commission of Foreign Economic Policy, under the chairmanship of Clarence B. Randall, was a compromise between Eisenhower and his Republican Congress. In return for Congress's renewing the trade act, Eisenhower promised to establish a legislative-executive commission to study and make recommendations on foreign and economic policy. The commission, made up of seventeen members, ten from Congress and seven chosen by the president, presented its final report in January 1954. Despite deep divisions within the commission, it articulated a clearly internationalist vision. In March, the president asked Randall to coordinate drafting legislation, which eventually became the 1958 trade act.

[74] Gaining congressional assent for executive trade acts had costs. To placate potential resistance, presidents routinely gave side payments in the form of trade relief to groups that could pose a problem for passage. In 1962, for example, to aid southern cotton producers, Kennedy facilitated a seventeen-nation textile conference in Geneva, which led to an agreement on the international control of cotton textiles. Thus the American Cotton Manufacturers Institute could say that it "believe[d] that the authority to deal with foreign nations proposed by the President [in the Trade Expansion Act] will be wisely exercised and should be granted." Kennedy also announced a six-point program for the lumber industry that granted, among other things, preferential procurement of U.S. timber by the Defense Department. He also accepted the recommendations of the Tariff Commission and granted increased tariffs on carpets and glass, which he retained even after the European Economic Community retaliated.

Similarly, in preparation for the 1973–74 act, President Nixon aided the steel industry with a voluntary export restraint agreement with Japan and Europe. Additionally, the cotton agreement was replaced with a long-term GATT textile agreement on man-made fibers, wool, and cotton textiles; promises were made to the footwear and dairy industries, and a trade statistics monitoring service was legislated to identify potential trade problems.

[75] Evans, *Kennedy Round*, p. 281.

tariffs were cut an average of 26 percent, raising world exports, according to one estimate, by $13 billion per year.[76]

Congress encouraged the liberalization process not only by granting negotiating authority but by expanding the bureaucracy that dealt with trade issues. In the 1962 trade act a new position was created, the special representative for trade negotiations (STR); the 1974 act made the STR a statutory unit in the executive branch. Later, as part of Congress's 1979 assent to the Tokyo Round proposals, the STR was expanded in size and scope. Providing trade leadership throughout this period, the STR has been protected by Congress from any recommendation—such as an 1983 proposal to subsume STR in the Commerce Department—that would undermine its authority.

The willingness of American central decision makers to open trade to foreign producers in the 1940s, 1950s, and 1960s presents few problems from an analytic perspective. America had a significant trade surplus, and leaders worried far more about markets for American exports than about foreign competition at home. Beginning in the 1960s, however, America's position in the international economic community began to erode (see Table 4.3). For long periods the dollar was overvalued, which aided the growing competition from European and Asian producers. Even so, the United States continued to open up home markets far more quickly and systematically than did its trading partners (see Table 4.4). As protectionist pressures increased, so did imports. Although a variety of import protections were granted, they did little to stem the influx of foreign goods. Thus by the first half of the 1980s, the rate of growth in U.S. imports had outstripped the rate of growth in world imports almost seven to one.[77]

Industries and organized labor did not ignore the surge in imports. The number of protectionist bills entered in Congress rose dramatically, especially in the 1980s. Only one or two bills had been entered in the early 1970s, but during the ninety-sixth Congress alone (1979–81), 127 protectionist acts were discussed in the House. The number rose to 137 in the ninety-seventh Congress, to 144 in the ninety-eighth, and leaped to 782 in the ninety-ninth. Measured differently, references to trade in the House and Senate increased by 70 percent between 1975 and 1980.[78]

[76] Alan Deardorff and Robert M. Stern, "Economic Effects of the Tokyo Round," *Southern Journal of Economics* 49 (January 1983): 606, 614.

[77] David Yoffie, "American Trade Policy: An Obsolete Bargain," in John Chubb and Paul Peterson, *Can the Government Govern?* (Washington, D.C.: Brookings Institution, 1989).

[78] These figures for the ninety-sixth to ninety-eighth Congresses are in I. M. Destler *American Trade Politics* (Washington, D.C.: Institute for International Economics, 1986), p. 75; on the ninety-ninth Congress see Yoffie, "American Trade Policy," p. 113.

Table 4.3. U.S. share of Organization of Economic
Cooperation and Development trade, 1950–1990

Year	U.S. share[a] (percent)
1950	50.2
1960	40.6
1970	17.3
1980	17.8
1990	16.1

Source: Organization of Economic Cooperation and Development, Monthly Statistics of Foreign Trade (Paris: OECD), Series
A, February 1962, p. 2; January 1973, p. 10; July 1982, p. 10; June
1991, p. 12.
[a]Computed as U.S. exports/OECD total exports.

Table 4.4. Percent change in import penetration, 1955–1990

Country	1955–1965	1965–1975	1975–1985	1985–1990
United States	7	104	38	9.2
Europe	−5	38	25	−6.5
Japan	−14	38	−11	−18.6

Source: International Monetary Fund, International Financial Statistics Yearbook (Washington: International Monetary Fund, 1988, 1991).
Note: Import penetration is measured as [import/GDP] × 1000. Europe category is a
composite of the United Kingdom, France, and Germany (1955–65 figure does not
include France).

Even in the face of this opposition and seeming attention to import-
sensitive industries, Congress was reticent to undercut the liberal regime. Throughout the period, opinion leaders characterized protectionists as self-serving and protectionism as counter to the general
interest.[79] The path to increased prosperity, they argued, was through

[79] This attitude is nowhere better exemplified than by the inordinate fear of a "return
to our protectionist past," even in the most liberal periods. For example, as early as in
1961, Jacob Viner argued that "the tide is running in a protectionist direction." "Economic Foreign Policy on the New Frontier," Foreign Affairs 39 (July 1961): 565. C. Fred
Bergsten later wrote that "since 1962 U.S. trade policy has been moving steadily away
from the liberal trade approach which had characterized it since 1934." "Crisis in U.S.
Trade Policy," Foreign Affairs 49 (July 1971): 619. More recently, as the Omnibus Trade
Act of 1988 wound its way through Congress, editorials in the major newspapers repeatedly prophesied an end to liberalism. For instance, on February 17, 1988, the Washington Post headlined an article "Poison Ivy" and condemned the protectionist elements
of the act. The Post editorial was not unusual. What was odd was the staff's surprise
when the protectionist parts of the bill were dropped. Even though the early versions
of most acts since 1974 had included protectionist elements as a gesture of concern for
those hurt by trade policy, which were removed in conference or on the floor, the Post

increasing trade, not through closing the American market. Industry-specific legislation aside, Congress had three chances to change the trade program substantially. In 1974, 1979, and 1988 the administration was forced to appeal to Congress to sustain its program of multilateral trade negotiations. In all three cases, Congress endorsed liberal trade, which, in an environment that was increasingly hostile to American producers, testifies to the widespread belief in liberal trade ideology among elites. But Congress extracted a price for renewing executive authority. With each renewal, Congress reinforced safeguards for industry and pushed for "fair" trade.

Congressional Support for Free and Fair Trade

In an atmosphere clouded by this century's first negative trade balance, double-digit inflation, and charges of presidential corruption, Richard Nixon gained bipartisan support for his 1974 trade reform act, which included an unprecedented provision that gave the president negotiating authority for five years to deal with tariff and nontariff barriers. Unlike in 1962, Nixon's trade legislation did not have the protection of Wilbur Mills and a subordinate House Ways and Means Committee.[80] Initially, the media portrayed Congress as hostile. Many groups, most notably organized labor, were pressuring members of Congress for help against import competition.

As with all trade legislation in the postwar period, the administration's strategy to gain congressional assent was to argue that liberalization benefited the nation's economy and its foreign policy. Congress was told that "protectionism produces catastrophe and there must be a commitment to the principle of strengthening the role of the market in the monetary, trade and investment area . . . the U.S. has a comparative advantage and much to gain from reliance on the market."[81] As explained by George Shultz, the secretary of the treasury, "The goal

---

remarked: "It continues to be truly remarkable: in an election year, the congressional conference on the trade bill—which touches countless special interests—keeps making good progress." *Washington Post*, March 22, 1989.

[80] Before the Watergate reforms, the House was controlled by a small group who held extensive power over rules and appointments. This enabled Wilbur Mills, a fervent free trader, to assure that the Ways and Means Committee supported trade liberalization. But after 1975, the House was no longer so easily managed. Ways and Means was stripped of its position as "committee on committees" and expanded from twenty-five to thirty-seven members. Perhaps more important, reforms created subcommittees that controlled the legislation. Destler comments that this change was good for liberal trade because it delayed product-restrictive proposals; it was bad, he says, because the subcommittee chair lacked the stature of the full committee head, which made it more difficult to block protectionist legislation from a powerful backer. Destler, *Trade Politics*, p. 60.

[81] Ibid., pp. 178–80.

[of the trade bill] must be to improve the efficiency of the U.S. economy ... we must not allow new protectionism to lead to a breakdown of multilateral and non-discriminatory trading arrangements of the post-war period."[82] But in 1974 Congress was asked to do more than just extend the authorization of previous trade bills. The administration now asked that negotiators be given the freedom to change domestic laws on a variety of commercial practices without congressional authorization. By the 1970s, tariffs were no longer the main impediment to trade. In return for further access to their markets, America's trading partners now wanted concessions on a range of American practices, from antidumping law to methods used in customs appraisals. The Nixon administration proposed an extension of executive authority to include such nontariff barriers. Noting that most of the concessions would require a revision in domestic codes, the administration bill included the proviso that either house of Congress could veto executive implementation within ninety days.

The congressional reaction was best expressed by Herman Talmadge of Georgia, who commented that this was "not the way we make laws."[83] Still, Congress was willing to devise a compromise that would both allow continued trade talks and assure that Congress controlled changes in domestic laws. The compromise was a new trade procedure known as the "fast track." Under this system, the president would negotiate concessions in consultation with relevant congressional committees. Then, at least ninety days prior, he would give notice of intent to enter into a nontariff barrier agreement. Both houses of Congress would be required to act within sixty days of his submitting the implementing legislation. In return for consultation, Congress would vote under a closed rule—no changes would be allowed either in committee or on the floor.

In practice, the legislative changes of 1974 worked far better than even the bill's creators had anticipated. Even though the trade environment bred increasing dissatisfaction in Congress, few problems marred the passage of the Tokyo Round accords. Congress's acquiescence to the significant changes agreed to in Geneva had much to do with the way it was brought into the process. In only one case, involving laws that protected the priority of minority-owned enterprises on certain government contracts, did Congress cancel promises made by negotiators. Not only were members of Congress and the bureaucracy present during trade talks, but once the president gave notice of intent to sign

[82] Congress, U.S. Senate, Committee on Finance, *Testimony on Trade Reform Act of 1974*, 74th Cong., 2d sess., p. 163.
[83] Quoted in Destler, *Trade Politics*, p. 64.

a nontariff barrier agreement, the House and Senate committees began a series of informal sessions to help the administration write the legislation. Differences in the two houses were reconciled in an informal conference. The final congressional version then went back to the president to be returned to Congress verbatim eighteen days later. The final passage on the 1979 trade act showed overwhelming and bipartisan support for the Tokyo Round negotiations.

Clearly, fears voiced in 1974 that the need for congressional endorsement of international agreements would undermine liberalization were unfounded. Both branches supported the liberal trade regime; they differed not over the idea of open trade but about what responsibility government officials had in assuring fair competition for American producers. Thus the key fight between the two branches in 1979 was over the rules for countervailing duty and antidumping laws. But, in the spotlight, Congress changed these laws only marginally more than the administration had desired. Congress did decide, however, to make fundamental changes in the organization of the trade bureaucracy. The big winner was the Commerce Department, which gained much of the responsibility previously held in unfair trade cases by the Treasury Department.[84] The intent of these changes was to define more clearly the grounds on which the besieged trade bureaucracy could and should grant import relief, not to undermine the trade liberalization program.

By 1988, America's trade balance had deteriorated to unprecedented levels. The deficit, $34.6 billion in 1981, was $171.2 billion by the end of 1987. The decline in America's trade position among the Organization of Economic Cooperation and Development Countries was apparent to all; the U.S. share had declined to a little over 16 percent (see Table 4.3). Structural changes in the economy hit labor particularly hard: according to the Bureau of Labor Statistics, an average of two million workers a year were out of work in the 1980s because of plant closings, layoffs, or the elimination of their jobs.[85] Despite planned depreciations of the dollar in 1985, 1986, and 1987 the trade deficit was climbing to unimagined heights. Again, the administration was rushing against a deadline for congressional authorization to engage in a new round of trade liberalization talks.

Congress had not neglected trade issues between 1979 and 1988. Aside from considering a variety of unsuccessful, politically volatile bills on reciprocity and domestic content, Congress in 1984, motivated by the impending expiration of trade preferences for developing coun-

---

[84] See Chapter 5 for an explication of the changes in unfair trade laws.
[85] Democratic Study Group, *Fact Sheet*, April 19, 1988, p. 1.

tries, had passed a trade bill.[86] The administration argued that, for foreign policy reasons, the United States should not abandon the General System of Preferences (GSP), which granted developing nations duty-free access to markets in the developed world. But with labor-intensive industries facing keen competition from just those countries being granted special access, the GSP had limited support. More to accede to the administration's wishes than to accord with members' agendas, the Senate Finance Committee combined the bill to renew GSP with a more popular bilateral free-trade agreement with Israel and a moderate bilateral reciprocity bill. All were then made part of a tariff bill that had already been approved by the House.

In floor discussions, the bill was loaded with protectionist amendments. The bill left the Senate with additional protection for the producers of copper, bromine, wine, footwear, ferroalloys, and dairy products and the promise of bilateral steel export agreements. In the House four separate bills passed and went to conference: GSP, the free-trade agreement, a steel import stabilization act, and a bill to aid the wine industry. Domestic content and bilateral reciprocity proposals were defeated.

The outcome in conference, as reported in the *Washington Post*, was "pretty respectable legislation . . . most of the bad stuff got thrown out and all of the good stuff stayed."[87] The act was essentially liberal with weak protections for wine and steel. The GSP, although unpopular, was renewed. Protection for copper, ferroalloys, shoes, and dairy products was dropped. Again, trade remedy laws were changed, making it slightly easier for American producers to get aid.

The same pattern was repeated in 1988; the potential of product-specific protectionism existed throughout the writing and passage of the bill but was removed by general consent in conference. Again, Congress passed an essentially liberal trade act, despite the politicization of the trade issue. In essence, the act condoned multilateral reductions of tariffs, censured unfair trade practices, and provided for adjustment for those hurt by import competition. Congress renewed the right of the president to negotiate the lowering of barriers to trade at home and abroad.[88] That renewal elicited relatively little debate, indicating

---

[86] For an excellent account of the 1984 act, see Destler, *Trade Politics*.

[87] "On Trade, A Happy Ending," *Washington Post*, October 12, 1984, quoted in I. M. Destler, "United States Trade Policymaking in the Eighties," p. 26, unpublished paper, 1990.

[88] The law extended negotiating authority for nontariff barriers for five years; it extended fast-track authority to 1991, with a proviso for a further two-year extension unless Congress disapproved. The executive was reauthorized to enter into tariff agreements through 1993. Tariffs could be cut up to 50 percent or, if they were currently at 5 percent or less, eliminated completely.

an endorsement for the expansion of the liberal trade regime into trade in services, investments, and intellectual property. Far more time was spent on how to stop countries from cheating on the liberal regime's rules. Here, Congress sent a clear message to the executive and other countries that it would feel no qualms about penalizing nations that practiced unfair trade. The 1988 trade act went beyond strengthening protections: it imposed sanctions against the Toshiba Corporation and one Norwegian firm that had sold sensitive technology to the Soviets.[89] Congress also returned to the issue of how to deal with the employment effects of increasing imports and moved to reinvigorate trade adjustment programs. In general, the congressional role, in 1988 as in 1945, was to keep the rules "fair," not to try to abrogate market forces.[90]

As with all other trade bills, many potentially protectionist provisions in the Omnibus Trade and Competitiveness Act of 1988 were dropped or modified in conference.[91] In the days before the conference, many parts of the bill were criticized as potentially protectionist. The most notorious was the Gephardt amendment, which called for trade penalties based on a measure of bilateral reciprocity, that is, on any country running an "excessive" surplus with the United States.[92] The act made

---

[89] Four changes were made to unfair trade laws. First, authority to determine whether a practice was unfair and subject to presidential action under section 301 was transferred from the president to the U.S. trade representative. Second, the act required the initiation of cases against violations of U.S. trade agreements or other unjustifiable practices except if so doing would cause serious harm to U.S. national security. Third, a new category of Super 301 cases was created in which the USTR identifies unfair practices and gives priority to negotiations with these nations to eliminate, reduce or compensate the United States for these practices. If any country does not comply within three years, the USTR resumes the unfair trade investigation and takes action under U.S. trade laws. Finally, the USTR was given the right to retaliate against export targeting by foreign nations. See Chapter 5.

[90] The most controversial part of the bill, ultimately vetoed by the president, required large employers to give sixty-day advance notice of plant closings and major layoffs.

[91] In the conference committee 99 members participated— 44 senators and 155 representatives, divided into seventeen subcommittees. The conference itself was preceded by "black Monday," which though clearly preoccupying members, may or may not have contributed to a fear that protectionism could further exacerbate the economic crisis.

[92] The history of the Gephardt amendment, more than anything else in the 1988 bill, shows the ambivalence of policy makers toward actions that run counter to the original conception of the GATT regime. Richard Gephardt supported mandatory retaliation against unfair foreign trade practices as an amendment to the 1988 bill, but it passed the House by only four votes. The Democratic Senate did not agree to the strong position. When Gephardt tried to make the trade issue, and especially his nationalist version of trade relations, a campaign issue, he was defeated in the presidential primaries. Although he argued rationally that the measure was the wisest way to use a valuable asset—the huge U.S. market—to open up foreign markets, the American public and elites agreed with the administration that this was protectionist reasoning and an inappropriate response to a declining trade balance.

it far easier to bring suits and win judgments against importers, ensured the right to bring legal action against any product from any country that did not protect workers' rights, and even required extensive public disclosure by any foreigner investing in the United States, a problematic issue given American protest against a similar provision enacted by the Canadian legislature. Also, upon entering conference, the bill contained a change in the U.S. antidumping code allowing a producer to claim that a foreign producer was dumping if the product was sold in the United States at a lower price than in the home market after the deduction of profit and selling costs from the U.S. price but *not* from the foreign price. Any importer cited more than three times within seven years for a trade violation would be prohibited from importing any goods for the next three years. The usual assortment of particularistic provisions also found their way to conference. For example, an amendment placed quotas on imports of lamb and demanded the abolition of quotas on American beef to Japan (which was somewhat ironic because the author also supported the first amendment), and the sugar industry would have received an enormous windfall from a provision that would have allowed it to claim a rebate of back duties on reexported sugar.

In the end, these well-publicized amendments were eliminated from the thousand page "balanced" bill.[93] The right of the president to decide on fair and unfair trade sanctions was sustained. In fact, the bill allowed the president greater, not less, flexibility to balance the benefits for the protected industry against the costs to the country as a whole.[94] With the relegislation of Trade Adjustment Assistance (TAA), the president's options of what to offer import-impacted industries were actually expanded.[95] Fears of protectionism resulting from the fractur-

---

[93] For a thorough legislative history of the passage of the bill see Destler, "Policymaking in the Eighties."

[94] The one provision that was maintained among those I have discussed was the retaliation against the two companies that sold sensitive military equipment to the Soviets. Perhaps it, too, would have been eliminated but for a concurrent decision by the Japanese court to give only minor sentences in the Toshiba case. (The court fined the subsidiary that had sold the technology only $15,750 and gave one-year suspended sentences to guilty company officials.) The author of the amendment, Senator Jake Garn, was close to giving way on the provision when news of the Japanese court's decision reached Capitol Hill. Members of both parties presented Garn with a coalition of support that could not have existed the day before. "I've got allies I didn't know I had," Garn said. "Everybody said, 'Don't give up.'" *Congressional Quarterly*, March 26, 1988, p. 798.

[95] In the House the vote on the conference report was an overwhelming 312 to 107 after only four hours of debate. Sixty-eight House Republicans voted with Democrats for the bill. Just two Democrats, Representatives Richard Gephardt and Robert Mrazek, voted against the bill. Gephardt's vote reflected the exclusion of his retaliation amendment in conference, making the act too liberal. For free-trader Mrazek, the bill was too protectionist. In the Senate, the vote was taken after four days of debate. The vote, 63

ing of trade into the purview of multiple committees were not borne out, even when the bill went to a conference committee that included 155 House members and 44 senators, representing thirteen House and eight Senate committees.

Nevertheless, the act had repeatedly been portrayed as protectionist and compared to Smoot-Hawley. Many claimed that it invited retaliation.[96] Many feared that administration officials would be unable to finesse the political dilemma of how to look tough on the issue of unfair trade while, at the same time, enacting a bill that would not elicit a harsh reaction from America's trading partners.[97] Their anxiety was unfounded. When the bill became law, America's trading partners saw it as a reasonable compromise that would not hinder the continued liberalization of world trade.

In sum, in the postwar period Congress consistently supported legislation allowing the United States to maintain its commitment to the liberal trade regime. Neither party attachment nor changes in America's relationship to the world economy has undermined this support. This is not to suggest that there has been no resistance to trade liberalization. Representatives have repeatedly used Congress as an arena in which to call attention to the plight of workers and producers who have suffered because of foreign trade. Thus Robert Pastor's description in 1980 of a "cry and sigh" syndrome, whereby protectionist

to 36, fell three short of the sixty-six-person majority needed to withstand the certain presidential veto. Senator Proxmire, the only Democrat to vote no, did so because of the way the bill dealt with the bribery of foreign officials. Both Alaskan senators voted against the measure because of the inclusion of restrictions on oil exports from a proposed Alaskan refinery. Support that did not exist in its first visit to the floor in the summer of 1987 was found in the bill's repeal of the "windfall" tax on certain oil revenues—a provision that had strong backing from states in which the depressed oil industry was active. In a like way, the inclusion of the plant-closing sections assured not only the support of organized labor but attention from a sympathetic media. In preparation for a potential veto, the House moved immediately to adopt a concurrent resolution that would eliminate from the trade bill the seventy thousand barrel-per-day limit on Alaskan oil exports from new refineries and the requirement that crude oil from the trans-Alaska pipeline sold to Canada be shipped through the lower forty-eight states. The vote was on a specialized "self-executing" rule that needed to go the Senate but not be signed by the president.

[96] For example, see Hobart Rowen, "A Trade Bill We Could Live Without," *Washington Post*, April 20, 1989, p. H1.

[97] This representation that trade legislation held the potential of sending the world down a "slippery slope" toward a world of beggar-thy-neighbor policies and depression existed in and out of the administration. Whether it was believed is difficult to discern, although in much of the press, such as the story cited below, writers repeatedly noted administration fears of foreign reaction to passage of the trade bill even though they recognized that the details of the bill did not support the vision of the act as protectionist. See Monica Langley and Walter S. Mossberg, "Congressional Conferees Clear Majority of Big Trade Bill, but Veto Is Possible," *Wall Street Journal*, April 1, 1988, p. 3.

threats are quelled to the relief of the representatives themselves, is as accurate today as then. But Congress's role is more complex. Because most believe that markets should control trade patterns and that overt interference leads to economic disasters such as the Great Depression, representatives are willing to allow the executive the right to have the United States continue to participate in the liberal regime. But legislators share in an equally strong tradition of protecting American producers against those who do not adhere to market demands; modern Congress defends the legal remnants of its earlier legislative actions that protect American producers from predatory trade practices. Thus, as more and more pressure was placed upon elected officials, government policy turned increasingly to market practices abroad in an attempt to force others to adhere to American standards.

The Coalition against Unfair Trade

By the 1980s, American economic decline led many to focus on the implications of continued adherence to a liberal trade policy. On the whole, these trade reform efforts were channeled away from solutions that would close American markets and toward those that emphasized the deregulation of foreign markets and industries. These efforts at increasing the autonomy of markets all fall under the fair-trade umbrella. As suggested in the preceding chapters, fair-trade ideas have a far longer and more entrenched history than free-trade ideas. Although policy makers in this century accepted that protectionism wreaks economic disaster, they never unanimously agreed on the converse—espoused by neoclassical economists—that even a unilateral lowering of barriers would increase economic wealth. Rather, policy makers' acceptance of a liberal regime at home was always contingent on liberalization abroad.

In American thought, protectionism connotes practices far broader than the height of a tariff. The United States has long declared that any predatory practice—from dumping to subsidies—is illegal under American law. In effect, however, the domestic practices of America's trading partners were not important to Americans in the first decades after World War II. Competition was muted as nations slowly recovered from the war's dislocations. And for security reasons, rapid economic recovery was viewed as more important than adherence to liberal rules. The United States either looked away or, in some cases, encouraged far more government involvement to aid home producers than was allowed by either GATT or U.S. law. But by the 1970s, American products were losing ground at home and in traditional export markets. In their own defense, manufacturers pointed to a range of practices in foreign countries which put them at a trading disadvantage.

Three factors explain why central decision makers found the criticism of foreign trade practices so salient. First, a range of neglected domestic laws provided recourse from at least some of these trade practices. Second, a strong coalition within Congress found that predatory practices against American business ran counter to their understanding of the spirit of free trade. And third, critics of conventional trade theory within the academic community successfully showed that government assistance policies boost comparative advantage and enhance the position of home producers. Such analyses legitimated the claims of American businesses that they had a right to government assistance.

Critics of Neoclassical Trade Policy

At about the same time that government officials became convinced that neoclassical trade theory was descriptively and normatively correct, members of the academic community began to abandon many of its basic assumptions. These writers, later labeled "strategic trade theorists," questioned a number of the policy assumptions derived from neoclassical thought. In particular, the economic community examined whether or not trade liberalization always leads to trade gains, how monopolies affect trade patterns, the effects of government intrusion into the markets, and the role of interest groups in either supporting or halting trade liberalization.[98] Their conclusions were not always as straightforward as originally envisioned. In fact, some found that under some conditions closure, not openness, increased domestic welfare.

The core criticism of classical doctrine derived from reexamination of the Ricardian assumptions of constant returns to scale and perfect competition. In its original form, free-trade doctrine suggested that national preferences, raw materials, and technology would distinguish each country and give each a comparative advantage in different products. Trade based on comparative advantage would offer the greatest benefit to all. But markets never operated that smoothly; imperfect

---

[98] See, for example, Paul R. Krugman, *Strategic Trade Policy and the New International Economics* (Cambridge, Mass.: MIT Press, 1986); Avinash Dixit and Joseph Stiglitz, "Monopolistic Competition and Optimum Product Diversity," *American Economic Review* 67 (June 1977): 297–308; Paul Krugman, "Trade in Differentiated Products and the Political Economy of Trade Liberalization," in Jagdish Bhagwati, *Import Competition and Response* (Chicago: University of Chicago Press, 1982); Robert Stern, *U.S. Trade Policies in a Changing World Economy* (Cambridge, Mass.: MIT Press, 1987).

markets led to trade flows that varied considerably from those envisioned by the neoclassicists. Economies of scale and foreign government manipulation of markets, not comparative advantage, often determined product competitiveness. The policy implications were that the United States could, and perhaps should, be similarly involved. In a sense, the academic community had provided the first new justification for protectionism since the nineteenth century.

Such protectionist ideas, of course, have a long legal history. Antidumping, countervailing, and unfair trade laws have repeatedly forced government officials to respond to the demands of U.S. producers, even when the former supported the liberal regime. In fact, by repeatedly demanding aid under statutes that left the president little discretion, American manufacturers forced an otherwise reticent government to respond to their trade problems. As it became clear that these cases had merit, Congress had tinkered with these laws, tightening the rules and expanding their jurisdiction.

Elected officials were especially drawn to a suggestion in the new strategic trade theory which advocated an aggressive response to other nations' subsidy policies. Although many still claimed that any act to close the American markets was the first step to world protectionism, more moderate officials could now find theoretical vindication for why the closing of the American market would provide American negotiators with increased clout to open foreign markets. Many academics, regularly testifying before Congress, endorsed this aggressive posture as a means to induce cooperation and assure a more liberal world.[99] Policies long associated with America's isolationist period were dusted off and reused to dissuade nations from adopting market-distorting policies.[100]

By the late 1970s, a new coalition in Congress articulated a nascent but widely believed position that trade should be both fair and free. Several themes characterized both the debate and the activities of this group. First, participants returned to the nineteenth-century image of reciprocity and demanded that the United States refrain from any trade concessions that did not directly follow a trading partner's bilateral concession. Access to the American market, sometimes labeled "sectoral reciprocity," was linked to the opening of some other market to a comparable U.S. product. In a similar form, the potential of closing the American market was used as a threat to balance bilateral trade.

[99] For example, see John Zysman and Stephen Cohen, *Manufacturing Matters: The Myth of the Post-Industrialist Economy* (New York: Basic Books, 1987), and other projects organized by the Berkeley Roundtable on International Economy.

[100] See Judith Goldstein and Stephen Krasner, "Unfair Trade Practices: The Case for a Differential Response," *American Economic Review* 74 (May 1984): 282–87.

In countries with which the United States was running considerable trade deficits, more American sales in the foreign market were to be a precondition of trade. Second, participants suggested that goods sold in the United States should be made with U.S. components. Recommended legislation would have established a proportion of the total value of goods which would have to be manufactured in the United States. Third, participants wished to isolate and punish countries and producers that broke international trading rules. Section 301, the censure of Toshiba in the 1988 act, and the closing of the American market for Japanese deviations from the semiconductor agreement all typify this approach. Unlike other trade laws, the criteria for government aid were less explicit but when the government responded, aid was highly efficacious because policy was targeted to a particular nation and product and orchestrated by the office of the president.

Section 301 of the 1974 trade act offers a good example of the new unfair trade policy; the law merged the institutional autonomy granted to the office of the president after 1934 with the more open-ended authorization traditional in matters of unfair trade. The statute allowed the president to assist businesses by providing protections unavailable under the injury requirements of the antidumping and countervailing duty statutues. Section 301 authorized the president to "take all appropriate and feasible" action to "enforce the rights of the United States under any trade agreement" or to respond to any foreign practice that is "unjustifiable, unreasonable or discriminatory and burdens or restricts United States commerce." Unlike many other statutes, presidential action is permitted even without proof of material injury. The provision was modified in 1984 and then expanded into Super 301 in 1988. The lack of clear criteria for the 301 cases makes them inherently political. Such political laws, however, give decision makers flexibility to carry out policies of their choosing. In the hands of predominantly free-trade administrators, the law has been used far more frequently to open markets than to close them.

The idea of fair trade resonates as well in contemporary Congress as it did in the nineteenth century. In interactions with the executive concerning the 1988 law, for example, Congress repeatedly indicated a desire for government to expand its efforts at keeping trade fair. Thus in 1988 Congress enacted a law that required the president to retaliate against violations of trade agreements and other unjustifiable trade practices. The president could waive retaliation only under specified circumstances. Additionally, in the Super 301 cases, the administration was asked actively to identify unfair trade practices and countries. Once targeted, the countries would have only three years to rectify the transgression or face penalties. The list of practices that justified American retaliation was far-ranging, from export targeting and the denial of workers' rights to the use of foreign cartels. Further to assure that action would be taken against unfair trade, Congress handed to the STR, not the president alone, the authority to determine and remedy a foreign unfair trade practice.

In sum, by the late 1980s, the lack of fairness in international trade was a popular explanation for the lack of competitiveness of American firms. But more than supplying an explanation for the trade imbalance, the issue of unfair trade defused the more politically charged issue of market closure. Congress could concentrate on assuring a level playing field within the liberal regime and thereby appear to be supporting both expanded trade and constituents' interests.

CONCLUSION

With the close of World War II, the United States became the world's dominant political, economic, and military power. As had its British predecessor, the U.S. government pursued an economic policy in this period that maximized trade openness. But although the international distribution of wealth may have sheltered some from the ill effects of trade liberalization, hegemony is an insufficient explanation for the timing, form, and extent of the change in trade policy. On the aggregate level, the mix of policies pursued in America's liberal period was far from classic laissez-faire; vestiges of the old protective regime not only remained as elements of policy but by the 1970s formed a crucial dimension in the politics of trade policy. Thus neither the form of state intervention in defense of particular industries nor the general level of protectionism can be derived from international variables alone.

Arguing the importance of domestic factors is not to suggest that American power was unimportant in making liberalism a viable policy. Especially when we consider security issues, structural factors explain the speedy acceptance by other nations of the essentially American-designed trade regime. But it is clear that the form of liberalism defended by the United States and the extent of GATT controls derive from a uniquely American set of beliefs about the world. Although the market skewed individual incentives, it was the aggregation of these interests into strategies and policy options that determined the direction of American policy.

As in previous periods, the explanation for American policy relies not only on changing interests but on two other variables: institutional structures and ideas. American liberalization had its origins in administrative changes legislated in the 1934 trade act. If Congress had not relinquished primary responsibility for trade, liberalization would not have begun nor could it have been sustained after World War II. As critical, the mechanisms set up in 1934 were managed by believers in free trade. The Roosevelt administration allowed a well-known free trader, Cordell Hull, to orchestrate commerical policy. Later appointments went to individuals who, influenced by the hegemony of classical ideas in American academia, shared Hull's support of free trade. Thus it was not enough that the state had the administrative capacity to liberalize trade; positions of power needed to be staffed with individuals who were committed to that liberalization. The executive-centered trade system created in 1934 could as well have been oriented toward alternative visions of trade reform such as that supported by the Agriculture Department and legislated for farm products.

Liberal trade policy rested on relatively weak ground in its early years. General support developed only because liberal ideas were tested in a benevolent environment. The United States was a rising giant with an advantage in almost all areas of production. Thus just as economic decline in the 1930s provided evidence of the failure of Smoot-Hawley, economic affluence in this period was interpreted by central decision makers as caused by the move away from protectionism. Free trade and affluence became commonly associated with trade liberalization, depression and unemployment with Smoot-Hawley and protectionism.

The outcome was an unequivocal shift in the politics of making commercial policy. Congress was the dominant partner in setting tariffs before 1934 but thereafter gave the executive office the power to set America's commerical policy. In the earlier period, Congress set rates to please specific constituents, but since 1934 the executive office has set levels of protection. Delegation to the executive by Congress was not without some safeguard provisions for industry. As is shown in the next chapter, Congress created the rules by which its two agents, the ITC and STR, would adjudicate among industries that claimed a right to trade protection. But on the whole, the congressional role in setting commerical policy is far more modest than is its constitutional prerogative. Executive control allowed Congress to use trade issues for symbolic purposes with little worry about the public policy implications of its voice. Thus a great disparity developed in the postwar period between the attention given to trade issues on Capitol Hill and actual policy change.

Although trade policy-making structures forestalled unilateral trade protectionism, they encouraged relief for unfair trade. By making unilateral protections unattainable, Congress inadvertently increased societal interest in other forms of relief. Unfair trade laws establish predictable standards for import relief. Industries need only show that practices of foreign countries undermine competition; the foreign policy discretion granted to the executive after the 1930s was never a part of these laws. The result was an increase in demand for relief under these statutes and the increased salience of fair-trade issues in Congress. Congress could defend fair trade and the efficacy of open markets and still claim to be helping American producers.

Finally, when trade politics in this period is compared with policy making in earlier periods, most obvious is the decline of trade as a partisan issue. Whereas in the 1880s the political struggle over control of government was clearly expressed in debates over tariff levels, one hundred years later we see marginal differences in the positions of parties on protectionism. The lack of partisan activity does not reflect a lack of interest in trade issues. By the 1980s, trade issues had once again emerged as a central element of American foreign policy; both the actions of politicians and the attention given to trade issues by academics show evidence of the increased salience of the trade policy debate. On the whole, however, the critics of liberal policies are not found in one or the other party. Rather, the modal position of leaders in both parties is to defend the liberal trade regime as critical to American foreign policy, to agree that markets and not states should set import prices and product availability, and to associate closure with economic disaster. The urge to use trade as a partisan issue existed throughout the period; certainly, given the trade imbalance, there was a potential constituency for trade protectionism. Yet neither party took up the call. The lack of such interest on the part of both parties speaks to the continuing commitment of elites to liberal trade ideas.

CHAPTER FIVE

The Pattern of Protectionism: Conflicting Rules, Conflicting Incentives

The three preceding chapters illustrated how beliefs can influence policy outcomes at a particular moment in time. Whereas trade policy in the antebellum period was consistent with predictions based solely on considerations of interest, commercial policy in the protectionist and liberal eras reflected the incorporation into politics of a particular economic and political vision. This chapter takes one additional step and suggests that ideas matter, even when they are no longer believed by policy makers.

This chapter demonstrates that ideas—if encased in institutional structures and norms—have a long-term and significant influence on policy. Rules and norms bias the incentives of those in organizations and those whose interests are served by these organizations. In particular, trade laws channel the behavior of groups that demand aid from imports and of policy makers who award that aid. Reflective of the period of their birth, these laws legitimate differing ideas about who should and should not be protected from foreign competition. These laws are the institutional vestiges of ideational eras; they provide evidence of the importance of past beliefs that may no longer be ascribed to by current political leaders.

What are the elements of the ideas reflected in contemporary trade laws? Reflecting the epoch in which free-trade beliefs dominated, there are a set of laws and administrative structures which give little legitimacy to social claims for protectionism. Policy makers' belief in the efficiency of markets is reflected in statutes that grant minimal and temporary aid to industries. Furthermore, in these laws, a petitioner will be granted aid only if other aspects of American foreign policy are not thereby undercut. The institutional design that accommodated such a purpose was insulated from group pressures and centered ultimate control for aid in the executive office.

But as suggested in earlier chapters, in the protectionist period Congress had far less regard for the play of market forces. Rather, members agreed that it was the responsibility of government to assure that American producers were treated equitably both at home and abroad. Instead of basing policy on the potential gains from trade, congressional actions after the Civil War reflected a belief that the United States should champion domestic producers. Laws of the period legitimated social claims for state intervention, especially in any case in which an American producer was being forced "unfairly" to compete with a foreign producer. These laws were Congress-centered, that is, either Congress or a Congress-appointed agent adjudicated cases.

Furthermore, starting in the 1960s, Congress began to mandate programs that redistributed the gains from trade to import-sensitive industries. Such programs introduced a welfare or entitlement component into trade policy. The state compensated uncompetitive sectors while helping capital and labor adjust to foreign competition. The administrative structures established as a result of the passage of these acts actually encouraged group petitions. Control was entrusted to sympathetic or "captured" agencies, assuring relatively easy access and high rates of success for petitions. These laws are best thought of as "side payments" legislated to allow continued liberalization. Reflecting the commitment of policy makers to openness, these laws responded to constituents' demands for protectionism without undercutting the liberal trade regime.

In sum, a review of contemporary American laws on protectionism finds policies based on fundamentally contradictory ideas about the government's obligations to import-sensitive industries. These laws reflect the economic beliefs of their creators, not necessarily contemporary American interests or beliefs. To demonstrate the importance of past economic ideas in explaining contemporary protectionist policy, this chapter reviews seven different forms of aid offered to injured parties. The statutes that regulate escape clause, adjustment assistance, Section 301, antidumping, countervailing duty, and unfair trade (Section 337) were all legislated in response to specific issues then thought important to American producers. Three of these forms of protectionism arose in America's liberal period; three date from the protectionist era. In addition, an extralegal form of protectionism, known as voluntary export restraint agreements, is studied. Often called the "new" protectionism, these agreements are commonly employed by the executive office as alternatives to aid under one of the other statutes.

This chapter makes three claims. First, the adjudication of trade laws reflects far more the era in which they were first written than the contemporary interests of the United States or her domestic producers. Although shifting markets correlate with increased demands by various groups for government aid, laws and thus policy did not change in line with changes in American economic and political power. Second, the history of use of each of these forms of protection suggests that the ability of later policy makers to alter the intent of earlier laws is limited, even if the laws run counter to their interests and beliefs. Third, and most important, the contemporary legacy of this institutional heritage is that similarly situated industries are treated differently depending on the specific piece of trade legislation under which they petition for assistance. Thus variation in government response to groups' demands for protection reflects far more systematic differences in laws than differences in the power of the petitioning party.

To demonstrate these points, this chapter is organized in three parts. First, the legal origins and administrative structures that adjudicate claims for protection are described for the six legislated trade remedies. Second, comparative data on the extent to which each of these laws has protected American producers are presented. And third, the extralegal VER is examined as a demonstration of how contemporary policy makers have responded to the constraints imposed by this legal environment.

PROTECTIONS LEGISLATED IN A LIBERAL PERIOD

As fitting of liberal Congresses, few new protectionist instruments were legislated in the postwar years. The three most visible legislated protectionist instruments are described below. The escape clause, conceived in the 1940s, reflects then contemporary fears of a loss of protections for constituents as the United States embarked on its trade liberalization program. The second example, that of adjustment assistance, was contrived in the 1960s as a means to bolster, not to undermine, competition in the American market. Section 301 of the 1974 trade act is the newest of the three. In one sense, the law is oriented toward a nineteenth-century objective, that is, keeping the American market fair, differentiating it from the other two legislated protections. But just as with the other two laws, Congress centered protectionist activity under Section 301 in the executive branch, not in Congress or a congressional agent. It is this administrative structure which is the critical feature of this and other liberal era laws.

Escape Clause Relief

The first escape clause was introduced by executive order in 1947 and incorporated into statute in 1951. Since then the United States has always included escape clauses in trade treaties and legislation allowing the president to "withdraw or modify trade concessions and impose duties or other restrictions on imports of any article which causes or threatens serious injury to the domestic industry producing a like or directly competitive article, following an investigation and determination by the International Trade Commission." Initially, the escape clause was designed to accomplish what the old "peril point" had failed to do, that is, to keep imports at a level that precluded injury to domestic producers.[1]

The concept of an escape clause first appeared as a provision in a 1942 trade agreement with Mexico which allowed the government to terminate trade concessions for particular products if it was determined that increased imports were causing serious injury to the domestic manufacturer. This idea reappeared in the debate over the Trade Agreements Act of 1945 as a compromise by the executive following congressional transference of increased tariff-making authority. The result was Executive Order 9832, which established that all future trade agreements would include an escape clause provision.[2]

To assure congressoinal assent, the United States pushed for the inclusion of an escape clause similar to that in domestic law in the General Agreement on Tariffs and Trade. President Harry Truman condemned the provision, Article XIX, calling it "an embarrassment to be avoided in the interest of maintaining an image of United States leadership and dependability in world and foreign affairs."[3] Once the escape provision was in place, however, the United States was the first to invoke it four years later in a case involving hatters' fur. The GATT Council held that the United States was "entitled to the benefit of the doubt" in its estimation of criteria of injury. This somewhat loose interpretation of Article XIX led to the prediction that the liberal tenets of GATT would unravel in an onslaught of cases using each nation's definition of injury as grounds for protection. But the use of Article

[1] For a general legal discussion, see Stanley Metzger, "Trade Agreements and the Kennedy Round," *Georgetown Law Journal* 51 (1963): 425–69.
[2] See William Ris, Jr., "'Escape Clause' Relief under the Trade Act of 1974: New Standards, Same Results," *Columbia Journal of Transnational Law 16* (1977): 297–325.
[3] Ibid., p. 300, n. 33.

XIX to avoid liberalization by the United States or any of its trading partners in no way mirrors the magnitude of changes in trade patterns over the postwar period. Rather, when protections have been granted, unilateral and bilateral arrangements have been used instead of Article XIX.

Whereas Gatt rules record the original intent of the escape clause, its domestic U.S. counterpart evolved over time. Since the 1951 trade act, escape clause procedures have been substantially revised three times. With each revision, Congress tinkered with some aspect of the statute's procedures and the criteria by which aid would be granted. Throughout, an escape clause investigation could be triggered by a request from the president, Congress, Senate Committee on Finance or House Ways and Means Committee, an ITC motion, or an application from an interested party (usually an industry, union, or association). According to the 1951 law, the investigation determines whether any industry product "on which a trade agreement concession has been granted is *as a result,* in whole or in part, of the customs treatment reflecting such concession being imported in such increased quantities either *actual or relative,* as to *cause or threaten to cause injury* to the domestic industry producing like or directly competitive products" (emphasis added). The ITC then has six months to investigate before submitting its findings to the president. If the ITC determines that imports threaten an industry, it can recommend increasing the import barrier. In the next sixty days, the president has three options: to ignore the finding, to accept the finding but choose a different remedy, or to accept the ITC's advice. All aid is temporary; its purpose is to allow gradual readjustment of industries to market pressures.

Changes in the law have affected the phrases emphasized in the paragraph above. The 1951 act required that imports must have "contributed substantially" to injury or the threat of injury. In 1962, this criterion was considered too permissive. Instead, imports had to be the "main factor" causing injury in order to justify aid. Under the trade act of 1974, the criterion again was eased. Increased imports had to be only a "substantial cause," not the "major cause" of injury.[4]

The 1951 law required proof that injury resulted from a customs concession, but Congress in 1962 voted for a stricter stipulation. The 1962 Trade Expansion Act stated that injury must have resulted "in major part" from the concession, not just "in whole or in part." When the law was reexamined in 1974, the newer requirement was dropped.

The 1951 law declared that increases in either absolute or relative terms constituted just cause for protection. In 1962, this provision was

---

[4] "Substantial" was defined as "important and not less than any other cause."

tightened. To obtain aid, an industry had to prove that there was an absolute increase in imports. Again, the 1974 law returned to the more flexible 1951 criteria.

The one criterion that consistently has been eased is the specification of what constitutes serious injury. In 1951, Congress mandated the ITC to consider, among other things, "a downward trend of production, employment, prices, profits, or wages in the domestic industry concerned, or a decline in sales, an increase in imports, either actual or relative to domestic production, a higher or growing inventory, or a decline in the proportion of the domestic market supplied by domestic producers." In 1962, this mandate was expanded to include "all economic factors which it considered relevant including idling of productive facilities, inability to operate at a level of reasonable profit, and unemployment or underemployment." More factors were added in 1974. In the legislation Congress specified that the ITC must consider, among other things, "a decline in sales, a higher and growing inventory . . . and a downward trend in production, profits, wages, or unemployment . . . in the domestic industry concerned."

If the ITC decides in favor of a petitioner, its report is sent to the president. According to the law, he must not only consider the economic factors in the report but also assess the impact of aid on the national interest.[5] For example, he must judge the feasibility of an adjustment to market forces and the effect of aid on consumers and market competition, along with general American foreign interests. In making his decision, the president relies on the advice of interagency groups. Depending on how controversial the case is, one, two, or three committees may convene before making a recommendation. These committees—the Trade Policy Staff Committee, the Review Committee, and the Policy Committee—include members from the STR and the Commerce, Labor, State, Treasury, Defense, and Justice departments. Before meeting, formal notice in the *Federal Register* invites public comment. If there are no pressures on the president from special interests and if there is a consensus among the staff, the first committee makes a recommendation. As the problem becomes more politicized, so does the process. As one observer noted, "The amount of and the quality

---

[5] Under section 202(c) of the 1974 trade act, the president must also consider the extent to which adjustment assistance is already provided to workers and firms; the effectiveness of import relief to promote adjustment to import competition; the efforts of the industry to adjust to import competition; the effect of import relief on consumers and on competition in domestic markets for the articles under investigation; and the effect of relief on U.S. international economic interests.

of access to this process will depend on the trade value of the case and political clout of the participants."[6]

In practice, the final step—obtaining presidential approval—has posed the greatest hurdle for petitioners. Although the ITC commissioners may be convinced of the legitimacy of the aid petition, the president often uses the discretion granted in the law to find protection against the national economic interest. As one government official reported, there is "a tale, perhaps apocryphal, of a meeting in the White House in the early 60s when it was decided to grant two of four petitions, the two to be selected by flipping a coin."[7]

If the president ignores the ITC recommendation, Congress may by joint resolution disapprove of his action and direct him to follow the ITC recommendation. The president can veto this resolution, but Congress can overturn that veto with a two-thirds majority. In practice, however, Congress has never disapproved of a president's action. Congress may groan and suggest that a resolution is forthcoming, but the president maintains the institutional upper hand. On two occasions, congressional resistance took the form of a committee request to conduct another ITC investigation. In both cases, the president went along with the second ITC decision, suggesting that if so motivated, Congress could make it politically costly for him to refuse.[8] But even if a president were inclined toward protectionism, he would face substantial constraints. Escape clause aid can be awarded for up to five years; an extension can be granted for no more than three additional years. In giving aid, the president cannot increase rates above 50 percent over the current ones. And if he restricts the number of imports, he must not let the level drop below the quantity or value imported during the most recent representative period.

In short, there are many constraints on the use of the escape clause as a protective device. These constraints reflect the original conception of an escape clause as a temporary mechanism to give industry time to adjust to market forces. Use of such a clause was never intended to keep market forces at bay. Although procedural issues have been challenged and changed by Congress, the fundamental relationship between executive and legislature has not been violated. In particular, Congress has never abrogated the president's jurisdiction as final arbi-

[6] William Perry, "Administration of Import Trade Laws by the ITC," *Boston University International Law Journal* 3 (1985): 375.

[7] Ibid. Likewise, Ronald Reagan's decision to grant relief to motorcycle producers was reputedly driven by his dislike for "bikers" and thus a lack of concern for an increase in the price of motorcycles.

[8] The two cases involved trade in footwear (1977) and bolts, nuts, and large screws of iron or steel (1978).

ter. Although sentiment has been expressed for renewal of a congressional role in aiding industries injured by imports, Congress's reaction has been to give more power to the bureaucracy by easing aid requirements, not to take authority from the president. Overall, it appears that Congress is satisfied to stay remote from those needing aid.[9]

In sum, two facts emerge from a review of the legal history of the escape clause. First, legislation has changed slightly in the postwar period. Before 1962 and after 1974, the criteria for escape clause aid were easier to meet than under the 1962 act. The decisions of the ITC should then reflect these changes in law. Second, although Congress has changed the legal criteria, the basic design of the legislation has remained essentially the same: Congress sets standards, the ITC adjudicates cases, but the president makes all final decisions on relief.

Adjustment Assistance

As when Congress first legislated the escape clause, policy makers initially envisioned adjustment assistance as a program to ameliorate the economic dislocation to labor and capital that resulted from the opening of American markets. The idea was first supported by David J. McDonald, then president of the United Steel Workers, in a paper for the Randall Commission. He suggested using federal financial aid in place of escape clause aid to injured workers, firms, and communities.[10] In the 1962 trade act, a weak version of trade adjustment assistance was passed by a one-vote margin. It appeared with union endorsement in the Automotive Products Trade Act of 1965 and was expanded in the 1974 bill.

When he first suggested it in 1962, President Kennedy was surprised that his rather unusual provision passed Congress unscathed. Although AFL-CIO support was contingent on inclusion of the provision, administration officials had privately agreed to water down the provision if the Republican party offered strong resistance. According to the 1962 trade act, both workers and firms were eligible to apply for TAA. Petitions were filed with the ITC, which conducted investigations (limited to sixty days) to determine whether the petitioners fulfilled the legisla-

---

[9] This is not to say the Congress has not acted strategically to assure that certain industries get protection. Even a petition initiated by Congress to the ITC indicates to the president that a veto of a positive ruling in such a case will have political costs. Rather, I suggest that Congress is more comfortable with informal rather than formal mechanisms of control. The lack of oversight by Congress may indicate that representatives are not unhappy with the low level of aid receipt.

[10] Daniel J. B. Mitchell, *Labor Issues of American International Trade and Investment* (Baltimore: Johns Hopkins University Press, 1976), p. 36.

tive criteria. The criteria of eligibility were met if injury was due in major part to a trade concession, if injury resulted in increased imports of a like or directly competitive product, and if imports were a major factor in causing or threatening to cause serious injury to the applicant firm, domestic industry, or group of workers. Once petitions were passed by the ITC, the president certified them; if the commission vote was tied, the president was empowered to decide the case. Because the criteria used in TAA cases were effectively the same as those dictating escape clause relief, a dilemma existed. The ITC "could not be liberal in approving adjustment assistance petitions without being liberal in approving escape clause petitions. Thus, adjustment assistance—which was supposed to foster freer trade—was included in the Trade Expansion Act in such a way as to make its actual use inconsistent with that objective."[11]

When the program was relegislated in 1974, the administration again showed limited enthusiasm for it. Within the administration, the STR and both the State and Labor departments had supported the program, suggesting that inclusion of adjustment assistance was the best way to get the new trade bill through Congress; the Office of Management and Budget and treasury secretary George Shultz opposed the program as expensive and unnecessary. Why, Shultz asked, should dislocation caused by imports be treated any differently than problems associated with technological change or government decisions, such as closing a military base?[12] The STR successfully argued, however, that adjustment assistance was not merely an attempt to assuage the labor lobby; it was a chance for representatives to demonstrate that they were looking out for labor's interests. Even if the AFL-CIO refused to support the bill, one hundred members of Congress could use it to show their sensitivity to the problems associated with increased imports.[13] Congressional action proved the STR prescient. Based on the recommendation of the Subcommittee on Foreign Economic Policy, the House not only made it easier to qualify for aid but substantially increased the dollar amount of benefits. The United Auto Workers (UAW) applauded these efforts, arguing that without an adjustment assistance program in the act, the union could not divert rank-and-file pressures for protection. UAW president Leonard Woodcock explained: "No matter how deeply I and the other leaders of the UAW may believe in liberal trade policies, the UAW will not be able to resist

---

[11] Ibid., p. 43.

[12] Robert Pastor, *Congress and the Politics of U.S. Foreign Economic Policy, 1929–1976* (Berkeley: University of California Press, 1980), p. 143.

[13] Ibid.

the protectionist tide to which, regrettably, a large part of the American labor movement has already succumbed, unless the nation's trade policy is humanized as well as liberalized."[14]

In its final form, the 1974 law revamped and expanded the TAA program. First, coverage was extended to communities as well as firms and workers. Second, the investigatory responsibilities and determination of injury were given to the Labor Department for cases involving workers and to the Department of Commerce for cases involving firms and communities. And third, eligibility criteria were eased. Petitioners now needed to demonstrate only that a significant number of workers were actually or potentially affected by imports, that there was an absolute decrease in sales and production, and that imports of a like or directly competitive article contributed importantly to a decline in sales or production. "Contributed importantly" was interpreted to admit the possibility of other, greater causes. This language distinguished TAA from escape clause claims. In 1974, the escape clause required imports to be a "substantial cause" of injury, a far more stringent requirement.[15]

Although the 1974 law was a boon for applicants, there were still complaints. For instance, the criterion that imports be of a similar nature to a U.S. product disqualified some otherwise legitimate applicants, especially in cases involving auto products. In the late 1970s, workers involved with auto parts, such as bumpers, were laid off as a result of the increased sales of foreign cars. Yet because no foreign bumper was imported, their case did not meet the legislated criteria.

Once certified, firms and communities received low-cost loans and other development assistance. Workers were paid a weekly adjustment allowance of 65 percent (in the 1962 act) or 70 percent (in the 1974 act) of their averge weekly wage for up to fifty-two weeks, with a twenty-six-week extension for workers in training or those over sixty years of age. In no case could aid exceed 65 percent (70 percent in the 1974 act) of the averge weekly manufacturing wage. Employment services and relocation allowances were offered to facilitate reemployment, but these were a small part of the program.

The original 1974 program was extended in 1981 for two years, but the Reagan administration soon announced opposition to it and asked Congress to eliminate all cash payments. Congress did not concur. After considerable effort, it legislated a reduced version of TAA in October 1981 (in Title 25 of the Budget and Reconciliation Act), mak-

---

[14] Quoted ibid., pp. 155–56.
[15] Compare this with the ITC's interpretation of serious injury in escape clause cases as injury caused by a financial downturn that is "crippling" or "mortal" and not "modest" or "transitory." See case of Electric Shavers and Parts Thereof, USITC Pub. 1819, Case No. 201-TA-57 (1986).

ing aid an extension to unemployment insurance for the long-term unemployed. No additional payment was offered to those unemployed because of imports, thus eliminating a provision added by the House in 1974. The 1981 act also stipulated that certification should be based on imports as a "substantial cause"—that is, imports as the primary cause—of industry malaise, the criterion used in the 1962 act. This criterion, which made it much harder to prove eligibility, was never implemented; Congress used the Miscellaneous Revenue Act of 1982 to reinstate the less restrictive "contributed importantly" test for certification. The program was extended for two years in September 1983 and again in 1986 for an additional six.

As import pressures increased, however, President Ronald Reagan found offering funds for retraining and adjustment relief a helpful tool in his arsenal against demands for more government regulation. Reagan's change of heart occurred even though his initial observations about the ineffectiveness of TAA were borne out in a series of Government Accounting Office (GAO) reports—the program was expensive and did little to adjust workers to import competition. Little use was made of job search, relocation, or training provisions.[16] But if TAA did little to provide adjustment, it did much to assure continued liberalization. TAA was an alternative to protection that kept markets open while showing a politically expedient concern for the plight of workers. Thus Reagan's own Task Force on Economic Adjustment and Worker Dislocation in 1987 called for a national program to assist workers in their search for jobs and training.[17] Even though he called for a balanced budget, Reagan's 1988 budget allocated funds for an expanded program for job search, counseling, and training.

Congress was more than happy to cooperate and incorporated a reinvigorated TAA program in the 1988 trade act. The act extended the TAA program until September 1993 and expanded it to include oil and gas workers and "secondary workers," that is, workers providing essential goods and services to industries hurt by increasing imports. No longer would the program be criticized for draining public funds;

[16] Among these reports were "Certifying Workers for Adjustment Assistance: The First Year under the Trade Act" (May 31, 1977); "Worker Adjustment Assistance under the Trade Act of 1974: Problems in Assisting Auto Workers" (January 11, 1978); "Adjustment Assistance to Firms under the Trade Act of 1974: Income Maintenance or Successful Adjustment?" (December 21, 1978); and "Restricting Trade Act Benefits to Import-Affected Workers Who Cannot Find a Job Can Save Millions" (January 15, 1980).

[17] The panel, consisting of twenty-one business, labor, and academic leaders, was brought together in late 1985 to review problems faced by industry and workers in adjusting to technological change and foreign competition. *New York Times*, January 12, 1987, p. 1.

instead, the act provided funding via receipts from a small import fee.[18] Eligibility was expanded, and the training portion of the TAA program became an entitlement; previously, workers could be retrained only if funds were available.

In sum, TAA is a program of transfer payments. Liberalism incurs differential costs and benefits. Adjustment assistance is an institutional response to these costs; it has acted both as a welfare policy and as a way to defuse potential opposition. The latter function fostered its creation, but the former has fueled its growth. Adjustment assistance or an equivalent is mandatory for a liberal American trade policy. The program ensures support for free trade through redistribution. Liberal trade policy was condoned because it brought wealth, not economic dislocation.

Section 301 of the 1974 Trade Act

In orientation, Section 301 of the trade act of 1974 mixes nineteenth-century unfair trade ideas with a mid-twentieth-century administrative structure. The original purpose of Section 301 was to give the president authority to provide ailing U.S. businesses with aid that was otherwise unavailable because of the injury requirements of the antidumping or countervailing duty statutes. Under Section 301 the president is authorized to "take all appropriate and feasible" action to "enforce the rights of the United States under any trade agreement" or to respond to any foreign practice that is "unjustifiable, unreasonable, or discriminatory and burdens or restricts United States commerce." For the most part, the statute has been aimed at the practices of foreign governments and corporations that hurt American exports, although the law covers any foreign violation of GATT and thus could be expanded to include imports.

Under the statute, after 1974 the president could deny or modify any trade concession or increase tariff or nontariff barriers on the products and services (after 1984) of any country. In 1988, the Super 301 was legislated, mandating quicker means to identify and prosecute

[18] Under the 1974 act, the TAA program was supposed to be financed by customs duties earmarked for an adjustment assistance fund. This fund was never created and TAA was financed instead by the Federal Unemployment Benefits and Allowances account. In reality, TAA funds came from general tax revenues. For an analysis of this financing, see Richard Hobbie, *Unemployment Insurance and Trade Adjustment Assistance: Reagan Budget Cuts*, Issue Brief IB81029, June 4, 1981 (Washington, D.C.: Library of Congress, Congressional Research Service, 1981). The 1988 act required the president to negotiate with trading partners on a small uniform fee, not to exceed fifteen-hundredths of 1 percent on imports. If negotiations are not successful, the president must decide whether unilateral imposition of the fee is in the national interest.

the unfair trade activities of America's trading partners. Such action by Congress parallels its attempts to push the STR and the president toward an increasingly aggressive stance against trade rule violators. Thus in 1988, Congress told the president that he should, as always, negotiate to minimize obstacles to trade; but if negotiations fail to reach an agreement, he is ordered to retaliate—even if GATT disagrees.

A 301 action can be initiated by the president, or, in response to a petition, by the STR. If the action is initiated by the executive, the president must publish his reasons in the *Federal Register* and consult the parties involved. A petition from a private party begins a somewhat more established routine. The STR immediately notifies the foreign government named in the petition and often requests information. The STR Section 301 committee then has forty-five days to decide whether to begin an investigation. If the committee decides not to accept the case, a notice with reasons is published in the *Federal Register.* If the STR accepts the petition, the notice in the *Federal Register* reproduces the petition and sets times for public hearings. By mandate, the STR must seek advice from both foreign and domestic actors. Upon receipt of a complaint, it must attempt a negotiated settlement, notify Congress of the result of negotiations, take public comments, and obtain the advice of appropriate industry representatives as part of its determination. The STR then advises the president on what action to take.[19] He then has twenty-one days to act. Twice a year, the STR must report to Congress on all pending Section 301 actions.

Section 301 petitions must either allege substantive violations of the provisions of a trade agreement, charge that benefits have been denied to the United States under a trade agreement, or show that some practice is unreasonable or discriminatory and a burden or restriction on commerce. If no international agreement clearly applies to the trade problem, the "unjustifiable, unreasonable, and discriminatory" criteria come into play. "Unjustifiable" has been defined to include policies or practices that are inconsistent with—as opposed to contrary to— international agreements. Thus this designation covers foreign government actions that are technically legal but violate the spirit of an agreement or violate common understandings or practices that are not themselves the subject of international agreements. "Unreasonable" has been broadly defined to mean "any act, policy or practice which

[19] The time limit for this investigation is seven months for export subsidies covered by the International Agreement on Subsidies and Countervailing Duties, eight months for others not covered by this agreement. If the petition involves an issue agreed to by Congress in the Tokyo Round of multilateral trade negotiations, that time limit is thirty days after the dispute settlement; if the problem falls in none of these categories, there is a twelve-month limit to the investigation.

although not inconsistent with international legal rights of the U.S. is otherwise unfair or inequitable." This definition allows rather sweeping condemnations of government practices. "Discriminatory" includes acts that uniquely discriminate against U.S. business in favor of others. It covers acts, policies, or practices that deny national or MFN treatment to U.S. goods, services, or investment.

Unlike the other unfair trade statutes that are discussed below, Section 301s do not require material injury. The petitions go through relatively little bureaucratic hassle because they are submitted directly to the STR or other trade policy review groups rather than to the Department of Commerce or the ITC. The list of possible actions is far longer than in other unfair trade cases, and, as with the escape clause, includes the entire gamut of state instruments. Unlike the escape clause, however, they can be used in a discriminatory manner to target a particular nation.

Because Congress failed to write clear guidelines into the law, this statute is more political than either of the two instruments discussed above. No rigid administrative procedures have developed to adjudicate these cases. They remain essentially a flexible instrument of the STR and the president to be used to promote "equitable" trade. For this reason, the potential impact of Section 301 is far greater than that of any of the other statutes discussed here. Unlike the other petition processes, both parties are encouraged to make their cases and to negotiate a settlement. Clearly, the STR considers retaliation a tool of "very last resort."[20] The United States has gone to great lengths to avoid taking action against other countries, instead seeing the legislation as a means to pressure other countries into stopping their most flagrant practices.

In sum, the Section 301 process is a hybrid of old ideas and new administrative structures. Because of its clear implications for foreign economic policy, presidents have claimed total jurisdiction in these cases. They are concerned about not undermining America's other interests and have used this powerful instrument infrequently. The intellectual basis of this law, however, predates 1934—a period when congressional laws were more oriented toward stopping unfair trade than increasing fair trade. This contradiction presents an interesting dilemma for presidents who, if they choose, could find no end of exam-

---

[20] Shirley A. Coffield, "Using Section 301 of the Trade Act of 1974 as a Response to Foreign Government Trade Actions: When, Why, and How," *North Carolina Journal of International and Commercial Regulations* 6 (Summer 1981): 399.

ples in which they could claim exclusion of American products in foreign markets.

Three forms of unfair trade legislation are examined below. Antidumping, countervailing duties, and Section 337 laws were first legislated in a protectionist economic era. Indicatively, they are all oriented toward the unilateral protection of American producers from foreign predatory practices.

Along with a divergent orientation, these unfair trade laws also differ from escape clause, adjustment assistance, and Section 301 legislation in that they grant far more autonomy to the bureaucracy and far less to the executive office. For example, in escape clause cases, the president can ignore an ITC decision on the amount and form of aid if he considers it in the national interest to do so. Executives have successfully used this exception to keep the American market open. Of the unfair trade laws studied here, only Section 337 gives any role to the executive, and that role has steadily diminished. Neither antidumping nor countervailing duty legislation gives the executive authority to counteract a protectionist ruling by the bureaucracy.

As America's world position changed, all three of these statutes took on new importance. When domestic industries increasingly found themselves unable to get aid under the escape clause, they began turning regularly to these less political laws to force a government response. Unfair trade laws were not of central importance to American policy until after the 1960s; only a few ardent followers of American trade law even knew of their existence. Although infringements of these statutes were prosecuted, American producers had little need to resort to them. But beginning in the 1970s, these laws posed a foreign policy problem. U.S. producers found that general business practices in other countries qualified them for state aid under unfair trade statutes. The resulting rise in petitions and potential impact on aid led liberal administrators and the executive to obfuscate the intent of these laws. With more public attention to issues of fair trade, however, administrators lost their flexibility and the laws began to adhere more closely to their original intent.

Antidumping Laws

The immediate impetus for legislating both an antidumping law and what became Section 337 of the 1930 trade act was Section 5 of the

Federal Trade Commission Act of 1914, which stated that "unfair methods of competition are declared unlawful." In 1919, the U.S. Tariff Commission submitted a report to the House Ways and Means Committee suggesting that current law did not protect domestic manufacturers from foreign governments' unfair trade practices. The report recommended that "some official body moving along lines sanctioned by Congress in the Federal Trade Commission Act, may reasonably be specifically instructed to deal with dumping as a manifestation of unfair competitive methods."[21] Antidumping legislation, in its modern form, appeared two years later in 1921.[22]

The intent of antidumping laws is to counter international price discrimination.[23] Unlike other laws that stop price discrimination, antidumping legislation targets competition and injury to individual competitors, not competition itself. Under 1947 GATT rules, dumping is defined as the introduction of products of one country into the market of another at "less than normal value of the products." "Less than normal value" is either a price that is less than the comparable price of a like product destined for consumption in the exporting country or, in the absence of such a domestic price, the highest comparable price for a like product in a third country or the cost of production of the product in the country of origin (plus selling costs and profits).[24]

Under one rubric, American antidumping law attempts to protect against three forms of dumping: sporadic, intermittent, and persistent sales at below-market prices.[25] Sporadic dumping refers to occasional sales on the American market of goods produced abroad at unusually low prices. Intermittent dumping occurs when a producer sells cheaply on the American market only until competition has been eliminated. Once in a monopolistic position, the importer raises prices in line with or greater than real production costs. The third type of dumping is

[21] U.S. Tariff Commission, *Information Concerning Dumping and Unfair Foreign Competition in the US and Canada's Antidumping Law* (Washington: USGPO, 1919), prepared for the House Ways and Means Committee, 66th Cong., 1st sess.

[22] The Revenue Act of 1916 condemned dumping, but the law was less specific in designating unfair trade practices. In fact, the distinction between antidumping and subsidies developed only in this century. Before, these practices were lumped together simply as unfair trade.

[23] See Frederick Davis, "The Regulation and Control of Foreign Trade," *Columbia Law Review* 66 (December 1966): 1428–59; and Lowell E. Baier, "Substantive Interpretations under the Anti-dumping Act and the Foreign Trade Policy of the United States," *Stanford Law Review* 17 (March 1965): 428–46.

[24] John Jackson, "Introduction: Perspectives on Antidumping Law and Policy," in *Antidumping Law: Policy and Implementation*, ed. Jackson (Ann Arbor: University of Michigan Press, 1979), p. 3.

[25] For types of dumping, see Bart Fisher, "Dumping: Confronting the Paradox of Internal Weakness and External Challenge," in Jackson, *Antidumping Laws*, pp. 11–33.

long term; the exporter sells at below the cost of production either, for instance, as part of a corporate strategy to achieve economies of scale or, more often, because of government assistance. In general, the first form of dumping has been ignored by government officials, although its effect may be especially pernicious during economic recessions. The second, predatory dumping, is what is classically decried as an unfair practice, although the last form has as deleterious an effect on American producers. If the government rules that any form of dumping is occurring, an additional duty equal to that price differential is assessed on the product.

Until the trade act of 1979, a request from a domestic producer to the Customs Bureau of the Treasury Department would trigger a preliminary appraisal of whether just cause existed for an antidumping investigation. If the bureau found just cause, the Treasury Department would launch an investigation, the major component of which was the determination of whether sales were at "less than fair value" (LTFV). Because preliminary judgment procedures, which determined the fate of many cases, were vague, the process was often charged with being inconsistent and highly discretionary. Compared with the three forms of aid already discussed, however, the criteria for such a determination were considerably more detailed.[26]

Within three months of its initial notice, the Treasury Department would make a final determination of LTFV sales. If the department made a final LTFV ruling, the case went to the ITC to determine whether domestic injury resulted from the dumping.[27] Until 1979, the ITC had wide discretion in its determinations.[28] No hearing was

---

[26] Before 1988, dumping was defined by three hundred lines of text in the Antidumping Act, with an additional one thousand lines on administrative regulation in the *Federal Register*. In contrast, the only criterion the trade act of 1974 imposed on the president's escape clause decision was "the national economic interest of the United States," and the criteria by which that act charged the ITC with judging injury fill only thirty-five lines. See J. M. Finger, H. Keith Hall, and Douglass R. Nelson, "The Political Economy of Administered Protection," *American Economic Review* 72 (June 1982); 452–66. In the 1988 act, both statutes are clearly stipulated. The escape clause receives nine pages of explanation (although just about all details ITC procedures), while antidumping procedures take up fifteen pages of text.

[27] The original act gave the Treasury Department authority to conduct both the LTFV and the injury determinations, but a 1954 amendment delegated the determination of injury to the ITC.

[28] Thus, for example, the ITC found injury when imports represented 1.1 percent of domestic consumption in the case of printed vinyl film from Brazil and Argentina in 1973 and denied aid when there were large margins of underselling, as in welded stainless steel pipe and tubing from Japan in 1978. A review of ITC decisions shows that neither lost sales not a decline in profitability always led to a determination of injury. See Judith Goldstein and Stephanie Lenway, "Interests or Institutions: An Inquiry into Congressional ITC Relations," *International Studies Quarterly* 33 (September 1989).

necessary, even if requested by the petitioners. If the ITC found injury, it sent a report to the secretary of the treasury, who issued a "finding of dumping" and collected duties retroactively.[29] Unlike escape clause cases, a tie vote in the ITC was considered an affirmative finding. Until 1979, the Treasury Department and the ITC mandate somewhat overlapped. In particular, the ITC could overturn the Treasury Department ruling that the foreign producer was dumping.[30]

The wide discretion allowed in determining injury was a central concern to foreign governments at the Tokyo Round of GATT negotiations.[31] Since 1967, they had repeatedly criticized the United States for not adhering to the GATT Antidumping Code. The problem was a congressional decision declaring the 1954 revisions of the antidumping law to have precedence over the international codes signed in 1967.[32] The Geneva antidumping code incorporated the notion of "material injury" caused by LTFV imports. At issue was whether any degree of injury other than *de minimus* constituted injury. The United States said that it did, although the other signatories disagreed. To conform with international standards, the Senate had instructed the ITC to define "material" injury as "harm which is not inconsequential, immaterial or unimportant."[33] But more generally, the American de-

---

[29] John Cutler claims that, under the 1921 act, the dumping duties the Treasury Department charged were usually small compared with the tentative dumping margins announced earlier, because "importers have raised prices to avoid dumping duties, or foreign producers have decided to seek other, friendlier markets." He thus claims that although producers were critical of the failure of the Treasury Department actually to collect dumping duties, the administrative procedures still worked to deter dumping. See Cutler, "The Antidumping Act: Comments for Business," in Jackson, ed., *Antidumping Law*, p. 118.

[30] Davis, "Regulation and Control of Foreign Trade," p. 1442; and Baier, "Substantive Interpretations," p. 418. The example most frequently noted is vital wheat glut in 1964 against Canada.

[31] American and foreign producers were critical of American antidumping procedures, but each saw the law as favoring the other. American producers were critical of the behavior of the Treasury Department, which they claimed rejected too many cases and failed to collect what duties were charged. Foreign producers pointed out that there was no preliminary estimation of injury, forcing importers to supply information that not only was proprietary and expensive to collect but that also endangered future sales since, with an investigation in process, buyers were wary of signing long-term contracts.

[32] The U.S. decision should not have been a surprise. When the United States agreed to the GATT code in 1967, it announced that it intended to comply without changing existing legislation. Members may have feared that new legislation could open the door to protectionist amendments that would finally make the law more, not less, restrictive. See Robert E. Hudec, "United States Compliance with the 1967 GATT Antidumping Code," in Jackson, ed., *Antidumping Law*, p. 209.

[33] In 1979, the Senate again addressed the issue of injury standards. The message to the ITC was that standards were to be lower than those set in escape-clause cases: "The issue [is not] whether less-than-fair-value imports are the principal, a substantial, or a significant cause of material injury. Any such requirement has the undesirable result of making relief more difficult to obtain for industries facing difficulties from a variety of

fense to charges of noncompliance was that, although the law appeared to vary with GATT codes, in practice it had the same effect. In fact, the ITC never determined injury using the "more than *de minimus*" criterion, and the Treasury Department used its discretion to sabotage, not increase, dumping rulings.

The changes in 1979 trade legislation reveal weaknesses in the previous administration of America's antidumping law. For example, Congress set a one-year limit for the collection of dumping duties. Formerly, collection had been delayed for long periods; most often cited was the example of the seven years it took to collect $400 million worth of duties on television receivers from Japan.[34] The Treasury Department's lethargy, however, was consistent with the original intent of dumping legislation, which was to halt intermittent dumping. Legislators in 1921 did not envisage that it would be economically rational to dump for extended periods of time. Thus if dumping margins were found to exist, yet were corrected before new merchandise entered the American market, no penalty was levied. It was assumed that the charge of dumping would lead to a change in foreign prices. Correspondingly, the Customs Bureau did not develop administrative structures to collect back taxes from intransigent producers. Legislation was aimed at stopping future infringements, not punishing past infractions.[35]

The 1979 legislation also raised the bonds posted after a preliminary determination of dumping. To many, light bonds supplied no incentive for an importer to stop dumping before the final judgment or to provide requested information to the Treasury Department or the ITC. After 1979, deposits of estimated dumping duties on merchandise imposed a far more substantial financial burden on importers. Increasing the bonds was consistent with practices in the European Community, with GATT codes, and with the intent of American law.

Perhaps most important, after the 1979 legislation, the Department of Commerce made LTFV determinations. As proponents of the bureaucratic transfer suggested, the Commerce Department would be more responsive than the Treasury Department to domestic producers. Time limits were set for all stages of the dumping process, and

---

sources; industries that are often the most vulnerable to less-than-fair-value imports." *Senate Report No.* 249, 96th Cong., 1st sess., pp. 74–75.

[34] Matthew Marks, "Recent Changes in American Law on Regulatory Trade Measures," *World Economy* 2 (February 1980): 434.

[35] Until the early 1970s, still another incentive existed to dump, at least until caught, on the American market. The Treasury Department had regularly suspended an antidumping proceeding if the exporter stated an intent to discontinue sales below value. This policy generally applied to cases in which the margins of dumping were under 1.5 percent. See Peter Ehrenhaft, "An Administrator's Look at Antidumping Duty Laws in United States Trade Policy," in Jackson, ed., *Antidumping Law,* p. 109.

petitions were to be sent simultaneously to the ITC and Commerce for a preliminary determination of both LTFV and injury before a full investigation.[36]

Many critics of American dumping legislation claim that the law overly favors home producers. The procedures alone, even if no dumping exists, are often cited as being as protectionist as is a final dumping determination.[37] For instance, when the notice of an investigation is published, foreign producers and importers are forced to supply what they often consider proprietary information. Customers are also contacted and asked to supply documentation of past sales. Even more problematic for the importer, the notice of a "Withholding of Appraisement," in which the Treasury Department gives an estimated dumping margin, is always higher than final determinations. At the time of publication, customs officials withhold appraisement on all shipments of the merchandise and require importers to post bonds on future imports to cover the possibility of a final dumping determination. And because importers are not allowed to pass on dumping duties to customers, it is said that the fear of a finding of dumping is enough to cause a decline in imports, an immediate increase in prices, or both.

Although some critics find the dumping law biased toward American producers, others claim it is still too difficult for American producers to get government action on their cases. Dumping cases are among the most expensive of the available trade remedies. Legal fees are high, and even if dumping is found, the final margins are nearly always a third to half of the preliminary rulings. Perhaps more important, the rules punish frivolous cases. Not only does a petitioner have to worry about legal fees that may be wasted if the case does not pass the preliminary judgment, but filing a poor case leaves him vulnerable to antitrust charges. Further, a rejected petition may backfire: the foreign producer may be encouraged to dump because a company would hesitate to file a second petition.[38]

Regardless of whether loopholes exist in the law, the U.S. antidumping legislation reveals a far more unambiguous censure of foreign trade than does other trading law. Although both the Sherman Antitrust Act

---

[36] Only final determinations are made by the entire ITC. Preliminary determinations are made by the ITC director of operations, who takes testimony, accepts briefs, and prepares a report with a recommendation for the commission. Final determinations are heard by the entire commission in a more formal setting. Cross-examination of witnesses is allowed and experts are brought in by both sides, as is typical in a judicial administrative law situation.

[37] Cutler, "Antidumping Act;" pp. 115–23.

[38] See, for example, Charlene Barshefsky and Richard O. Cunningham, "The Prosecution of Antidumping Actions under the Trade Agreements Act of 1979," *North Carolina Journal of International Law and Commercial Regulations* 6 (Summer 1981): 307–62.

and the Clayton Act could potentially apply to the regulation of foreign as well as domestic trade, American policy makers had no liking for some of the "balance" in those laws. The arguments that low prices combat inflation, provide consumers with cheap goods, or are a healthy part of trade hold no weight when the goods are foreign.

But even such protectionist machinery has limits: when in the hands of liberal central decision makers the law was undermined. Thus, while in the control of the Treasury Department, the law was little enforced. By imposing low bonds, dropping cases when continued prosecution was politically unwise, accepting foreign producers' promises to raise prices, and foot-dragging when it was time to collect assessed duties, the department shirked its legal responsibilities. But as trade problems increased and growing numbers of producers turned to antidumping law for import relief, such behavior ultimately caused Congress to re-delegate LTFV determinations to the Commerce Department to assure petitioners a better chance of a fair hearing.

Countervailing Duty Laws

Dumping involves corporations; countervailing duties apply to practices of governments. Through subsidization of home producers, nation-states attempt to increase their share of world trade. Because long-term dumping often reflects such a state policy, the two laws work in tandem. Both counteract what are considered illegitimate forms of international trade. As stated in a 1979 Senate report, subsidies and dumping are "two of the most pernicious practices which distort international trade to the disadvantage of United States commerce.[39]

If a nation directly or indirectly gives a bounty or a grant—that is, a subsidy—to one of its domestic producers, U.S. law stipulates that an additional duty equal to the net amount of the subsidy will be levied on that product when it is imported into the United States. Current countervailing duty legislation appeared in the tariff act of 1930, but similar mandates against such foreign practices were promulgated in 1909 and 1913. In 1909, countervailing duties (CD) were part of the maximum and minimum arrangements. These stipulated two tariff schedules, with the higher applied to nations using undue discrimination against the United States through "tariff rates or provisions, trade or other regulations, charges, exactions in any other manner," or an export bounty or duty. In the 1913 trade act, the secretary of the trea-

[39] *Senate Report No.* 249, 96th Cong., 1st sess., p. 37, quoted in William E. Perry, "Administration of Import Trade Laws by the United States International Trade Commission," *Boston University International Law Journal* 3 (Summer 1985): 349.

sury was authorized "to impose additional duties equal to the amount of any grant or bounty on exportation given by any foreign country."

The procedures in countervailing duty cases are straightforward and, in virtually all aspects, mirror procedures for antidumping investigations. Upon complaint, the Customs Bureau (Department of Commerce after 1979) initiates an investigation. Until 1979, the law did not delineate how the investigation should be conducted, nor did it describe the appropriate criteria to consider. Upon completion of the investigation, the secretary of the treasury would decide whether to impose the duty and assign the appropriate "equalizing" amount.

The 1974 and 1979 trade acts addressed the problem of unclear criteria in determining aid. In 1974, Congress had empowered the executive branch to negotiate an international agreement limiting the use of subsidies by foreign governments. In return, foreign governments asked that the United States adopt a material injury test for countervailing duty investigations.[40] Later, as part of the Tokyo Round, the United States formally agreed to such a stipulation and signed the Subsidies Code, establishing a framework for conducting investigations. Thus the 1979 law specified, for the first time, actual procedures and guidelines to be followed in the investigations conducted by the new oversight agency, the Commerce Department.

Accordingly, upon receipt of a petition, Commerce Department investigators examine the foreign regulations that authorize subsidies to the industry. The department assesses their value, which is then weighted by the volume of exports, and a rate is established to offset the subsidy. If the ITC rules that there is injury, this amount is collected from the importer.[41]

As with antidumping cases, the ITC determines injury based on questionnaires sent to importers and domestic producers and on information obtained by the ITC staff through personal interviews, briefs, and other submissions. The ITC can subpoena any information not voluntarily supplied. Also as with antidumping cases, the ITC determines three issues: What is the domestic industry in question? Has there been material injury?[42] If so, did subsidies contribute to that

---

[40] The United States opposed the inclusion of injury criteria for both countervailing duty and antidumping cases under the GATT grandfather clause, which they claim exempted legislation in effect before the signing of the General Agreement in October 1947. In the 1974 law, items on the free list were subject to an injury test; in 1979, all items needed to have caused injury to an American producer.

[41] See Perry, "Administration of Import Trade Laws," pp. 382–430.

[42] In the 1979 act, the ITC was given three specific criteria in Section 771(7) on which to make its injury determination: volume of imports, effect of imports on U.S. prices of like products, and impact of imports on domestic producers. In 1984, Congress further specified what was meant by "threat of material injury" in Section 771(7)(f).

injury? The ITC need only show that the imported product caused injury—not that the subsidy itself was the culprit. Once the ITC makes a final determination (or if the preliminary determination was negative), petitioners have thirty days to appeal the decision to the U.S. Court of International Trade. On the basis of the record, the court determines whether the finding was arbitrary, capricious, or an abuse of discretion. Its decision can be appealed to the Court of Appeals for the Federal Circuit. Further appeals go to the U.S. Supreme Court. Two years after a final determination, a foreign producer can request a review of the ITC finding of injury in either antidumping or CD cases. The commission then determines whether there is still a reason to tax the producer. The ITC informs the Commerce Department of its decision; the department will then revoke or modify the order.

Between 1930 and 1979, great latitude characterized the procedures in CD cases. The size of the duty imposed was not subject to judicial review, and the Treasury Department generally had much freedom to interpret the law as it saw fit. Although the law had protectionist overtones when first written fifty years earlier, its adjudication by the Treasury Department meant that few cases were prosecuted. Many perceived that such discretion had been at the cost of the petitioner,[43] further inspiring the 1979 reforms. As with antidumping legislation, Congress no longer wanted the liberal administrators to sabotage its protections.

In sum, the standards for receipt of aid in both antidumping and CD cases are much lower than those stipulated for escape clause cases. The provisions, however, are designed not only to stop the importation of goods; rather, they are part of an overall strategy to create incentives for foreign nationals to play by the rules of the game.

Section 337 of the 1930 Trade Act

Section 337 of the tariff act of 1930 empowers the ITC to investigate complaints of unfair competition in the importation or sales of foreign products. Although it potentially applies to a wide variety of predatory import practices, most cases deal with patent and copyright violations.[44]

---

[43] See, for example, prepared statement of Charles Carlisle to the U.S. Senate Subcommittee on International Trade, Senate Committee on Finance, *Trade Agreements Act of 1979*, 96th Cong., 1st sess., pp. 489–96.

[44] Since 1974, the commission has tried to expand the jurisdiction of Section 337 cases. This attempt has met with limited success; in jurisdictional conflicts with other agencies, the ITC has generally lost. In one case in which the commission attempted to rule on predatory pricing, the president set aside the finding claiming that there was a conflict with antidumping law and that the complainant needed to exhaust relief possibilities through those channels first. See Harvey Kaye and Paul Plaia, Jr., "The Filing and De-

As with the 1921 Anti-dumping Act, Congress was motivated to write this legislation by charges that American manufacturers were protected from domestic infringements of unfair trading laws but not from foreign violators.

The modern unfair trade statute first appeared as Section 316 of the tariff act of 1922. The act instructed the Tariff Commission to report to the president all cases of unfair import competition. He could increase duties or exclude imports from the American market if he agreed with the finding.[45] Section 337 superseded Section 316 in the tariff act of 1930. The president retained the right to exclude unfair trade items, but the power to raise duties on such imports returned to Congress.[46] In practice, the ITC interprets Section 337 (and 316) as parallel to Section 5 of the Federal Trade Commission Act. As a result, the ITC uses the law almost exclusively to maintain American patent rights. The commission considers other acts of unfair trade to be largely under the purview of other statutes. Congress expanded the powers of the ITC in the 1974 act, which transferred the authority to issue exclusion orders to the ITC (changing its role from an advisory to an adjudicatory agency) and placed a one-year limit on investigations.[47] In 1979, new trade legislation gave the ITC the additional authority to fine violators up to $10,000 per day. Finally, in the 1988 trade bill, certain portions of Section 337 were revised, establishing a separate track for certain intellectual property rights claims, further reducing the evidence necessary to satisfy the domestic industry requirements, and deleting the injury requirement.[48]

Not surprisingly, these administrative changes led American corporations to look with increasing favor at filing for Section 337 protection. Unlike antidumping and CD laws—and even escape clause requirements—Section 337's injury requirement was never difficult to meet. Neither falling profits nor declining sales were necessary for relief.

---

fending of Section 337 Actions," *North Carolina Journal of International Law and Commercial Relations* (1980–81): 464–82.

[45] The president issued three exclusion orders under Section 316: synthetic phenolic resin, May 26, 1927; revolvers, July 14, 1925; manila rope, April 1927.

[46] The House version eliminated the president's right to increase duties on imports; the Senate eliminated the right of petitioners to go to the Supreme Court. *Senate Report No. 37*, 71st Cong., 1st sess., p. 67.

[47] In very complicated cases, the commission may take up to eighteen months to complete its investigation.

[48] Before the 1988 changes, the ITC had been criticized for decisions that barred relief to offshore manufacturers and licensing companies because they were ruled not to be part of a domestic industry. Thus in Title 19 of the 1988 bill, Congress stipulated a specific definition of a domestic industry, which includes any producer that either has significant investment, employment, or research and development facilities in the United States.

Whereas the definition of the industry makes it difficult for many to qualify for escape clause aid, the very narrow definition used in unfair trade cases makes it easier for the petitioners to claim damages. In sum, the injury standard, the use of a narrow designation of affected industry, and the stipulation that a decision must be rendered within one year of the date of petition make this statute a potentially powerful protectionist device.

Investigations under Section 337 of the tariff act of 1930 can be initiated through a petition by a company or by action of the ITC itself. Upon receipt of a complaint, the Office of Unfair Import Investigations undertakes an informal examination to determine whether there is sufficient evidence to begin a complete investigation. The ITC votes on whether to initiate an investigation. If it decides to investigate, notice is published in the *Federal Register* and the appropriate parties are notified. The commission has one year from this date to make its decision. In practice, cases are heard by an administrative law judge in procedures akin to a civil trial. The judge makes a recommendation to the ITC, and the commission determines whether the law has been violated.[49]

Of all the laws examined, the processes following Section 337 violations most resemble conventional litigation. The two major differences are time limitations, which impose constraints at all levels of court activity, and the presence of a third-party litigant (the commission's investigative attorney), who represents the public interest. Although neither the petitioner nor the respondent may have any claim to the "public interest," Congress has mandated that decisions be based not only on the evidence but also on a more generalized interpretation of America's interests.[50] Any of the parties can take a case to the Federal Court of Appeals.

If the ITC finds that unfair methods of competition are being used either in the importation or sale of products in the United States and that the practice has substantially injured, or threatens to injure, an industry "efficiently and economically operated in the U.S.," the prod-

---

[49] The commission has forty-five days to determine whether it will review the entire case to study points in which it disagrees with the judicial findings. Only one of the commissioners needs to ask for a review for the case to be reopened. If the commission does reopen the case, another notice then appears in the *Federal Register,* asking for the submission of briefs and giving the time of hearings.

[50] In 1974 hearings, the Senate Finance Committee stated that the ITC needed to ensure that "the public health and welfare and the assurance of competitive conditions in the United States economy must be the overriding considerations in the administration of this statute." *Senate Report No. 93-1298,* 93d Cong., 2d sess., p. 197.

uct can be excluded from entry.[51] Following an ITC exclusion order (a cease-and-desist order after 1974), the president has sixty days (under the 1974 law) in which to intervene and override the ITC's decision "where he determines it necessary because of overriding policy reasons." Policy reasons given in 1974 were the economic and political effect of the action on U.S. foreign relations, the public health and welfare, competitive conditions in the economy, and the production of like or directly competitive articles in the United States.[52] Even so, presidents have rarely overturned an ITC decision. Since 1974, only four cases have been vetoed.[53]

Unlike escape clause, CD, and antidumping cases, Section 337 cases involve standards set in the Constitution and established by international treaty. The Constitution provides clear guidance on patent and copyright protection; Section 337 cases are simply a broader enforcement of rules on intellectual property. Not surprisingly, then, the injury standards are mild; even before the 1988 law, the ITC made the criteria in these cases the loosest of those in its jurisdiction. Even in situations in which the domestic industry's profits were still increasing and use of capacity was near 100 percent, the ITC found in favor of petitioners.[54] Since the logic of these cases suggests that patent rights guarantee owners monopoly rights on the trade good, any decrease in sales was accepted as evidence of a relationship between patent violation and decline in sales. These standards indicate that Congress wants to encourage fair competition; if foreign producers are cheating and cannot defend their practices using contemporary legal standards, they deserve to be punished.[55]

THE USES OF PROTECTIONIST LAWS

Six legal mechanisms available to those who have suffered from American trade policy have been outlined above. Below data are presented on the implementation of these statutes. The analysis focuses on two specific questions relating to protection against imports. First,

[51] On issues of industry efficiency and the extent of injury, standards favor domestic producers; the ITC has never denied aid because an American industry was run inefficiently.

[52] Perry, "Administration of Import Trade Laws," p. 451.

[53] The reasons given in these cases were the detrimental effect of the remedy on national economic interests, the potential detrimental effect on international relations, the need to avoid conflicts in the administration of the unfair trade practice laws, and the probable lack of any significant benefit to U.S. procedures.

[54] Perry, "Administration of Import Trade Laws," p. 432.

[55] Kaye and Plaia, "Filing and Defending of Section 337 Actions," p. 480.

has the rise in requests for aid led to a corresponding increase in protectionism? If protection varies as much or more across types of aid as over time, then shifts in America's world economic position and society's resultant discontent alone cannot explain protectionism. Rather, policy may be determined by legal structures as critical intermediaries between changes in interest and outcomes. Second, if institutions are critical in translating societal demands into policy outcomes, what is the impact of a different ideational logic on who is granted aid under each of these statutes? If laws reflect different ideas about the legitimacy of protectionism, there should be significant variation in who gets how much of each form of aid.

Escape Clause and Adjustment Assistance Data

Table 5.1 displays the aggregate data on petition activity, ITC response, and final presidential decision in escape clause cases. The table, which shows data for all cases decided between 1958 and 1991, is organized according to major legislative periods.

Table 5.1. Escape-clause cases (in effect 1958–1991)

Year[a]	Average number petitions/year (total)	ITC acceptance rate[b]	Presidential acceptance rate	
			Approved[c]	Approved with ITC relief
1958–1962	11 (56)	.27	.14	.07
1963–1974	3 (31)	.30	.13	.03
1975–1978	10 (40)	.60	.23	.03
1979–1991	2 (30)	.48	.27	.11

Source: U.S. International Trade Commission, *Annual Report* (Washington: USGPO, 1975–82); U.S. President, *Annual Report of the President of the U.S. on the Trade Agreements Program* (Washington: USGPO, 1958–91); U.S. Tariff Commission, *Annual Report* (Washington: USGPO, 1958–89), *Federal Register,* 1958–1991.
[a] Organized by legislative periods.
[b] Includes split votes and cases to extend relief due to expire.
[c] An award of adjustment assistance alone is not considered.

Two points immediately stand out. First, petition activity is not a good predictor of either ITC or presidential acceptance rates. The years of greatest interest in the escape clause were the early 1960s, when congressional standards made it difficult to receive aid. After the 1974 act, there was again a relatively large number of applicants and a relatively high acceptance rate. In both periods, presidential action reversed ITC rulings. Further, as shown in the last two columns on approval rates, even the minimal relationship between ITC behavior and petition activity disappeared. The period showing the highest final acceptance rates was 1979 to 1991, when petition activity was extremely low. The president's high rate of acceptance in this twelve-year period could have resulted from general political pressure to aid industry, but if so, such pressure was not successful: the form and amount of relief in the 1979–91 period (11 percent) does not differ significantly from the 1958–62 period (7 percent).

Second, legislated changes in the law appear to be prima facie explanations for variation in ITC acceptance rates. The ITC increased its acceptance rate from 27 to 48 percent between 1958 and 1991, with the greatest increase occurring after passage of the 1974 law. This relationship between congressional legislation and ITC votes is less apparent in the 1958–62 period. Although the legislation was similar to that after 1974, the acceptance rate was relatively low. This discrepancy occurred because fewer industries met the technical criteria of injury.

Although ITC behavior seems to be linked to congressional action, presidential actions cannot be so explained. Table 5.1 does, however, reveal two aspects of presidential behavior. First, presidents have routinely vetoed ITC decisions. On more than half the cases that the ITC decided in favor of an industry, the president overruled that decision on grounds of the national economic interest. In this manner, the president minimized the effect of congressional changes in injury criteria. This is not to suggest that the president is immune from generalized pressures to aid industry—the rise in acceptance rates after 1975 bespeaks such pressure. Rather, the evidence suggests that the president uses his authority, given these constraints, to undermine protectionist ITC decisions. Second, presidents who accept ITC decisions use their authority to blunt the protectionist instrument. We can assume that ITC decisions on aid reflect the advice of technical experts.[56] The president has repeatedly deviated from the suggested remedy, awarding less than the ITC has suggested, and so has minimized closure of the American market.

In sum, the adjudication of escape clause cases reflects the biases of its creators. Compared with earlier forms of protectionism, the escape clause allows for significant presidential discretion in awarding aid. The executive has on occasion granted protection; under enough pressure, any elected leader will respond to the demands of his constituency. But overall, the institutional arrangement that characterizes escape clause

---

[56] Although there is probably some strategic behavior on the part of the ITC, it should bias the commission toward underestimating, not overestimating, the necessary remedy.

protectionism has allowed liberal presidents to be more isolated from constituent pressure than would otherwise be the case. As a result, the nation has experienced less protectionism than shifting constituent and international interests would suggest.

Table 5.2. Trade adjustment under the 1962 and 1974 trade adjustment assistance statutes, 1963–1989

Year[a]	Average petitions per year		Acceptance rate	
	Commerce[b]	Labor	Industry	Worker
1963–1974	5	19	.37	.30
1975–1978	8	882	.91	.45
1979–1981	623	2,071	.81	.28
1982–1989[c]	251	1,311	.97[d]	.47

Source: Department of Labor data; Department of Commerce data: ITC, *Annual Reports* (Washington: USGPO), 1963–75.

[a] By legislative mandate.

[b] Some pre-screening at regional offices reduces number of cases and increases possibility of aid.

[c] Between 1975 and 1989, although the average rate of acceptance of labor petitions was only 36%, these cases represented 51% of workers who applied for aid.

[d] This was distributed as $94.8 million in technical assistance and $63.3 million in loans.

Comparing Table 5.1 with Table 5.2, we can see clearly that government reluctance to assist those adversely affected by imports did not extend to adjustment assistance. Table 5.2 shows that requests for adjustment assistance have increased significantly over time: the number of cases jumped from under twenty a year, when the program was administered by the Tariff Commission, to about a thousand a year for labor petitions and to over two hundred each year for corporate petitions in the Reagan years. The increase in petitions, beginning in 1975, indicates that petitioners quickly reacted to the easing of legal aid requirements. Further, although both laws serve similar constituencies, the number of petitioners receiving aid is significantly higher than for the escape clause cases. After the 1974 law went into effect, a little over 40 percent of the labor petitions and over 85 percent of the business petitions were successful. And even though adjustment assistance is a redistributive program, its use has little to do with partisanship; Reagan's acceptance rate is closest to Jimmy Carter's—two administrations whose stated positions were diametrically opposed on the responsibility of government to ease market forces.

Tables 5.3 and 5.4 take the comparison of escape clause and adjustment assistance cases one step further. These tables examine the effectiveness of different industries in gaining state aid, using a twenty-year sample period for each of the two types of aid.[57]

Table 5.3. Predicting escape-clause aid, 1958–1978

Variable	B (Standard error)
Change in number of employees	−1.51[a]
	(.32)
Government petitions	.28[b]
	(.17)
New capital expenditures	10.78[a]
	(2.00)
Association petitions	−1.18[a]
	(.26)
Average import penetration	−6.29[a]
	(1.30)
Industry petitions	.93[a]
	(.17)
Intercept	1.16
	(.179)

Sources: See Table 5.1; U.S. Department of Commerce, *Census of Manufactures* (Washington: USGPO, 1964, 1967, 1972, 1977, 1982); U.S. Department of Commerce, *U.S. Imports, SIC Based Products, FT 210 Annual* (Washington: USGPO, 1964, 1972, 1978, 1979, 1980, 1981); U.S. Department of Commerce, *U.S. Exports, SIC Based Products, FT 610 Annual* (Washington: USGPO, 1965, 1972, 1978, 1979, 1980, 1981).
[a] Significant at the .01 level.
[b] Significant at the .10 level.

If the aggregate data portray the escape clause as legitimating freer trade, so, too, does the regression model. The data on petitions filed between 1958 and 1978 show that a number of variables significantly affected who received escape clause aid. First, who petitions is important. Data were collected on five catgories of petitioners—single industries, trade associations, government, unions, and unions and in-

[57] The information in Tables 5.3, 5.4, and 5.7 was modeled from the same data set. That data set included all industries that applied for at least two of these three types of aid between these years, disaggregated by eight-digit product categories and then reorganized into four-digit Standard Industrial Classification codes. This method allows petitions covering large product groups to be weighted appropriately. The estimations of the model were produced using weighted least squares.

The variables that are used to explain government response were organized into seven analytic groups: indicators of international competitiveness; measures of import penetration or export strength; indicators of relative industrial size; measures of relative industrial strength; measures of success of previous petitions; measures of change in industry characteristics; for the unfair trade table, the country that would be affected if a positive ruling were made.

Table 5.4. Adjustment assistance model, 1963–1978

Variable	B (Standard error)
Average value of imports	5.76[a]
	(.74)
Value of shipments	.34[a]
	(.05)
Growth in exports	−.24[a]
	(.03)
Change in number of production plants	−.14[a]
	(.03)
Change in labor costs	.28[a]
	(.07)
Average capital intensity	.03[a]
	(.01)
Change in number of employees	.02[a]
	(.004)
Change in export shipments	.21[a]
	(.04)
Change in level of technological sophistication	.34[b]
	(.16)
Intercept	−5.53
	(.63)

Source: Computed from data in Tables 5.2 and 5.3.
[a]Significant at the .01 level.
[b]Significant at the .05 level.

dustries filing jointly. Government and industry petitions had a better chance of getting aid; conversely, petitions from associations were inversely related to success rate. That government petitions would be more favorably received was expected. These petitions to the ITC— either from Congress, the president, or the ITC itself—get special attention. Often they are cases that have been refused before. Although repeated petitioning generally does not seem to increase an industry's propensity to receive aid, a repetition from a government agency probably does.

It is less clear why industry petitions are more likely to get aid than association petitions. The explanation may lie in the types of cases filed by single industries and those filed by associations. If association petitions represent smaller industries or ones that have had less previous contact with the government petition process, they may have a more difficult time receiving government assistance. On further examination, this proved to be the case. Petitions from industries were from larger manufacturers with relatively high petition activity. "Petitioning agent" may be an indirect surrogate for industry size.[58]

Three other factors help explain who gets escape clause aid: change in number of employees is negatively related to success; new capital expenditures are positively related to success; and average import penetration is negatively related. All three findings contradict what is commonly envisioned as the typical aided industry. Of the industries asking for aid, those that receive escape clause aid are not the relatively unsophisticated industries or the ones suffering from the greatest import penetration. They are, however, the industries having relatively large declines in employment, which perhaps makes an executive veto politically unfeasible.

These findings are revealing. First, import penetration does not affect aid receipt in the way one would expect. All the industries in the sample were import-competing, but those that did receive aid were not necessarily those with the most penetrated markets. Second, who petitions seems to matter as much as the merits of the case. This finding suggests a political, rather than an economic, explanation for protection. Third, industries that received aid were relatively healthier than the bulk of industries in the sample. These industries still invested in capital improvements, which in these equations serve as proxies for a range of other industry attributes. In short, it appears that the more competitive members of the sample received more aid. Last, there is a strong relationship between the size of the industry and aid receipt. Large industries suffering declines in employment are more apt to get a favorable response from the state.

These results are not wholly compatible with any of the traditional explanations of the nature of protectionism. It is clear that the results are far from what would be predicted from a review of the legislation. The neediest are not those that are receiving aid. The finding that who petitions affects outcome, that declines in employment elicit a state response, and that aid goes to the most competitive of the industries that petition fits broadly with an interest group or political explanation of aid. If capital expenditures and employment decline are indicative of the ability to organize and get results, and if government petitions are assumed in the name of powerful constituents, then it may be that the ITC and president are heeding the needs of the socially powerful by aiding the upper strata of manufacturers. But alternately, it is coun-

---

[58] The Pearson correlation between average employment (1963–77) and petition activity is .69 (P = .oo). The correlation between employment and petitioning as an industry (not through an association) is .45 (P = .oo).

terintuitive to think that association petitions would be inversely related to success and that import penetration would not lead to far greater interest and organization to get aid. From the perspective of international structural theories, both the lack of longitudinal change in import relief and the inverse relationship between imports and outcomes are counterintuitive. Although it is difficult to generate clear hypotheses at this level of analysis from a systemic theory, a structural perspective would suggest that a change in America's position in the world— as evidenced by import increases and interest in aid—should, but does not, result in an increase in protection.

The comparison across types of aid is even more revealing. Table 5.4 displays a similar regression analysis on a sample of adjustment assistance cases.[59] The results show that industries receiving aid face heavy import competition, are relatively small in size, have declining exports, are closing factories, and show increasing labor costs. They are the industries economic theorists predict will be victimized in international competition.

The other attributes of those that receive adjustment assistance, however, are less intuitive. Relative to all industries that applied for adjustment assistance, those that were successful were more capital-intensive and had gone through relatively greater changes in industry technology during the years examined. These industries have declining export markets and resultant fluctuations in their employment numbers. These findings can be explained by the type of industry facing stiff import competition after the 1970s. The sample of adjustment assistance petitioners is dominated by the large "boom" industries of the postwar period. The government targeted these industries, which included steel and autos, as the logical recipients of adjustment assistance.

The legislative intent of escape clause and adjustment assistance legislation explains some of the variation in their uses. The discretionary nature of escape clause legislation translates into a state policy that uses criteria other than need. Comparatively, as a transfer payment or an illusory form of protectionism, adjustment assistance is given to industries that are suffering as a result of the opening of the American market, as was intended. Although the same industries demand both forms of aid, the state differentiates its package of rewards. Variation, however, is caused by more than legislative mandate. Individuals en-

[59] Fewer years are covered than in escape clause cases. Adjustment assistance was legislated in the 1962 act.

trusted to carry out these laws were biased toward giving transfer payments and away from restrictions that close the American market.

Section 301 Data

There are significant differences between the use of Section 301 and the other forms of import relief examined here. Section 301 is the only form of unfair trade relief in which the executive has primary jurisdiction. But also, the intent of this law is different; instead of punishing offenses through an increased tariff to equalize the market, the law is oriented toward changing the practices of other nations. If necessary, presidents are unconstrained in their response to unfair trade—they could hike tariffs sky high if they thought that such pressure would bring a nation to the negotiating table. The goal of this law, however, was to make the unilateral closing of the American market a last resort. Import restrictions were to be used strategically, keeping in mind America's foreign policy needs. Section 301 was not seen as a tool for making a "level playing field" in the United States but rather as an instrument to assure liberal world trade.

This purpose is evident from government behavior. Table 5.5 lists the average number of 301 petitions filed since passage of the 1974 trade act. The numbers are far smaller than in any of the other categories examined. The effectiveness of each petition, however, is far greater. Although the STR states that two-thirds of the petitions were either terminated or turned down, a review of each case reveals that in only six had government action not led to some change in the behavior of the targeted foreign nation. In the rest of these cases, termination meant that the petitioner was satisfied with the reaction of the trading partner. Since 1974, the president has been forced to use his authority to increase tariffs on imports under this statute only five times. In each case, the action gained the immediate attention of the foreign nation and quite quickly led it to the negotiating table.[60]

Although presidents have been loath to use their 301 authority unilaterally to close the American market, if American producers are uncompetitive because of international cheating, even free-trade presidents, such as Ronald Reagan, will punish offenders. Presidents have found protection to be acceptable when oriented toward the further liberalization of markets, not to protect uncompetitive producers. Countries should negotiate to remove trade barriers, not unilaterally

---

[60] Tariffs were increased in response to problems in citrus and pasta, semiconductors, European Community enlargement and exports to Spain, Brazil pharmaceutical and Canadian softwood.

Table 5.5. Section 301 petitions, 1975–1991

Year	Average number of petitions
1975–1979	4
1980–1984	5
1984–1991	5

Source: U.S. Trade Representation, "Trade Action Monitoring System," August 19, 1993.

increase them. But the United States will not accept the "sucker's pay-off"—all nations that benefit from open trade borders must play by the same rules. Foreign policy concerns may temporarily lead central decision makers to ignore trade infractions, but such cheating has never been condoned.

Unfair Trade Data

Table 5.6 displays petition activity and acceptance rates for the three other unfair trade laws. As was suggested by the review of their legal histories, petition activity increased in all categories after passage of the 1974 law and remained high or higher after 1979. This general increase in interest in all forms of unfair trade remedies, however, is not mirrored by increases in acceptance rates.

Table 5.6. Antidumping (AD), countervailing duty (CD), and Section 337 cases, 1958–1991

Year[a]	Average petitions per year			Acceptance rate		
	AD	CD	337	AD	CD	337
1958–1962	28	1	1	.04	1.00	.00
1963–1974	24	1	4	.22	.93	.13
1975–1978	42	37	12	.15	.30[b]	.28
1979–1991	40	18	22[c]	.38	.30	.29

Source: See Table 5.2; U.S. Government, *Federal Register* (Washington: USGPO, 1958–83).
[a] Organized by legislative periods.
[b] Of these cases, only 8 percent were not waived.
[c] Data are from 1990 only.

In countervailing duty cases, the high rate of acceptance in the early period reinforces the argument that subsidies were never considered legitimate. As the number of cases accelerated, however, the acceptance rate undermined America's commitment to the further liberalization of world commerce. One possible response was for the president to use the provision in the 1974 act allowing him to waive the CD if the country in question was negotiating with the United States over its subsidy policy. In the last years of the Tokyo Round, over 90 percent of the products that had technically qualified for aid were so waived. And although there was a fear that the 1979 change in jurisdiction to the Commerce Department would lead to an increase in CDs, the joint efforts of Commerce and the ITC led to about the same number of petitions approved as had the Treasury Department from 1974 to 1979.

One of the most surprising features about the antidumping law is its long history of use. The law has been used consistently as a mechanism to keep the American market fair. Its low approval rates in the late 1950s may be attributed to America's economic strength—few foreign manufacturers had yet acquired the capacity to threaten American producers at home. With increased competition, however, antidumping legislation became what its creators in 1921 envisioned: a foreign policy equivalent of American fair-trading laws. From an acceptance rate of under 5 percent in the early 1960s, dumping findings increased to an average of 15 percent under the 1974 act and 38 percent under the 1979 act.

Section 337 determinations are the most technical of the types of protection examined. They typically involve complex issues and procedures that encourage settlement between parties. Thus the 28 to 29 percent acceptance rate that has held since 1974 underestimates the number of instances in which American producers have used the petition process to stop an unfair trade practice.[61] Also, although the president is so empowered, he vetoed only four rulings in the cases covered by this study. Two factors explain such presidential reticence. First, a favorable finding clearly signifies that a particular foreign producer has taken predatory action toward American technology. International and domestic norms have been violated. Patent violations or other forms of industrial espionage are not accepted anywhere. Second, a favorable ruling arises from a complex process. The ITC's clout resides in the sophistication of the procedures used to adjudicate the cases. Thus both the content of the ruling and the method of its determination serve to dampen the incidence of a presidential veto.

[61] The number of settlements in the 1963–78 period equaled the number of favorable rulings. Since 1979, they have exceeded the number of positive decisions. There were eighty-one settlements, sixty violations, and eighty-seven terminations (fifty without prejudice) between 1979 and 1989.

Table 5.7 compares these laws with each other and with the fair-trade laws. Since the 1960s, there have been far more cases involving unfair trade than the escape clause. Although the adjustment assistance figures dwarf all four of the other legal remedies, the escape clause has clearly been underused. The reason may be found in the strategic behavior of petitioners. Relative to all the other types of aid, it is most difficult to get a favorable escape clause ruling. The drop in the number of CD cases most probably stems from the use of Section 301 as a more generalized remedy for foreign subsidization. In general, the government seems to respond more favorably to assertions of foreign dumping, subsidization, and patent stealing than to claims that a manufacturer cannot compete because of lowered tariffs. The data are compatible with the interpretation of the legislation already offered.

Table 5.7. Final outcomes of EC, AA, and U.S. unfair trade cases by legislation period, 1963–1991

Year	EC	AA[a]	AD	CD	337
1963–1974	(3) .03[b]	(24) .31	(24) .22	(1) .93	(4) .13
1975–1978	(10) .03	(890) .45	(42) .15	(37) .30	(12) .28
1979–1991	(2) .11	(1871) .47	(40) .38	(18) .30	(22) .29

Source: See Tables 5.1, 5.2, and 5.5
Note: Top number indicates average number of petitions; bottom number indicates percentage approved.
[a] Weighted average of worker and industry rates; data only through 1989.
[b] With percent approval of ITC remedy.

Again, although the number of affirmative findings has increased, that increase has been slight over time. Only in antidumping cases did the number of favorable findings double in the last period over the two earlier periods. Either changes in the law or an increase in the incidence of dumping would explain the increased determinations of dumping. Since the increase occurred without a rise in petition activity, it is more likely caused by changes in the adjudication of the law by the Commerce Department. Similarly, in both CD and 337 cases, response rates are far more closely associated with changes in the law than with increased numbers of petitions.

As with fair trade cases, these data suggest the importance of the law itself as well as who administers it. For example, the ITC decides both Section 337 and escape clause cases; Commerce and the ITC together consider antidumping and CD cases. Yet we see no pattern based on agency jurisdiction. Similarly, presidents have undermined the escape clause provision but allowed ITC decisions on Section 337 cases to pass unaltered.

In comparisons of who actually received aid based on unfair trade, relative to fair trade, differences are again apparent. Table 5.8 repeats the modeling exercise found in Tables 5.3 and 5.4.

Table 5.8. Unfair trade aid model, 1958–1978

Variable	B (Standard error)
Petitions from Europe	1.23[a] (.35)
Total number of unfair trade petitions	−0.42[a] (.12)
Average value of export shipments	2.04[a] (.73)
Average new capital expenditures	−6.24[b] (2.82)
Intercept	.85 (.13)

Source: Sources listed in Tables 5.3 and 5.5.
[a] Significant at the .01 level.
[b] Significant at the .05 level.

When all these decisions are grouped, they reveal a pattern of aid receipt that varies greatly from that found for the other cases. First, a national bias is apparent. Although Japan is the competitor nation most often named in petitions for relief, the petitions against European nations have a higher probability of receiving aid. This high success rate cannot be explained by a greater incidence of cheating. Two likelier explanations are that the numbers reflect executive involvement—for foreign policy reasons, CD cases were waived, the trigger price system instituted, and VERs negotiated, undermining the number and type of positive unfair-trade rulings—and that part of the variation speaks to legal issues—it is easier to document unfair trade by some countries than others.

Three other attributes of petitioners are associated with success rates. Industries that are relatively more export-oriented gain more aid. Those that have spent relatively less on new capital expenditures benefit more. And finally, industries that have petitioned less often seem to elicit more favorable government responses.

The negative relationship between aid and capital expenditures is the most intuitively obvious of the three findings. The industries that receive aid are the least competitive in the applicant pool. They have chosen not to reinvest, perhaps because business practices in other nations have led to a more competitive foreign product. The other two findings need more explanation. The negative relationship between number of petitions and aid receipt is counterintuitive. Most theories of American politics look to pressure on government officials as the primary explanation for protectionism. Here the relationship runs in the opposite direction. The most likely explanation is that repetition may indicate a relatively weak case. The more one needs to apply, the less likely it is that one initially had strong cases.[62]

The relationship between exports and aid can be explained in a similar way. The firms that are most involved with world trade are most affected by the trading practices of their competitors. They are also most aware of the trading practices of different countries and firms. Both contribute to the legitimacy of their claims.

In sum, the politics of obtaining aid based on unfair trade is unlike that for escape clause, adjustment assistance, or Section 301. Although the same industries apply for relief, different laws dictate a different purpose for each type of aid.

EXPORT RESTRAINT AGREEMENTS

The use of VERs provides further insight into the constraints imposed on liberal central decision makers by the legal protectionist apparatus just presented. Since the 1960s, the most visible method for ameliorating the ill effects of trade has been the VER. VERs are similar to quotas; in effect, they place some limit on the amount of a product that can enter the United States.[63] Although producers gain relief from import pressures, this form of aid is far from optimal from the perspective of the national interest. Tariffs and even quotas can help the

---

[62] There is also the possibility that, given the sample years, we are seeing the effects of the trigger price mechanism, which led to the withdrawal of an unusually large number of petitions. Since such an action is coded as a petition that did not receive aid, the model may be biased on such cases.

[63] There are distinctions, often pedantic, among export restraint agreements. A VER is a response to pressures from an industry or government in an importing country, which formally remains a unilateral action by the exporting nation. The restriction is voluntary in the sense that the country formally has a right to eliminate or to modify it unilaterally and it is essentially monitored and enforced at the exporting country's border. In the second type of agreement, the voluntary restraint agreement (VRA) the importing country and the exporting country share responsibility for the administration of the agreement. Elimination or modification of the agreement requires the consent of both countries. Within this category, the term "orderly marketing arragement" (OMA) is reserved for government-to-government negotiations while VRA is often used to cover, in addition to OMAs, arrangements with industry participation. See Michel Kostecki, "Export-Restraint Arrangements and Trade Liberalization," *World Economy* 10 (December 1987): 425–28.

blighted industry while they add dollars to the national treasury, but VERs give all the "rents" to the exporting country. For the exporting nation, a VER is preferred to either quotas or tariffs because it is often equivalent to a global cartel, especially in industries with high entry barriers and limited numbers of suppliers.[64] Through upgrading, controlled markets, and transshipment, VERs yield high prices for the importing consumer and high profits for the exporting industries.[65] All this makes the VER a poor substitute for a tariff increase.

[64] See Vinod Aggarwal, Robert Keohane, and David Yoffie, "The Dynamics of Negotiated Protectionism," *American Political Science Review* 81 (June 1987): 347.

[65] The repeated use of the VER as American policy has also created legal problems. The premise of the Sherman Act is that "competition produces the best allocation of resources, the lowest prices, the highest quality and the greatest progress." Jacqueline Nolan-Haley, "The Trigger Price Mechanism: Protecting Competition or Competitors?" *New York University Journal of International Law and Politics* 13 (Spring 1980): 3. Thus the decision to control prices through both implicit and explicit agreements with foreign competitors contradicts both the letter and the spirit of the law. For example, programs such as the trigger price mechanism forced the Treasury Department to consult with foreign producers when their invoices indicated that their prices were too low. As one legal analyst concluded: "To the extent that it attempts to control competition from imported steel mill products, the TPM thus is 'in restraint of trade or commerce among the several States, or with foreign nations' within the meaning of Section 1 of the Sherman Act. To the extent that it determines or controls prices at which imported steel mill products enter the domestic market, the TPM also is a species of price fixing, manipulation or stabilization." Ibid., p. 12. Both the issues of antitrust violations and the legality of VERs were raised in the courts shortly after the first set of agreements. In *Consumers Union of the United States* v. *Kissinger,* a consumer group questioned the legality of the 1972 steel agreements. The suit made two claims. First, it said the VER violated the Sherman Act and second, that the VER was an ultra vires of the executive branch because of failure to conform to the procedural requirements laid out in escape clause cases. Not surprisingly, the District Court agreed that "very serious questions can and should be raised as to the legality of the arrangements under the Act." Carl Green, "The New Protectionism," *Northwestern Journal of International Law and Business* 3 (Spring 1981): 8. As to the role of the executive branch, the court argued that Congress had jurisdiction, but since the VER was nonbinding, the court would, in this case, uphold the authority of the executive branch. But the court questioned the future ability of the executive to negotiate VERs, whether or not they were in the national interest. "The President clearly has no authority to give binding assurances that a particular course of conduct, even if encouraged by his representatives, does not violate the Sherman Act or other related congressional enactments any more than he can grant immunity under such laws. . . . When representatives of the Executive Branch venture into areas where the antitrust laws have apparent application, they must proceed with strict regard for legislation outlawing restraints of trade so that no action taken will be inconsistent with the clear requirements of settled national policy. . . . The court declares that the Executive has no authority under the Constitution or acts of Congress to exempt the Voluntary Restraint Arrangements on Steel from the antitrust laws and that such arrangements are not exempt." Nolan-Haley, "Trigger Price," p. 15. In response, Congress enacted a limited waiver in Section 607 of the trade act of 1974 to exempt steel agreements made before January 1975 from antitrust prosecution.

Similar problems arose over the auto agreement. There was no specific congressional exemption for autos, although the House had passed a resolution suggesting the negotiation of an export agreement. The lack of the exemption, however, put the administration and the auto companies in a legal bind. Negotiating the agreement without a specific

Much attention since the 1970s has focused on the use of these agreements as indicative of a new protectionism. As a government response to ailing industries, these interstate agreements did not appear in regular use until this time. In that sense they were a new protectionism. Whether or not these agreements constitute a deviation from general liberal trade policy, however, is far from self-evident. Most academic studies show VERs to be inefficient and short-term remedies for structural deficiencies in the American economy.[66] At best, one can argue that the extent of protectionism afforded by these marketing arrangements is indeterminate. With the exception of the textile accords, which may be best explained by European, not American, insistence on higher barriers to trade, VERs may be the most liberal of possible American options.[67] The three examples below suggest that the American executive—institutionally constrained as well as politically compelled to offer some response to beleaguered industries—often finds VERS an attractive alternative to the more deterministic and protective forms of aid described above.

Carbon Steel

The American steel industry lost its international competitive edge in the late 1950s; by the mid-1960s, foreign competition was hurting home producers. Although steel was under the somewhat protective barrier of a 6 to 8 percent ad valorem tariff, new discoveries of iron ore deposits, declining shipping costs, rising American wages, and improved foreign technologies stimulated foreign competition.[68]

---

congressional waiver risked not only antitrust suits against the exporters but legal issues for the American officials who negotiated the agreement.

The solution was a bit of creative legal manipulation. The United States could not have a formal agreement with Japan, for that would surely be an ultra vires under the *Consumers Union* rationale. In fact, the administration had to avoid any use of the words "agreement" or "negotiations" with Japan. The Japanese government needed to say that the restraints were entirely voluntary; the Japanese car manufacturers needed to say that they were wholly involuntary. This way, if sued under American antitrust law, the companies could claim the defense of foreign legal compulsion. American courts would then recognize that the actions of firms were compelled by a foreign sovereign. Green, "New Protectionism," p. 10. Assurances against legal action were requested and given to the government of Japan in the form of a written opinion by the Department of Justice assuring them of the legality of this arrangement.

[66] See, for example, David B. Yoffie, *Power and Protectionism: Strategies of the Newly Industrializing Countries* (New York: Columbia University Press, 1983).

[67] See Vinod K. Aggarwal, "The Unraveling of the Multi-Fiber Agreement, 1981: An Examination of International Regime Change," *International Organization* 37 (Autumn 1983): 617–45.

[68] See Robert Crandall, *The U.S. Steel Industry in Recurrent Crisis: Policy Options in a Competitive World* (Washington, D.C.: Brookings Institution, 1981), for a general analysis of the industry and its problems with international competition.

In response to an articulate, well-organized steel lobby, Congress in the fall of 1968 considered a steel quota bill that would have rolled back imports to the share held during 1964–66. The act would have reduced the share to 9.6 percent from the 13.4 percent level in 1968.[69] As with the textile industry, the administration's response was to attempt to negotiate bilateral VERs with major competitors. In 1969, the first steel accord restrained imports from Japan and the European Community (EC), then totaling 82 percent of steel imports. Not unexpectedly, because the VER restricted only total imports, exporters switched to more expensive stainless and alloy steel products, reneging on the Japanese promise not to change their export mix.[70] As a result, the renewed agreement in 1972 contained specific tonnage limitations for the next three years.[71] Although pressure from imports temporarily subsided, they had risen to over 18 percent of the domestic market. By 1978 profit margins had dropped to under 1 percent on sales.[72] This time the steel industry changed its tack: its leaders did not simply claim that imports were hurting the domestic industry; instead, they made a concerted effort to prove that foreign producers were engaging in unfair competition. In particular, they claimed that foreign dumping was causing their lack of competitiveness.

Initially, the Carter administration was sympathetic to this claim and encouraged the industry to apply for relief under existing antidumping statutes. But it soon became apparent that under the law only European producers would be charged with selling products at less than fair value. In addition, if dumping duties were laid on the European producers, the Japanese, who were operating under capacity, could be expected to supplant them. The outcome would not be a reduction in steel imports but a windfall for Japanese producers and further divisiveness in European-U.S. trade relations. The administration found this unacceptable for obvious foreign policy reasons.

But the administration was in a quandary. It had no way to stop the Treasury Department from making unfavorable rulings on these dumping cases. To circumvent the possibility, the administration devised an alternative that it convinced steel producers was superior to antidumping procedures. The new system—the trigger price mecha-

---

[69] Gary C. Hufbauer, Diane T. Berliner, and Kimberly A. Elliot, *Trade Protection in the United States: 31 Cases* (Washington, D.C.: Institute for International Economics, 1986), pp. 154, 156.

[70] Ibid., p. 154.

[71] In addition, the annual increase was lowered from 5 to 2.5 percent. Ibid., p. 155.

[72] Edmund Ayoubin, "Comment," in U.S. Department of Labor, *The Impact of International Trade and Investment on Employment* (Washington: USGPO, 1978). Most analysts agree that the administration had not done enough to protect the industry. See also Crandall, *U.S. Steel Industry.*

nism (TPM)—was devised by Treasury Secretary Anthony Solomon as an alternative route for assuring fair market prices. Under the TPM, if imports were priced below an acceptable level, the treasury secretary would automatically initiate an antidumping investigation. For home producers, the TPM served the function of setting acceptable prices for foreign steel at the Japanese cost of production with 8 percent for profit. For Europeans, TPM prices allowed them to dump steel that otherwise would be subject to a tariff.

But even with the TPM in place, imports continued to rise.[73] By 1980, the industry had reverted to its earlier strategy of filing massive numbers of antidumping and countervailing duty petitions. Since the Carter administration and the industry had agreed to substitute TPM for petitions for aid, the monitoring system was suspended by Carter in March 1980 (and was permanently eliminated by Reagan in 1982). In October, having gained approval from the industry, Carter renewed the TPM but with significantly higher trigger prices and a special provision to limit quantities during import surges. Even with the new TPM, however, imports continued to increase. In February 1982, the industry again filed a massive number of petitions. In one day alone, U.S. steelmakers jointly delivered 494 boxes containing three million pages of support for 132 countervailing duty and antidumping petitions.[74] The industry was operating at less than 50 percent capacity with fewer shipments and lower production than at any time since the late 1940s.[75] This time the administration returned to the bargaining table and its strategy of negotiated export restraints. In fall 1982, the Europeans agreed to restrain trade; the industry withdrew its petitions for aid.

No agreement, however, stemmed imports from third-country suppliers. Although Japan, Mexico, Brazil, and South Africa had agreed to set quotas, the industry (specifically, Bethlehem Steel and the United Steel Workers) increased pressure on the administration by filing an escape clause petition.[76] Working the halls of Congress, the industry

---

[73] The TPM could not close the gap between Japanese and European production costs. Since Japan was the low-cost producer, European producers could cut their export prices and still be competitive on the American market.

[74] I. M. Destler, "United States Trade Policymaking in the Eighties," unpublished paper, 1990, pp. 23–24.

[75] Hufbauer, Berliner, and Elliot, *Trade Protection*, p. 163.

[76] This was not the only escape clause action on the part of the steel industry. The manufacturers of specialty steel began their quest for aid with a successful escape clause ruling in 1976; afterward, President Ford ordered negotiation of a marketing agreement with leading suppliers. Only Japan negotiated such an agreement (it was terminated in February 1980). Quota restrictions were placed on the other suppliers for three years (some protections terminated in June 1977 and April 1978; all were removed in February 1980). In 1982, the STR responded to complaints of unfair trade practices under Section

claimed that 201 representatives were willing to cosponsor an import quota bill. Almost simultaneously, in June 1984, the ITC ruled that the industry was injured by imports of carbon and alloy steel products. It recommended a mixture of tariffs, quotas, and tariff-rate quotas on 70 percent of all imports for five years. The Reagan administration, opposed to any further unilateral action but forced to respond as the 1984 election approached, pursued a policy of negotiating "surge control" agreements with major suppliers while sanctioning the enforcement of all unfair trade laws. The ITC was directed to monitor modernization of the industry and the Commerce Department was ordered to initiate countervailing duty petitions if it suspected unfair trade. These agreements were calculated to hold imports to 18.5 percent of the market (imports stood at 25 percent in 1984). In October 1984, the Trade and Tariff Act passed Congress with a "sense of Congress" resolution limiting imports to between 17 and 20.2 percent of the market, authorizing Reagan to negotiate the necessary arrangements. The following month, the U.S. Customs Bureau embargoed steel pipe and tube imports from the EC because they would have exceeded the 5.9 percent market share agreed to in 1982. But unlike the U.S. Customs Bureau, the EC Council of Ministers did not believe that the 1982 restraint agreement was a formal arrangement. Consequently, the council sought redress under GATT rules. The dispute was resolved in January 1985 when both sides agreed to an export limit of 7.6 percent.

In 1989, the Bush administration reexamined the quota benchmarks (which twenty-nine nations had agreed to) established by the Reagan administration in 1984. Although domestic steelmakers sought a five-year extension of quotas, the administration stated that it would address the needs of domestic steel-using manufacturers but once more. The president declared an increase in the quota from 18.4 to 20.2 percent of the market for thirty months, to be eliminated thereafter.[77] The administration declared that it would not again review the decision.[78] Instead of announcing VERs, administration officials declared their intent to end market-disrupting policies, which they claimed were the

---

301 of the 1974 trade act and sent the ITC a request to determine whether these imports were harming the industry. The ITC determined that they were, and Reagan granted four years of import relief with tariffs and quotas. The EC claimed the right to compensation under GATT rules and, when negotiations broke down, retaliated with increased tariffs on several American products.

[77] Under the Reagan plan quotas were set on two-thirds of imports from twenty-nine nations. In total, imports from controlled and not controlled nations could not rise above 21 percent. The Bush administration plan increased quotas on controlled imports 1 percentage point a year up to 21 percent in 1992.

[78] Quotas were eliminated in March 1992; this was the first time since 1984 that steel was not under some import regulatory regime.

source of the industry's problems. The plan, called the Steel Trade Liberalization Program, sought an international pact on steel subsidies within GATT.

Did the steel agreements restrain steel imports and so protect the home market? Clearly not; nor was this the intent of policy makers. In the late 1960s and early 1970s, voluntary agreements did ameliorate penetration of the American market. By the mid-1970s, the state of the economy and industry would have required an explicit government commitment to save the steel producers. Although the government negotiated VERs that covered the majority of importers, they did not quell the repeated surges onto the American market.[79] Effective aid to American steel producers would have required both domestic and import aid. But no elected official has ever suggested such a commitment to the industry, and the American steel industry continues to lose market share nationally and internationally.

Textiles

Of the marketing arrangements to which the United States has been party, the agreements over trade in textiles have most effectively put the private movement of textile products under public control. Because of their longevity and effectiveness, these agreements have been characterized as a textile "regime."[80]

Benefiting from regional concentration, the textile lobby had long been a formidable political force in American politics. As early as the mid-1950s, southern mill owners successfully pressured Washington for relief from Japanese exports. Looking to protections guaranteed under Section 204 of the Agricultural Act of 1956, the textile lobby claimed it needed government intervention to stabilize the market. Prodded by southern representatives, Congress threatened late in the summer of 1956 to pass a unilateral quota. Almost simultaneously, the Tariff Commission ruled favorably in an escape clause injury determination. Under increasing pressure to respond yet unwilling to advocate unilateral barriers to trade, the government negotiated its first textile export restraint agreement with Japan, effective from 1957 through 1962.

In its first year, the VER appeared to be a success. In 1957–58,

---

[79] The impact of aid on imports of carbon and alloy steel products (as percent of total American market) had not led to a decline in imports but to a controlled but steady increase in import share: in 1968, imports were at 16.7 percent; in 1984, imports were at 26.7 percent. Hufbauer, Berliner, and Elliot, *Trade Protection*, pp. 156, 165, 176.

[80] For a history of the textile regime see Vinod Aggarwal, *Liberal Protectionism* (Berkeley: University of California Press, 1985).

imports decreased though as much from a general economic slowdown as from Japanese action. As would become a common pattern in the ensuing thirty years, the president then vetoed the Tariff Commission recommendation, claiming the VER was sufficient aid. Soon afterward, however, inefficiencies with the VER solution became apparent. Transshipment inflated the agreed-upon quotas, despite the Japanese government's efforts to abide by the negotiated settlement.[81] By 1958, cotton imports had increased over their 1956 levels. Velveteen and gingham exports from Japan, the products that would have benefited from the affirmative escape clause finding, were 120 percent over quota.[82] To worsen matters, noncotton imports, not covered by the agreement, rapidly increased the value of total textile imports; Japanese synthetic textile exports to the United States increased 400 percent during the life of the VER; wool shipments doubled.[83] By 1960, it was obvious that the textile problem had not been solved. Article XIX of GATT, which specifies the escape clause response to such domestic problems, was not an answer that appealed to the administration. Even though Article XIX was written by the United States in the 1940s, by the late 1950s, Americans feared its enactment would be inconsistent with America's commitment to trade liberalization. Thus the United States again turned to export controls, responding to inefficiencies by seeking to increase the number of importing and exporting nations that were parties to the agreement. In 1961, the Short Term Agreement on Cotton Textiles was initialed by all parties; it was followed a year later by the Long Term Agreement on Cotton Textiles (LTA).

Thirty interested nations participated in the first GATT-sponsored trade talks on textiles. The LTA itself was a forum, a mechanism for negotiating bilateral and multilateral agreements. If textile trade qualified under the eased standards for a market disruption, then importing countries could request a restraint agreement from exporters.[84] If a

[81] Yoffie notes that one reason the Japanese government was committed to enforcing the VER was to avoid the reputation Japanese manufacturers had acquired during the 1930s. Before World War II, the Japanese had become notorious for cheating on international trading regulations by allegedly violating copyrights, falsely labeling country of origin, and attempting to destroy competition by flooding foreign markets with underpriced products. This reputation, the Japanese government felt, was responsible for early discrimination against Japanese goods in the United States. Yoffie, *Power and Protectionism*, pp. 59, 60.
[82] Ibid., p. 61.
[83] Ibid., p. 62.
[84] In 1959, GATT had held discussions on the cotton textile trade. Out of these talks a definition of market disruption was agreed upon which eased the injury test established for escape clause cases under Article XIX. The new criteria included potential increases in imports, price differences at home and abroad, and selective restraints by country. Hufbauer, Berliner, and Elliot, *Trade Protection*, p. 118.

complaint was issued that received no response from the exporting nation, Article III of the LTA allowed unilateral quotas. All actions, however, had to include a minimum 5 percent annual growth in quotas and be set at a level not lower than imports during the twelve-month period ending two or three months before the restraint agreement.

In the first year of the LTA, unilateral quotas were imposed 115 times. Such actions became more and more rare as an increasing numbers of agreements were signed.[85] The result was that trade in cotton became comparatively stable; imports only doubled during the 1960s. At the same time, however, producers moved into unregulated areas; synthetic imports, for example, increased 1,700 percent.[86] But the LTA should not be judged as a traditional act of protectionism—far more efficient mechanisms were available to quell textile trade. Foremost, it was a successful attempt to obtain support from the textile industry for trade legislation.

Although on some levels the LTA was a failure, the interests of producers in importing and exporting nations and those of the United States coalesced around this agreement. For producers, market-sharing arrangements were superior to uncontrolled trade; for American leaders, the LTA was in America's enlightened self-interest—the alternative, old-style protectionism, was avoided. This explains why, even though imports were not checked, the United States responded to failure by expanding the LTA, not rejecting it. In 1969, the United States engaged the major exporting nations in bilateral negotiations on non-cotton products. Once again, under threats of unilateral congressional action, an agreement was reached. Despite U.S. interests, all allowed considerable growth rates in quotas.[87] These agreements, however, were constructed so they could be easily undermined. Thus it was not surprising, for instance, that while the export of specific products covered in Taiwan's agreement declined 26 percent between 1971 and 1973, the value of all Taiwanese textiles sent to the United States increased 45 percent.[88]

---

[85] The United States imposed unilateral quotas on imports from eighteen countries in the first year, but acted quickly to transform these restraints into bilateral agreements and by 1965 had concluded eighteen such agreements, leaving only five unilateral restraints under Article III or VI(b). Benjamin Bardan, "The Cotton Textile Agreement, 1962–1972," *Journal of World Trade Law* (1973): 15.

[86] Yoffie, *Power and Protectionism*, p. 119.

[87] The initial agreement with Hong Kong, Korea, and Taiwan allowed 7.5 percent annual growth rates. In subsequent negotiations, Korea's growth rate increased to 9 percent for the first year and 8 percent for the second. Taiwan's increased to 9.5 percent for the first year. Japan negotiated an agreement for three, not five, years but with only a 5 percent growth rate. Ibid., pp. 152–54.

[88] Ibid., p. 159.

In 1974, these new bilateral agreements were incorporated into the Multifiber Textile Arrangement (MFA) and a board, the Textile Surveillance Body, was established to monitor compliance. The minimum growth rate for quotas was set at 6 percent, but American producers continued to push for the right to negotiate for lower quotas and the freedom to depart from an original agreement if they had reasonable cause. In 1981, such an agreement was reached. By 1985, the United States had negotiated 650 separate quotas under the MFA covering all important suppliers of textiles and apparel outside Europe and Canada.[89]

As currently constituted, the MFA functions efficiently from the perspective of the values held by American central decision makers. Although the MFA allows the United States to protect producers by unilateral action, the administration has never chosen to resort to such action.[90] The government has shown support for the industry, has slackened import penetration, and has offered product-specific aid when necessary without unraveling the general liberal trade regime.[91] And in fact, producers did receive some closure, far more than other industries.

Autos

The last example of the contemporary response to interest-group pressure for protection is aid to the automobile industry. The automobile industry has long held a premier place among American manufactures, alone accounting for almost 4 percent of the Gross National Product.[92] In the 1970s, however, the market share held by American cars began to erode. Rising oil prices, cheaper, more efficient Japanese cars, and consumers' displeasure with the reliability of American automobiles increased the demand for foreign vehicles. Significantly, there was a fivefold increase in domestic sales of Japanese cars during the 1970s. Imports rose from 17.7 to 26.7 percent of the U.S. market and sales of American-made cars declined from 9.3 to 6.6 million, the number sold in the early 1960s. By the 1990s, imports accounted for 25

---

[89] Hufbauer, Berliner, and Elliot, *Trade Protection*, p. 139.

[90] As with the steel case, the success of the trade restrictions, as measured by market share for textile imports, was mixed. In 1960, market penetration was about 6 percent; in 1985 it had risen to over 15 percent—still less than the foreign market share of steel products. Ibid., pp. 144, 131, 121.

[91] Although the textile industry was excluded from tariff cuts in the 1962 trade talks, tariffs were rolled back thereafter. Thus the tariff on threads went from 11.5 percent in 1962 to 9 percent at the close of the Tokyo Round; fabric tariffs declined from 24 to 11.5 percent in the same period. Ibid., p. 123.

[92] U.S. Department of Census, *Survey of Current Business* (Washington: USGPO, 1991).

percent of the market, the Japanese alone holding 18 percent.[93] Generally poor economic conditions and increased competition resulted in employee layoffs, a 30 percent unemployment rate, and plummeting profits. Given this level of dislocation, American policy may be far more noteworthy for its limited intervention than for its responsiveness.

In 1980, the United Auto Workers of America and the Ford Motor Company filed for escape clause relief.[94] (Other manufacturers chose not to join in the petition.) At the same time, hearings were held in the House Trade Subcommittee fueling both congressional and interest-group pressures on the ITC to respond to the industry's malaise. In its report the ITC agreed that the industry had suffered serious injury but concluded that the cause was factors other than imports, specifically, changing consumer preferences, high interest rates, and the recession. No relief was recommended under existing statutes. Further appeal to the Carter administration in the wake of his reelection campaign led to the authorization of trade adjustment assistance benefits.

By year's end the industry's requests to Congress for relief had gained wide support. Newly elected President Reagan had made campaign promises that relief from Japanese imports would be forthcoming. Too, the new Republican chair of the trade subcommittee, John Danforth (R-Mo.), was quick to assure the industry that hearings and legislation were on his agenda. Soon after, several auto trade bills were introduced, the most notorious being the Danforth bill, which proposed to limit auto imports from Japan to 1.6 million units annually until 1983.[95] No one expected these bills to become laws; the Reagan White House was far too committed to free-market solutions to intervene directly in the industry. Rather, the administration publicly proclaimed the legislation a violation of America's obligations under Article XI(1) of the GATT and Article XIV of the 1953 Japan–United States Treaty of Friendship, Commerce, and Navigation. Citing the finding of the ITC and potential violations of GATT agreements, the administration supported a laissez-faire policy.

[93] Destler, "United States Trade Policymaking," p. 17; Wards Communication, *Automobile Yearbook* (Detroit: Wards, 1991).

[94] The ITC was under substantial pressure in this case. President Carter had requested the ITC in July 1980 to speed up its investigation because of the large number of businesses, workers, and consumers for whom an investigation taking the full six months "could cause major uncertainties." Similar requests were made by several senators and representatives and the UAW. Hufbauer, Berliner, and Elliot, *Trade Protection*, p. 249.

[95] At the initial hearings in January 1981, auto industry representatives requested different quota targets. The UAW requested a 1.2 million unit ceiling, Chrysler, a 1.3 million limit; Ford argued for the legislation to cover five years. U.S. Senate Committee on Finance, *Hearings Before the Subcommittee on International Trade, Part 2*, 97th Cong., 1st sess.

But the administration found itself in an awkward position. The auto industry increasingly united in favor of protection. Even General Motors, which had favorable relations with Japanese producers, joined other manufacturers in asking for aid. Reagan was being forced to act on a variety of nonspecific pledges he had made in the election campaign to aid America's top industry.

The problem was solved by opening discussions with the Japanese to restrain imports. When Senate Majority Leader Robert Dole (R-Kan.) announced that he had two-thirds of the Senate lined up in support of the Danforth bill, Tokyo announced that it would reduce exports. In April 1981, the Japanese Ministry of International Trade and Industry (MITI) offered a voluntary program to give American manufacturers time to adjust to import competition. MITI proposed an auto agreement that would limit exports to 1.7 million cars a year, a 7.7 percent cut, which would be enforced through quotas for individual manufacturers.[96] This figure was slightly higher than the quota mandated in the Danforth bill and did not stipulate further reductions should auto sales in the United States decline further.

As the depression deepened, even these voluntary controls did not stop the Japanese from increasing their market share. Concern led Congress the following February to consider a domestic content bill, mandating that large companies such as Toyota and General Motors manufacture 90 percent of their automobile parts in the United States. Because the bill was introduced to control production and not trade, it went to the more favorably disposed House Energy and Commerce Committee and not the more cautious Ways and Means Committee.[97] Perhaps in response, at the end of March 1982, Japan declared its intention to extend the VER through March 1983 at 1.68 million units. The month before this extension expired, a new version of the domestic content bill was introduced into the House. Again, Japan renewed the VER, this time through March 1984. In both cases, the domestic content bill passed the House but was not taken up by the Senate. By fall 1984, however, the industry was split on the merits of extension for a

---

[96] Hufbauer, Berliner, and Elliot, *Trade Protection*, pp. 249–51. Japan did far better with the VER than it would have done with legislated quotas. The quota would have reduced imports of all automobiles by 42 percent; Japan's 80 percent of all imports would have been reduced considerably more than the 8 percent reduction in the VER.

[97] The story of trade protectionism is nested in some degree in changes in committee structures in Congress. Committees such as Energy and Commerce were using trade legislation as a means to increase their general influence in the House, thereby undermining the traditional hegemony of Ways and Means. Domestic content would have been dropped by Ways and Means, but this internal dynamic led to its inclusion on the political agenda. The energy subcommittee twice considered and reported the bill favorably. It was twice passed by the House: 215 to 188 in December 1982 and 219 to 199 in November 1983. Destler, "United States Trade Policymaking," p. 20.

fifth year. Ford, Chrysler, American Motors, and the UAW wanted a renewal; General Motors and the American International Automobile Dealers Association opposed an extension. MITI declared that it would not renew the agreement because the American auto manufacturers had high earnings and unemployment in the industry had dropped. Japan would, however, observe some quota guidelines to prevent a sudden surge of foreign autos on the American market. In February, Reagan announced his assent to the Japanese agreement. Thus the four-year accord expired on April 1, 1985. Japan announced that it would limit its exports to 2.3 million cars in 1985, an increase of 24 percent over imports under the VER.

Both American and Japanese producers prospered under the VER. Correspondingly, the American public paid more for cars and found only the highest-priced vehicles for sale. The result was a slow but controlled rise in Japanese imports in the late 1980s accompanied by rather steep increases in prices.[98] By all traditional measures, the industry had been in trouble. One of the big three automakers needed a bailout, and unemployment exceeded three hundred thousand in an industry of one million employees. Congress had made it clear that some response to these problems was in order. The ITC did not rule that the economic problems of the industry were largely caused by imports, but Congress nevertheless wanted to do something to relieve the industry's economic plight.

As was the case with steel and textile agreements, the answer was an accord with the exporting nation. Congress did not want to impose quotas through legislative action; during the final days of the Ninety-sixth Congress, the House had approved a resolution that called on the president to negotiate an export restraint agreement with Japan. The administration was happy to have Japan impose its own quotas, thereby taking the matter entirely out of the hands of the American government. This move accommodated the president's aversion to unilateral protectionism yet fulfilled his campaign pledge. It also gave auto manufacturers time to recoup losses from the late 1970s, ultimately leading to more direct investment in the United States and coproduction with the Japanese.

Conclusion

American laws on trade protectionism serve fundamentally different purposes. They serve different constituencies, they legitimate different

---

[98] The sharp appreciation of the yen and the declining value of the dollar exacerbated price hikes.

roles for the government, and their efficiency varies greatly. Depending upon the protectionist instrument on which analysis focuses, the United States appears more, or less, open to international trade. Some forms of protection respond to interest-group pressures for aid; others seem immune from such societal pressures. Some serve America's interests in the liberal trade regime; others seem to oppose that purpose.

Why do domestic institutions work at such cross-purposes? This chapter has provided the key with which to solve this puzzle. Laws are the mechanism by which trade preferences are translated into government policy. Laws influence both the supply of and demand for protection; by determining the level and form of aid to be awarded, laws channel social interests in particular directions. And once enacted, laws are slow to change. Old and new ideas about trade protectionism have legal counterparts.

The data presented here on the general level of protection and its variation across the seven types cannot be explained by a simple interest-group or international-structural theory. Aggregate measures of import policy indicate that America has consistently allowed imports to penetrate the market at a rate far ahead of GNP growth (see Table

Table 5.9. Change in U.S. real GNP, imports, and tariffs, 1948–1991 (in percent)

Years	GNP	Imports	Tariffs
1948–1958	38	20	− 20
1958–1968	58	110	2
1968–1978	26	69	− 47
1978–1988	35	75	− 50
1988–1991	3	8	− 1.9

Sources: Calculated from U.S. Government, *Historical Statistics of the United States from Colonial Times to the Present* (Washington: USGPO), pt. 1, 1970, 1975, p. 224; pt. 2, pp. 884–900; *Statistical Abstract of the United States* (Washington: USGPO, 1973); Office of the President, *Economic Report of the President* (Washington: USGPO, 1991), Table B-2.

5.9). This move has been part of a general policy commitment to trade liberalization. Yet liberalization did not benefit all sectors of the economy equally (see Table 5.10). The opening of American markets incurred significant costs; the rise in the number of petitioners asking for import relief is one of many indicators of those costs. But the government response to increasing pressures is perplexing from conventional perspectives. In some arenas, officials were responsive to group demands; in others, however, it was almost impossible to gain effective state aid. Most important, the same industry would get refused one form of aid and receive another, with no change in condition. The power of private groups and the change in America's place in the

Table 5.10. Rates of change in U.S. trade by sector, 1958–1988 (in percent)

Category	Imports	Exports
Food and live animals	65	210
Beverages	224	167
Crude materials	49	287
Mineral fuels	232	36
Animal and vegetable oils	126	41
Chemicals	554	496
Machinery (transport)	3333	422
Other manufactures	746	197
Automobiles	2437	741
Clothing	3114	335
Textiles	335	122

Sources: U.S. Department of Commerce, *Overseas Business Reports* (Washington: US-GPO, 1958); U.S. Department of Commerce, *Statistical Abstract of the United States* (Washington: USGPO, 1990), Nos. 762, 1410–1411.

world economy were good predictors of the demand for aid. They fared poorly, however, as determinants of who gets effective protection.

This chapter has suggested that protectionism is not merely a response to domestic and international forces. This is not to say that the interests these forces engender are not important. Rather, the data suggest that these interests—when channeled through legal and institutional structures—lead to a policy outcome not predictable from interest alone. As well as interests influencing policy, legal and institutional structures color who gets what amount of trade protection. Laws vary in their bias, reflecting the political climate in which their enabling legislation was first written. As was demonstrated above, laws diverge on what constitutes a legitimate claim against the state for aid, on the institutional structures used to adjudicate aid, and on the discretion granted to administrators. In the United States, this reflects liberal, protectionist, and redistributive policy ideas translated into law.

Liberal laws were written after the United States opened its borders to trade. Limited state intervention reflected the generalized belief that governments serve their societies most efficiently when they do not interfere with market mechanisms. But laissez-faire was only the preferred option. When imports endangered American jobs, central decision makers created programs that would cloister liberalism. Thus redistributive programs became a second wave of liberal policies. From the start, administration of these laws was given to sympathetic agencies that assured high acceptance rates. In effect, the state bolstered its liberal policies by mitigating the most painful aspects of open markets.

But another set of ideas is also evident in American law. Fair-trade ideas legitimate a government role in trade that ensures active state commitment to enforcing competition on an equal basis. Three of the laws examined, written in the years preceding World War II, reflect an era in which trade was a major congressional issue, administrators were given detailed criteria to adjudicate cases, and presidents were granted little discretion to coordinate commercial policies with other foreign policies. Liberal decision makers have done what they could to sabotage these laws. Yet these laws do not grant the executive branch many of the rights it gained in post-Depression legislation.

Ideas on trade policy have life cycles. But their institutional incarnations are far more long-lived. Thus ideas matter—not only because trade policy makers believe in "free" trade or "free and fair" trade, but because the legal system that crystallized these ideas creates institutions that offer incentives to social actors to keep even old, defunct ideas alive.

CHAPTER SIX

Ideas and American Foreign Policy

The central problem addressed in this book can be stated simply. American commercial policy is riddled with inconsistencies that cannot easily be explained by either of the dominant modes of analysis—structural realism and domestic interest-group politics. The inadequacies of these approaches result from their paying undue attention to changes in market forces and to their impact on national and group interests. Such analyses are not wrong, but they are insufficient.

This book has argued that beliefs about the causal connections between interests and policies are at least as important as is the nature of the interests themselves. Even if we assume that political entrepreneurs fully understand their own interests, those of their constituents, and those of the nation as a whole, they still have to rely on an explicit—or implicit—theoretical model in making choices about policy strategies. This is because in a world clouded with uncertainty, entrepreneurs cannot predict with any assurance what policy or range of policies will lead to their preferred outcomes. Thus the focus of this book has been on causal ideas, explaining why some were selected over others at different times, analyzing the impact of the choice of an economic model on the constitution of trading rules and procedures, and exploring the lasting effects of these institutions on trade politics.

Two distinct arguments have been made. The first is a general understanding of the role of ideas in politics. Throughout history, political entrepreneurs have faced choices among competing policy options. In most cases, policy makers have incomplete information about their environment and thus must rely on causal models in making policy choices. Here, ideas are like road maps, linking policies to a constellation of interests. But ideas also serve other purposes. Even when political entrepreneurs understand the effects of changes in market forces, they still depend on ideas about how to translate these forces into a political and economic program. It is not markets but ideas that establish the rules of the game, that demarcate for policy makers the proper form of new policies, and that privilege particular constituencies. At moments of great flux, ideas serve as focal points for political entrepreneurs in their selection of political coalitions.

This book has also made a longitudinal argument about the historical processes of policy change. Ideas not only condition the action of political leaders at one point in time, but, through their incorporation into institutional structures, they also affect the evolution of policy over time. American trade policy has been very "sticky"; the creation of rules and procedures to enforce a particular economic strategy at one point has acted as a constraint not only on current behavior but also on the range of options available to future entrepreneurs. In particular, laws have remained in force long after the economic conditions and political interests originally underpinning them have changed. Old statutes have constrained newer policies by giving standing to particular claims for protection from foreign goods. They have also affected the fundamental constitution of social interests.

Trade policy making proved a good arena in which to evaluate these general arguments about politics and ideas for both theoretical and empirical reasons. Explanations of trade policy are overwhelmingly dominated by rationalist accounts. Whether it is the role played by domestic interest groups or the effects of position in the international economy on the national interest, commercial policy has been viewed as a classic example of the materialist basis of public policy. Thus if beliefs have a significant impact in this "hard" case, they should also be important in other policy areas where interests are less clearly defined.

It is, however, more than a concern to engage these rationalist accounts that has motivated this study. As well, the focus on trade has facilitated a concentration on the selection of ideas rather than on their generation. Some view ideas as technologies—they are discovered out of necessity and then used to solve the problems that brought them forth.[1] Such an approach directs attention to factors that influence the generation of ideas and assumes that "good" ideas, like science, will be recognized for their objective merits. But in the case of trade there has been a fixed supply of economic ideas, whose influence on politics has varied widely over time. Throughout American history elected officials

---

[1] For example, see Peter Haas, *Saving the Mediterranean* (New York: Columbia University Press, 1990), and essays in *International Organization*, special issue, Winter 1992.

have confronted clear but contradictory statements by experts on the economic effects of particular trade policies. This ever-available and unchanging supply of prescriptions by lay and academic economists facilitates the search for the explanation for why an idea, once generated, becomes politically salient at a particular moment in time.[2]

Finally, this book attempted to explain four empirical anomalies that derive from prevailing rationalist accounts of American trade policy:

First, current laws in the United States reflect fundamentally different notions of the proper relationship between government and those who are hurt by trade. Laws which suggest that government should take a laissez-faire approach to competition coexist with those which imply that government should defend the home market against foreign producers. Depending on the claim a given industry has made for protection, outcomes have varied from market closure, to monetary compensation, to government facilitation of a market-sharing arrangement, or to the request simply being denied. These disparate outcomes are anomalous from the perspective of international market and domestic interest-based theories because similarly situated industries have been treated very differently depending on the statute under which their cases have been examined.

Second, in the late eighteenth and early nineteenth centuries, a U. S. polity emerged that would later be characterized as exceptionally liberal. That characterization was based on the incorporation into American thought and government of the ideas espoused by eighteenth century liberal philosophers. But what this history fails to note is that while they embraced John Locke, Americans shunned Adam Smith. This rejection of the logic of liberal trade occurred not only with full knowledge of Smithian ideas but also with the understanding that these ideas were more compatible with the American conception of limited government than was the protectionist alternative.

Third, in the 1930s, the federal government responded to the severe economic and social dislocations of the Great Depression by instituting a set of interventionist policies. Government intervention reached almost all aspects of the economy except commercial policy. Concurrent with the passage of programs that guaranteed active government help in assuring the economic viability of producers and consumers, Congress declared a policy of abstention from protection of industries adversely affected by international competition. Furthermore, the

---

[2] American commercial policy is not a story of enlightenment in which a progressive idea—liberal free trade—triumphed. Liberal policy gained support in the United States in the 1930s for the same reasons as did protectionism in the 1860s: elected leaders conceived of each policy as the best means to further their interests.

decision to support trade liberalization extended only to manufacturing and not to agricultural trade, even though it was in agriculture that the United States held its greatest comparative advantage.

Finally, those who study American tariff history often use a simple shorthand: Republicans have been the party of protection and Democrats have advocated free trade. Policy is seen as the product of the electoral fortunes of each party. Yet this view obscures systematic changes in the meaning of protection and free trade over time. For example, in the early nineteenth century, free trade meant a tariff under 20 percent; in the late nineteenth century, free traders advocated tariff levels under 40 percent; and in the twentieth century, a tariff over 5 percent was considered a violation of liberal policy. Similarly, in the 1890s, those who advocated protectionism also proposed negotiated reciprocal trade agreements, to the chagrin of the free-trade community. Forty years later, however, it was the free traders, not the protectionists, who favored that policy. And again, whereas in the nineteenth century tariffs were considered legitimate distributive instruments, by the mid-twentieth century even the notion of a log-rolled tariff was anathema to members of both political parties.

There also is a problem with the proposition—intrinsic to the rationalist literature—that party positions are based on the material interests of their political constituencies. But by the time the Democrats became articulate supporters of tariff reform, southern producers (the backbone of support for liberal trade in the antebellum period) were far less competitive abroad than they had been in the period when the party equivocated on tariff issues. How did central and western farmers, large industry, and northeastern commercial interests all find their material well-being to be enhanced by closure of the American market? It is easy to explain why the state of Pennsylvania supported a protective policy. The problem, however, is understanding the behavior of other members of the coalition who could as easily have been found on the other side.

All those outcomes suggest that the translation of interest into appropriate policy is not unproblematic. It is frequently assumed that trade policy is a functional response to domestic or international constraints. History may "dress up" the expression of functional necessity, but over the long run policies can parsimoniously be derived from a set of rational assumptions about how political entrepreneurs are influenced by the environment in which they make policy. Yet policy has been sticky, constituencies have ended up in the "wrong" political party, and "correct" well-articulated policy proposals have been regularly ignored. Why? Because more than one policy invariably has had the minimum necessary attributes to fulfill the interests of these entrepreneurs. If insufficient attention is paid to the agent who interprets changes in domestic group demands and in the national interest—often through institutionally biased lenses—the essence of the politics of making economic policy may be overlooked. It is the political entrepreneur who matches a political constituency with some set of policies. Much attention has focused on the objective interests of different constituencies. This book has argued, however, for the need to direct research into the choice among the range of policies that is compatible with the constellation of interests.

The remainder of this chapter examines the general findings of this book. A set of issues for future research is discussed by way of conclusion.

MARKETS, IDEAS, AND INSTITUTIONS

The basic results of the study are synthesized in Figure 1. The figure is divided into six time periods, corresponding to the logical divisions suggested in the preceding chapters. Three variables are central to the analysis. "Markets" refer to the domestic interests that derive from the international division of labor. A number of factors potentially affect the impact on groups of increased trade; here, interests are considered as the self-expression of preferences by groups and political parties, not as a set of intrinsic interests deductively derived from market forces. Second, "ideas" are operationalized as the extent of conviction to a trade theory on the part of policy makers. Third, "laws and institutions" connote the rules and norms biasing policy in the direction of either trade openness or closure. The " + " refer to the incentives for trade closure and the " − " those for openness. The most important causal variable in each period of time is in a box. The arrows indicate the causal processes of intertemporal change. Policy outcomes at each point in time are described in the final column.

Arraying the historical data in this manner points out a cyclical pattern in the relative importance of the three variables: markets, ideas, and laws and institutions. At the beginning of each cycle, demarcated by a disequilibrating shock, market conditions largely shape policy. These market forces privilege certain economic ideas over others. In time, the ideas diffuse broadly and become a powerful independent explanation of policy, even when not supported by domestic and international interests. The shared belief in the efficacy of a particular economic strategy leads political entrepreneurs to institutionalize elements of their economic program. But since these institutions change far more slowly than do market conditions, social interests or both, in a

Figure 1. The determinants of American trade policy

Years	Markets/ interests	Ideas	Laws/ institutions	Outcome
I. The protectionist cycle				
1816–1870	+/–	+/–	+	+/– revenue tariffs
1870–1896	+	+ +	+ +	+ + protective tariffs
1897–1933	– –	+	+ + +	+ + + high protective tariffs
II. The free-trade cycle				
1934–1962	– – –	–	–/+	– trade liberalization
1963–1978	–	– –	– –/+	– – liberal trade
1979–present	–	–	– –/+ +	–/+ free and fair trade

"+" indicates protectionism
"–" indicates liberalism

third stage, laws and institutions cause policy to drift away from that dictated by market forces. This equilibrium is upset at a later stage by some political "shock," motivating entrepreneurs to seek alternatives more in line with the objective needs of the economy. But the cycle does not begin tabula rasa: the institutional legacy of the previous policy idea remains embedded in norms and rules and thus continues to influence policy outcomes.[3]

These policy cycles have two interesting features. First, even at the head of a cycle, market forces dictate only the general direction of policy. Markets define a viable policy space; they do not determine which particular policy is selected.[4] The choice by entrepreneurs of a

[3] Although there are historical cases in which exogenous shocks—usually wars—do lead to the total revamping of existing institutional structures, such cases are rare. Economic shocks more often lead to the redirecting of existing structures, which accounts for much of the variation in the outcome of similar types of policies in different polities. For example, on the adoption of Keynesian thought see Peter Hall, *The Political Power of Economic Ideas* (Princeton: Princeton University Press, 1988).

[4] The United States is somewhat unusual in the limited extent to which markets select particular policies. Because of its size, its rich endowments, and, for much of its history, its overwhelming relative power, the United States faced more choices in trade policy than other nations. Thus, for example, pure free trade may not have been in the interest of newly industrializing constituents in the 1870s, but a far more moderate trade policy would have been as satisfactory as high levels of protection. Similarly, in the postwar period, one can imagine a range of policies—either more open or more closed—that would have led to the reinvigoration of the American economy and acceptance by political elites.

particular strategy is as significantly affected by the fit between the constellation of political power and the available pool of policy ideas as by market constraints.

Second, although there was choice among potential economic models to be selected by political entrepreneurs at the beginning of the cycle, once one was chosen, political leaders were then constrained from radical departures in policy. In a sense, the initial ideational choice pushes out alternatives, narrowing the band of possible future policies. The choice has lasting implications because political elites, operating in a world of great uncertainty, make economic policy decisions according to rules suggested by the economic model to which they ascribe. And even after policy makers no longer believe in their precepts, old models remain influential—a result of the existence of organizational and legal procedures that have been created to facilitate policy making in line with these economic rules. These institutions in turn can dictate policy, even in the face of declining elite consensus and divergent social interests. Policies are maintained because existing institutions influence the articulation of social interests and constrain—both cognitively and politically—the ability of political entrepreneurs to change the direction of economic policy.

This temporal process is well demonstrated in trade policy history. In the United States, the cycle began with the search for a commercial policy in the antebellum period. The selection of protectionism by the Republican party reflected both the economic needs of groups in the Republican coalition and the prevailing understanding of who gained and lost from trade. Once accepted, the protectionist economic model took on a life of its own. Leaders, confronted by a rapidly changing economy, relied on tariffs as the appropriate response to myriad economic ills. Further, the hegemony of the protectionist vision ultimately manifested itself in the creation of institutions that made it difficult for political leaders to stop the repeated escalation of general tariff levels.

American policy became increasingly dysfunctional after the turn of the century. On the heels of the Great Depression, political entrepreneurs became convinced that high tariffs were responsible for economic decline. As in the 1860s, an alternative economic model was selected that was better suited for the prevailing economic conditions. The experiment with liberal trade ideas coincided with a period of rapid economic recovery, which facilitated the nearly universal acceptance of trade liberalism.

By the early 1960s, political elites in both parties believed that the use of protectionism to shield industries from market forces not only hurt American competitiveness but also held the potential for pushing the world down a slippery slope to recession. The result was the institutionalization of free-trade ideas in successive trade acts. After 1979, however, as after 1896, political consensus on the worth of the prevailing economic model began to decline in accord with increasing American economic problems. But even in the face of this decline, American policy makers did not implement an alternative economic platform. In the absence of a change in economic beliefs, trade policy continued to reflect existing institutional structures. These institutions, however, were themselves a hybrid, embodying not only the idea of free trade but also America's earlier experiment with protectionism.

The following sections examine this theoretical cycling in the context of American policy. The first examines the initial phases in the protectionist and free-trade cycles and analyzes the role of market forces. The second section examines the phases in which the force of ideas and institutions ran counter to market forces. The third section returns to the top of the cycle and explains why political entrepreneurs selected a particular economic policy from the set of policies that were compatible with social interests.

Markets and the Selection of Economic Ideas

The 1816–60 and the 1934–62 periods mark the beginning of trade cycles. In both periods, market forces significantly constrained policy choice.

The United States faced a significant developmental task in the antebellum years. Not only did new industries encounter stiff and often predatory competition from Britain, but regional interests rapidly diverged. The South advocated low tariff barriers because of its need to import most finished products. Northern interests were divided. One camp—involved in commerce— concurred with the South on the evils of any restraint on trade. The new manufacturers that needed aid against the more advanced British products, however, favored protectionism. Thus, market forces in the antebellum years went in two directions in accordance with the interests of these regional groups.

In this period, economic ideas were similarly bifurcated. Both the free-trade and protectionist arguments were clearly articulated and embraced by the appropriate constituencies. Congressional representatives from the South defended what would become classical economic thought while those who represented the early industrial areas spoke in favor of Hamiltonian logic. Before midcentury, it would have been difficult to predict which set of ideas ultimately would be adopted as national policy. In terms of the rules and procedures used to set duties, the attractiveness of tariffs as a source of government revenues generated an institutional bias in favor of protection. But likewise, general

American political values were inclined not to support active state intervention of the sort suggested by the protectionist coalition.

Policy was volatile during the period, changing with partisan control of government. High tariffs were maintained through the 1830s. These were subsequently lowered with the growing ascendance of southern Democrats in Congress. Both policies were consistent with market constraints. Throughout, policy choice was conditioned by partisan politics. Low tariffs served the agrarian economy; high tariffs facilitated the construction of an industrial base in the North. The victory of the Republican party on the eve of the Civil War heralded the demise of the cotton economy and the ascension of protectionism.

A similar pattern ensued in the years after the Great Depression. The 1930s was a decade of readjustment. From the perspective of now competitive American manufacturers, the protective tariffs of the previous era were highly counterproductive. In the wake of the Depression, market forces for all products—except agriculture—favored freer trade. Thus any policy that entailed the opening of markets at home and abroad was likely to meet with success.

In this period, political elites had considerable latitude to address what they perceived to be the failures of the protective system. But the antiprotection consensus did not engender agreement over an alternative set of liberal trade policies. Although closure and tariffs as political "pork" were universally rejected, elites remained uncertain over which of the possible internationalist solutions would maximize American interests. This is evidenced by the significant variation in legislative statutes passed in the 1930s and the limited clout granted to newer liberal institutions. Thus the 1934 law facilitated a change in tariff policy by allowing the executive to negotiate reductions, but the empowerment of the executive was for a specified period, the structure of tariffs was set by Smoot-Hawley, and the laws on unfair trade remained operative. In short, the new liberal rules were placed on top of the older protectionist base. Only with the change in the trade position advocated by the Republican party in the late 1950s, followed by the passage of the 1962 trade act, did the classical trade model gain near universal acceptance among political leaders.

Both these periods were prefaced by a shock to the system.[5] The

[5] Shocks may be neither sufficient nor necessary for the adoption of new policy ideas. Change in the ideational basis of policy occurs when carriers of an alternative model for economic activity gain political power. Shocks appear to precede such change because in periods of great political flux, it is easier for political entrepreneurs to recast coalitional patterns. But ideational change does occur in more "normal" times. For example, neither the deregulation movement in the United States nor democratization in Eastern Europe was prefaced by the two traditional shocks: war and depression.

Great Depression unseated the Republican party and undermined in the minds of many the efficacy of existing economic policies, including protectionism. Liberal trade was one of many economic programs used by the Democratic party to attract a political coalition. The demise of the Whig party and the Civil War created a similar opportunity for the Republican party, which used an economic strategy—protectionism— as a means to attract and keep its new political constituency. In both cases, the policy latitude of the early part of this period declined with the growth of a widespread consensus on the virtues of the chosen economic model.

Ideas and Institutions

In the two periods following the choice of a general trade policy, market conditions changed far more rapidly than did policy. This divergence was generated in two stages. First, popular consensus on the virtue of a particular set of economic policies gave the ideas themselves a significant impact on policy. In this period, entrepreneurs increasingly used only one economic model as a guide for policy. This elite consensus led to a subsequent institutionalization of these ideas, making policy even more resilient to changes in economic conditions.

The years from 1870 to 1896 were the heyday of protectionist ideas. No other economic model had political appeal, and even the Democratic party acceded to many of the policy prescriptions of the theory of protection. This is not to suggest that the parties did not differ substantially on tariff issues; in fact, tariffs were the dividing issue of the period. Nevertheless, both sides in the debate accepted the basic principle of the right and obligation of government to extend protection to particular producers. Even western agricultural groups, which had an objective interest in any form of tariff revision, became convinced that their interests were served by protection of the home market.

The institutional effects of the dominance of protectionist ideas became manifest between 1897 and 1933. As industries grew more competitive, business groups pressured government for policies that would increase their access to new markets. Political entrepreneurs responded by experimenting with new policies, reciprocity in particular. Still, higher levels of protection ensued, reflecting the institutional and cognitive constraints facing entrepreneurs in this period. A range of institutional structures—from the existence of a particular tariff structure to the control of committees by protectionist congressmen—served to translate demands for economic assistance into even greater levels of protectionism. The widespread belief in the virtues of protection made it difficult for leaders and constituents even to conceive of a radically different trade policy.

The weight of the past was most evident in the years after World War I. The war thrust the United States onto the world stage, revealing its great economic and military strength. Paying no attention to the 1913 tariff—an act in line with American power—policy in the 1920s reveals the constraints imposed by the institutional vestiges of America's protectionist past. The manner in which commercial policy was set—encouraging the organization of special interests and the use of tariffs as "pork"—could lead only to increasingly higher barriers to trade. Tariffs remained high even though few policy makers thought the levels of protection they granted were in the national interest and even in the face of powerful interest-group pressures for reform.

Trade policy after 1962 followed a similar path. Elite support for liberalism was at its zenith following the passage of the 1962 trade act and the completion of the Kennedy Round of GATT. As predicted by the small band of free-trade advocates in the 1930s, liberal trade had led to large profits for industry and cheap prices for consumers. Accordingly, institutional rules and norms increasingly came to reflect a belief in the efficacy of a free-trade policy. But these new rules on import protections were layered on top of the old: protectionist rules were not removed from existing statutes.

As consensus developed over the virtues of free trade, and as institutions were created to enforce these ideas, market conditions began to pressure groups that previously had benefited from trade liberalization. Perhaps the best indicator of the weight of ideas in this period was the reaction of political leaders to the rediscovery by industry of fair-trade laws. The broad trend in policy in the 1960s and 1970s was toward increasing openness. But such a policy was not without costs to American industries that now were threatened by products made with relatively cheaper foreign labor. With rising demands for protection, the existence of old laws became a problem to liberal elites. Under these statutes, protection was available to specific groups, even though this countered the executive-centered liberalization program. The response of both the executive office and high-level officials was a systematic attempt to finesse these laws through the use of side payments, illusory aid, and extralegal alternatives.

But after 1979, as at the turn of the century, both market-driven interests in openness and the ideological conviction of elites in liberalism eroded. Competition from Asian and European producers led to a marked increase in American industry demands for government assistance. Although few advocated radical market closure, many industries were no longer willing to offer unqualified support for free trade.

Similar ambivalence crept into the views of elected officials. Although no alternative model emerged to direct American commercial policy, both legislative and executive fears about foreign competition led policy makers to question the efficiency of existing trading practices.

As in the years after 1897, however, policy did not change markedly, reflecting the entrenchment of economic ideas in institutional structures. The creation of free-trade rules based on previous faith in openness promoted continuity in trade policy even in the face of growing domestic resistance. A behavioral change, however, resulted from the decline in elite support for free trade. In the 1980s, the use of old trading statutes—unfair trade laws—became less of a problem for elected officials. Whereas they had attempted to undermine their use in the past, elites began to propound—not eliminate—the policy prescriptions found in these hybrid institutions. American trade policy defended both free and fair trade.

Supply of Policy Ideas

If markets constrain the range of feasible policy choices but do not determine a unique outcome, what, then, explains the initial policy choices of political entrepreneurs? For example, in the 1860s the Republican coalition could have endorsed a tariff for revenue with mild protection. Roosevelt in 1934 could have pushed through Congress a liberalization scheme that foreclosed both congressional and executive discretion. How are demands for new policies translated into the choice of one particular policy?

Three previously detailed cases can now be compared to shed light on this process. Two of the examples, in the 1860s and the 1930s, are of policy change. New ideas were selected by government officials and came to influence their behavior. The other is a counterfactual. Why did the Republicans after the turn of the century ignore calls for tariff reform from within their own party when reform would have served their constituents' and the party's long-term interests? This last problem is particularly puzzling because at that time, as opposed to thirty years earlier, classical economic ideas were hegemonic among academic economists.

Analysis of the two periods of policy change illuminates the factors explaining the lack of change in the third case. The choice of a new policy in the 1860s and 1930s derives from the interpretation by political elites of the strategy best suited to furthering their interests. In the 1860s, the new Republican coalition was held together by little other than a commitment to antislavery. In selecting the tariff as central in their policy platform, Republican leaders relied on the one model that asserted a clear causal relationship between trade expansion and wages. Because higher wages were a common interest for this diverse group, the party supported high tariffs. Not only did the policy promote the interests of both workers and industry but—according to the analysis at the time—it also guaranteed a large home market for agriculture, a constituency sought by both parties.

In the 1930s, the choice of an executive-centered trade system was perceived to have similarly wide-ranging benefits. The granting of tariff rights to the executive sat well with Roosevelt's broader interest in an enlarged office of the president. Negotiated reciprocal reductions were also salient to the Democratic Congress for they legitimated the congressmen's disregard for the Republican Tariff Commission. Although not explained alone by the earlier Democratic allegiance to tariff reform, the newer ideas clearly conformed with the traditional Democratic platform, just as Republican protectionism had complemented Whig economic programs.

In short, as policy ideas, executive-centered trade liberalization in the 1930s and congressional-centered protectionism in the 1860s had similar political attributes. The policies had positive externalities; they were articulated in a manner that made them readily available to political entrepreneurs; and the policies had at least the minimum necessary market attributes to assure success.

In contrast, no idea had these features at the turn of the century. Lacking any salient alternative policy idea, elites responded to changing market forces and demands from interest groups in accord with the entrenched protectionist logic. Entrepreneurs were constrained on two sides. Institutional arrangements made it difficult to deny groups tariffs, and political leaders were cognitively constrained by their protectionist visions.

But if free-trade ideas were as theoretically advanced in this period as they would be at their adoption thirty years later, why did they lack political salience? Although well articulated in classrooms, classical economic ideas at the turn of the century were far too abstract to be appealing guides for political action. On the whole, economists commanded little respect. They were either uninterested in or incapable of applying their theories to policy. Thirty years later, a generation of students would be trained in classical economics. It was the diffusion of classical thought, not a change in the political status of economists, that underlay the shift in the theoretical basis of American trade policy.

Thus without a motivating idea, lowering tariffs seemed to be a costly strategy for the Republican party. After establishing a coalition based on the distribution of tariff benefits, entrepreneurs needed some alternative conception of how to cement their constituency. That vision could have been—but was not—supplied by economic theorists. Thus in the decades after 1897—similar to the years after 1979—the weight of history on current policy was most visible. In both periods, the lack of an alternative economic model precluded change, even in the presence of voter unhappiness and elite disagreement.

If the past is any guide, the United States is ripe for a policy shift. That change could begin with some shock—such as a deep recession—that reveals the extent of the disjuncture between market-determined interests and government policy. But though a shock would "grease the wheels," change will not occur without an additional factor: an alternative idea that is available to and salient for use by political decision makers. In its absence, policy in the 1990s, just as at the turn of the century, will not deviate far from the status quo.

In sum, policy change is prefaced on the existence of a salient alternative idea because, as suggested by Weber, ideas are the "switches" that channel interests down particular paths. Political entrepreneurs' choice of the path reflects their perception of what policy, including the status quo, will further their varying interests. Policy choice, however, involves more than the evaluation of "ideas as technology." Change is contingent upon the existence of a new solution, the realization by elites that some new policy is superior to the old, and their political savvy in being able to create political support for new ideas.

RESEARCH ON IDEAS AND POLITICS

This book has suggested that there are limits to the use of rationalist assumptions and functional analysis for understanding politics. The analysis began with the assumptions that individuals were maximizers of self-interest, that policy makers' foremost concern was their reelection, and that, on the whole, nations maximized wealth. Thus the critique of rationalist approaches has not been aimed at its "Lakatosian" core, but rather at the inability of such analyses to explain particular political outcomes. This underdetermination reflects political reality: interests alone are an insufficient guide for action. Politics is about choice. Political entrepreneurs must select from a wide range of strategies the policy that maximizes the interests of their constituents. In a world of incomplete information, however, such choices are conditioned by beliefs about cause-effect relationships that interpret for leaders how their interests are affected by changes in market forces and then indicate the appropriate policy response.

This suggests a larger research agenda that looks beyond objective social interests to the beliefs of political entrepreneurs. Here, the role for ideas is not that imputed by psychological theory; individuals do rely on cognitive models to interpret a complex environment, but here ideas are not conceived in terms of the psychological needs of central decision makers.[6] Although political entrepreneurs are the key agents translating beliefs into policies, their selection and use of ideas do not derive solely from individual-level factors. Rather, beliefs are simply strategies, that can be abandoned if they fail to deliver the goals sought by political leaders.

To show the importance of beliefs to political outcomes, this book attempted to show that the empirical anomalies generated from a purely interest-based explanation of trade policy could be resolved by taking ideas into account.[7] Here and in all analyses of foreign economic policy, interest explanations pose the null hypothesis. Markets and material interests should not be ignored; they form a formidable constraint in the setting of policy in that they direct domestic interests and determine the payoffs from an economic policy.[8] Such analysis, however, is rarely sufficient. The international economy, as Peter Gourevitch correctly points out, works "through domestic actors, shaping their

[6] There is a large body of work in international politics that looks at the implications of cognitive psychology for how individuals interpret political reality. Although this genre of work is also about beliefs, it is not about how particular generalized ideas about the nature of the world influence politics. For examples of the former see Alexander George and Juliette George, *Woodrow Wilson and Colonel House* (New York: Dover, 1956); Robert Jervis, *Perception and Misperception in International Politics* (Princeton: Princeton University Press, 1976); Deborah Welch Larson, *Origins of Containment: A Psychological Explanation* (Princeton: Princeton University Press, 1985); Richard Ned Lebow, *Between Peace and War: The Nature of International Crisis* (Baltimore: Johns Hopkins University Press, 1981); Robert Jervis, Richard Ned Lebow, and Janice Gross Stein, *Psychology and Deterrence* (Baltimore: Johns Hopkins University Press, 1985).

[7] For a variety of essays using this technique see Judith Goldstein and Robert O. Keohane, *Ideas and Foreign Policy* (Ithaca: Cornell University Press, 1993).

[8] Following on the classic works of Gershenkron, Barrington Moore, and others, few cross-national comparisons of economic policy fail to consider the origins of coalitional patterns. In looking for sources of group alliances over trade policy, most analyses pay due attention to the impact of changing market conditions on social actors. For example, Ronald Rogowski suggests that changes in the level of trade flows differentially reward factors of production (land, labor, capital) and thus dictate interests for trade policy. Helen Milner and Peter Gourevitch also argue for the importance of changing trade patterns; Gourevitch focuses on the impact of trade on economic sectors and Milner on the interests of firms. Similarly, Peter Katzenstein argues that the economic policies designed by the small European states reflect their need to adjust to market forces because the options pursued by large states—exporting or preempting the costs of economic change—are unavailable to them. See Ronald Rogowski, *Commerce and Coalitions: How Trade Affects Domestic Political Alignments* (Princeton: Princeton University Press, 1989); Peter Gourevitch, *Politics in Hard Times: Comparative Responses to International Economic Crises* (Ithaca: Cornell University Press, 1986); Helen Milner, *Resisting Protectionism: Global Industries and the Politics of International Trade* (Princeton: Princeton University Press, 1988); Peter Katzenstein, *Small States in World Markets: Industrial Policy in Europe* (Ithaca: Cornell University Press, 1985).

policy preferences and their propensities to conflict and to align with other groups."[9] Accepting the importance of markets, however, does not mean that markets alone explain policy decisions. As Peter Hall suggests, "structural accounts can tell us a great deal about the constraints facing policy makers, but policy making is based on creation as well as constraint."[10] Thus market forces may explain the preferences of social actors but rarely policy itself. Along with changing coalitional patterns, analysts must pay attention to political entrepreneurs and the ideas they hold; their beliefs are a critical link between market forces and policy outcomes.

This suggests a two-stage research program for the analysis of ideas and foreign policy. First, analyses must focus on the degree to which ideas affect policy. Specifically, researchers need to assess how much of the variation in policy is due to the existence of some cognitive framework, as opposed to other sets of variables. Ideas may merely be "hooks" on which interests hang—they may have no independent causal weight. One cannot assume that an idea is important just because the idea was present in policy discussions. To have causal weight, ideas must have an independent effect on policy, apart from the interests of the actors who defend them.

Second, research should focus on why policy ideas vary in their salience to political entrepreneurs over time. Analysis should consider both the demand and supply sides; shifting environments and constituencies explain why leaders seek new ideas, but it is the pool and salience of the set of possible solutions that determine policy choice. Four hypotheses can organize research under these two headings.

(H.1) Numerous policies are consistent with the political interests generated by market forces. *The greater the range of feasible economic and political policies, the greater the reliance of political entrepreneurs on policy ideas.*

Many studies show that ideas—to differing extents—funnel policy in particular directions. This has been argued in the area of monetary policy by John Odell, in macroeconomic policy by Hall, and in deregulation by Martha Derthick and Paul Quirk and John Kingdon.[11] Similarly, many agree with Stephen Krasner that hegemonic nations

[9] Gourevitch, *Politics in Hard Times,* p. 24.

[10] Hall, *Political Power of Economic Ideas,* pp. 661–62.

[11] John Odell, *U.S. International Monetary Policy: Markets, Power, and Ideas as Sources of Change* (Princeton: Princeton University Press, 1982); Peter Hall, *Governing the Economy: The Politics of State Intervention* (New York: Oxford University Press, 1986); Martha Derthick and Paul Quirk, *The Politics of Deregulation* (Washington, D.C.: Brookings Institution, 1987); John Kingdon, *Agendas, Alternatives and Public Policies* (Glenview, Ill: Scott, Foresman, 1984).

are able to further ideological goals, in addition to those that are tradi-tionally thought of as national interests.[12] In this latter case, interna-tional forces are said to pose little constraint on policy making, and thus political leaders are able to select goals based on internal values. In the former instance, markets are a structural constraint, but they do not determine the particular policies that serve the interests of constituents or the nation as a whole. Thus all these studies recognize some independent influence for the "vision" that directs policy.

Research that focuses on beliefs as the filter between interests and policy faces a twofold task. First, analysts must delineate the arenas in which structure is more or less determinative. Few dispute the role played by international forces in setting foreign economic or security policy in times either of high compulsion or of complete indifference.[13] For small nations, the market is always driving policy; for larger or more autarkic economies, only at moments of great economic upheaval is there an overwhelming influence of market forces.[14] In practice, however, these ideal types are rarely operative. There is considerable variation in the economic politics of even the smallest and most vulner-able states, and these are explicable only in terms of domestic politi-cal processes.[15]

In research into ideas and economic policy, market forces operate as the baseline from which to judge the power of ideas at different points in time. Once cognitive models are identified—whether they are about macroeconomic coordination or currency stabilization—their importance can be measured by comparing policy outcomes with those predicted by pure market forces or by market-induced domestic interests.

According to this logic, ideas are most important when constraints are least acute. At such times, a range of possible policies appear to suit the interests of domestic constituents and the nation as a whole.

---

[12] Krasner asks: "Why has ideology only become important at a certain period in the nation's history?" He responds: "The answer is basically found in the international distribution of power among states. Ideological goals can be pursued only by the very powerful and perhaps also the very weak, by those who can make things happen and those who cannot change what happens." Stephen Krasner, *Defending the National Interest* (Princeton: Princeton University Press, 1978), p. 340.

[13] Arnold Wolfers, *Discord and Collaboration: Essays on International Politics* (Baltimore: Johns Hopkins University Press, 1962). For two excellent studies on the importance of structure—economic and security—on politics, see Jeffry A. Frieden, *Debt, Development and Democracy* (Princeton: Princeton University Press, 1991), and Joanne Gowa, *Allies, Adversaries and International Trade* (Princeton: Princeton University Press, 1994).

[14] Katzenstein, *Small States in World Markets,* and *Corporatism and Change* (Ithaca: Cornell University Press, 1985).

[15] John Goldthorpe, ed. *Order and Conflict in Contemporary Capitalism* (New York: Oxford University Press, 1984).

253

But at all times—except on the rare occasions of high compulsion—there will invariably be more than one policy option consistent with market forces. Ideas both select and legitimate for political entrepreneurs particular foreign policy strategies.

> (H.2) Policy making occurs in highly uncertain environments, forcing political actors to rely on theoretical models that suggest how to translate interest into policy. *The role of ideas increases, the greater the policy uncertainty.*

Ideas are critical not only because they serve as mechanisms by which entrepreneurs choose from a wide range of policies but also by virtue of their role as road maps supplying policy makers with a vision of cause-effect relationships. Policy makers live in a world of uncertainty. The interests of their constituents or of the nation as a whole may be unclear; when these interests are clarified, they may be contradictory. Furthermore, even when policy makers know the interests they wish to maximize, they are still likely to be uncertain about which policy is optimal.[16] In this world of incomplete information, ideational models provide the entrepreneur with a means for linking actions with outcomes.

If uncertainty is the motivation for reliance on ideational models, there should be variation in their use over issue areas. In policy arenas where there is a clear delineation of interests and unambiguous feedback on the appropriateness of particular strategies, beliefs should be less important in explaining the behavior of policy makers. Where elites have less information about constituents' interests or where the environment cannot quickly select out "bad" policies, however, there should be increased reliance on ideas in both the selection and constitution of a policy and its application over time. By implication, there should be far more reliance on ideas in the realm of foreign policy than in domestic issue areas; among domestic issues, economic policies—in which outcomes are far more difficult to control by state officials than other policies—should have more ideational content than purely distributive policies.

These first two hypotheses suggest the conditions under which policy makers might have an incentive to rely on theoretical models as a guide

[16] Such conceptualizations of the policy-making situation are far more prevalent than are those that assume pure rationality and complete information. See, for example, James March and Johan Olsen, "Garbage Can Models of Decision Making in Organizations," in *Ambiguity and Command: Organizational Perspectives on Military Decision Making*, ed. March and Roger Weissinger-Baylon (Cambridge, Mass.: Ballinger, 1986); James March and Herbert Simon, *Organizations* (New York: Wiley, 1958).

for action. They say little, however, about the content of a particular model and the influence on future policy of the use of one set of ideas rather than another. Research must also address these two issues.

(H.3) Objectively functional policies are not necessarily politically salient. *The greater the perceived divergence between underlying social values and domestic institutions and a policy prescription, the less likely the policy idea will be selected.*

In his analysis of the politics of Keynesianism, Hall proposes a number of variables that might explain the propensities of nations to incorporate new economic ideas into policy. The content of Keynesian ideas themselves was important only to the extent that there was variation in the economic problems in nations to which Keynesian ideas could be applied. More important in explaining the adoption of the Keynesian model were domestic coalitions and institutions that made these ideas more or less appealing.[17] Hall concludes that ideas are not powerful in themselves but that they are made powerful by an existing constellation of interests and institutions.

Similarly, in the case of American trade policy, entrepreneurs ignored economic models that held assumptions deemed inappropriate for the American case. For example, models that presumed abundant labor or that were based on a pessimistic vision of the future—such as that suggested by Malthus—were routinely ignored. The biggest impediment to the adoption of free-trade ideas in the first one hundred years of American history was that its supporters argued that cheap prices lowered wages, a prospect feared by all politicians in the 19th century. Even at the turn of the century, when free trade should have been appealing, at least to business groups, the inability of those who carried the message to articulate how free trade fit within America's institutional and social norms meant that few found its logic compelling. In retrospect, such a case could have been made, but it was not.

These examples suggest two general phenomena. First, underlying social, institutional, and cognitive patterns affect how political entrepreneurs regard policy ideas. Ideas vary in their "fit" and thus their affinity to political environments. Efficiency is valued only to the extent that the means to a goal adhere to existing ideas, values, and institutions. And second, to be sold to both elites and the mass public, ideas must be "packaged"—again, usually in terms of existing social, institutional, and normative patterns. Ideas are politically salient only when

[17] Hall, *Political Power of Economic Ideas,* pp. 361–91.

embedded within some set of existing cognitive and political structures. If entrepreneurs do not make these connections, even the most functional of ideas invariably will be ignored.

Thus, inquiry into the selection of ideas must include analysis of both the "selling" of policies and their intrinsic content. Even ideas that are inherently compatible with existing institutions, such as deregulation and a weak state, will be adopted and institutionalized only if political entrepreneurs make the case for their "natural" appeal.

> (H.4) Institutions are sticky; once an idea is institutionalized, its impact may long outlive its functional efficacy. *The greater the institutionalization of a policy idea, the longer lasting and more pervasive will be its impact on the policymaking process.*

Once a policy is chosen, it has long-lasting effects. For example, in the case of American agricultural supports, even though few farm groups supported the programs in 1933, their existence came to elicit farm interest in continued subsidization. The outcome was an organization of interests that created a formidable obstacle to any policy change. Similarly, contemporary American trade laws, written almost one hundred years ago, continue to affect public policy because they influence the incentives of industry by making it easier to get one form of aid rather than another. Although Congress could have changed these laws at some earlier time, to take away these protections now would elicit unacceptable levels of political criticism. The outcome is that U. S. policy is far broader and more explicit in its sanctioning of industrial policies in foreign countries and in its defense of fair trade than would be expected from other actions taken by the government. Again, to see the influence of the inculcation of ideas into institutions, we need to look no further than the American Constitution to see how reigning notions of democracy at the time of its writing have fundamentally affected all aspects of government—federal and state.

These examples suggest that it is not the objective worth of an idea that predicts its longevity but the extent to which other policies, institutions, and/or social groups form a protective belt around the idea, making it difficult for entrepreneurs to disentangle interests from a given set of casual beliefs. Thus attention should be directed to the process by which ideas become inculcated into laws, institutional procedures, and general norms. Such an investigation suggests two related issues.

First, analysis must consider why certain policies and not others become embedded in organizations. It is likely that institutionalization is a reflection of the functional fit between a policy and its environment.

Once the policy proves itself to its supporters, laws are passed that facilitate the enforcement of this "good" policy idea. This finding is consistent with the trade data presented here. But as well, explicit choices could be made, even in environments detrimental to the success of the idea, that cause the idea to be sustained over time. Organizations could be designed to ensure support for a policy even though the policy idea never proved itself to meet the needs of any majority. The implementation of Stalinist economic planning in East Europe and China may be such an example.[18]

Second, once in place, the process by which institutions create an ideational bias must be investigated. Institutions can be so envisioned in two different ways. First, institutions could affect the choice of strategy used by groups to maximize their interests. Alternatively, institutions may actually induce a change in preferences by making institutional rules valuable in themselves.

The former case is the easier to prove. Few dispute that an actor's behavior changes under differing structural situations. As the rules of the game change, so does the behavior of individuals. Such behavioral changes, however, are not indicative of alterations in interests but rather are alterations in strategies. In the case presented here, the rules on trade protectionism in the modern period made it easier for an industry to receive protection if it could prove that the foreign competitor was cheating than if economic decline was simply the result of an inability to compete with a more efficient firm. Industries sought to make claims of unfair trade for rational reasons—their interest in state aid led them to select the strategy with the highest success rate.

But rules do more than affect the strategic behavior of individuals and groups. They might be valued in themselves and thus lead to a change in preferences. For example, the existence of democratic institutions and their accompanying rituals have changed the way Americans think about politics. Democratic norms have been inculcated into all aspects of behavior and influence the way other nations are perceived. Democratic rules are thought to be valuable in themselves and are sustained for reasons having little to do with the strategic behavior of individuals. Instead of seeing preferences as always exogenous and fixed, analysts should entertain the possibility that they are endogenous, pliable, and, among other things, determined by institutions. Thus James March and Johan Olson suggest that there may be some

---

[18] Nina Halpern, "Stalinist Political Economy," in *Ideas and Foreign Policy,* ed. Goldstein and Keohane.

institutional designs that foster collective identity or promote homogeneity of preferences better than do other forms of organization.[19]

If preferences are determined by existing structures and these structures incorporate ideational patterns, we have an additional explanation for policy stickiness. It is not only that embedded ideas affect strategic choice. They also influence the basis of politics—the preferences of actors.

CONCLUDING THOUGHTS

Let us briefly return to the initial problem posed in this book. How can contemporary American commercial policy be explained and what are the prospects for the future?

For much of the postwar period, American policy has had two distinct sides: actions that both bolster and undercut trade openness have characterized American behavior. This bifurcation in policy is not surprising in light of the foregoing review of the legal basis for American policy of trade protectionism. The move to openness after the 1930s did not result in the mechanistic replacement of protectionist laws, institutions, and beliefs with a consistent liberal alternative. Policy change occurred far more subtly and incorporated many vestiges from the protectionist period. Thus today, laws exist that fundamentally differ in their prescriptions for legitimate government action. These laws are products of history; they are the contemporary manifestation of the past. Their use should not be viewed as a harbinger of a protectionist future.

This book also suggested that the explanation for the existence of concurrent contradictory forms of trade protectionism was found in the interaction between interests, beliefs, and institutions. Although the book began with the fundamentals of economic policy making—domestic and international interests—it was suggested that the choice among a range of possible strategies to realize economic interest was as important, if not more so, in explaining behavior. Further, it was proposed that the choice of strategy reflected the economic and political beliefs of political entrepreneurs. Once selected, strategies that were at least minimally effective became institutionalized and thereafter affected the incentives of those in and dependent upon political institutions.

What is implied here for the future of American policy? Since most

[19] James March and Johan Olsen, *Rediscovering Institutions: The Organizational Basis of Politics* (New York: Free Press, 1989).

analysts believe that economic openness is contingent upon either societal support or U.S. national interests as the dominant economic power, predictions of imminent protectionism and economic closure have become increasingly common since the 1970s. Additionally, many fear that a decline in American support for free trade will lead the world again, as in the 1930s, down a slippery slope toward high protective barriers to trade, beggar-thy-neighbor policies, and perhaps depression. The analysis offered here suggests a slightly different reality. Even if one agrees with commentators that there has been change in both national and domestic interests, there is still no reason to believe that a significant alteration in policy is imminent. Changing interests alone do not explain the course of policy. The web of norms, practices, and legal statutes that have existed since the 1930s suggest that American policy is immune to all but radical shifts in market conditions. Only if some radical shift downward should occur—and, given the powerful interests that are still served by openness, we should not expect it soon—should we expect the search for some alternative policy.

But even in a period of economic decline, it would not be enough that entrepreneurs are disenchanted with policy. A trade policy shift can occur only after some new economic policy idea has become politicized. Currently, there are few alternatives to neoclassical trade theory. Strategic trade theory might be the precursor of such an ideational option, but as yet, no entrepreneur has successfully translated this still evolving set of economic theories into a politically powerful program. Even if this were to transpire, however, policy generated from this new trade analysis would be layered on top of the old. As many found America's protectionist past to deter an aggressive stance on trade liberalization, so too will future leaders—even if they seek closure—be confronted with the rules from America's liberal past.

Index

Adams, Brooks, 91
Adams, John Quincy, 56, 58
AFL-CIO, 190–91
Aggarwal, Vinod, 222–23, 227
Agricultural Act of 1948, 157
Agricultural Act of 1956, 227
Agricultural Adjustment Act (AAA) of
  1933, 139–40, 154–55; §22, 156; §32,
  156
Agricultural Adjustment Administration,
  155
Agriculture, 25–28, 30–32, 34, 37–40,
  44–45, 64–65, 76, 81, 102, 111, 116,
  118, 124, 125, 129–30, 161, 164–65,
  181, 240, 249, 256; East, 74; Farm
  Bureau, 155–56; Grange, 155–56;
  Midwest, 19, 240; South, 24–26, 47,
  50, 54–62, 66–68, 71–72, 74, 77, 79,
  82, 105, 166, 240, 244–45; West, 26,
  57, 62, 73, 78, 79, 94, 240. See also
  individual laws and products
Aldrich, Nelson, 112, 116, 117
Allen, William, 143
Almonds, 156
American Cotton Manufacturers
  Institute, 166
American Economic Association, 85,
  88–89, 91, 134
American Historical Association, 134
American International Automobile
  Dealers Association, 233
American Motors, 233
American Tariff League, 164
American Trade Council, 164
Antidumping, 130, 171, 174, 197–205,
  206, 208, 218, 219, 224, 225. See also
  individual laws
Anti-dumping Act of 1921, 199, 200,
  206, 218; 1954 amendments to, 199,
  200
Appleton, Nathan, 59
Argentina, 199
Arthur, Chester, 98, 99, 129, 150
Arthur, W. B., 11
Atlantic Charter, 158
Austria-Hungary, 113
Automotive Products Trade Act of
  1965, 190
Autos, 190–92, 222–23, 230–33
Ayoubin, Edmund, 224

Baier, Lowell, 198, 200
Banking, 76, 141
Barbour, John, 52
Barbour, P. P., 54
Bardan, Benjamin, 229
Barley, 156
Barnburners, 75
Barshefsky, Charlene, 202
Bates, Isaac, 69
Bauer, Raymond, 4
Beef, 174
Bell, John (W-Tenn.), 68
Bell, John C. (D-Colo.), 114
Bellamy, Edward, 134
Bergsten, C. Fred, 168
Bernstein, Marver, 17
Bethlehem Steel, 225–26
Bhagwati, Jagdish, 7, 177
Block, Fred, 13
Blaine, James G., 106, 129
Board of General Appraisers, U.S., 103,
  122
Bounties, 104, 114
Bowen, Francis, 86, 87

Brazil: film, 199; pharmaceuticals, 216; steel, 225
Bretton Woods Conference (1944), 158
Britain, 15, 35, 37, 39, 45–47, 52–53, 55–56, 59, 61, 64, 66, 67, 71–72, 79, 81, 82, 112, 113, 125, 129, 133, 138, 158–61, 180, 244; academic influences on U.S., 27–31, 33–42, 49, 67–68, 76, 85–90, 135, 177, 239, 255; Corn Laws, 37, 67, 71; Navigation Acts, 37
Brock, William, 7
Brougham, Lord, 45
Buchanan, James, 54, 69, 70, 76–77
Budget and Reconciliation Act of 1981, 192–93
Bush, George, 226–27
Business and industry, 5, 23–26, 30–33, 34, 37–50, 57, 60, 64, 66–69, 76–77, 82, 83–84, 86, 90, 98, 101, 102, 103, 105, 108, 109, 120, 121, 123, 125, 128–31, 134, 135–36, 167, 181–82, 187–88, 212–15, 234–35, 239–40, 242, 246–47, 255–57; East, 94, 100, 240; Middle Atlantic, 47, 52, 55; Midwest, 26, 61; New England, 26, 47, 50, 54–56, 65, 74; North, 24, 47, 50, 52, 54–55, 58, 68, 73, 74, 78, 79, 240, 244–45; South, 227; West, 52. See also individual industries, products, corporations
Butt, Isaac, 87
Butter, 156, 157

Calhoun, John C., 54
Cambreleng, Churchill, 52
Canada, 93, 107, 118, 158, 174; lumber, 216; oil, 175; textiles, 230; wheat, 200
Cardozo, J. Newton, 36
Carey, Henry, 26, 36, 38–41, 74, 86–88, 91
Carey, Matthew, 36, 50
Carnegie, Andrew, 144
Carpets, 166
Carter, Jimmy, 211, 224–25, 231
Cattle, 156
Chase, Salmon P., 77
Cheese, 156, 161
China (PRC), 161–62, 257
Choate, Rufus, 59
Chrysler Corporation, 233
Clay, Henry, 52, 53, 54, 57, 58, 60, 68, 71
Clayton Act, 203
Cleveland, Grover, 101, 108, 109, 111, 118
Coal, 79, 84, 116
Cocoa, 58

Coffee, 58, 77, 78, 97, 98, 112
Coffield, Shirley, 196
Colton, Calvin, 36–38
Commissioner of Revenue, U.S., 132
Commission of Foreign Economic Policy (Randall Commission), 166, 190
Committee for Reciprocity Information, 153
Commodity Credit Corporation, 157
Congress, U.S., 14, 50, 256; Agricultural Committee, 133; Danforth Bill, 231–32; Full Employment Bill, 160; Gephardt Amendment, 173; House Energy and Commerce Committee, 232; House Foreign Economic Policy Subcommittee, 191; House Manufactures Committee, 52, 56, 58; House Trade Subcommittee, 231; House Ways and Means Committee, 96–98, 102, 109–12, 116–17, 119, 124–25, 143, 164, 169, 187, 198, 232; Mills Bill, 103; pre–Civil War years compared to antebellum period, 42–43; Senate Finance Committee, 103–4, 107, 110, 112, 117, 119, 123, 125, 172, 187, 207; Speaker of the House, 96, 97, 100. See also individual members, parties, laws
Consumers Union of the United States v. Kissinger, 222–23
Cooper, Richard, 14, 15
Cooper, Thomas, 36, 37
Copper, 84
Corn, 155, 156
Corn Laws, British, 37, 67, 71
Cotton, 38, 52, 59, 62, 65, 79, 105, 106, 155–58, 166, 245. See also Textiles
Countervailing duties (CDs), 171, 197, 203–6, 208, 217–19, 225
Court of Appeals for the Federal Circuit, U.S., 205, 207
Court of Customs Appeals, U.S., 122
Court of International Trade, U.S., 205
Crandall, Robert, 223
Cripps, Stafford, 160
Crisis of 1837, 38–39, 57, 61–62
Culbertson, William, 123, 149, 150
Cunningham, Richard, 202
Customs Bureau, U.S., 103, 199, 201, 204, 226
Cutler, John, 200, 202

Dallas, George M., 62
Danforth, John, 231
Davis, Frederick, 198, 200
Davis, John, 69
Democratic party: 1800–1850, 20, 51,

Democratic party (*cont.*)
62, 65, 245; 1850–1900, 20, 24, 44, 66, 73–79, 82, 83, 92, 94–95, 97–98, 99, 100–108, 109, 110–11, 113–14, 128, 129–32, 135–36, 240, 246; 1900–1930, 16, 20, 44, 82, 95, 117–22, 125–31, 143, 151; 1930s (Depression), 20, 44, 82, 140–43, 145, 147, 148, 151, 246, 249; 1940s–(postwar), 16, 130, 164, 165, 174–75, 182. *See also* Congress, U.S.; *individual politicians and administrations*
Derthick, Martha, 252
Destler, I. M., 5, 167, 169, 170, 172, 174, 225, 231–32
Dew, Thomas B., 36
Dingley, Nelson, 92, 111, 114
Dingley Tariff of 1897, 82, 111–17, 144; §5, 114
Dixit, Avingsh, 177
Dobson, J. M., 5, 77
Dole, Robert, 232
Domestic content, 171, 172, 179
Downs, Anthony, 17
Dumping. *See* antidumping
Dunbar, Charles, 84–85, 88, 90
DuPont, 123
Dyes, 123

Economic Basis of Protection (Patten), 90
Edwards, Richard, 92
Eggs, 157
Ehrenhaft, Peter, 201
Eisenhower, Dwight D., 165–66
Elements of Political Economy (Perry), 85, 87
Ely, Richard T., 85, 134
Escape clause, 5, 165, 185–91, 192, 196, 197, 199, 200, 200–201, 205–16, 219–21, 225–26, 227, 228, 231
Essays on the Principles of Population (Malthus), 28
Essays on the Rate of Wages (Henry Carey), 38
European Community, 166, 201, 216; steel, 224–26
Evans, George, 72
Evans, John, 164, 166
Everett, Alexander, 36
Executive Commercial Policy Committee, 153

Farm Bureau, 155–56
Fast track, 170, 172
Federal Register, 188, 195, 199, 207
Federal Trade Commission Act of 1914, 197–98, 206

Filberts, 156
Film, 199
Findlay, Ronald, 7
Finger, J. M., 199
Fish, 84
Fisher, Bart, 198
Flax seed, 156
Foner, Eric, 73–75
Footwear, 166, 189
Ford, Gerald, 225
Ford Motor Co., 231, 233
Fordney-McCumber Tariff of 1922, 123–26, 128, 144, 145–46, 152; §315, 123; §316, 206; §317, 149–50
Foreign and Domestic Commerce, U.S. Bureau of, 132
France, 30–31, 38, 112, 113; Physiocrats, 27–30, 34; treaties, 115, 148
Franklin, Benjamin, 29–30
Free Soil party, 75
Frieden, Jeffry, 253
Friedman, Milton, 9
Friends of American Industry, 68
Friends of Protection, 69
Fruit, 101, 216
Fur, 186

Gardner, Richard, 158–62
Garfield, James A., 129
Garn, Jake, 174
GATT (General Agreement on Tariffs and Trade), 156, 173, 176, 180, 194–95, 204, 226, 227; Annecy Round, 163; Antidumping Code, 198, 200–201; Article XI, 231; Article XIX, 186–87, 228; creation of, 158–59; Dillon Round, 163, 164, 166; Geneva Round (1947), 161–63; Geneva Round (1956), 163; Kennedy Round, 163, 166, 247; Long Term Agreement on Cotton Textiles (LTA), 228–29; Multifiber Textile Arrangement (MFA), 166, 230; Part II, 162; Short Term Agreement on Cotton Textiles, 228; Subsidies Code, 204; Tokyo Round, 163, 166–67, 170–71, 195, 200, 204, 218; Torquay Round, 163; Uruguay Round, 163
Geertz, Clifford, 11
General Motors, 232, 233
General System of Preferences, 172
George, Alexander, 251
George, Juliette, 251
Gephardt, Richard, 173, 174–75
Germany, 86, 87, 89, 116; reciprocity treaty, 115; Zollverein trade agreement of 1844, 93

Gershenkron, Alexander, 4, 251
Glass, 59, 107, 166
Gloves, 112
Gold, 84, 118, 160
Goldstein, Judith, 11, 146, 155, 178, 199, 251
Goldthorpe, John, 253
Gould, Stephen Jay, 11
Gourevitch, Peter, 13, 14, 251–52
Gowa, Joanne, 253
Grady, Henry, 147
Grain, 19
Grange, 155–56
Grant, Ulysses, S., 78, 97
Great Depression, 14, 16, 20, 61, 82, 95, 107, 127, 133, 136, 138–39; 143–44, 176,181, 239, 243, 246, 249, 256; Agricultural Adjustment Act of 1933, 139, 140, 154–56; Agricultural Adjustment Administration, 155; described, 126; National Industrial Recovery Act, 139–40; National Recovery Administration, 140; Reciprocal Trade Agreements Act of 1934, 137, 139–43, 146–47, 149–56, 163–64, 179–81, 245; Soil Conservation and Domestic Allotment Act of 1936, 154–55
Greeley, Horace, 57, 70, 78
Green, Carl, 222
Grieco, Joseph, 4

Haas, Ernst, 11, 15
Haas, Peter, 15, 238
Hadley, Arthur T., 89
Hale, Eugene, 106
Hall, H. Keith, 199
Hall, Peter, 2, 13, 15, 242, 252, 255
Halpern, Nina, 257
Hamilton, Alexander, 26, 29–37, 39, 45, 46, 61, 65–66, 129, 244
Harding, Warren G., 123–24, 149
Harrison, Benjamin, 103, 106, 107
Hartz, Louis, 28
Hayes, John, 99
Hayne, Robert, 55, 58
Hewitt, Abram, 128
Hides, 112, 116
Hogs, 155
Holsti, Ole, 4
Home League, 69
Hong Kong, 229
Hoover, Herbert, 124, 141, 142, 151
Hopkins, Albert, 113
Houston, Samuel, 54
Hudec, Robert, 200

Hufbauer, Gary, 224, 225, 227, 228, 230, 232
Hughes, Charles Evans, 149
Hull, Cordell, 139, 140, 142, 143, 147, 152, 158, 181
Hume, David, 30
Hunter, Robert, 71
Hunt's Merchants' Magazine, 57
Huston, James, 74

Ideas and policymaking, 181; British influences, 27–31, 33–42, 49, 67–68, 76, 85–90, 135, 177, 239, 255; early American thought, 26–42; foreign policy role of, 237–59; French influences, 27–30, 34; Gilded Age, American thought in, 84–94, 134–35; political role of, 9–18; strategic trade theory in 1970s and 1980s, 177–80
India, 41, 162
Infant industry, 104–5, 122
Inland Steel Corporation, 165–66
Internal Revenue Act of 1865, 78
International Agreement on Subsidies and Countervailing Duties, 195
International American Conference (1890), 106
International Chamber of Commerce, 162
International Trade Commission (ITC), 5, 140, 181, 186–91, 192, 196, 199–202, 204–14, 218–20, 226, 231, 233
International Trade Organization (ITO), 158–63
Interstate Commerce Commission, 145
Ireland, 41
Iron, 47–48, 58, 59, 65, 84, 97, 116, 189, 223
Italy, 115

Jackson, Andrew, 54, 58, 59, 74, 75, 129
Jackson, John, 198, 200, 201
Japan, 166, 220; autos, 223, 230–33; beeef, 174; MITI, 232, 233; semiconductors, 179; steel, 199, 224–25; technology to Soviets, 173, 174; televisions, 201; textiles, 227–28, 229; Treaty of Friendship, Commerce, and Navigation, 231
Jefferson, Thomas, 30
Jenifer, Daniel, 59
Jervis, Robert, 251
Johnson, Hugh, 142
Johnson, Richard, 54
Jones-Costigan Act of 1934, 156

J. W. Hampton Jr. and Co. v. *United States*, 145–46

Kaplan, A. D. H., 39
Kasson, John A., 75–76, 113
Katzenstein, Peter, 4, 251, 253
Kaye, Harvey, 205, 208
Kelly, William, 129, 150
Kennedy, John F., 164, 166, 190
Keohane, Robert, 4, 8, 9, 11, 18, 222, 251
Keynes, John Maynard, 2, 3, 255
Kingdon, John, 10, 13, 252
Know-Nothing party, 75
Kostecki, Michel, 221
Krasner, Stephen, 4, 8, 178, 253
Kratochwil, Friedrich, 8
Kreps, David, 6
Krugman, Paul, 177

Labor, 5, 35, 36, 133; 1700s, 23, 30–33, 43–44, 255; 1800–1850, 23, 38, 46, 49, 53, 61, 66–70, 255; 1850–1900, 19, 24–26, 42, 66–67, 73, 74, 76, 80, 82, 86, 90–92, 94, 98, 99, 100, 102, 103, 107, 129, 132, 249, 255; 1900–1930, 82, 116, 132; 1930s (Depression), 126, 141, 181; 1940s– (postwar), 160, 167, 171, 173, 175, 188, 192–94, 212–15, 223, 231, 233, 235. *See also individual unions and industries*
Labor Statistics, Bureau of, 171
Lake, David, 4, 88–84, 93
Lamb, 174
Larkin, John, 145, 147–48, 150, 151, 153
Larson, Deborah Welch, 251
Laughlin, James Laurence, 89, 93, 115
Lebow, Richard Ned, 251
Lee, Henry, 51
Lend-Lease Act of 1941–42, 156–58
Lenroot, Irvine, 146
Lenway, Stephanie, 199
Leslie, T. E. Cliffe, 85, 86
Lewis, Dixon, 71
Liberty Lobby, 164
Liechtenstein, Walter, 141
Lincoln, Abraham, 73, 74, 75
Linseed oil, 156
Liquor, 65, 101
List, Fredrick, 34, 135
Locke, John, 239
Long Term Agreement on Cotton Textiles (LTA), 228–29
LTFV, 199–203
Lumber, 84, 107, 110, 166, 216

McCulloch, John Ramsay, 33, 90
McDonald, David J., 190
McDuffie, George, 68, 72
McKeown, Timothy, 5
McKinley, William, 111, 112, 130–31
McKinley Tariff of 1890, 82, 102–9, 113–14, 128, 144; §3, 150
McLane, Louis, 54
McVickar, John, 36, 37
Madison, James, 43–44
Magee, Stephen, 7
Malthus, Thomas, 28–29, 33, 36, 39, 41–42, 67–68, 76, 86, 88, 255
March, James, 7, 17, 254, 257–58
Marks, Matthew, 201
Martindale, Henry, 53
Marx, Karl, 14
Meat-packing, 113–14
Metzger, Stanley, 186
Mexico, 161, 186; steel, 225
Milgrom, Paul, 8
Milk, 155–57, 166
Mill, John Stuart, 29, 85, 90
Mills, Roger Q., 110
Mills, Wilbur, 164, 169
Milner, Helen, 4, 251
Miscellaneous Revenue Act of 1982, 193
Mitchell, Daniel, 190, 191
Moe, Terry, 7, 8, 9
Molasses, 58, 77, 78
Moley, Raymond, 142
Monroe, James, 52
Moore, Barrington, 251
Morill Act of 1861, 77
Morrell, Daniel, 44–45
Most-favored-nation (MFN) status, 140, 148–53, 196
Motorcycles, 189
Mrazek, Robert, 174–75
Multifiber Textile Arrangement (MFA), 166, 230

National Association of Manufacturers, 130–31
National Foreign Trade Council, 162
National Industrial Recovery Act (NIRA), 139–40
National Recovery Administration (NRA), 140
Nation-Wide Committee on Import-Export Policy, 164
Navigation Acts, British, 37
Nelson, Douglass, 199
Netherlands, 162
New York Evening Post, 76
Niles, Hezekiah, 36, 45–46, 51, 56
Niles, John, 65

Niles' Weekly Register, 46, 50
Nixon, Richard M., 166, 169–71
Nolan-Halay, Jacqueline, 222
Noll, Roger, 3
North, Douglass, 8, 14
Norway, 173

Oats, 156
Odell, John, 5, 252
Oil, 84, 116, 175, 230
Old Protective Tariff League, 164
Olson, Johan, 7, 254, 257–58
Omnibus Trade and Competitiveness
    Act of 1988, 5, 168–69, 172–75,
    193–94, 206, 208; Super 301, 173,
    179–80, 194–95; Title 19, 206
Organization of Economic Cooperation
    and Development (OECD), 171

Pace, Stephen, 157
Panic of 1857, 65, 70–71, 76, 80
Panic of 1873, 98, 135
Panic of 1904, 116
Panic of 1907, 116, 118
Parity, 154–55
Parrington, V. L., 83–84
Parsons, Talcott, 14
Past, Present and Future (Henry Carey),
    39
Pasta, 216
Pastor, Robert, 5, 141, 164, 175–76, 191,
    192
Patten, Simon, 88, 90–91, 134
Payne, Sereno, 117
Payne-Aldrich Tariff of 1909, 116–19,
    121, 203
Peanuts/peanut oil, 156
Peek, George, 139, 140, 152
Perry, Arthur Lathan, 85–87
Perry, William, 189, 203, 204, 208
Pharmaceuticals, 216
Phillips, Willard, 36–37
Physiocrats, 27–30, 34
Pincus, Jonathan, 5
Plaia, Paul Jr., 205, 208
Policy Committee, 188
Polk, James K., 62
Populist party, 110, 111
Portugal, 41, 115
Potatoes, 157
Preeg, Ernest, 5, 164
Principles of Political Economy, The
    (McCulloch), 33
Principles of Social Science (Henry Carey),
    40
Proposals for Expansion of World Trade and .

Employment (State Department),
    158–59
Proxmire, William, 175

Quarterly Journal of Economics, 119–20
Quinine, 98
Quirk, Paul, 252

Rae, John, 36
Rau, Allan, 155–57, 162
Railroads, 19, 81
Randall, Clarence, 165–66
Randall Commission (Commission of
    Foreign Economic Policy), 166, 190
Randolph, John, 56
Rankin, Christopher, 53, 67
Raymond, Daniel, 26, 33–35, 38, 57
Reagan, Ronald, 13, 189, 192–93, 211,
    216, 225, 226, 231–33
Reciprocal Trade Agreements Act: of
    1934, 137, 139–43, 146–47, 149–56,
    163–64, 179–81, 245; of 1937,
    163–64; of 1940, 163–64; of 1943,
    163–64; of 1945, 156, 157, 163–64,
    186; of 1948, 164; of 1949, 164; of
    1951, 157, 164, 186–88; of 1954, 164;
    of 1955, 164; of 1958, 164, 166
Reciprocal Trade Agreements Act of
    1947, 166, 167, 169–71, 179, 187–88,
    190–93, 194, 199, 204, 206, 208–11,
    216–18; §202(c), 188; §301, 173, 179,
    184–86; 194–97, 216–17, 219, 221,
    225–26; §607, 222
Reciprocal Trade Agreements Act of
    1979, 169, 171, 199–201, 204–6, 218;
    §771(7), 204; §771(7)(f), 204
Reciprocity, 93–94, 105–7, 112–15,
    117–18, 126, 127, 128–29, 130–32,
    133, 136, 143, 148–53, 162, 171, 172,
    178–79
Report on Manufactures (Hamilton),
    30–32, 46
Republican party, 240; 1850–1900, 19,
    24–26, 43, 66–67, 73–80, 92–95,
    97–105, 107–8, 110–15, 128, 129–32,
    135–36, 137 245, 248–49; 1900–1930,
    19, 44, 95, 116–23, 125–31, 145, 150,
    151, 248; 1930s (Depression), 141–42,
    145, 147, 246, 249; 1940s– (postwar),
    16, 164, 165, 166, 174–75, 182, 190,
    231, 245. *See also* Congress, U.S.;
    individual politicians and administrations
Resin, synthetic phenolic, 206
Revenue Act of 1916, 198
Review Committee, 188
Revolvers, 206

Ricardo, David, 26, 28–29, 33, 36–41, 49, 76, 177
Rice, 155
Ris, William, Jr., 186
Robbins, Asher, 60
Rogowski, Ronald, 4, 25, 251
Roosevelt, Franklin D., 94, 139–43, 145, 146, 151, 153, 156, 181, 248, 249
Roosevelt, Theodore, 116
Root, Elihu, 116
Rope, manila, 206
Ross, John, 47
Ruggie, John, 8, 11
Rye, 156

Salt, 58, 98
San Francisco Conference (1945), 158
Say, Jean Baptiste, 29, 33, 35
Sayre, Francis, 146
Schattschneider, E. E., 4, 5, 144
Scott, C. James, 93
Section 301, 179–80, 194–97, 216–17
Seligman, Erwin, 89
Semiconductors, 179, 216
Shepsle, Kenneth, 3, 7
Sherman, John, 97, 98
Sherman Antitrust Act, 202–3, 222
Sherwood, Sidney, 85
Short Term Agreement on Cotton Textiles, 228
Shultz, George, 169–70, 191
Silver, 84, 109, 111
Simon, Herbert, 17
Skocpol, Theda, 13
Smith, Adam, 27–31, 33–36, 41, 49, 239
Smith, Peshine, 86–88
Smoot, Reed, 144, 149
Smoot-Hawley Tariff of 1930, 82, 123–27, 128, 133, 140, 141–42, 147–49, 152–53, 175, 180, 197–98, 203, 205–8, 245; §337, 184, 197–98, 205–8, 206, 207, 208, 218–20
Soil Conservation and Domestic Allotment Act of 1936, 154–55
Solomon, Anthony, 225
Sorghum, 104
South Africa, 225
South America, 106–7, 113, 143
South Korea, 229
Soviet Union, 5, 173, 174
Spain, 30–31, 216
Special representative for trade negotiations (STR), 180, 181; creation of, 167; unfair trade complaints and, 188, 191, 195, 196, 216, 225–26
Spices, 97

Stanwood, Edward, 45, 52, 55, 56, 57, 62, 70, 99
Steagall Amendment of, 1941, 157
Stein, Janice Gross, 251
Steel, 82, 166, 189, 190, 199, 222, 223–27, 230
Steel Trade Liberalization Program, 227
Steenerson, Halvor, 144
Stern, Robert, 177
Stevenson, Andrew, 56
Steward, John, 104
Stewart, Andrew, 72
Stiglitz, Joseph, 177
Sturtevant, Julian Monson, 87, 88
Subsidies, 130, 156–57, 161
Sugar, 47, 59, 77, 78, 97, 103, 104, 106, 110, 112, 119, 121, 128, 16, 174
Suggested Charter for an International Trade Organization of the United Nations (State Department), 158–59
Sumner, William Graham, 89
Supreme Court of the United States, 145–46, 205, 206
Surplus Property Act of 1940, 157

Taft, William H., 116–18
Taiwan, 229
Talbert, W. Jasper, 114
Talmadge, Herman, 170
Tarbell, Ida, 144
Tariff: of 1816, 44–47, 49, 50, 53–55; or 1818, 47–48, 52–53; 1824, 36, 48, 52, 53–57; of 1828, 36, 48, 50, 55–57, 59, 70–71; of 1832, 36, 48, 57–60, 62; of 1833, 48; 1842, 39, 48, 62; of 1846, 48, 65, 76, 110, 118; of 1857, 48, 76; of 1870, 97; 1872, 78, 97–98; of 1875, 97–98; of 1883, 99–100; of 1894, 108–11, 108–9, 110, 144. *See also trade legislation by name*
Tariff and Trade Act of 1984, 171–72, 179, 204, 226
Tariff Commission (TC), U.S., 118, 120–21, 123, 124, 132, 133, 144–45, 147, 149, 151, 165, 166, 206, 211, 226–28, 249; antidumping and, 198; creation of, 98–99, 145
Tartar, 113
Tarullo, Daniel, 144
Tasca, Henry, 147, 150, 153
Task Force on Economic Adjustment and Worker Dislocation, 193
Taussig, Frank William, 55, 89, 90, 97, 109, 116, 119–20, 121, 122, 127, 144
Tea, 58, 77, 78, 97, 98, 112
Televisions, 201
Terrill, Tom E., 5, 102, 128

Textiles, 26, 45, 47–49, 55–56, 58–59, 99, 112, 116, 121, 166, 223, 227–30
Textile Surveillance Body, 230
Thompson, Richard, 5
Thompson, William Ellis, 86, 87
Tin, 104–5, 107
Tobacco, 52, 101, 105, 155, 156, 158
Tocqueville, Alexis de, 23
Tod, John, 52
Todd, Albert, 113–14
Tonka beans, 112
Toshiba Corp., 173, 174, 179
Toyota, 232
Trade Adjustment Assistance (TAA), 174, 184, 185, 188, 190–94, 209–16, 221
Trade Agreements Committee, 153
Trade Expansion Act of 1962, 164, 166, 167, 169, 187–88, 190–93, 215, 245, 247
Trade Information Committee, 153
Trade Policy Staff Committee, 188
Treatise on Political Economy (Say), 29
Trigger price mechanism (TPM), 220, 222, 224–25
Truman, Harry, 186
Tugwell, Rexford B., 139, 142
Turkey, 41
Turkeys, 157
Twine, 107

Underwood, Oscar, 119
Underwood Tariff of 1913, 82, 83, 94, 95, 118–22, 128, 131, 203–4, 247
Unfair Import Investigations, Office of, 207
Unfair trade complaints, 210, 212, 214, 221; antidumping, 197–205, 206, 208, 218, 219, 224, 225; countervailing duties, 197, 203–6, 208, 217–19, 225; §337, 184, 197–98, 205–8, 218–20
United Auto Workers (UAW), 191–92, 231, 233
United Nations, 158–59, 161
United Steel Workers, 190, 225–26

Van Buren, Martin, 54, 75

Vandenberg, Arthur, 125
Vanilla beans, 112
Veblen, Thorstein, 134
Vest, George G., 110
Viner, Jacob, 147, 168
Voluntary export restraints (VERs), 5, 220–33
von Schmoller, Gustav Friedrich, 87

Walker, Amasa, 86
Walker, Francis, 89
Walker, Robert, 62–67, 70, 72, 76
War Industries Board, U.S., 122
Washington Post, 168–69, 172
Wealth of Nations, The (Adam Smith), 27–28, 41
Weber, Max, 12, 250
Webster, Daniel, 56, 65, 68, 69, 93
Weingast, Barry, 7, 8, 146
Wellisz, Stanislaus, 7
Wells, David A., 77, 78, 129, 135, 136
Wheat, 155–58, 200
Whig Almanac, 70
Whig party, 24, 246, 249; 1800–1850, 44, 51, 65; 1850–1900, 66, 69, 70, 73, 75–76
Wilcox, Clair, 159
Wilgress, Edna, 159
Williams, Lewis, 49
Williamson, Oliver, 7
Willis, H. Parker, 115
Wilson, Marcius, 87, 88
Wilson, William Lyne, 92, 109–11
Wilson, Woodrow, 82, 118–19, 121, 123, 124, 142, 145
Wine, 78, 101, 112, 113
Wolfers, Arnold, 253
Wood, Silas, 53, 54
Woodcock, Leonard, 191–92
Wool, 55–56, 58–59, 65, 66, 107, 109, 110, 119, 121, 128, 156, 157, 161, 166. See also Textiles
Wool Manufacturers' Association, 99

Yoffie, David, 167, 222, 223, 228, 229

Zysman, John, 178

Cornell Studies in Political Economy

EDITED BY PETER J. KATZENSTEIN

Collapse of an Industry: Nuclear Power and the Contradictions of U.S. Policy, by John L. Campbell

Power, Purpose, and Collective Choice: Economic Strategy in Socialist States, edited by Ellen Comisso and Laura D'Andrea Tyson

The Political Economy of the New Asian Industrialism, edited by Frederic C. Deyo

Dislodging Multinationals: India's Strategy in Comparative Perspective, by Dennis J. Encarnation

Rivals beyond Trade: America versus Japan in Global Competition, by Dennis J. Encarnation

Democracy and Markets: The Politics of Mixed Economies, by John R. Freeman

The Misunderstood Miracle: Industrial Development and Political Change in Japan, by David Friedman

Patchwork Protectionism: Textile Trade Policy in the United States, Japan, and West Germany, by H. Richard Friman

Ideas, Interests, and American Trade Policy, by Judith Goldstein

Ideas and Foreign Policy: Beliefs, Institutions, and Political Change, edited by Judith Goldstein and Robert O. Keohane

Monetary Sovereignty: The Politics of Central Banking in Western Europe, by John B. Goodman

Politics in Hard Times: Comparative Responses to International Economic Crises, by Peter Gourevitch

Closing the Gold Window: Domestic Politics and the End of Bretton Woods, by Joanne Gowa

Cooperation among Nations: Europe, America, and Non-tariff Barriers to Trade, by Joseph M. Grieco

Pathways from the Periphery: The Politics of Growth in the Newly Industrializing Countries, by Stephan Haggard

The Politics of Finance in Developing Countries, edited by Stephan Haggard, Chung H. Lee, and Sylvia Maxfield

Rival Capitalists: International Competitiveness in the United States, Japan, and Western Europe, by Jeffrey A. Hart

The Philippine State and the Marcos Regime: The Politics of Export, by Gary Hawes

Reasons of State: Oil Politics and the Capacities of American Government, by G. John Ikenberry

The State and American Foreign Economic Policy, edited by G. John Ikenberry, David A. Lake, and Michael Mastanduno

The Paradox of Continental Production: National Investment Policies in North America, by Barbara Jenkins

Pipeline Politics: The Complex Political Economy of East-West Energy Trade, by Bruce W. Jentleson

The Politics of International Debt, edited by Miles Kahler

Corporatism and Change: Austria, Switzerland, and the Politics of Industry, by Peter J. Katzenstein

Industry and Politics in West Germany: Toward the Third Republic, edited by Peter J. Katzenstein

Small States in World Markets: Industrial Policy in Europe, by Peter J. Katzenstein

The Sovereign Entrepreneur: Oil Policies in Advanced and Less Developed Capitalist Countries, by Merrie Gilbert Klapp

International Regimes, edited by Stephen D. Krasner

Business and Banking: Political Change and Economic Integration in Western Europe, by Paulette Kurzer

Power, Protection, and Free Trade: International Sources of U.S. Commercial Strategy, 1887–1939, by David A. Lake

State Capitalism: Public Enterprise in Canada, by Jeanne Kirk Laux and Maureen Appel Molot

France after Hegemony: International Change and Financial Reform, by Michael Loriaux

Economic Containment: CoCom and the Politics of East-West Trade, by Michael Mastanduno

Opening Financial Markets: Banking Politics on the Pacific Rim, by Louis W. Pauly

The Limits of Social Democracy: Investment Politics in Sweden, by Jonas Pontusson

The Fruits of Fascism: Postwar Prosperity in Historical Perspective, by Simon Reich

The Business of the Japanese State: Energy Markets in Comparative and Historical Perspective, by Richard J. Samuels

In the Dominions of Debt: Historical Perspectives on Dependent Development, by Herman M. Schwartz

Europe and the New Technologies, edited by Margaret Sharp

Europe's Industries: Public and Private Strategies for Change, edited by Geoffrey Shepherd, François Duchêne, and Christopher Saunders

Ideas and Institutions: Developmentalism in Brazil and Argentina, by Kathryn Sikkink

Fair Shares: Unions, Pay, and Politics in Sweden and West Germany, by Peter Swenson

Union of Parts: Labor Politics in Postwar Germany, by Kathleen A. Thelen

Democracy at Work: Changing World Markets and the Future of Labor Unions, by Lowell Turner

National Styles of Regulation: Environmental Policy in Great Britain and the United States, by David Vogel

International Cooperation: Building Regimes for Natural Resources and the Environment, by Oran R. Young

Governments, Markets, and Growth: Financial Systems and the Politics of Industrial Change, by John Zysman

American Industry in International Competition: Government Policies and Corporate Strategies, edited by John Zysman and Laura Tyson

Library of Congress Cataloging-in-Publication Data

Goldstein, Judith.
  Ideas, interests, and American trade policy / Judith Goldstein.
    p.   cm.—(Cornell studies in political economy)
  Includes bibliographical references and index.
  ISBN 0-8014-2695-2 (cloth : alk. paper).—ISBN 0-8014-9988-7 (pbk. : alk. paper)
  1. Protectionism—United States—History. 2. Tariff—United States—History.
3. United States—Commercial policy—History. 4. Pressure groups—United States—
History. 5. United States—Foreign relations. I. Title. II. Series.
  HF1455.G65 1995
  382'.73'0973—dc20
                                                   93-29481